Cisco UCS Cookbook

Over 40 practical recipes to get your hands dirty with the powerful Cisco UCS and overcome various challenges

Victor Wu

BIRMINGHAM - MUMBAI

Cisco UCS Cookbook

First published: March 2016

Production reference: 1140316

Published by Packt Publishing Ltd.
Livery Place
35 Livery Street
Birmingham B3 2PB, UK.

ISBN 978-1-78588-898-4

www.packtpub.com

Credits

Author
Victor Wu

Reviewer
Michael Ciulei

Acquisition Editor
Kirk D'costa

Content Development Editor
Trusha Shriyan

Technical Editor
Devesh Chugh

Copy Editor
Sneha Singh

Project Coordinator
Kinjal Bari

Proofreader
Safis Editing

Indexer
Hemangini Bari

Graphics
Kirk D'Penha

Production Coordinator
Shantanu N. Zagade

Cover Work
Shantanu N. Zagade

About the Author

Victor Wu has over 10 years of IT experience. Currently, he works as a Solution Architect at BoardWare Information System Limited in Macau. It is one of the most reputable and leading companies in Macau that provides products and services along with systems integration. He is responsible for storage implementation, architecture, upgrades, and migration (such as EMC Clariion/VNX, HP 3PAR StoreServ 7200/7400, HP P-Series and IBM DS-Series, and so on). He is also responsible for virtualization solutions (such as VMware vSphere/View, Microsoft Hyper-V, Novell PlateSpin, Double-Take, and Citrix XenServer/App/Desktop).

He has lots of experience with virtualization solutions. This includes VMware vSphere/View, Microsoft Hyper-V, Novell PlateSpin, Double-Take, Citrix XenServer, Citrix XenApp, Citrix XenDesktop, and Cisco UCS deployment. He is interested in some deployments of virtualization solutions and troubleshooting, such as VMware version upgrades, storage data migration, and so on.

He is the only qualified person in Macau with a certificate in VMware VCAP5-DCD and VCAP5-DCA, and he was awarded vExpert in 2014/2015/2016.

His professional qualifications include EMCIE, EMCPE, EMCTAe, vExpert 2014/2015/2016, VCP6-DCV, VCP6-CMA, VCP6-NV, VCP6-DTM, VCAP5-DCD, VCAP4/5-DCA, VCP5-DT, VCP-Cloud, VCP-NT, VCP3/4/5, CDCUCSS, CDCUCDS, CCA, MCITP, and MCP.

He was the author of *Mastering VMware vSphere Storage*, published by *Packt Publishing* in July 2015.

You can find him on LinkedIn at `https://www.linkedin.com/in/victor-wu-95a07022`.

About the Reviewer

Michael Ciulei has more than 15 years of experience in the IT field. He has a bachelor's degree in computer science and has obtained several certifications including CCIE Collaboration, NetApp Certified Clustered Data ONTAP Administrator, and CCNA Wireless. He has always been fascinated by virtualization technologies and the Cisco UCS platform. He has been actively involved in a significant number of complex projects and has successfully completed several UCS deployments with VMware ESXi. Michael has always been aware of the importance of staying abreast of the latest technologies and claims that pro-active learning and real-word deployments are what helped him to be on top of his game. When not spending time in his lab, Michael enjoys spending time with family and friends.

I am thankful to my friend and mentor Florin Ramboiu, who has always encouraged me to pursue my dreams and has played an important role in my professional development. I am also thankful to my wife, Cristina, who has an impressive tolerance for my Cisco endeavours.

I would also like to thank my colleagues, who are a wealth of information and a constant source of fun and have always supported me.

www.PacktPub.com

eBooks, discount offers, and more

Did you know that Packt offers eBook versions of every book published, with PDF and ePub files available? You can upgrade to the eBook version at `www.PacktPub.com` and as a print book customer, you are entitled to a discount on the eBook copy. Get in touch with us at `customercare@packtpub.com` for more details.

At `www.PacktPub.com`, you can also read a collection of free technical articles, sign up for a range of free newsletters and receive exclusive discounts and offers on Packt books and eBooks.

`https://www2.packtpub.com/books/subscription/packtlib`

Do you need instant solutions to your IT questions? PacktLib is Packt's online digital book library. Here, you can search, access, and read Packt's entire library of books.

Why subscribe?

- Fully searchable across every book published by Packt
- Copy and paste, print, and bookmark content
- On demand and accessible via a web browser

Instant updates on new Packt books

Get notified! Find out when new books are published by following `@PacktEnterprise` on Twitter or the *Packt Enterprise* Facebook page.

Table of Contents

Preface

This book is for competent system, network, or storage administrators who are working with Cisco UCS, but they now want to learn innovative ways to compute or deploy UCS to leverage its full potential.

What this book covers

Chapter 1, Cisco UCS to SAN Connectivity, is about how to upgrade firmware on Fibre SAN Switch and how to set up the interconnection of Cisco UCS to Brocade FC Switch and Cisco UCS to Cisco FC Switch.

Chapter 2, Cisco UCS to LAN Connectivity, describes how to configure the Ethernet uplink, LAN pin groups and Ethernet port channel on UCS Fabric Interconnect, and set up NIC Teaming on Microsoft Windows and VMware vSphere ESXi.

Chapter 3, Installing an Operating System on Cisco UCS, covers the system platform installation on Cisco UCS. It includes Microsoft Windows and VMware vSphere Server in local boot and SAN boot.

Chapter 4, Data Migration to Cisco UCS, describes how to migrate the physical machine and virtual machine from HP Server to Cisco UCS.

Chapter 5, System Integration on Cisco UCS, describes how to set up system integration on Cisco UCS, for example, UCS Management Pack in VMware vRealize Operation Manager, and UCS Central best practices.

Chapter 6, Cisco UCS Site Planning, describes how to use Cisco UCS compatibility Support Matrix and other vendor interoperability tools, such as EMC E-lab, HP Single Point of Connectivity Knowledge (SPOCK), VMware Compatibility Guide, and IBM System Storage Interoperation Center (SSIC).

Chapter 7, Cisco UCS Backup Solutions, describes how to backup and restore Cisco UCS configurations, the backup solutions on Cisco UCS in detail, for example, VMware Data Protection, HP 3PAR array's virtual copy/remote copy, and EMC VNX array's SnapClone and MirrorView.

What you need for this book

This book requires the following software: Cisco UCS Manager 2.2, Cisco UCS Central 1.4, VMware vSphere 5.5, VMware vCenter Server 5.5, vCenter Operation Manager 6.0, Microsoft Windows 2008/2012, HP 3PAR Management Console 4.6, and EMC Unisphere 1.3.

Who this book is for

This book is for competent system/network or storage administrators who are working with Cisco UCS but now want to learn new ways to compute UCS.

Sections

In this book, you will find several headings that appear frequently (Getting ready, How to do it..., How it works..., There's more..., and See also).

To give clear instructions on how to complete a recipe, we use these sections as follows:

Getting ready

This section tells you what to expect in the recipe, and describes how to set up any software or any preliminary settings required for the recipe.

How to do it...

This section contains the steps required to follow the recipe.

How it works...

This section usually consists of a detailed explanation of what happened in the previous section.

There's more...

This section consists of additional information about the recipe in order to make the reader more knowledgeable about the recipe.

See also

This section provides helpful links to other useful information for the recipe.

Conventions

In this book, you will find a number of text styles that distinguish between different kinds of information. Here are some examples of these styles and an explanation of their meaning.

Code words in text, database table names, folder names, filenames, file extensions, pathnames, dummy URLs, user input, and Twitter handles are shown as follows: "After finishing the FOS download, the example of the FOS file name would be `v7.1.1c1.zip`."

Any command-line input or output is written as follows:

```
portCfgFillword port, mode
```

New terms and **important words** are shown in bold. Words that you see on the screen, for example, in menus or dialog boxes, appear in the text like this: "Select **SAN Switches** in the **Download by** menu and download the Fabric Operating System (FOS) version you want."

Warnings or important notes appear in a box like this.

Tips and tricks appear like this.

Reader feedback

Feedback from our readers is always welcome. Let us know what you think about this book—what you liked or disliked. Reader feedback is important for us as it helps us develop titles that you will really get the most out of.

To send us general feedback, simply e-mail `feedback@packtpub.com`, and mention the book's title in the subject of your message.

If there is a topic that you have expertise in and you are interested in either writing or contributing to a book, see our author guide at `www.packtpub.com/authors`.

Customer support

Now that you are the proud owner of a Packt book, we have a number of things to help you to get the most from your purchase.

Downloading the color images of this book

We also provide you with a PDF file that has color images of the screenshots/diagrams used in this book. The color images will help you better understand the changes in the output. You can download this file from `https://www.packtpub.com/sites/default/files/downloads/CiscoUCSCookbook_ColorImages.pdf`.

Errata

Although we have taken every care to ensure the accuracy of our content, mistakes do happen. If you find a mistake in one of our books—maybe a mistake in the text or the code—we would be grateful if you could report this to us. By doing so, you can save other readers from frustration and help us improve subsequent versions of this book. If you find any errata, please report them by visiting `http://www.packtpub.com/submit-errata`, selecting your book, clicking on the **Errata Submission Form** link, and entering the details of your errata. Once your errata are verified, your submission will be accepted and the errata will be uploaded to our website or added to any list of existing errata under the Errata section of that title.

To view the previously submitted errata, go to `https://www.packtpub.com/books/content/support` and enter the name of the book in the search field. The required information will appear under the **Errata** section.

Piracy

Piracy of copyrighted material on the Internet is an ongoing problem across all media. At Packt, we take the protection of our copyright and licenses very seriously. If you come across any illegal copies of our works in any form on the Internet, please provide us with the location address or website name immediately so that we can pursue a remedy.

Please contact us at `copyright@packtpub.com` with a link to the suspected pirated material.

We appreciate your help in protecting our authors and our ability to bring you valuable content.

Questions

If you have a problem with any aspect of this book, you can contact us at `questions@packtpub.com`, and we will do our best to address the problem.

1

Cisco UCS to SAN Connectivity

In this chapter, we will cover the following topics:

- Firmware upgrade on the Brocade Fibre Channel Switch
- Firmware upgrade on the Cisco Fibre Channel Switch
- Cisco UCS to Brocade FC Switch connectivity
- Cisco UCS to Cisco FC Switch connectivity
- Zoning configuration in UCS Fibre Channel Switch mode
- HP 3PAR Storage connectivity of the Cisco UCS B-Series Server
- EMC Storage connectivity of the Cisco UCS B-Series Server

Introduction

In this chapter, you will learn to accomplish tasks related to Cisco UCS to SAN connectivity, how to upgrade firmware on Brocade Fibre Channel Switch, Cisco Fibre Channel Switch, and how to set up the interconnection of Cisco UCS to Brocade and Cisco UCS to Cisco FC Switch; we will also learn how to create an FC Zone on Cisco UCS in FC Switch mode. You will also learn how to present the SAN disk to the Cisco UCS B-Series Server in a different model of SAN storage; for example, EMC CLARiiON CX4 Series and HP 3PAR 7200.

Firmware upgrade on the Brocade Fibre Channel Switch

In this recipe, we will learn how to upgrade FOS on Brocade Fibre Channel Switch ranging from version `7.0.0a` to `7.1.1c1`; its model is Brocade DS-300B.

Getting ready

We need to prepare an FTP or TFTP Server for the Brocade FOS upgrade, which can either be a physical or a virtual server.

This FTP Server has the following requirements:

- The Operation System platform should be Microsoft Windows XP or 7
- Two vCPUs at 2 GHz if it is a virtual server, and one CPU at 2 GHz if it is a physical server
- 2 GB memory and 6 GB disk space
- The IP address of this FTP Server can access the management network of the Brocade Fibre Channel Switch (DS-300B)

How to do it...

In this recipe, we will learn how to download the **Fabric Operating System** (**FOS**) on a Brocade website and upgrade FOS on Brocade Fibre Channel Switch (DS-300B).

Download

Following are the steps to download FOS:

1. Navigate to `http://my.brocade.com` and login to **MyBrocade** account and select **downloads**, as shown next:

Note: Access to product downloads and documentation is limited to users with an active Technical Support Contract with Brocade.

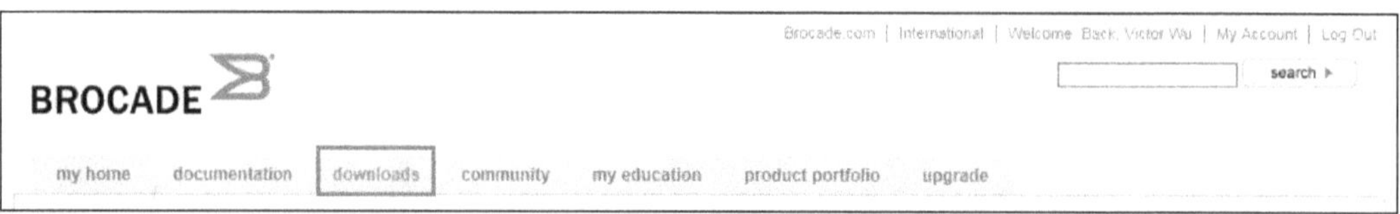

2. Select **SAN Switches** in the **Download by** menu and download the Fabric Operating System (FOS) version you want:

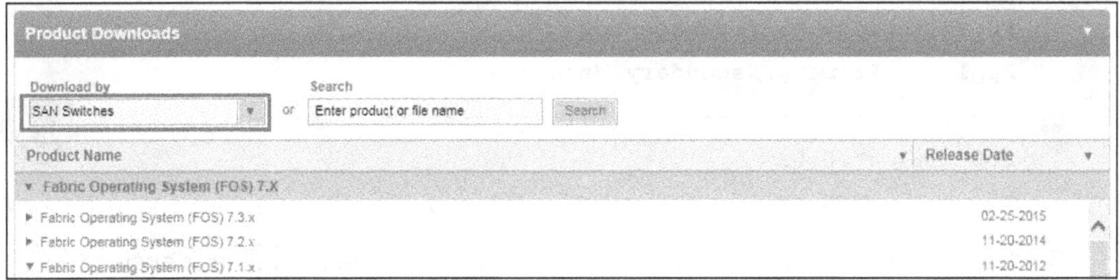

3. After finishing the FOS download, the example of the FOS file name would be `v7.1.1c1.zip`.

Upgrade

We assume that you are installing the FTP software **3CDaemon** on a Microsoft Windows XP.

Following are the steps to install 3CDaemon on Microsoft Windows:

1. First, you need to prepare an **FTP Server 3CDaemon**, which is an FTP freeware on Microsoft Windows XP; then, create a user named `user1`, who has full-access rights and set up the FOS upload path as `C:\temp\brocade\`:

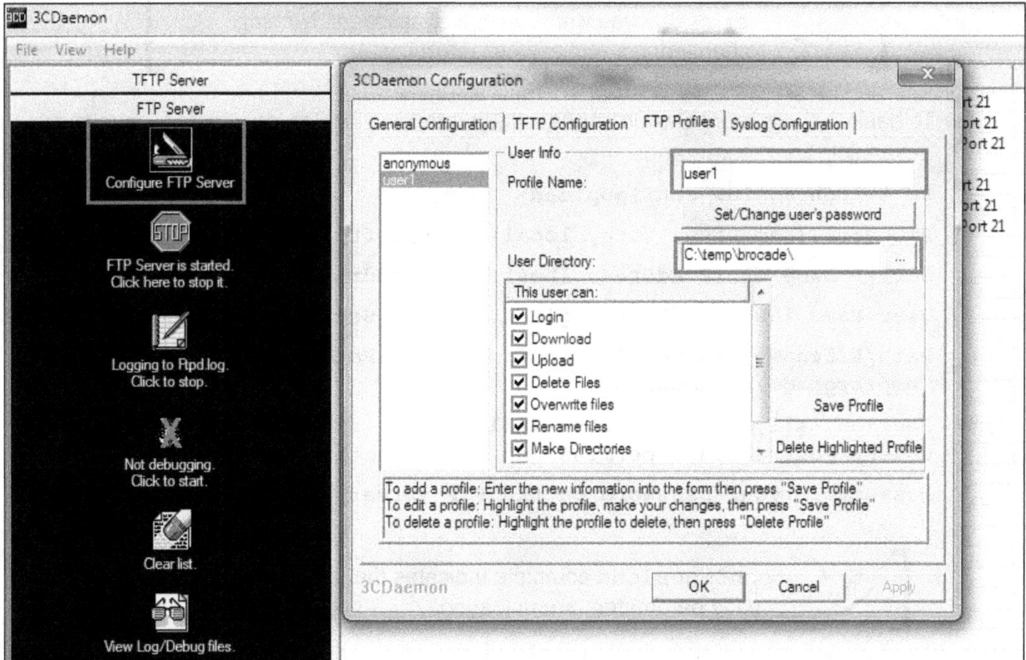

2. Use SSH to log in to your Brocade DS-300B using the admin account and execute `firmwareshow` to identify the current version of FOS. In the following output, it is listed that the current version of **FOS** is **v7.0.0a**:

```
FC_Switch:admin> firmwareshow
Appl      Primary/Secondary Versions
------------------------------------------
FOS       v7.0.0a
          v7.0.0a
```

3. Save the current Switch configuration. Issue the `cfgSave` command to ensure that the zoning information in the Switch's flash is preserved after the reboot. The following output is for reference:

```
FC_Switch:admin> cfgsave
You are about to save the Defined zoning configuration. This
action will only save the changes on Defined configuration.
Any changes made on the Effective configuration will not
take effect until it is re-enabled.
Do you want to save Defined zoning configuration only?<yes, y, no,
n:[no] y
```

Note: If nothing has changed since the most recent `cfgSave`, you will receive the message: "Nothing changed: nothing to save, returning...".

4. To backup the current Switch configuration into the FTP Server, you can issue the `configUpload` command:

```
FC_Switch:admin> configUpload
Protocol (scp, ftp, sftp, local) [ftp]: ftp
Server Name or IP Address [host]: {IP address of FTP Server}
User Name [user]: {Your login ID on FTP Server}
Path/Filename [<home dir>/config.txt]: {Path to the file} i.e./
temp/brocade/origconfig.txt
Section <all|chassis|switch [all]>: all {all should be accepted
unless your account permissions dictate otherwise}
Password: {your password on the FTP server}
```

`configUpload` complete indicates that all the selected config parameters are uploaded.

5. Execute the `firmwaredownload` command to upgrade FOS on Brocade Switch; the details of the same are as shown:

```
FC_Switch:admin> firmwaredownload
Server Name or IP Address: <FTP Server IP address>
User Name: <FTP Server User Name>
File Name: /v7.1.1c1
Network Protocol(1-auto-select, 2-FTP, 3-SCP, 4-SFTP) [1]:
Password: *****
Checking system settings for firmwaredownload...
Server IP: <FTP Server IP address>, Protocol IPv4
System settings check passed.
You can run firmwaredownloadstatus to get the status of this
command.
This command will cause a warm/non-disruptive boot but will
require that existing telnet, secure telnet or SSH sessions be
restarted.

Do you want to continue [Y]: y
Firmware is being downloaded to the switch. This step may take up
to 30 minutes.
Preparing for firmwaredownload...
Start to install packages...
dir                         ######################################
############
ldconfig                    ######################################
############
glibc                       ######################################
############
~
awk                         ######################################
############
Removing unneeded files, please wait ...
Finished removing unneeded files.

All packages have been downloaded successfully.
Firmware has been downloaded to the secondary partition of the
switch.
HA Rebooting ...
```

Note: The SSH session will be disconnected after the HA Rebooting. You should use SSH to connect to Brocade Switch again.

How it works...

In this recipe, we will learn how to verify the new firmware on Brocade FC Switch.

Validation

After finishing the FOS upgrade, you should use SSH to connect to Brocade FC Switch again and issue the `firmwaredownloadstatus` command to identify whether the firmware download has completed successfully; the details are given in the following screenshot:

```
DS300B01:admin> firmwaredownloadstatus
[1]: Fri Jan 10 09:32:47 2014
Firmware is being downloaded to the switch. This step may take up to 30 minutes.

[2]: Fri Jan 10 09:36:51 2014
Firmware has been downloaded to the secondary partition of the switch.

[3]: Fri Jan 10 09:38:24 2014
The firmware commit operation has started. This may take up to 10 minutes.

[4]: Fri Jan 10 09:41:06 2014
The commit operation has completed successfully.

[5]: Fri Jan 10 09:41:06 2014
Firmwaredownload command has completed successfully. Use firmwareshow to verify
the firmware versions.
```

Note: This operation may take up to 30 minutes.

Finally, execute the `firmwareshow` command to ensure that the new firmware is active on primary and secondary partition in Brocade Switch, as shown; the new FOS is running on `v7.1.1c1`:

```
FC_Switch:admin> firmwareshow
Appl      Primary/Secondary Versions
------------------------------------------
FOS       v7.1.1c1
          v7.1.1c1
```

Firmware upgrade on the Cisco Fibre Channel Switch

In this recipe, we will learn how to upgrade NX-OS on Cisco MDS SAN Switch from version `5.2.8e` to `6.2.13`. The model we are using is the Cisco MDS-9148.

Getting ready

We need to prepare one TFTP Server for the Cisco NX-OS upgrade, which can either be a physical server or a virtual server.

The TFTP Server has the following requirements:

- The Operation System platform is Microsoft Windows XP or 7
- Two vCPUs at 2 GHz if it is a virtual server, one CPUs at 2 GHz if it is a physical server
- 2 GB memory and 6 GB disk space
- The IP address of this FTP Server can access the management network of Cisco MDS Switch (MDS-9148)

How to do it...

In this recipe, we will learn how to download NX-OS on a Cisco website and upgrade NX-OS on Cisco Fibre Channel Switch (MDS-9148).

Download

Following are the steps to download NX-OS:

1. Navigate to `https://software.cisco.com/download/navigator.html` and log in to **My Cisco** account. Select **Products**, the details are as shown in the following screenshot:

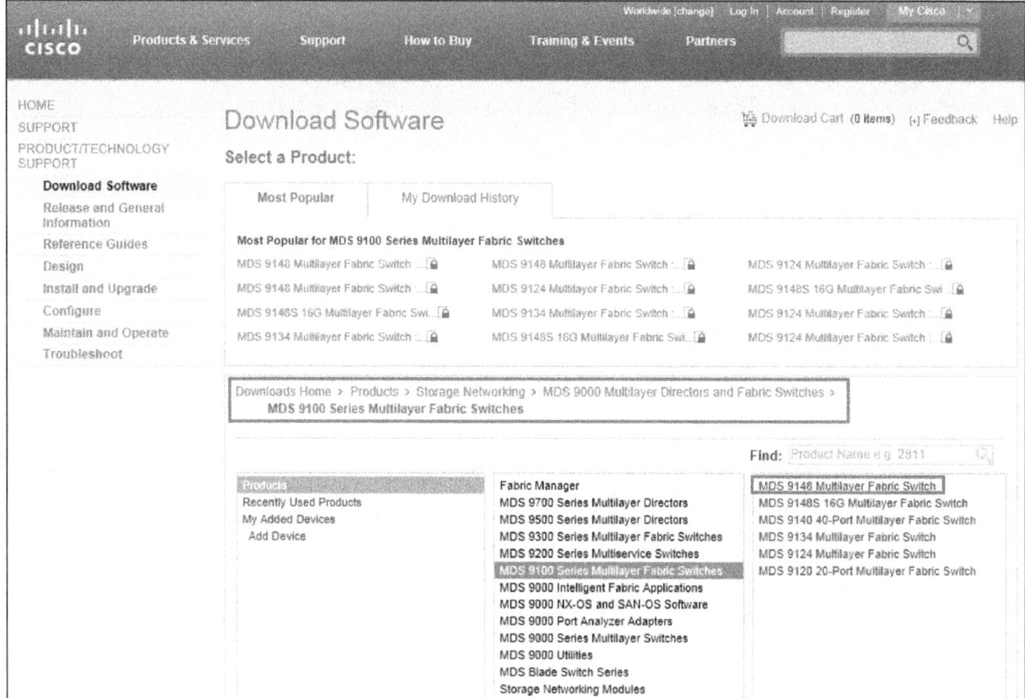

Note: Access to download Cisco NX-OS is limited to users with an active Technical Support Contract with Cisco.

2. Download MDS **NX-OS Kick Start** 6.2(13) and **NX-OS** system images 6.2(13) on the software menu:

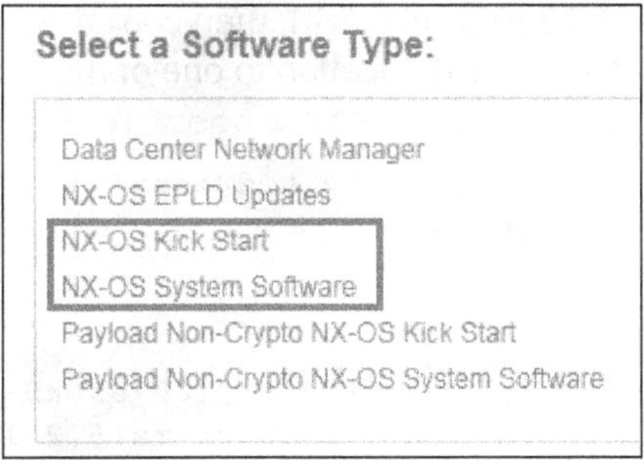

3. After finishing the NX-OS kick-start and system image download, the example of the file name will be `m9100-s3ek9-kickstart-mz.6.2.13.bin` and `m9100-s3ek9-mz.6.2.13.bin`.

How it works...

Upgrade

We assume that you are installing TFTP **3CDaemon** on Microsoft Windows XP:

1. First, prepare one FTP Server **3CDaemon**, which is an FTP freeware, on Microsoft Windows XP. Then set up the firmware upload path `C:\cisco\` and store all NX-OS firmware files on this path:

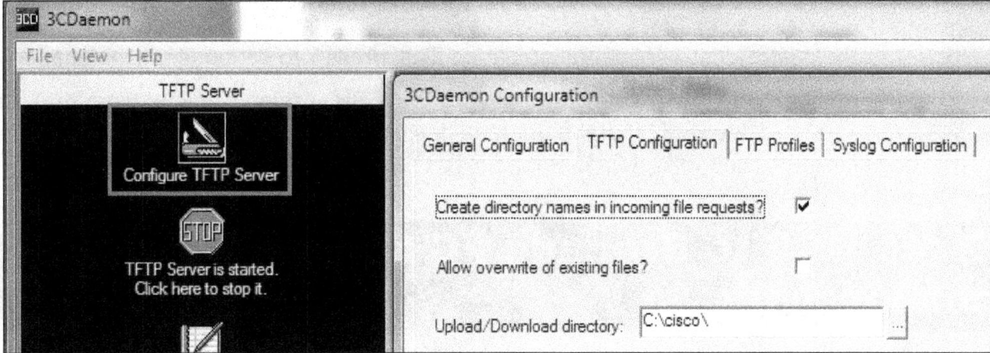

2. Log in to the MDS-9148 Switch with SSH, then copy the Cisco NX-OS kick-start and system image from the TFTP location to one of the two bootflashes. Issue the following command to copy the files to the `bootflash`:

   ```
   switch# copy tftp://<server IP address>/<filename in TFTP>
   bootflash:<image filename>
   ```

   Example:

   ```
   switch# copy tftp://192.168.1.2/ m9100-s3ek9-kickstart-mz.6.2.13.
   bin bootflash:/m9100-s3ek9-kickstart-mz.6.2.13.bin
   ```

   ```
   switch# copy tftp://192.168.1.2/ m9100-s3ek9-mz.6.2.13.bin
   bootflash:/m9100-s3ek9-mz.6.2.13.bin
   ```

3. Verify the running version of NX-OS for MDS-6148 by issuing the `show version` command. You can see that the running version is `5.2.(8e)`.
4. Back up the current Switch configuration into TFTP by issuing the following command:

   ```
   switch# copy startup-config tftp://<server IP address>/<startup-
   config_switch name_date>
   Example:
   switch# copy startup-config tftp:// 192.168.1.2/<startup-config_
   MDS-6148
   ```

5. Issue the following command to perform the upgrade:

   ```
   switch# install all kickstart bootflash:m9100-s3ek9-kickstart-
   mz.6.2.13.bin system bootflash: m9100-s3ek9-mz.6.2.13.bin
   ```

6. After the process has verified the uploaded files, press *Y* to continue the installation.
7. After the installation is complete, it will drop your SSH session. Login and perform the `show version` to verify that the upgrade has been completed successfully. You can see kick start and the system is version `6.2(13)`.

Cisco UCS to Brocade FC Switch connectivity

In this recipe, we will learn how to set up Cisco UCS 6248UP to Brocade Fabric connectivity.

Getting ready

Prepare one **Cisco UCS 5108 Chassis** with two installed UCS IOM 2208XP; each UCS IOM is connected to one Cisco UCS 6428UP. Configure two ports on each Cisco UCS 6428UP, as an FC uplink port which is connected to Brocade SAN Fabric (DS-300B) by Fibre Channel cables. The Brocade fabric is an 8 GB SAN Switch. The UCS service profile (defined by two vHBA1/2) is associated with the UCS Server and can boot up the OS successfully. The details are listed in the following diagram:

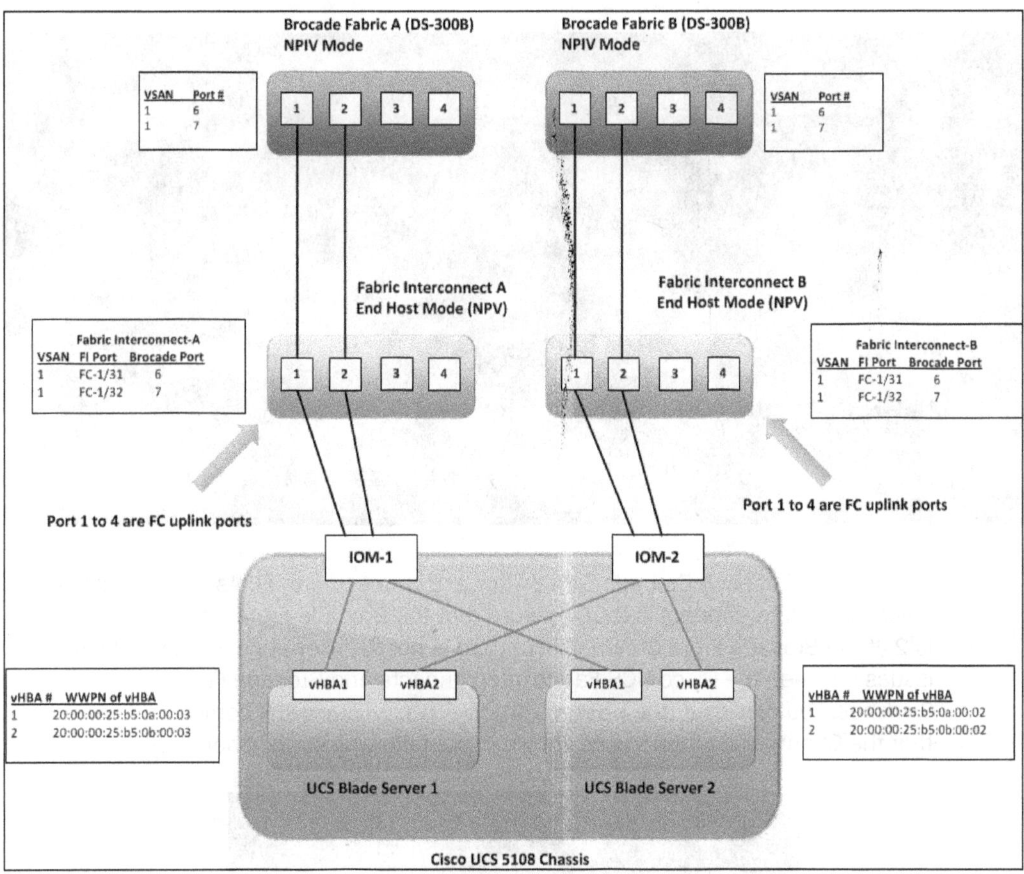

How to do it...

We assume that the compatibility of the Cisco UCS Fabric Interconnect (FI) and Brocade DS-300B Switch is supported. The FC mode of each FI is End Host:

1. We need to verify that the **NPIV** (**N_Port ID Virtualization**) status of all ports is **ON** and then issue the `portcfgshow` command on the Brocade command interface by SSH. The **NPIV capability** parameter will display **ON** if the NPIV feature is enabled per port, as shown in the following screenshot:

```
DS300B01:admin> portcfgshow

Ports of Slot 0         0   1   2   3     4   5   6   7     8   9  10  11    12  13  14  15
-----------------------+---+---+---+---+-----+---+---+---+-----+---+---+---+-----+---+---+---
Speed                   AN  AN  AN  4G    AN  AN  8G  8G    4G  AN  AN  AN    AN  AN  AN  AN
Fill Word(On Active)    3   3   3   3     3   3   3   3     3   3   3   3     3   3   3   3
Fill Word(Current)      3   3   3   3     3   3   3   3     3   3   3   3     3   3   3   3
AL_PA Offset 13         ..  ..  ..  ..    ..  ..  ..  ..    ..  ..  ..  ..    ..  ..  ..  ..
Trunk Port              ON  ON  ON  ON    ON  ON  ON  ON    ON  ON  ON  ON    ON  ON  ON  ON
Long Distance           ..  ..  ..  ..    ..  ..  ..  ..    ..  ..  ..  ..    ..  ..  ..  ..
VC Link Init            ..  ..  ..  ..    ..  ..  ..  ..    ..  ..  ..  ..    ..  ..  ..  ..
Locked L_Port           ..  ..  ..  ..    ..  ..  ..  ..    ..  ..  ..  ..    ..  ..  ..  ..
Locked G_Port           ..  ..  ..  ..    ..  ..  ..  ..    ..  ..  ..  ..    ..  ..  ..  ..
Disabled E_Port         ..  ..  ..  ..    ..  ..  ..  ..    ..  ..  ..  ..    ..  ..  ..  ..
Locked E_Port           ..  ..  ..  ..    ..  ..  ..  ..    ..  ..  ..  ..    ..  ..  ..  ..
ISL R_RDY Mode          ..  ..  ..  ..    ..  ..  ..  ..    ..  ..  ..  ..    ..  ..  ..  ..
RSCN Suppressed         ..  ..  ..  ..    ..  ..  ..  ..    ..  ..  ..  ..    ..  ..  ..  ..
Persistent Disable      ..  ..  ..  ..    ..  ..  ..  ..    ..  ..  ..  ..    ..  ..  ..  ..
LOS TOV enable          ..  ..  ..  ..    ..  ..  ..  ..    ..  ..  ..  ..    ..  ..  ..  ..
NPIV capability         ON  ON  ON  ON    ON  ON  ON  ON    ON  ON  ON  ON    ON  ON  ON  ON
NPIV PP Limit           255 255 255 255   255 255 255 255   255 255 255 255   255 255 255 255
QOS E_Port              AE  AE  AE  AE    AE  AE  AE  AE    AE  AE  AE  AE    AE  AE  AE  AE
```

2. Ports 6 and 7 of each Brocade SAN Switch are connected to FI. As each FC uplink of Cisco Fabric Interconnect is 8 GB, ensure that the Brocade Fibre Channel fill pattern is 2. If the Brocade Fibre Channel fill pattern is not 2, it develops interoperability issues between the Cisco UCS Fabric Interconnects and Brocade Fibre Channel Switches. You can issue the `portcfgshow <port number>` command to ensure that the Channel fill pattern is as shown in the following screenshot:

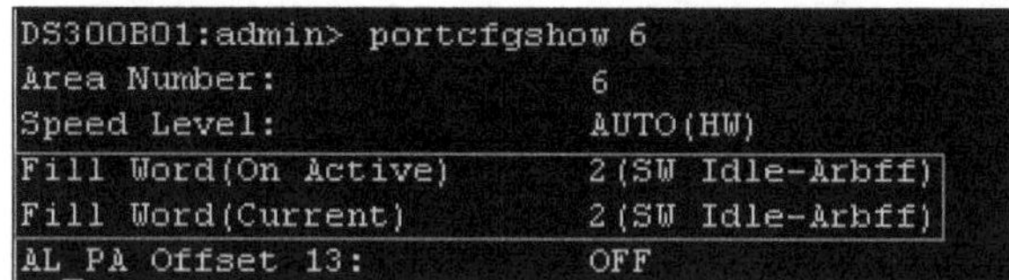

```
DS300B01:admin> portcfgshow 6
Area Number:                6
Speed Level:                AUTO(HW)
Fill Word(On Active)        2(SW Idle-Arbff)
Fill Word(Current)          2(SW Idle-Arbff)
AL_PA Offset 13:            OFF
```

> Brocade Channel fill pattern in mode **2 (SW Idle-Arbff)** can match the Cisco UCS configuration.

If the Channel fill pattern of the port is not 2, you can issue the `portCfgFillword` command to change the fill pattern. The syntax is as follows:

```
portCfgFillword port, mode
```

> The Brocade 16 GB SAN Switch does not support the `portCfgFillword` command, as this platform automatically detects and sets the correct Fibre Channel fill pattern.

3. Go to **Show Interface** of **General** tab of each FC uplink port, and ensure that the **Fill Pattern** of each FC uplink port on FI is **Arbff**, as shown in the following screenshot:

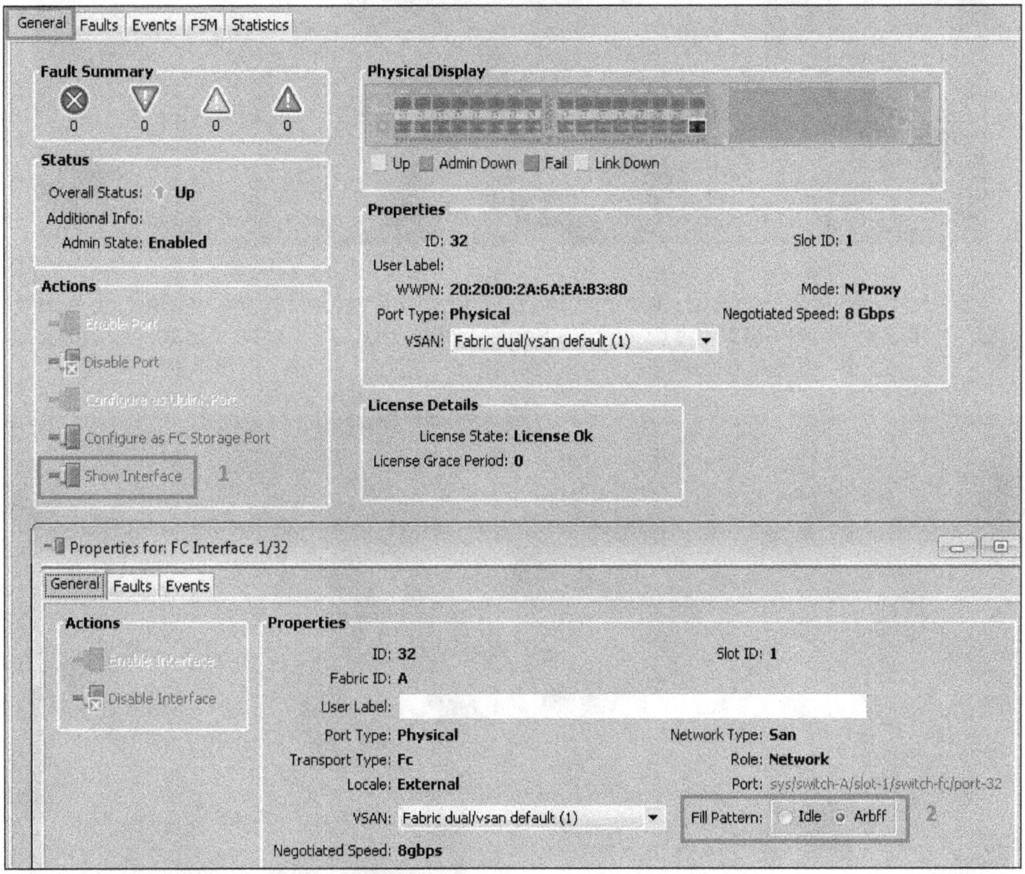

4. Repeat the preceding procedure from Steps 1 to 3 on another FI and Brocade SAN Switch. Make the connection between Cisco UCS FI and the Brocade SAN Switch by two Fibre Channel cables, and then finally the Cisco UCS to Brocade FC Switch connectivity will be completed.

How it works...

1. Log in to Brocade SAN Switch by SSH and issue the `switchshow` command; you can see that ports 6 and 7 have 2 NPIV logins, as shown in the following screenshot:

```
Index Port Address Media Speed State     Proto
==============================================
  0   0   010000   id    N4   Online      FC  F-Port  50:06:01:64:47:20:25:eb
  1   1   010100   id    N8   Online      FC  F-Port  20:11:00:02:ac:00:8e:5b
  2   2   010200   id    N8   No_Light    FC
  3   3   010300   id    4G   Online      FC  F-Port  50:06:01:6d:47:20:25:eb
  4   4   010400   id    N8   No_Light    FC
  5   5   010500   id    N8   Online      FC  F-Port  21:11:00:02:ac:00:8e:5b
  6   6   010600   id    8G   Online      FC  F-Port  1 N Port + 2 NPIV public

  7   7   010700   id    8G   Online      FC  F-Port  1 N Port + 2 NPIV public

  8   8   010800   --    4G   No_Module   FC  (No POD License) Disabled
  9   9   010900   --    N8   No_Module   FC  (No POD License) Disabled
```

2. Next, issue the `portShow` command on port 6 or 7 to identify the **WorldWide Port Names** (**WWPNs**) of the Cisco UCS Server vHBAs that are logged into the Brocade F-port, as shown in the following screenshot:

```
DS300B01:admin> portshow 6
portIndex:   6
portName: port6
portHealth: No Fabric Watch License

Authentication: None
portDisableReason: None
portCFlags: 0x1
portFlags: 0x20b03       PRESENT ACTIVE F_PORT G_PORT U_PORT NPIV LOGICAL_ONLINE LOGIN NOELP ACCEPT FLOGI
LocalSwcFlags: 0x0
portType:  18.0
POD Port: Port is licensed
portState: 1    Online
Protocol: FC
portPhys:  6    In_Sync         portScn:   32   F_Port
port generation number:    0
state transition count:    1

portId:    010600
portIfId:    43020012
portWwn:   20:06:00:27:f8:bd:c7:85
portWwn of device(s) connected:
        20:00:00:25:b5:0a:00:02   WWPN of UCS2 vHBA1
        20:00:00:25:b5:0a:00:03   WWPN of UCS1 vHBA1
        20:1f:00:2a:6a:ea:b3:80   WWPN of UCS Fabric Interconnect FC Uplink port
Distance:  normal
portSpeed:  8Gbps
```

3. Repeat the preceding procedure from Steps 1 to 2 on another Brocade SAN Switch. After that, you can create the FC zone Brocade SAN Switch for the connection between the Cisco UCS Blade Server and external SAN storage.

There's more...

The following table lists the comparison of FC uplinks between Cisco UCS and other band Blades:

Number of Chassis	Case1	Case2
Cisco UCS Chassis x 3	This does not require the installation of any additional FC module on each Chassis for FC connection. Summary This does not require additional FC module for FC uplink connections on Blade Chassis	If each Fabric network requires two uplinks, it is necessary to connect those two FC uplinks to the Fabric Interconnect. Summary Totally it has four FC uplinks throughput shared between three Blade Chassis
Other Band Chassis x 3	This needs to install one pair of FC modules on each Chassis for FC connection. Summary This requires an additional FC module for FC uplink connections on each Blade Chassis	If each Fabric network requires 2 uplinks, it is necessary to connect two FC uplinks to each FC module on each Blade Chassis. Summary This requires four FC uplinks shared between each Blade Chassis. Totally it is necessary to use 12 FC uplinks for three Blade Chassis .

Cisco UCS to Cisco FC Switch connectivity

In this recipe, we will learn how to set up Cisco UCS 6248UP to Cisco MDS 9000 SAN Switch connectivity.

Getting ready

Prepare one Cisco UCS 5108 Chassis with two installed UCS IOM 2208XP, each UCS IOM is connected to one Cisco UCS 6428UP. Now, configure two ports on each Cisco UCS 6428UP as an FC-uplink port, which is connected to Cisco MDS Fabric by Fibre Channel cables, this Cisco MDS is an 8 GB SAN Switch.

The UCS service profile (defined by two vHBA1/2) is associated with the UCS Server and can boot up the OS successfully. The details are listed in the following diagram:

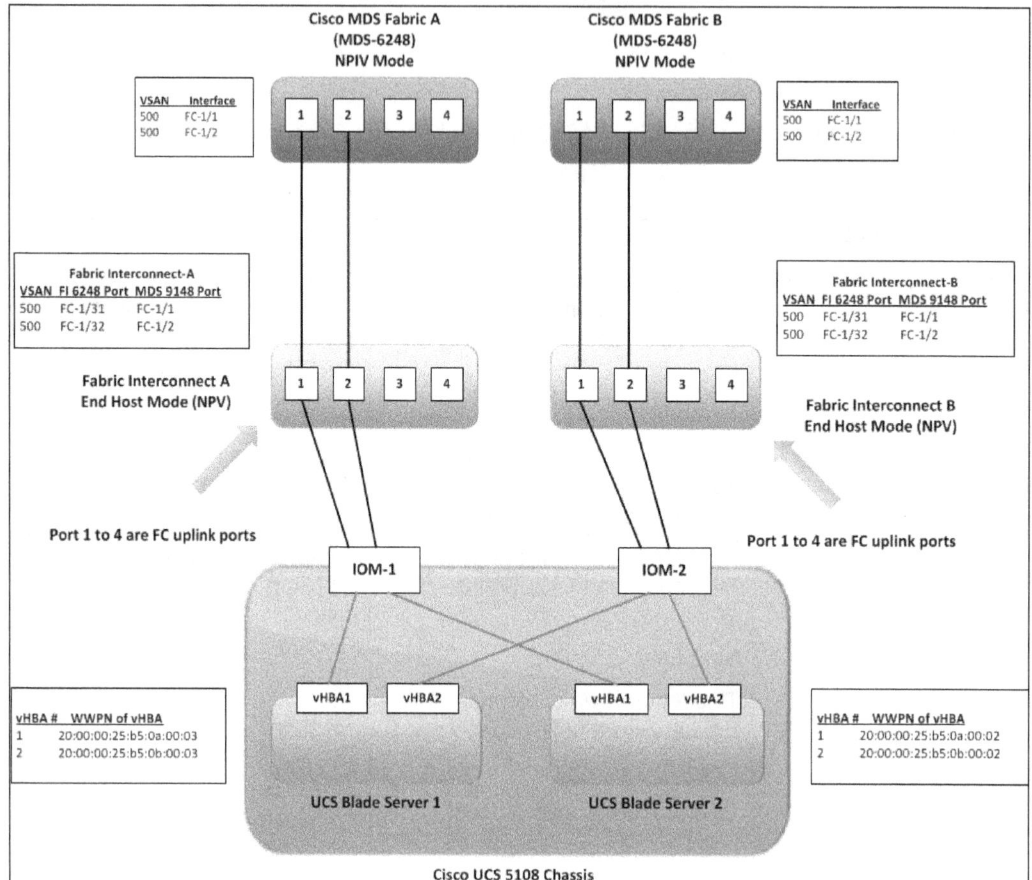

How to do it...

We will assume that the compatibility of the Cisco UCS Fabric Interconnect (FI) and Cisco MDS-9148 is certificated and the FC mode of each FI is End Host.

1. First, we need to make sure that the NPIV feature is **enabled** on Cisco MDS 9148. Log in to MDS 9148 with Cisco Fabric Manager and choose **Feature Control...** on the **Admin** tab menu. The details are as shown in the following screenshot:

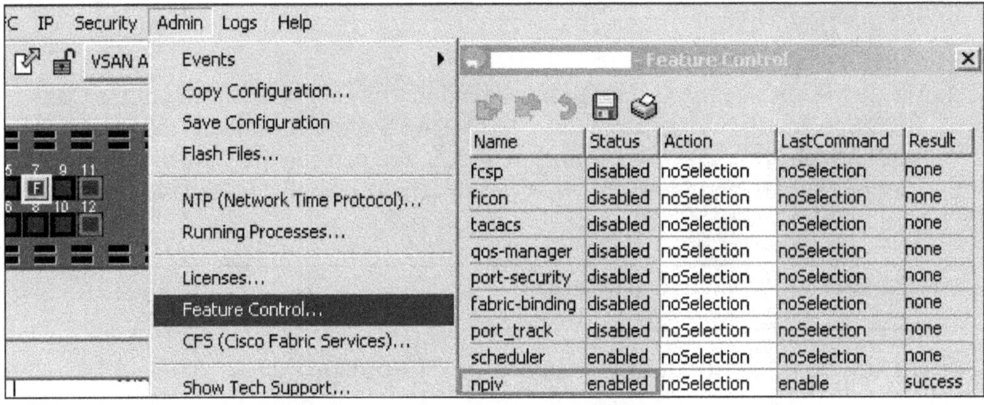

You can enable this feature by CLI via SSH if NPIV is not enabled; the procedure is as shown:

```
switch#  config t (Enter configuration mode)
switch(config)#  feature npiv (Enable NPIV feature for all VSANs
on the switch)
```

2. Make sure that the VSAN (ID=500) configuration is created and assigned to each vHBA:

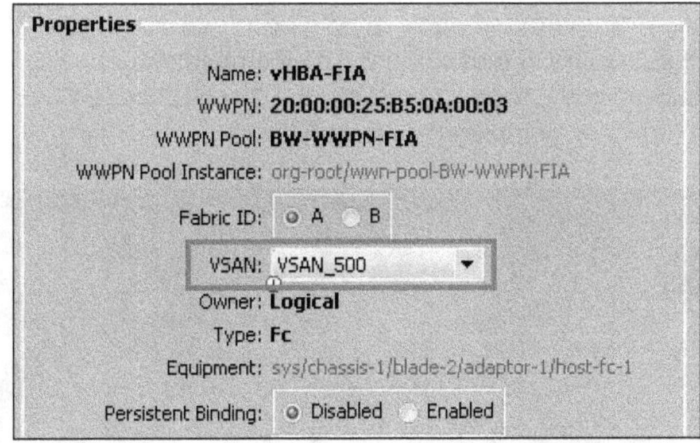

3. Make the connection between Cisco UCS FI and MDS SAN Switch with two Fibre Channel cables. Finally, the Cisco UCS to Cisco MDS Switch connectivity will be completed.

How it works...

1. Issue the `show flogi database` command to identify the WWPNs of the Cisco UCS Server vHBAs logged into Cisco MDS 9148 Switch. This means that the MDS SAN Switch is successfully connected to UCS. You can see the WWPN of UCS Server1's vHBA and Server2's vHBA, which can log in to this MDS 9148, as shown in the following output:

```
Switch1-MDS-9148# show flogi database
--------------------------------------------------------------------
INTERFACE VSAN   FCID      PORT NAME                NODE NAME
--------------------------------------------------------------------
fc1/1       500  0x010601  20:00:00:25:b5:0a:00:03  20:00:00:25:b5:00:00:03
fc1/2       500  0x010701  20:00:00:25:b5:0a:00:00  20:00:00:25:b5:00:00:00
fc1/2       500  0x010707  20:00:00:25:b5:0a:00:01  20:00:00:25:b5:00:00:01
fc1/1       500  0x010607  20:00:00:25:b5:0a:00:02  20:00:00:25:b5:00:00:02
Total number of flogi = 4.

Switch1-MDS-9148#
```

2. Issue the following command `show npv flogi-table` on the UCS Fabric Interconnect in the NX-OS mode. If the UCS Fabric Interconnect Switch returns four flogi sessions in the following output, the Cisco UCS and Cisco MDS Switch connectivity has been completed successfully:

```
BW-UCS-A(nxos)# show npv flogi-table
--------------------------------------------------------------------------------
SERVER                                                               EXTERNAL
INTERFACE VSAN FCID             PORT NAME               NODE NAME    INTERFAC
E
--------------------------------------------------------------------------------
vfc974    500  0x010601 20:00:00:25:b5:0a:00:03 20:00:00:25:b5:00:00:03 fc1/31 WWPN of UCS1 vHBA1
vfc990    500  0x010701 20:00:00:25:b5:0a:00:00 20:00:00:25:b5:00:00:00 fc1/32
vfc996    500  0x010707 20:00:00:25:b5:0a:00:01 20:00:00:25:b5:00:00:01 fc1/32
vfc1034   500  0x010607 20:00:00:25:b5:0a:00:02 20:00:00:25:b5:00:00:02 fc1/31 WWPN of UCS2 vHBA1

Total number of flogi = 4.

BW-UCS-A(nxos)#
```

3. Repeat the preceding steps on another Fabric Interconnect and Cisco MDS Switch. After that, you can create the FC Zone on Cisco MDS SAN Switch for the connection between the Cisco UCS Blade Server and external SAN Storage.

There's more...

When you increase the number of links for the connection of UCS Chassis and Fabric Interconnect, the bandwidth per chassis also increases. The following table shows the comparison between them:

Model of Chassis	Number of Links per Chassis	Bandwidth per Chassis
Cisco UCS 5108 Chassis	2	20 GBs
	4	40 GBs
	8	80 GBs
	16	160 GBs

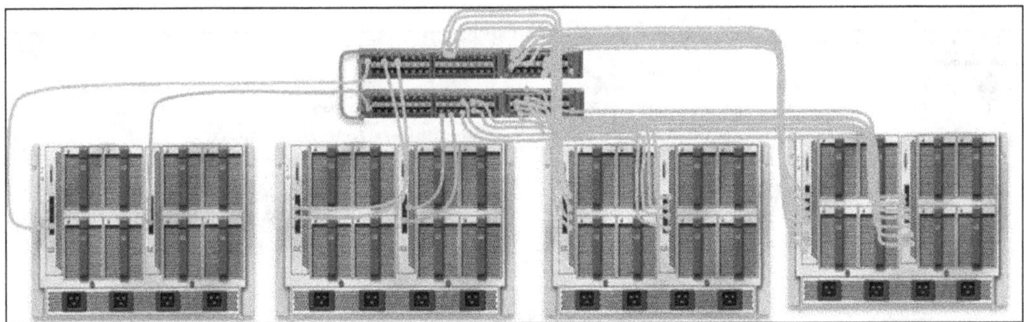

Zoning configuration in UCS Fibre Channel Switch mode

In this recipe, we will learn how to enable Cisco UCS 6248UP in the FC Switching mode, create FC Zoning on FI, and configure it into Cisco UCS service profile.

Getting ready

Prepare the Cisco UCS 5108 Chassis and install two UCS IOM 2208XP; each UCS IOM is connected to one Cisco UCS 6428UP. Then, configure the two ports on each Cisco UCS 6428UP as an FC Storage port, which is connected to the two FC ports of the SAN Storage controller by Fibre Channel. This SAN storage has two controllers, which in turn has two FC ports. There is one UCS B200M3 installed into this UCS Chassis.

How to do it...

In this recipe, we will learn how to enable the Cisco UCS Fabric Interconnect in FC Switching mode and create Local FC Zoning.

Enable Cisco Fabric Interconnect in FC Switching mode

Assume that it has configured the FC port in the UCS Fabric Interconnect.

Follow these steps to enable Cisco Fabric Interconnect in FC Switching mode:

1. First, log in to the Cisco UCS Manager and identify the **FC Mode** of the Cisco UCS Fabric Interconnect (FI) in the FC Switching mode. You should change the **FC Mode** in FC Switching if it is in the **End Host**, as shown in the following screenshot:

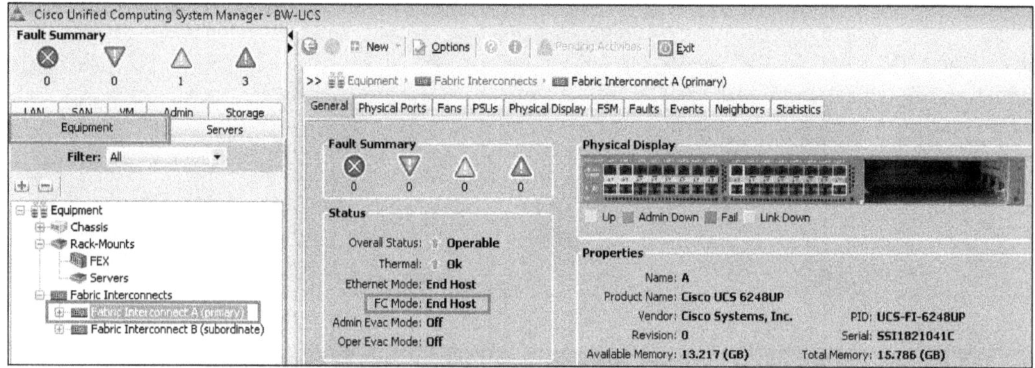

By default, the Ethernet Mode and FC Mode are in the End Host.

2. Set the FC Switching Mode to active on the **Actions** menu of the **General** tab, as shown:

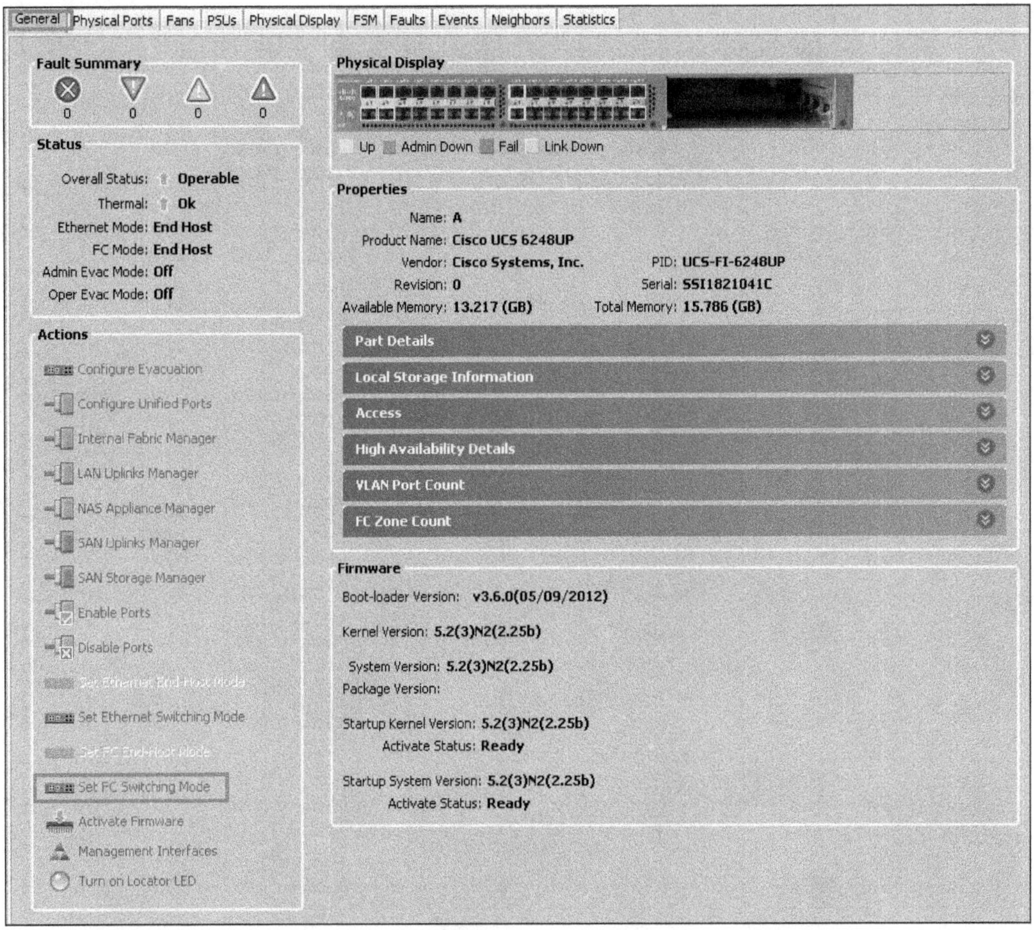

General | Physical Ports | Fans | PSUs | Physical Display | FSM | Faults | Events | Neighbors | Statistics

Fault Summary

0 0 0 0

Status

Overall Status: Operable
Thermal: Ok
Ethernet Mode: End Host
FC Mode: End Host
Admin Evac Mode: Off
Oper Evac Mode: Off

Actions

Configure Evacuation
Configure Unified Ports
Internal Fabric Manager
LAN Uplinks Manager
NAS Appliance Manager
SAN Uplinks Manager
SAN Storage Manager
Enable Ports
Disable Ports
Set Ethernet End-Host Mode
Set Ethernet Switching Mode
Set FC End-Host Mode
Set FC Switching Mode
Activate Firmware
Management Interfaces
Turn on Locator LED

Physical Display

Up Admin Down Fail Link Down

Properties

Name: A
Product Name: Cisco UCS 6248UP
Vendor: Cisco Systems, Inc. PID: UCS-FI-6248UP
Revision: 0 Serial: SSI1821041C
Available Memory: 13.217 (GB) Total Memory: 15.786 (GB)

Part Details
Local Storage Information
Access
High Availability Details
VLAN Port Count
FC Zone Count

Firmware

Boot-loader Version: v3.6.0(05/09/2012)
Kernel Version: 5.2(3)N2(2.25b)
System Version: 5.2(3)N2(2.25b)
Package Version:
Startup Kernel Version: 5.2(3)N2(2.25b)
Activate Status: Ready
Startup System Version: 5.2(3)N2(2.25b)
Activate Status: Ready

The Fabric Interconnect will restart after you click on the **Yes** button and all the ports of the Fabric Interconnect will disconnect:

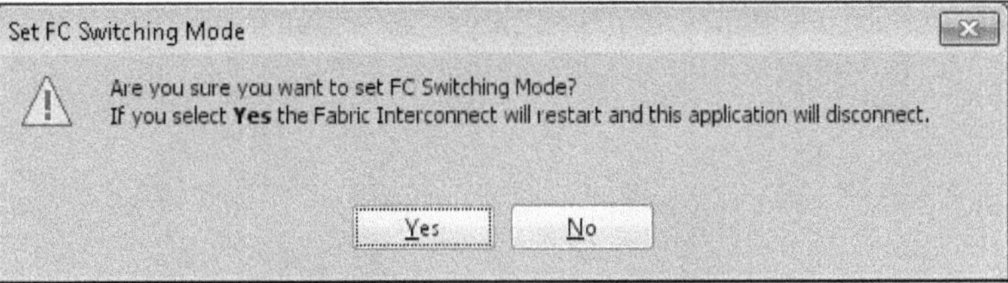

After the Fabric Interconnect restart is complete, the **FC mode** displays **Switch** and **Set FC Switching Mode** displays in gray. Now the Switch mode of FI is active.

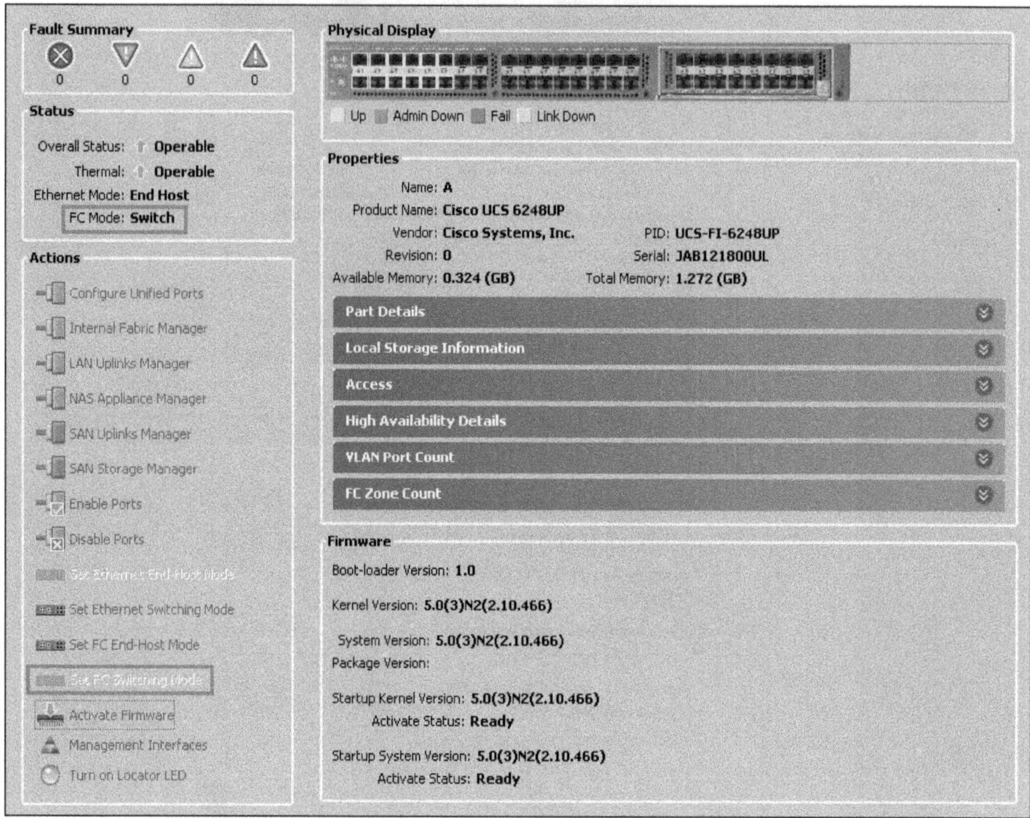

Create local FC Zoning on Cisco UCS Fabric Interconnect

The following diagram describes the concept of local FC Zone on Cisco UCS Fabric Interconnect (FI). It mainly consists of four components, **Service Profile**, **SAN Connectivity Policy**, **Storage Connection Policy**, and **SAN Target**, as shown in the following screenshot:

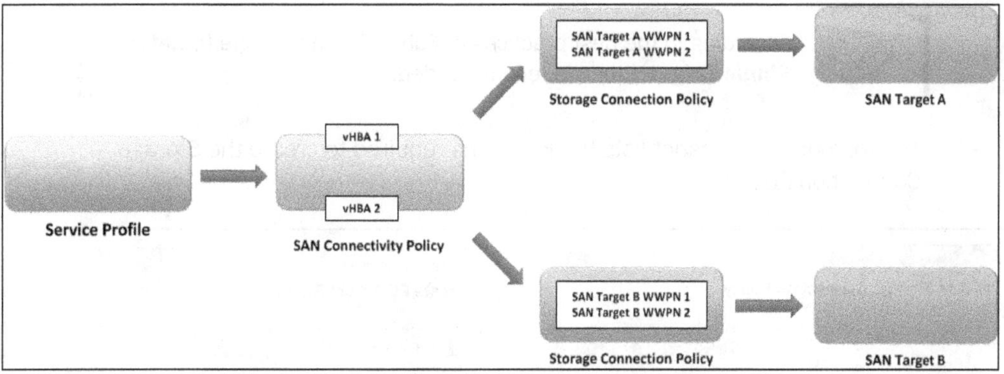

Following are the steps to create Local FC Zoning on Cisco UCS Fabric Interconnect:

1. First, create two **Storage Connection Policies**: `SAN-TargetA` and `SAN-TargetB`, in **Policies** on the **SAN** tab of the UCS Manager. The following table lists the sample configuration for reference:

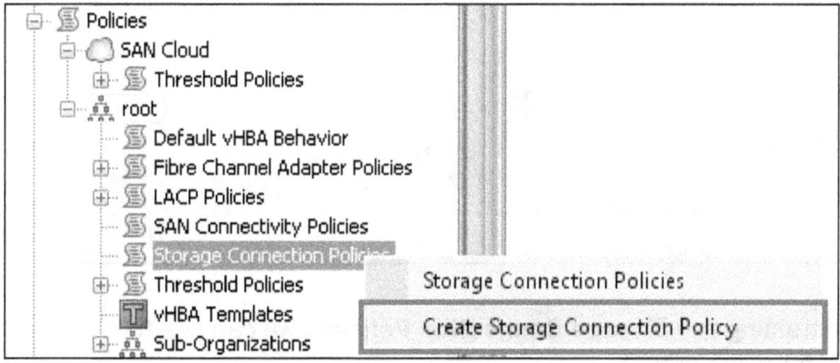

Storage Connection Policy	Zoning Type	WWPN	Path	VSAN
SAN-TargetA	Single Initiator Single Target	50:06:01:60:47:20:25:EB	A	default(1)
SAN-TargetA	Single Initiator Single Target	50:06:01:61:47:20:25:EB	A	default(1)
SAN-TargetB	Single Initiator Single Target	50:06:01:68:47:20:25:EB	B	default(1)
SAN-TargetB	Single Initiator Single Target	50:06:01:69:47:20:25:EB	B	default(1)

According to the best practices of Fabric Zoning, **Single Initiator Single Target** option is recommended.

The following screenshot lists the key items required to create the Storage Connection Policy:

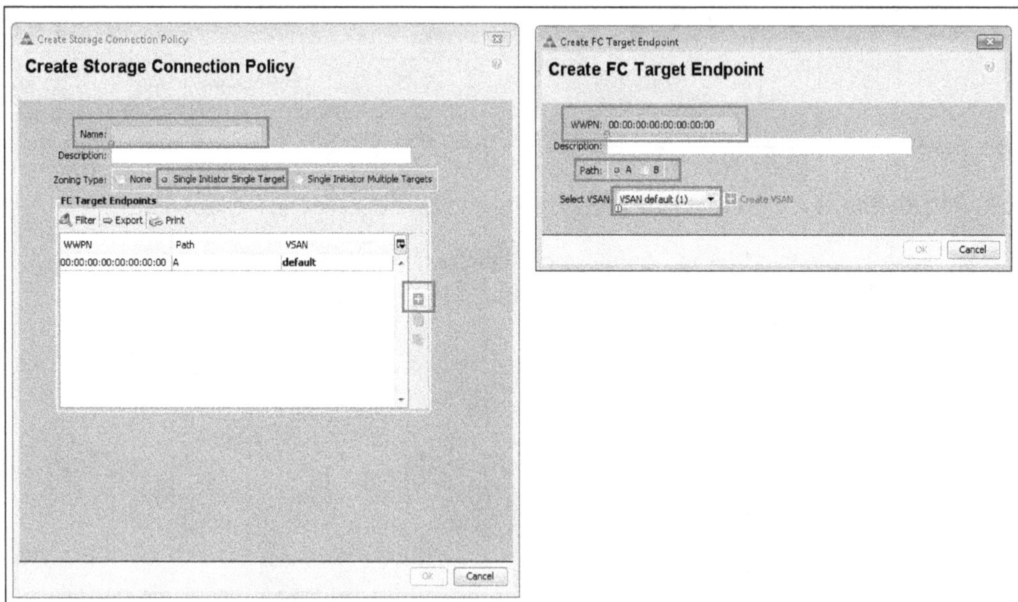

After creating two **Storage Connection Policies**, we can see that it is listed as shown in the following output:

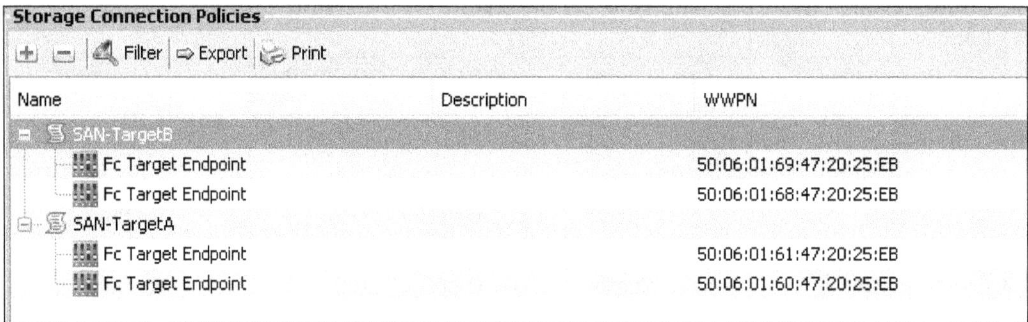

2. Create one SAN Connectivity Policy `SAN_Con_Policy` in the **Policies** on the **SAN** tab of the UCS Manager. The following table lists a sample configuration for reference:

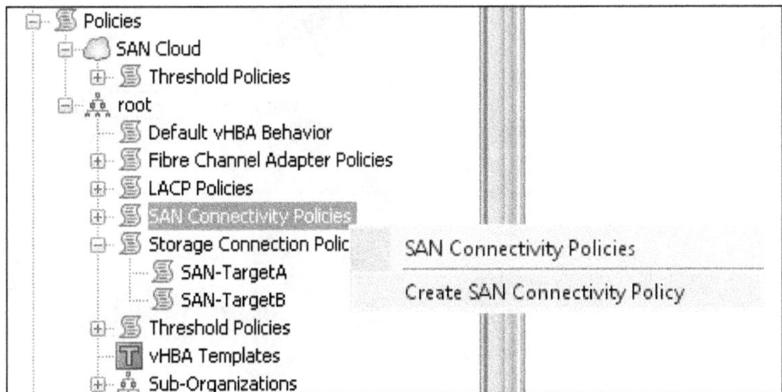

Storage Connectivity Policy	vHBA Name	vHBA Initiator Groups	Storage Connection Policy
SAN_Con_Policy	vHBA1	FabA_Zone	SAN-TargetA
	vHAB2	FabB_Zone	SAN-TargetB

3. Assume that vHBA1 is connected to FI-A and vHBA2 is connected to FI-B. The following screen is listed in the key items to create the **Storage Connectivity Policy**:

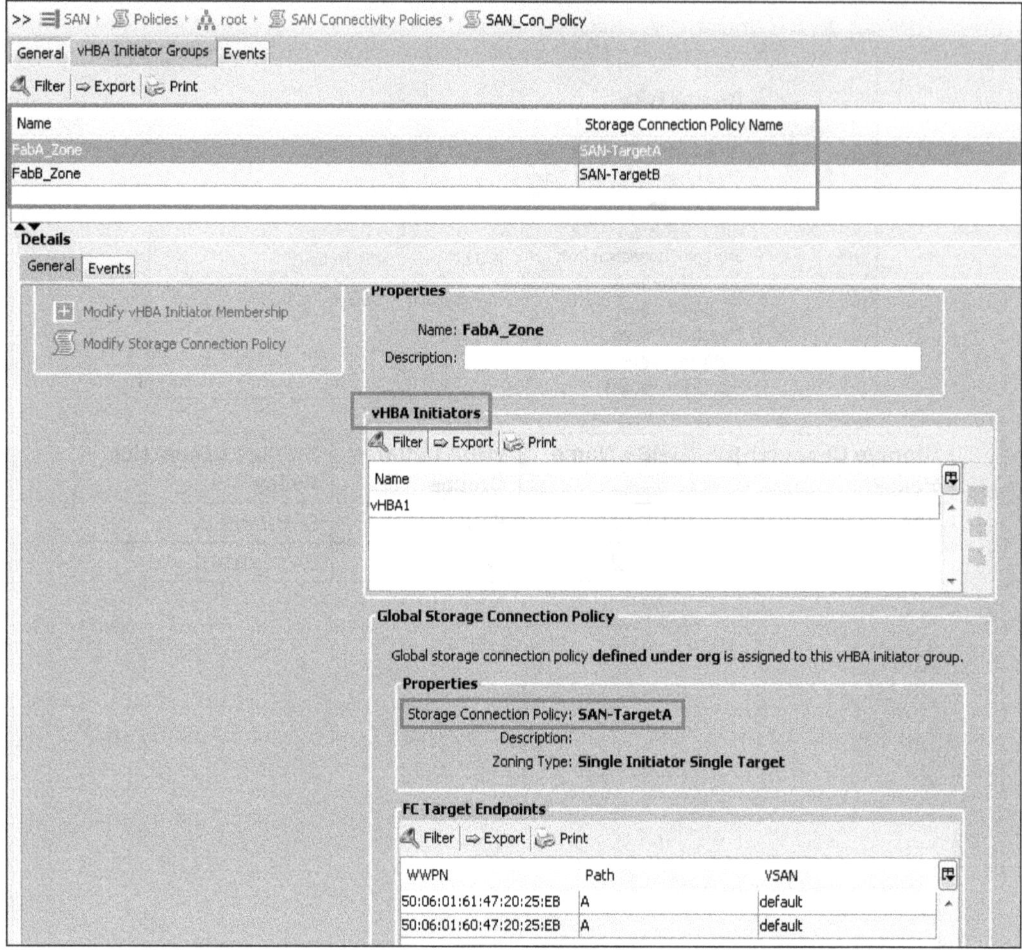

4. After creating the **Storage Connectivity Policy** named **SAN_Con_Policy**, it has two **vHBA Initiators Groups**, **FabA_Zone** and **FabB_Zone**. **FabA_Zone** includes two zones: vHBA1 to SAN-TargetA1 and vHBA1 to SAN-TargetA2. FabB_Zone includes two zones: vHBA2 to SAN-TargetB1 and vHBA2 to SAN-TargetB2.

How it works...

In this recipe, we will learn how to apply the Local FC Zone to the service profile.

Validation

You should choose the SAN connectivity during the creation of a service profile; select **Use Connectivity Policy**. In the following example, you can select the **SAN_Con_Policy**, which is defined in the preceding example:

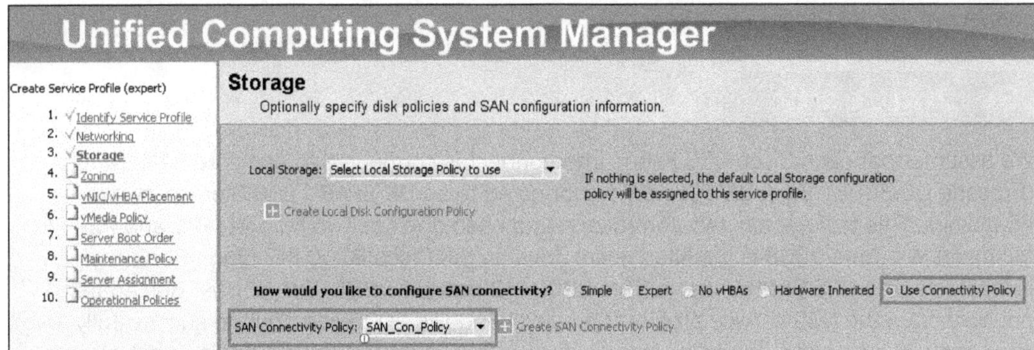

After you select the **SAN Connectivity Policy**, you can see two **vHBA Initiator Groups**: **FabA_Zone** and **FabB_Zone,** which is defined in the preceding example. This service profile includes four Local FC Zones:

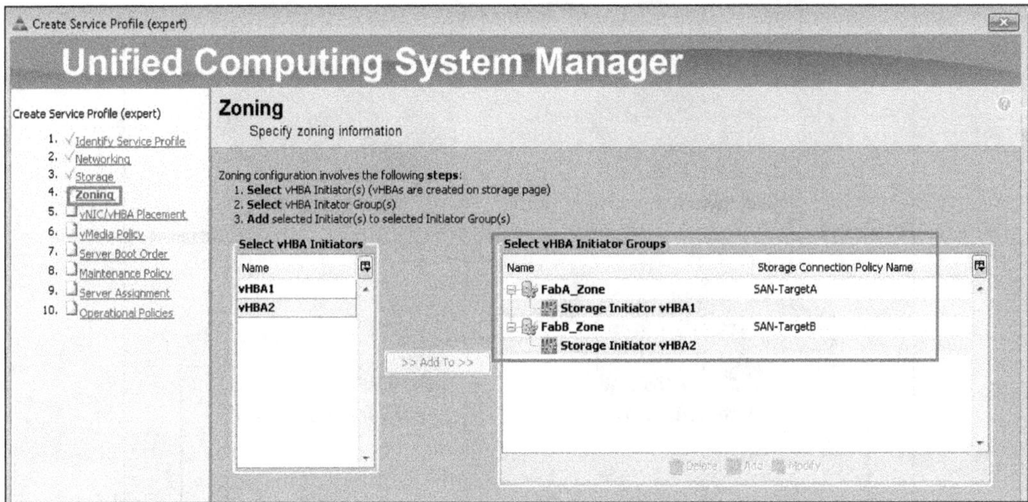

HP 3PAR Storage connectivity of the Cisco UCS B-Series Server

In this recipe, we will learn the concept of how to set up the **HP 3PAR 7200** Storage connectivity of the Cisco UCS B-Series Server.

Getting ready

We assume that each Cisco UCS Fabric Interconnect is connected to one core SAN Switch (Brocade DS-300B). Each SAN Switch is connected to an HP 3PAR 7200 Storage by two FC uplinks. This storage has two controllers, and each one has two FC ports (P1 and P2). Microsoft Windows 2008 is installed (local drive) in the Cisco B200 M3 Blade Server, which is located in the UCS 5108 Chassis. This B200 M3 has two vHBA (Virtual Host Bus Adapter) pre-defined in the UCS service profile; Microsoft Windows 2008 can boot up successfully from this service profile. The following screenshot lists the detail of this demo environment:

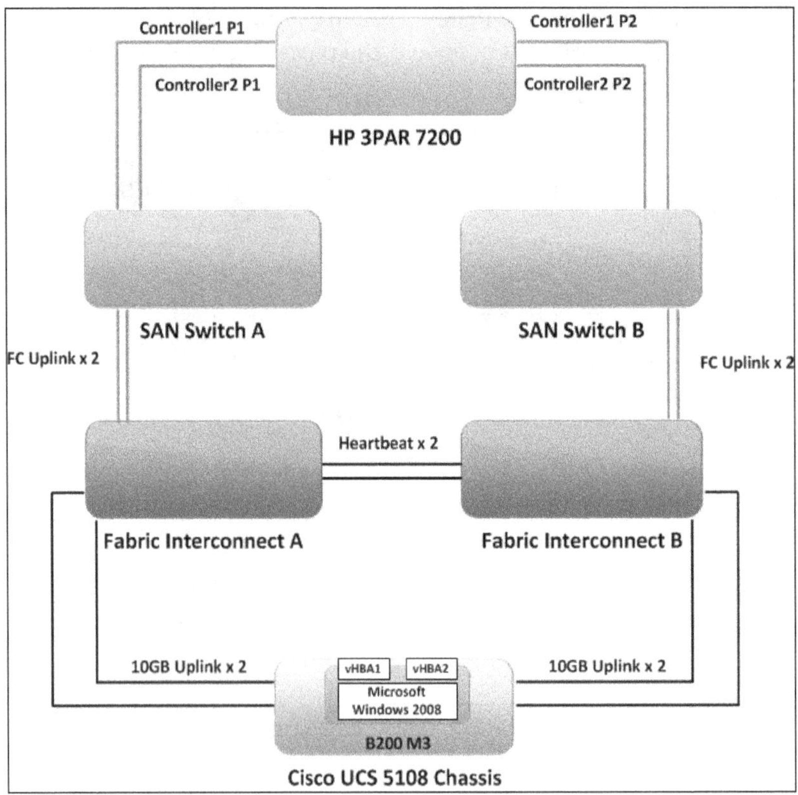

The FC mode of Cisco UCS Fabric Interconnect is End Host, each FC Zone is defined on a SAN Switch.

How to do it...

Follow these steps to create HP 3PAR Storage connectivity of the Cisco UCS B-Series Server:

1. First, go to note **WWPN** of **vHBAs** on the **Storage** tab of this service profile, as shown in the following screenshot. The **WWPN** of **vHBA-FIA** is **20:00:00:25:B5:0A:00:00** and **vHBA-FIB** is **20:00:00:25:B5:0B:00:01**:

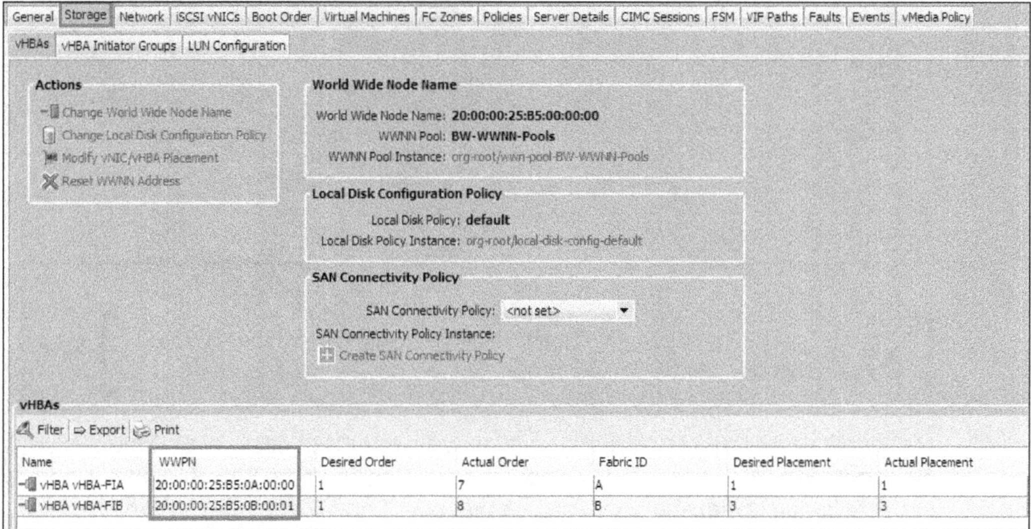

2. Log in to the **HP 3PAR Management Console** and go to **Systems** and choose **Host** of **Ports**; you can note the **WWN** of each port on each Controller. **0:1:1** is port1 and **0:1:2** port2 on Controller1 and **1:1:1** is port1 and **1:1:2** port2 on Controller2. The **WWN** of Controller1-P1 is **20110002AC008E5B** and of Controller1-P2 is **20120002AC008E5B**. The WWN of Controller2-P1 is **21110002AC008E5B** and of Controller2-P2 is **21120002AC008E5B**:

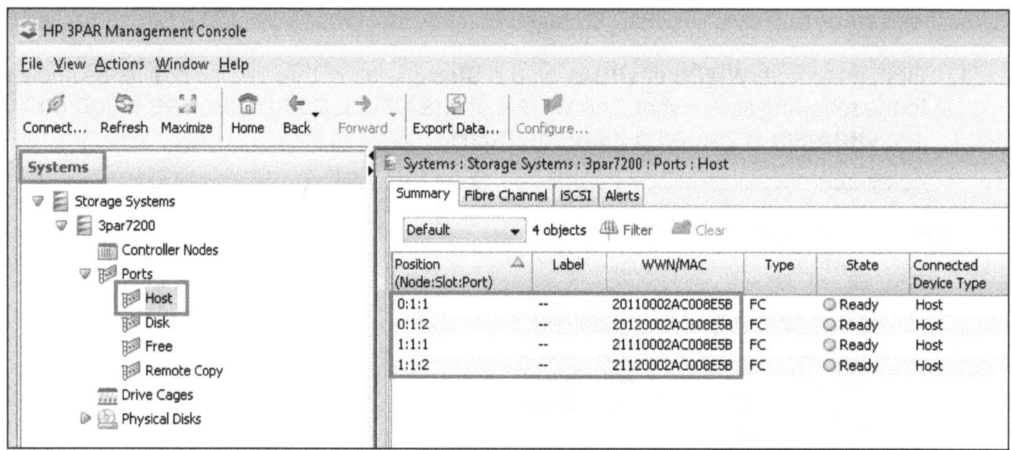

3PAR Management Console is a management tool that is used to manage HP 3PAR Storage.

3. Log in to SAN Switch-A by SSH and verify that the WWPN of each 3PAR Controller's FC port and WWN of each vHBA can successfully log on to the SAN Switch. According to the following screenshot, you can see that port **1** and **5** are the WWPN of **Controller1-P1** and **Controller2-P1** by executing the `switchshow` command. Port **6** and **7** is **FIA's FC uplinks**:

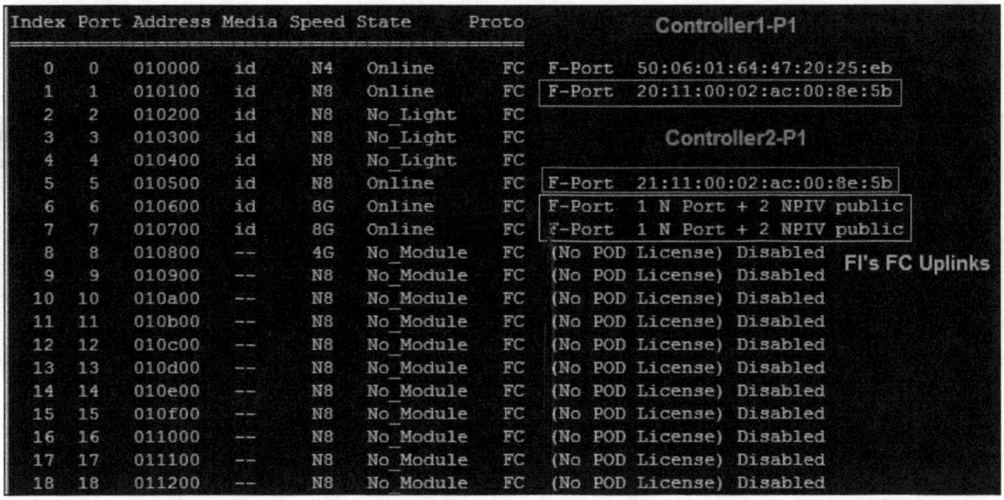

```
Index Port Address Media Speed State     Proto              Controller1-P1
=================================================
  0    0   010000   id    N4   Online      FC  F-Port   50:06:01:64:47:20:25:eb
  1    1   010100   id    N8   Online      FC  F-Port   20:11:00:02:ac:00:8e:5b
  2    2   010200   id    N8   No_Light    FC
  3    3   010300   id    N8   No_Light    FC                 Controller2-P1
  4    4   010400   id    N8   No_Light    FC
  5    5   010500   id    N8   Online      FC  F-Port   21:11:00:02:ac:00:8e:5b
  6    6   010600   id    8G   Online      FC  F-Port   1 N Port + 2 NPIV public
  7    7   010700   id    8G   Online      FC  F-Port   1 N Port + 2 NPIV public
  8    8   010800   --    4G   No_Module   FC  (No POD License) Disabled   FI's FC Uplinks
  9    9   010900   --    N8   No_Module   FC  (No POD License) Disabled
 10   10   010a00   --    N8   No_Module   FC  (No POD License) Disabled
 11   11   010b00   --    N8   No_Module   FC  (No POD License) Disabled
 12   12   010c00   --    N8   No_Module   FC  (No POD License) Disabled
 13   13   010d00   --    N8   No_Module   FC  (No POD License) Disabled
 14   14   010e00   --    N8   No_Module   FC  (No POD License) Disabled
 15   15   010f00   --    N8   No_Module   FC  (No POD License) Disabled
 16   16   011000   --    N8   No_Module   FC  (No POD License) Disabled
 17   17   011100   --    N8   No_Module   FC  (No POD License) Disabled
 18   18   011200   --    N8   No_Module   FC  (No POD License) Disabled
```

4. As ports 6 and 7 are NPIV, you need to perform the `portloginshow <port number>` command to verify that the WWN of each vHBA can successfully log on to the SAN Switch. You can see the WWN of vHBA-FIA can login to port 7, as shown in the following screenshot:

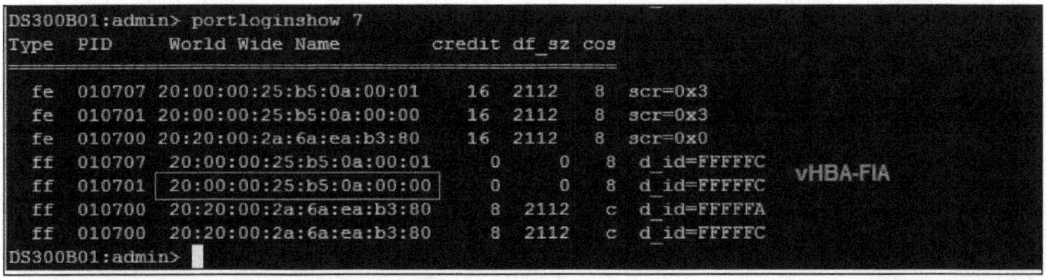

```
DS300B01:admin> portloginshow 7
Type  PID     World Wide Name          credit df_sz cos
=====================================================
 fe  010707 20:00:00:25:b5:0a:00:01    16   2112   8  scr=0x3
 fe  010701 20:00:00:25:b5:0a:00:00    16   2112   8  scr=0x3
 fe  010700 20:20:00:2a:6a:ea:b3:80    16   2112   8  scr=0x0
 ff  010707  20:00:00:25:b5:0a:00:01     0      0   8  d_id=FFFFFC
 ff  010701  20:00:00:25:b5:0a:00:00     0      0   8  d_id=FFFFFC   vHBA-FIA
 ff  010700  20:20:00:2a:6a:ea:b3:80     8   2112   c  d_id=FFFFFA
 ff  010700  20:20:00:2a:6a:ea:b3:80     8   2112   c  d_id=FFFFFC
DS300B01:admin>
```

5. Finally, you can see all the WWN login to SAN Switch-A successfully, the details are given in the following table:

SAN Switch	Port Number	WWPN/WWN	Devices
SAN Switch-A	1	20:11:00:02:AC:00:8E:5B	Controller1 Port1
	5	21:11:00:02:AC:00:8E:5B	Controller2 Port1
	7	20:00:00:25:B5:0A:00:00	vHBA-FIA

6. Repeat the procedure in Step 3 to verify all the WWPN/WWN on SAN Switch-B. You can see that all the WWN can log in to SAN Switch-B successfully, as shown in the following screenshot:

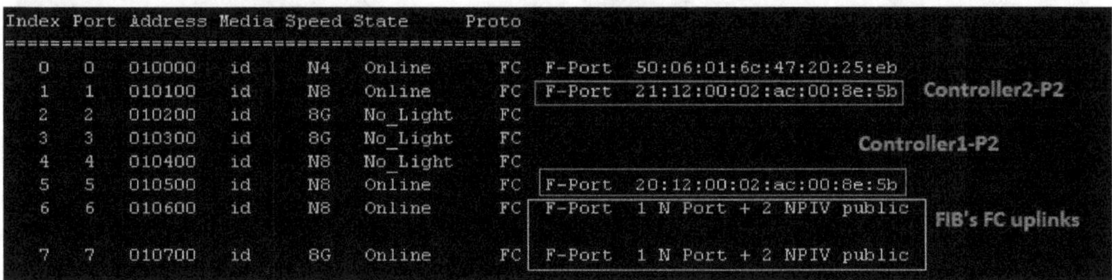

7. The following table has the listed summary of all the WWPN/WWNs on SAN Switch-B:

SAN Switch	Port Number	WWPN/WWN	Devices
SAN Switch-B	1	21:12:00:02:AC:00:8E:5B	Controller2 Port2
	5	20:12:00:02:AC:00:8E:5B	Controller1 Port2
	7	20:00:00:25:B5:0B:00:01	vHBA-FIB

8. Finally, create two zones on each SAN Switch. The following table lists the summary of each FC zone:

SAN Switch	Zone Name	Zone Member1	Zone Member2
SAN Switch-B	vHBA-FIA_Controll1-P1	vHBA-FIA	Controller1 Port1
	vHBA-FIA_Controll1-P2	vHBA-FIA	Controller2 Port1
SAN Switch-B	vHBA-FIB_Controll1-P2	vHBA-FIB	Controller1 Port2
	vHBA-FIB_Controll1-P2	vHBA-FIB	Controller2 Port2

According to the best practices of FC Zoning, single initiator zoning is recommended (one initiator to one target).

How it works...

In this recipe, we will learn how to create a new host group in the **HP 3PAR Management Console** and assign Cisco UCS's vHBA into this host group. You can then assign 3PAR's SAN disk into this host group.

Validation

1. After the FC Zoning is created on both the SAN Switches, log in to **HP 3PAR Management Console** and go to **Hosts** and click on **Create Host...** to create a host group, as shown:

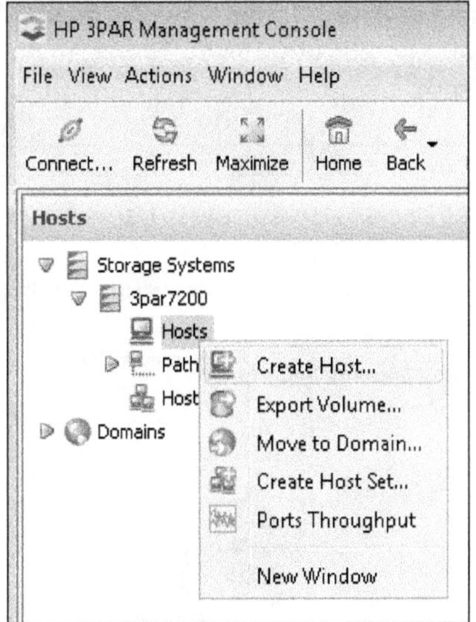

2. Input the name for this host group and select the **Host OS** as **Windows 2008/2008 R2**, as shown in the following screen:

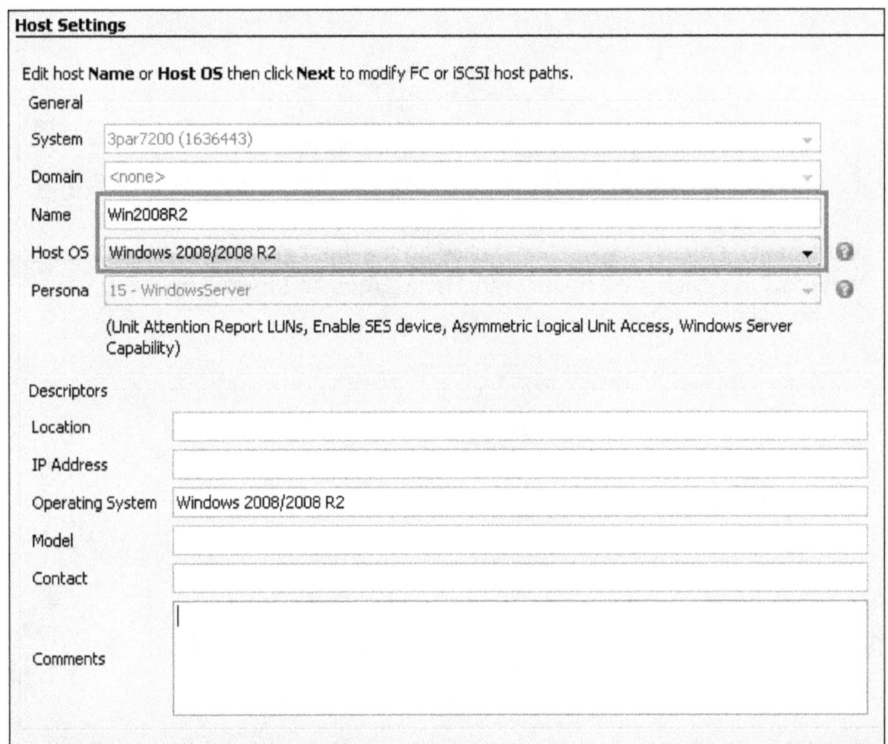

3. Assign all the **Available WWNs**, which are related to vHBA-FIA and vHBA-FIB that is, **20000025B50A0000** and **20000025B50B0001**, to **Assigned WWNs** as shown in the following screenshot:

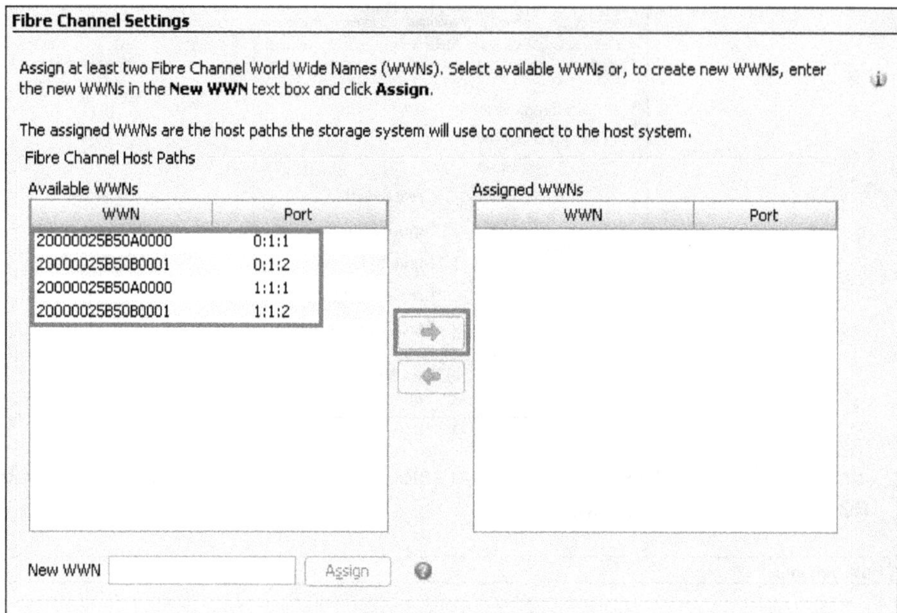

There are two zones for each vHBA on each SAN Switch; so, it there are four WWNs available in the preceding screenshot.

4. After creating the host group, right-click on the host group and select **Export Volume...** to assign the volume to this host Group on the volume menu, as shown in the following screenshot:

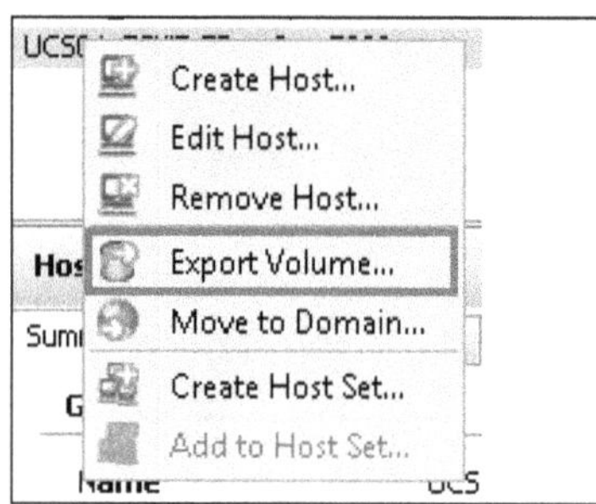

There's more...

When you configure a multipath software on Microsoft Windows 2008, according to the HP 3PAR best practice, the Microsoft MPIO needs to be enabled for HP3AR's multipath configuration.

EMC Storage connectivity of the Cisco UCS B-Series Server

In this recipe, we will learn the concept of how to set up the EMC CLARiiON Storage connectivity of the Cisco UCS B-Series Server.

Getting ready

We assume that each Cisco UCS Fabric Interconnect is connected to one core SAN Switch (Brocade DS-300B). Each SAN Switch is connected to an **EMC Storage** by two FC uplinks. This storage has two controllers and each one has two FC ports (A0 & A1 and B0 & B1). The VMware vSphere is installed (local drive) on a Cisco B200 M3 Blade Server, which is located in the UCS 5108 Chassis. This B200 M3 is pre-defined as two vHBA and associate into the UCS service profile. The VMware vSphere host can boot up successfully from this service profile. The following diagram lists the details of this demo environment:

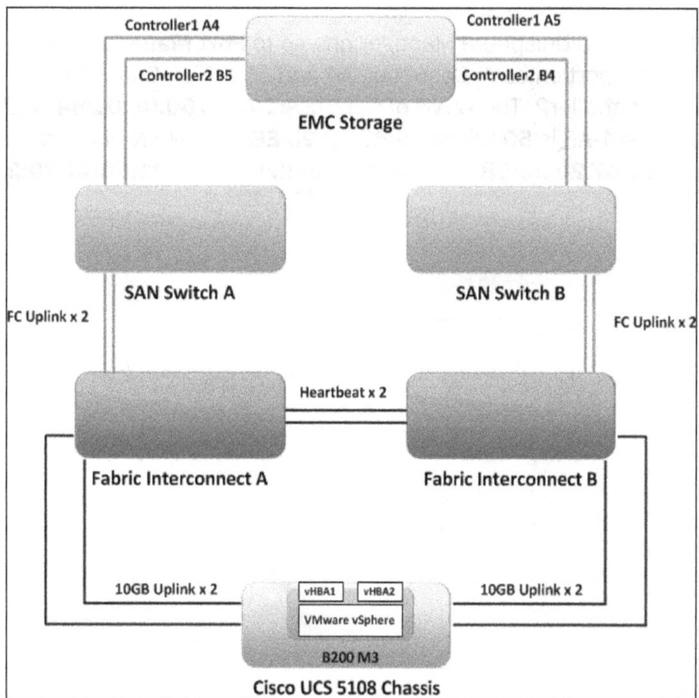

How to do it...

1. First, go to note **WWPN** of each vHBA on **Storage** tab of this service profile as shown in the following screenshot. The **WWPN** of **vHBA-FIA** is **20:00:00:25:B5:0A:00:02** and **vHBA-FIB** is **20:00:00:25:B5:0B:00:02**:

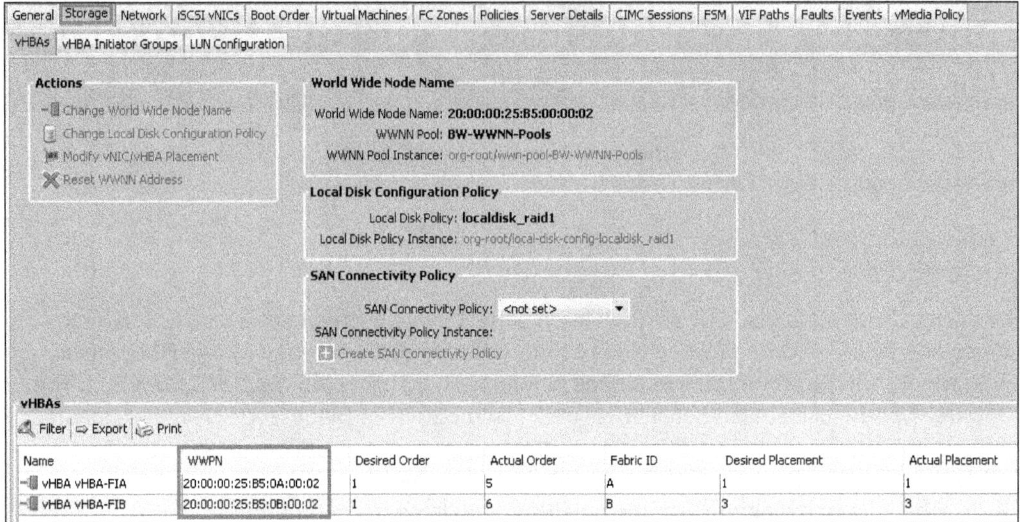

2. Log in to the EMC Unisphere Manager and go to **Port Management**, you can note **WWN** of each port on each Controller. A4 and A5 are on Controller1 and B4 and B5 are on Controller2. The **WWN** of Controller1-A4 is **50:06:01:64:47:20:25:EB** and Controller1-A5 is **50:06:01:65:47:20:25:EB**. The WWN of Controller2-B4 is **50:06:01:6C:47:20:25:EB** and Controller2-B5 is **50:06:01:6D:47:20:25:EB**:

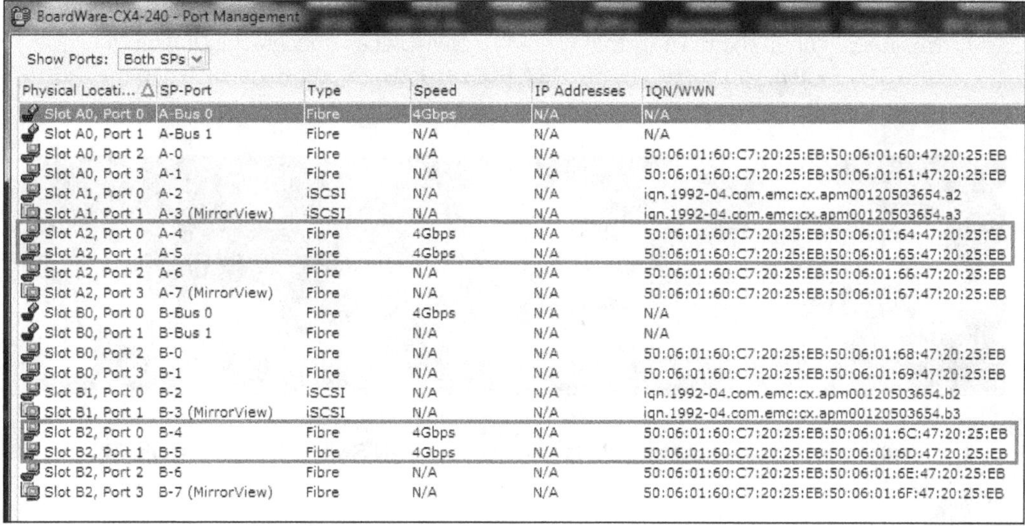

BoardWare-CX4-240 - Port Management

Show Ports: Both SPs

Physical Locati...	SP-Port	Type	Speed	IP Addresses	IQN/WWN
Slot A0, Port 0	A-Bus 0	Fibre	4Gbps	N/A	N/A
Slot A0, Port 1	A-Bus 1	Fibre	N/A	N/A	N/A
Slot A0, Port 2	A-0	Fibre	N/A	N/A	50:06:01:60:C7:20:25:EB:50:06:01:60:47:20:25:EB
Slot A0, Port 3	A-1	Fibre	N/A	N/A	50:06:01:60:C7:20:25:EB:50:06:01:61:47:20:25:EB
Slot A1, Port 0	A-2	iSCSI	N/A	N/A	iqn.1992-04.com.emc:cx.apm00120503654.a2
Slot A1, Port 1	A-3 (MirrorView)	iSCSI	N/A	N/A	iqn.1992-04.com.emc:cx.apm00120503654.a3
Slot A2, Port 0	A-4	Fibre	4Gbps	N/A	50:06:01:60:C7:20:25:EB:50:06:01:64:47:20:25:EB
Slot A2, Port 1	A-5	Fibre	4Gbps	N/A	50:06:01:60:C7:20:25:EB:50:06:01:65:47:20:25:EB
Slot A2, Port 2	A-6	Fibre	N/A	N/A	50:06:01:60:C7:20:25:EB:50:06:01:66:47:20:25:EB
Slot A2, Port 3	A-7 (MirrorView)	Fibre	N/A	N/A	50:06:01:60:C7:20:25:EB:50:06:01:67:47:20:25:EB
Slot B0, Port 0	B-Bus 0	Fibre	4Gbps	N/A	N/A
Slot B0, Port 1	B-Bus 1	Fibre	N/A	N/A	N/A
Slot B0, Port 2	B-0	Fibre	N/A	N/A	50:06:01:60:C7:20:25:EB:50:06:01:68:47:20:25:EB
Slot B0, Port 3	B-1	Fibre	N/A	N/A	50:06:01:60:C7:20:25:EB:50:06:01:69:47:20:25:EB
Slot B1, Port 0	B-2	iSCSI	N/A	N/A	iqn.1992-04.com.emc:cx.apm00120503654.b2
Slot B1, Port 1	B-3 (MirrorView)	iSCSI	N/A	N/A	iqn.1992-04.com.emc:cx.apm00120503654.b3
Slot B2, Port 0	B-4	Fibre	4Gbps	N/A	50:06:01:60:C7:20:25:EB:50:06:01:6C:47:20:25:EB
Slot B2, Port 1	B-5	Fibre	4Gbps	N/A	50:06:01:60:C7:20:25:EB:50:06:01:6D:47:20:25:EB
Slot B2, Port 2	B-6	Fibre	N/A	N/A	50:06:01:60:C7:20:25:EB:50:06:01:6E:47:20:25:EB
Slot B2, Port 3	B-7 (MirrorView)	Fibre	N/A	N/A	50:06:01:60:C7:20:25:EB:50:06:01:6F:47:20:25:EB

The EMC Unisphere Manager is a web-based tool to manage and monitor EMC CLARiiON/VNX SAN Storage.

3. Log in to SAN Switch-A by SSH and verify that the WWPN of each Controller's FC port and WWN of each vHBA can successfully log on to the SAN Switch. According to the following screenshot, you can see that ports **0** & **3** are the WWPN of Controller1-SPA4 and Controller2-SPB5 by executing the `switchshow` command. Port **6** & **7** is **FI-A FC uplinks**:

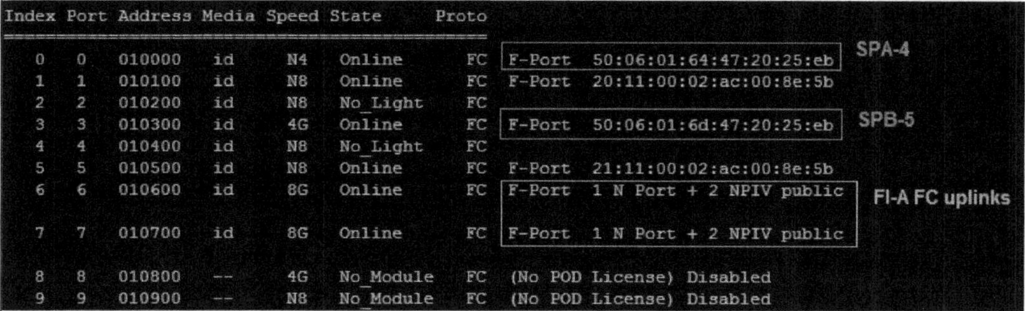

```
Index Port Address Media Speed State     Proto
==============================================
  0    0   010000   id    N4   Online     FC  F-Port  50:06:01:64:47:20:25:eb
  1    1   010100   id    N8   Online     FC  F-Port  20:11:00:02:ac:00:8e:5b
  2    2   010200   id    N8   No_Light   FC
  3    3   010300   id    4G   Online     FC  F-Port  50:06:01:6d:47:20:25:eb
  4    4   010400   id    N8   No_Light   FC
  5    5   010500   id    N8   Online     FC  F-Port  21:11:00:02:ac:00:8e:5b
  6    6   010600   id    8G   Online     FC  F-Port  1 N Port + 2 NPIV public

  7    7   010700   id    8G   Online     FC  F-Port  1 N Port + 2 NPIV public

  8    8   010800   --    4G   No_Module  FC  (No POD License) Disabled
  9    9   010900   --    N8   No_Module  FC  (No POD License) Disabled
```

As ports 6 and 7 are NPIV you need to perform the portloginshow <port number> command to verify that the WWN of vHBA can successfully log on to the SAN Switch, you can WWN of **vHBA-FIA** can login to port 6, as shown in the following screenshot:

```
Type  PID     World Wide Name          credit df_sz cos
=========================================================
 fe   010607 20:00:00:25:b5:0a:00:02    16   2112   8   scr=0x3
 fe   010601 20:00:00:25:b5:0a:00:03    16   2112   8   scr=0x3     vHBA-FIA
 fe   010600 20:1f:00:2a:6a:ea:b3:80    16   2112   8   scr=0x0
 ff   010607  20:00:00:25:b5:0a:00:02     0      0   8   d_id=FFFFFC
 ff   010601  20:00:00:25:b5:0a:00:03     0      0   8   d_id=FFFFFC
 ff   010600  20:1f:00:2a:6a:ea:b3:80     8   2112   c   d_id=FFFFFA
 ff   010600  20:1f:00:2a:6a:ea:b3:80     8   2112   c   d_id=FFFFFC
```

4. Finally, you can see that all WWNs can log in to SAN Switch-A successfully. The details are as follows:

SAN Switch	Port Number	WWPN/WWN	Devices
SAN Switch-A	0	50:06:01:64:47:20:25:EB	Controller1-A4
	3	50:06:01:6D:47:20:25:EB	Controller2-B5
	6	20:00:00:25:B5:0A:00:02	vHBA-FIA

5. Repeat Step 3 to verify that all WWPN/WWN on SAN Switch-B log in SAN Switch-B successfully, as shown in the following screenshot:

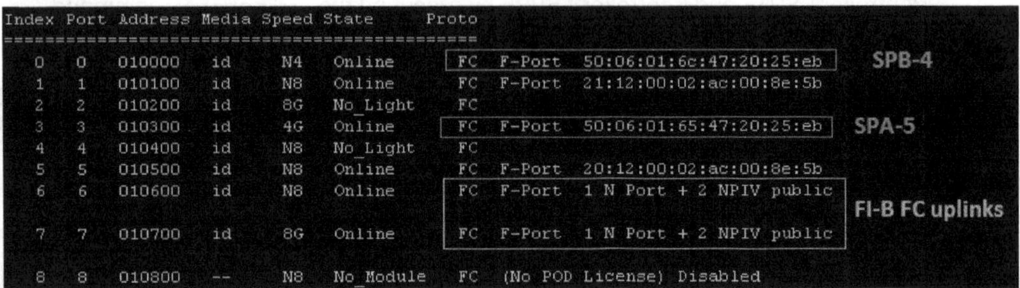

```
Index Port Address Media Speed State     Proto
==============================================
  0   0   010000   id    N4   Online      FC  F-Port  50:06:01:6c:47:20:25:eb
  1   1   010100   id    N8   Online      FC  F-Port  21:12:00:02:ac:00:8e:5b
  2   2   010200   id    8G   No_Light    FC
  3   3   010300   id    4G   Online      FC  F-Port  50:06:01:65:47:20:25:eb
  4   4   010400   id    N8   No_Light    FC
  5   5   010500   id    N8   Online      FC  F-Port  20:12:00:02:ac:00:8e:5b
  6   6   010600   id    N8   Online      FC  F-Port  1 N Port + 2 NPIV public

  7   7   010700   id    8G   Online      FC  F-Port  1 N Port + 2 NPIV public

  8   8   010800   --    N8   No_Module   FC  (No POD License) Disabled
```


6. The following table lists the summary of all WWPN/WWN on SAN Switch-B:

SAN Switch	Port Number	WWPN/WWN	Devices
SAN Switch-B	0	50:06:01:6c:47:20:25:EB	Controller2-B4
	3	50:06:01:65:47:20:25:EB	Controller1-A5
	6	20:00:00:25:B5:0B:00:02	vHBA-FIB

7. Finally, create two zones on each SAN Switch, the following table lists the summary of each FC Zone:

SAN Switch	Zone Name	Zone Member1	Zone Member2
SAN Switch-B	vHBA-FIA_Controll1-A4	vHBA-FIA	Controller1-A4
	vHBA-FIA_Controll2-B5	vHBA-FIA	Controller2-B5
SAN Switch-B	vHBA-FIB_Controll1-A5	vHBA-FIB	Controller1-A5
	vHBA-FIB_Controll2-B4	vHBA-FIB	Controller2-B4

According to the best practice of FC Zoning, a single initiator zoning is recommended (one initiator to one target).

How it works...

In this recipe, we will learn how to create a new storage group in EMC Unisphere Manager and assign Cisco UCS's vHBA into this storage group. Then you can assign EMC's SAN disk into this storage group.

Validation

1. When all the FC Zoning is created on both the SAN Switches, then log in to EMC Unisphere Manager, right-click on the **System** and choose **Connectivity Status**, as shown in the following screen:

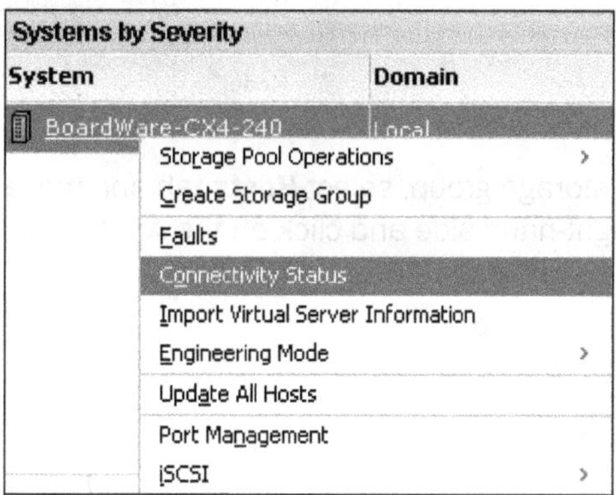

2. Then you can see that all UCS's initiators (WWN of each vHBA) will be registered automatically in one host esxi55b:

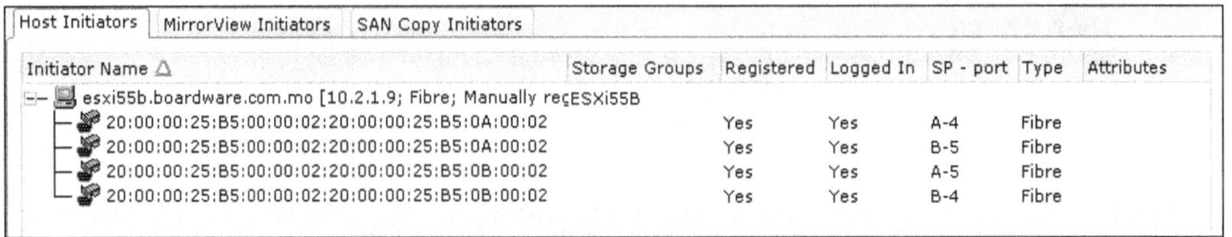

The host initiator can be registered automatically in one group, if the ESX is version `5.0` or above.

3. Go to **Storage** and create a new storage group by clicking on the **Storage Groups** in the **Storage** menu, enter the name of the storage group:

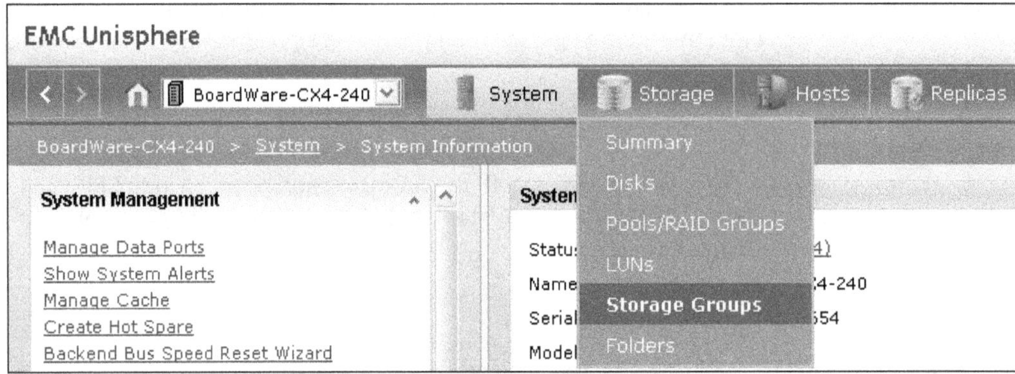

4. After creating the storage group, select **Hosts** tab and move the host initiator group "esxi55b" to the right-hand side and click on the **Apply** button. Finally, the EMC Storage connectivity of Cisco UCS is completed:

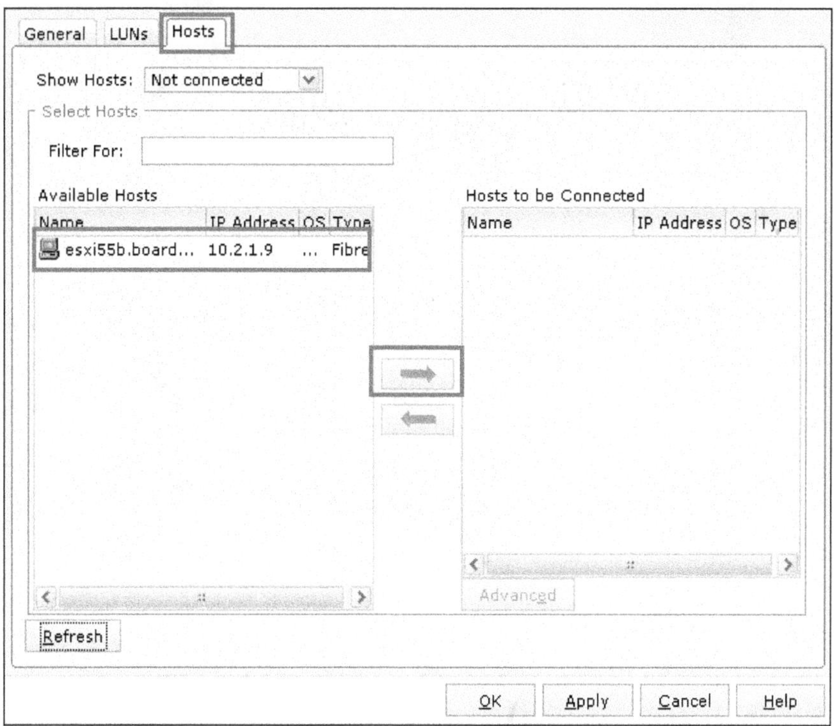

There's more...

By default, the VMware vSphere uses the VMware **Native Multipathing Plugin** (**NMP**) for multipath management. NMP is also supported in EMC CLARiiON storage's multipathing. EMC also provides its multipath software for VMware vSphere. This is an EMC Powerpath/VE that is used to automate and optimize data path pools in virtual environments.

In the next chapter, we will learn how to set up Cisco UCS to LAN connectivity.

2

Cisco UCS to LAN Connectivity

In this chapter, we will cover the following topics:

- Configuring an Ethernet uplink on Cisco UCS Fabric Interconnect
- Configuring an Ethernet Port Channels uplink on UCS Fabric Interconnect
- Installing and configuring the NIC Teaming on Microsoft Windows
- Configuring the load-balancing and failover on VMware vSphere
- Configuring LAN pin groups on UCS Fabric Interconnect
- Installing and configuring VMware vSphere Distributed Switch on Cisco UCS

Introduction

In this chapter, you will learn how to accomplish tasks related to Cisco UCS and LAN connectivity; how to configure the Ethernet uplink, LAN pin groups, and Ethernet Port Channels on UCS Fabric Interconnect; how to install and configure the NIC Teaming on Microsoft Windows Server; and set up the load-balancing and failover on the VMware vSphere Server. You will also learn how to install and configure the VMware vSphere Distributed Switch (DvSwitch) on Cisco UCS Server.

Configuring an Ethernet uplink on Cisco UCS Fabric Interconnect

In this recipe, we will learn how to configure the Ethernet uplink on Cisco Fabric Interconnect.

Getting ready

Prepare a **Cisco UCS 5108 Chassis** with two UCS IOM 2208XP installed, each UCS IOM is connected to one Cisco UCS 6428UP, and configure two ports on each Cisco UCS 6428UP as the Ethernet uplink port (port 17/18), which is connected to a Cisco LAN Switch by Fibre Channel cables. The details are shown in the following diagram:

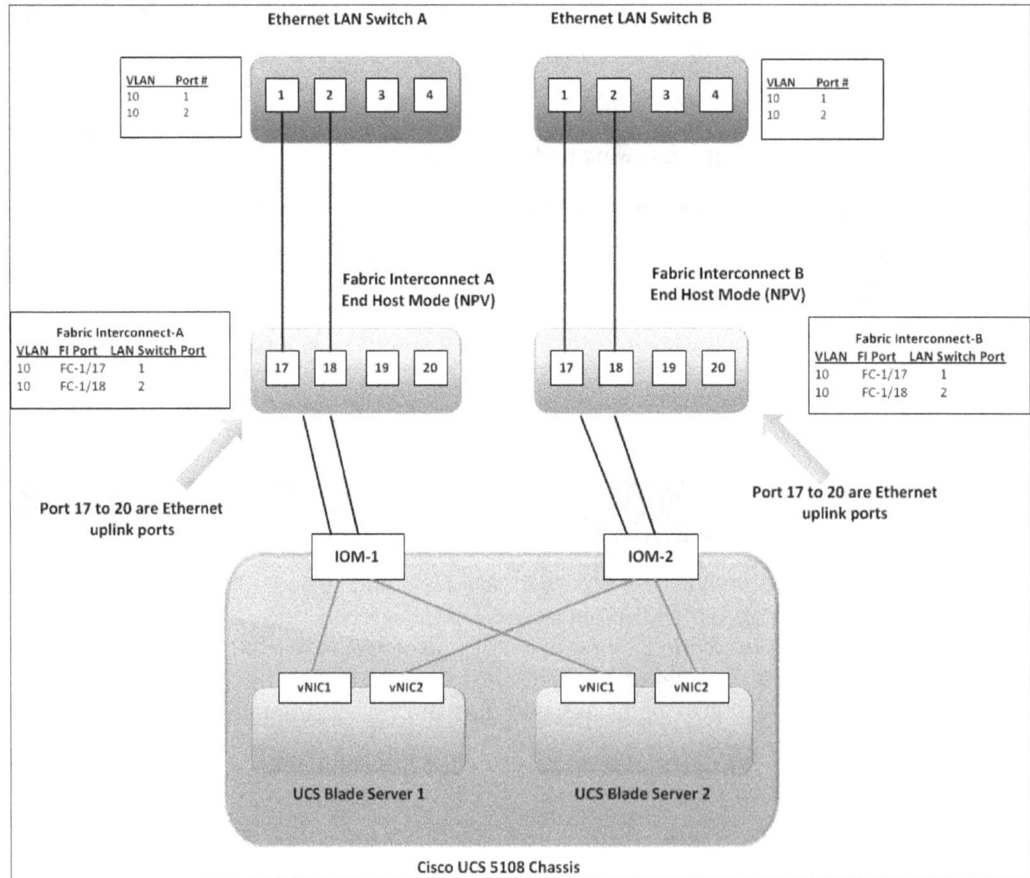

How to do it...

In this recipe, we will learn how to configure an individual Ethernet uplink on **Fabric Interconnect** (**FI**).

The following steps configure the Ethernet uplink:

1. Assume that ports 1 to 24 are the Ethernet ports on each Fabric Interconnect.
2. Log in to UCS Manager and click on the **Equipment** tab in the navigation pane. In the **Equipment** tab, click on **Fabric Interconnects**, as shown:

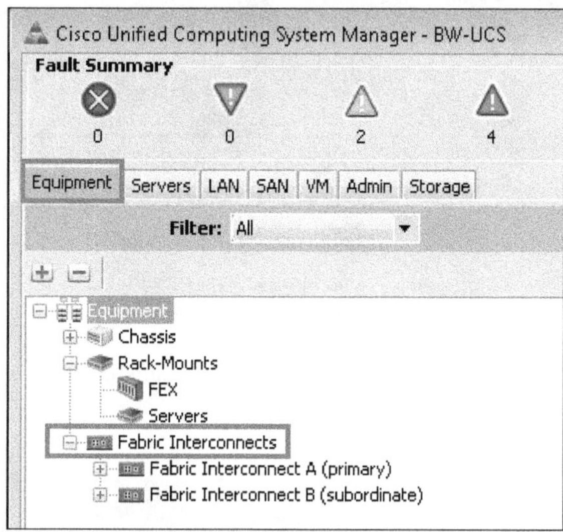

3. Verify that the **Ethernet Mode** of FI is **End Host**, as shown in the following screenshot:

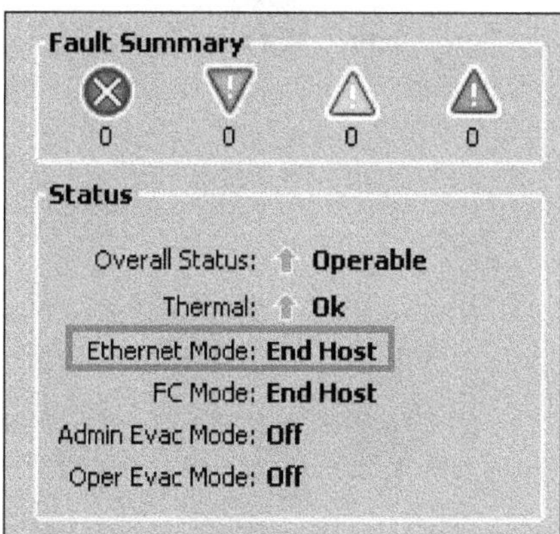

[You need to change the Ethernet Mode to the End host if the mode is in the Switching Mode. Fabric Interconnect is required to reboot if it changes the Ethernet Mode.]

4. Assume that ports 17 and 18 are not configured, now configure these two ports as uplink port by right-clicking on port 17 and 18 and selecting **Configure as Uplink Port**, as shown in the following screenshot:

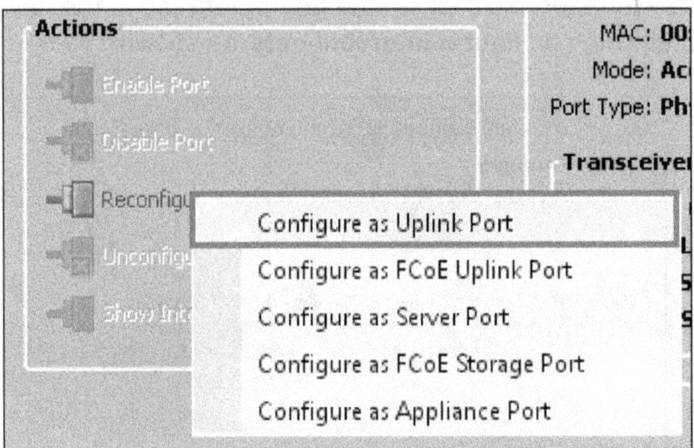

Repeat the preceding steps to configure all the uplink ports on another Fabric Interconnects.

How it works...

In this recipe, we will learn how to verify the state of an Ethernet uplink on FI.

Validation

The **Role** of the port (17 and 18) is to display **Network** after configuring the port as an uplink port. The **Admin State** displays **Enabled** and **Overall Status** displays **Up**, as shown in the following screenshot:

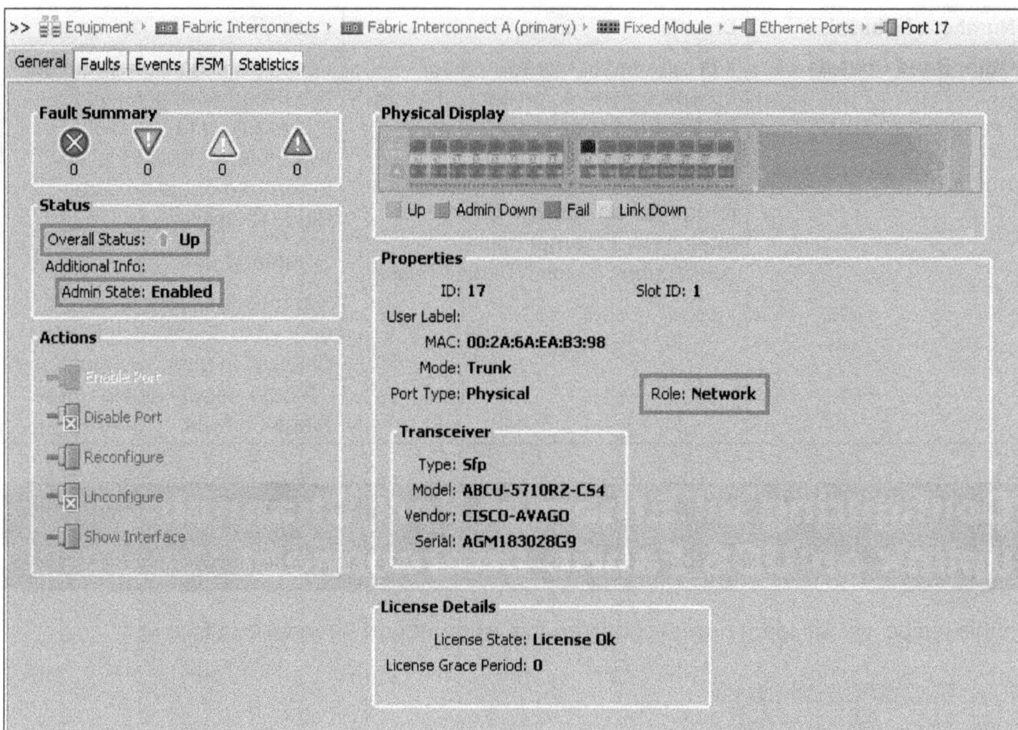

Repeat the preceding procedure to verify all the uplink ports on another Fabric Interconnects.

There's more...

The following table lists the comparison of Ethernet uplinks between Cisco UCS and other band Blades:

Number of Chassis	Case 1	Case 2
Cisco UCS Chassis x 3	It is not necessary to install an additional Ethernet module on each Chassis for Ethernet connection. Summary: An additional FC module for Ethernet uplink connections on each Blade Chassis is NOT required.	If each Fabric network requires two Ethernet uplinks, it is required to connect two Ethernet uplinks to each Fabric Interconnect. Summary: In total, four Ethernet uplinks are required to share three Blade Chassis

Number of Chassis	Case 1	Case 2
Other Band Chassis x 3	It is required to install a pair of Ethernet modules on each Chassis for Ethernet connection. Summary: It requires an additional Ethernet module for Ethernet uplink connections on each Blade Chassis	Each Fabric network requires two Ethernet uplinks and it is required to connect two Ethernet uplinks to an Ethernet module on each Blade Chassis. Summary: You must use four Ethernet uplinks to share each Blade Chassis. In total, you must use 12 Ethernet uplinks for three Blade Chassis.

Configuring an Ethernet Port Channels uplink on UCS Fabric Interconnect

In this recipe, we will learn how to configure the Ethernet port channel on Cisco FI.

Getting ready

Prepare a Cisco UCS 5108 Chassis with two UCS IOM 2208 XP installed and each UCS IOM is connected to a Cisco UCS 6428 UP. Configure four ports on each Cisco UCS 6428 UP, as Ethernet uplink ports (port 17/18/19/20), which are connected to Cisco LAN Switch by Fibre Channel cables. The details are listed in the following diagram:

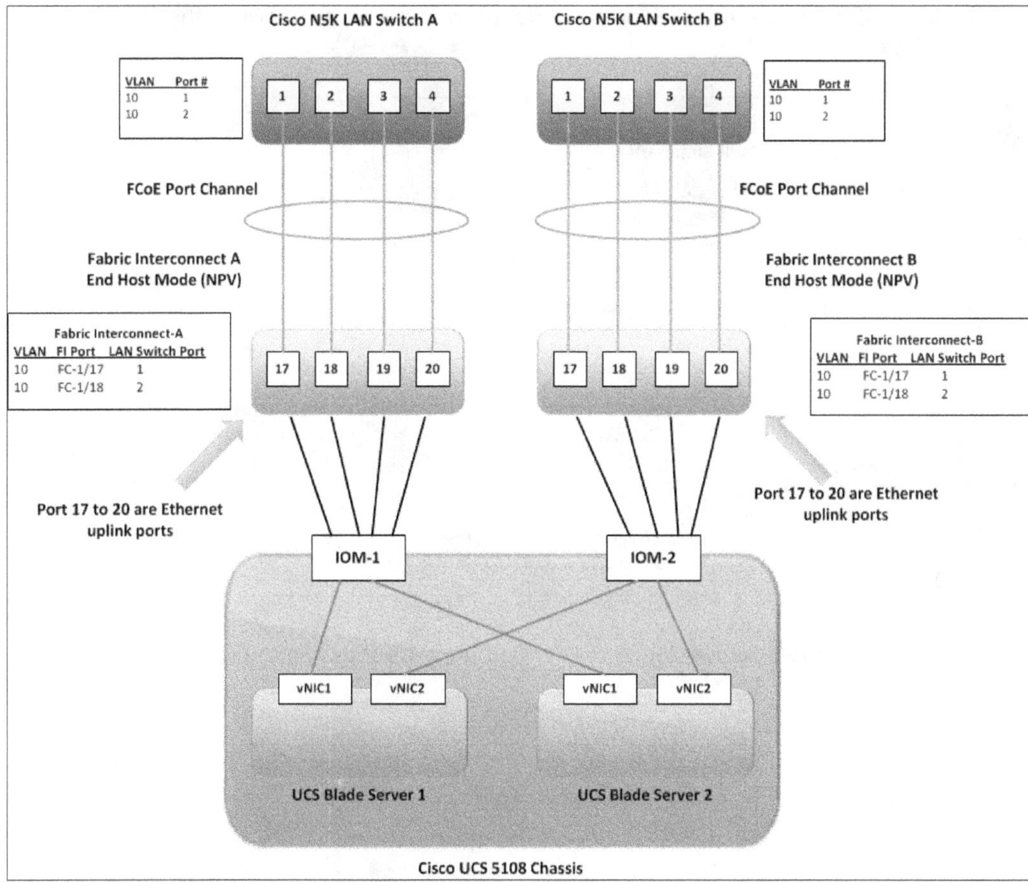

How to do it...

In this recipe, we will learn how to configure the Ethernet Port Channel on FI.

The following are the steps to configure the Ethernet uplink:

1. Assume that ports 1 to 24 are the Ethernet ports on each Fabric Interconnect.
2. Open an Internet Browser, such as IE or Firefox and enter the FI Cluster address and log in to the UCS Manager. Click on the **Equipment** tab in the navigation pane.

3. In the **Equipment** tab, click on a **Fabric Interconnects**, as shown in the following screenshot:

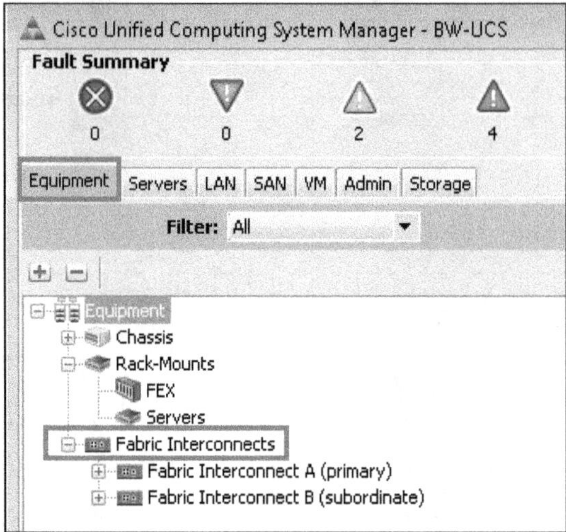

4. Verify that the **Ethernet Mode** of FI is **End Host**, as shown in the following screenshot:

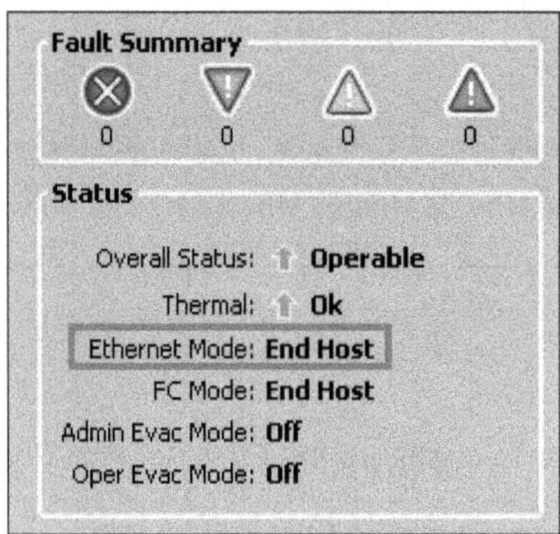

You need to change the Ethernet Mode in the end host if the mode is Switching Mode. Fabric Interconnect is required to reboot if it changes the Ethernet Mode.

5. Right-click on port 17/18/19/20 and select **Configure as Uplink Port**:

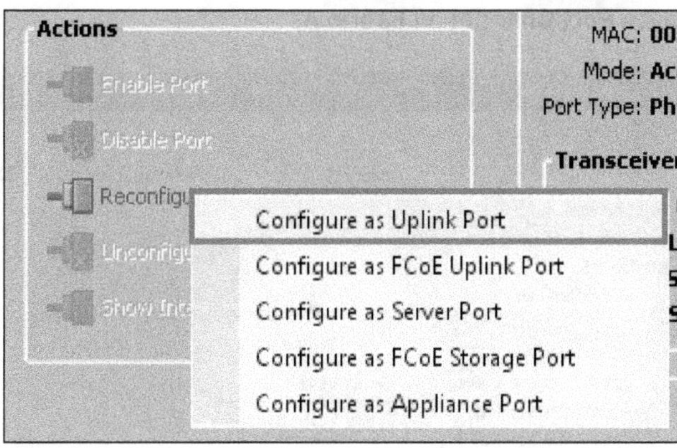

6. After all the Ethernet uplink ports are configured, go to **LAN Uplinks Manager** in the **Actions** area on **Fabric Interconnect A (primary)**:

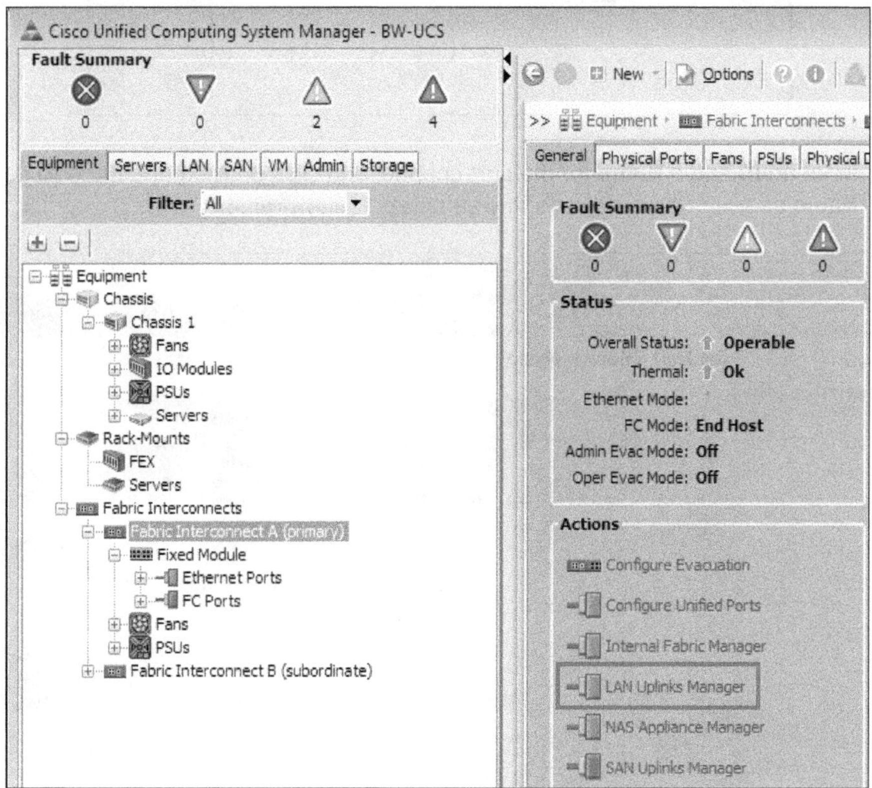

7. Click on **Create Port Channel** on **Fabric A**:

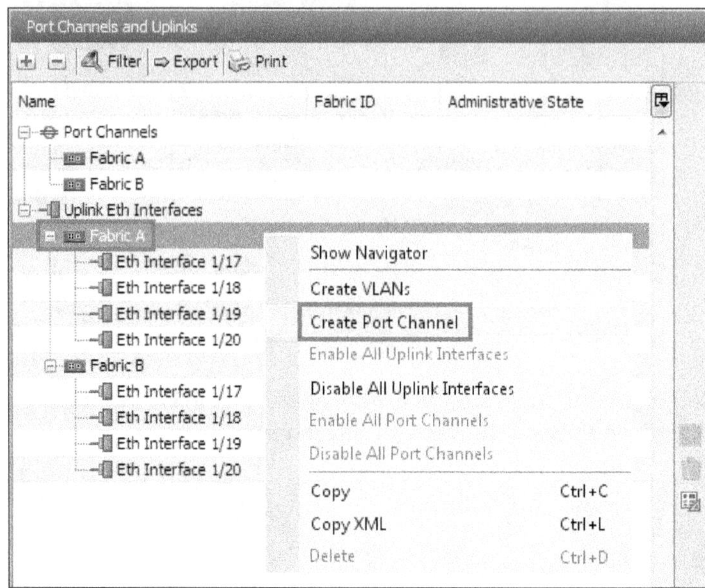

8. Input an **ID** and a **Name** for the port channel and click on **Next** (input the **ID** as `1` and **Name** as `Port_Channel1` for the sample):

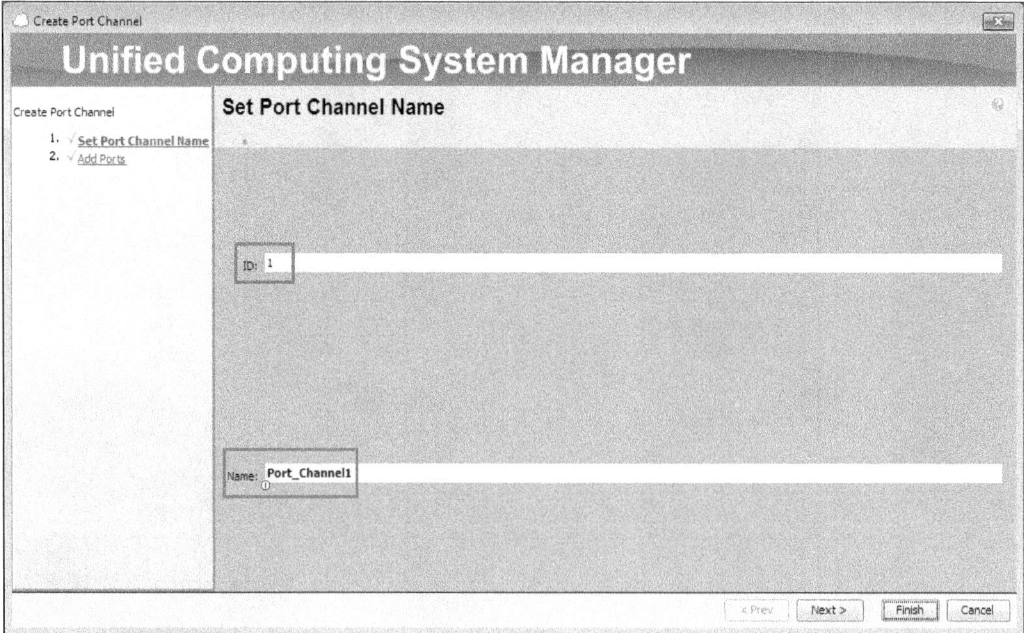

9. Select the uplink ports that should be added to the port channel and click on the arrow sign to add these ports to the port channel. Then click on the **Finish** button:

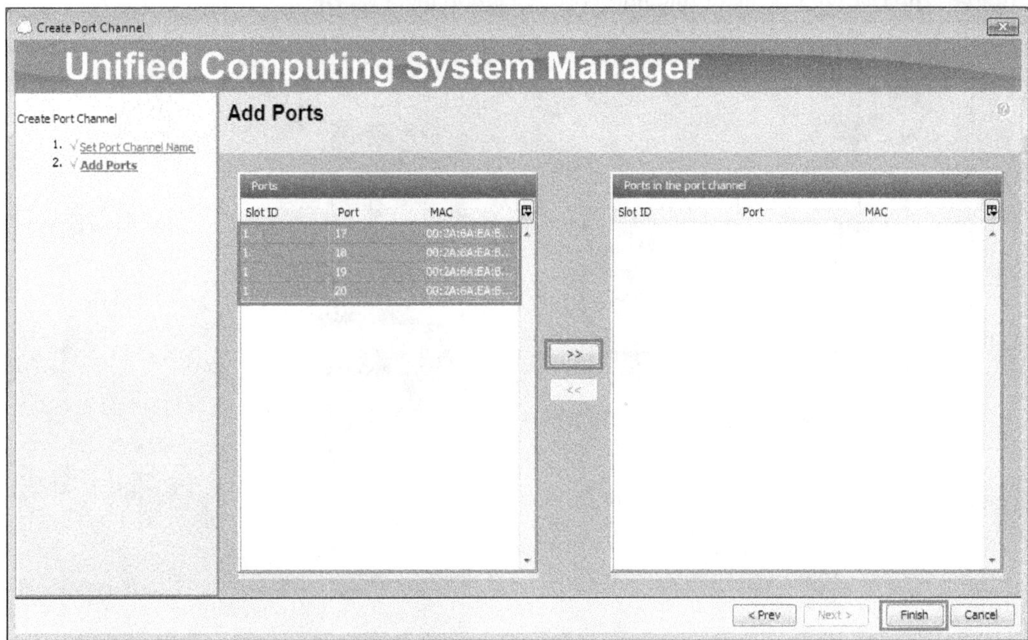

The port channel ID and the name configured on the Fabric Interconnect should match the name and ID configuration on the upstream Ethernet Switch.

How it works...

In this recipe, we will learn how to verify the state of Ethernet Port Channel on FI.

Validation

In the **LAN** tab, click **Fabric A** under **LAN Cloud**. The **Port Channels** group **Port_Channel1** is created. The **Overall Status** of this port channel group displays **Up**:

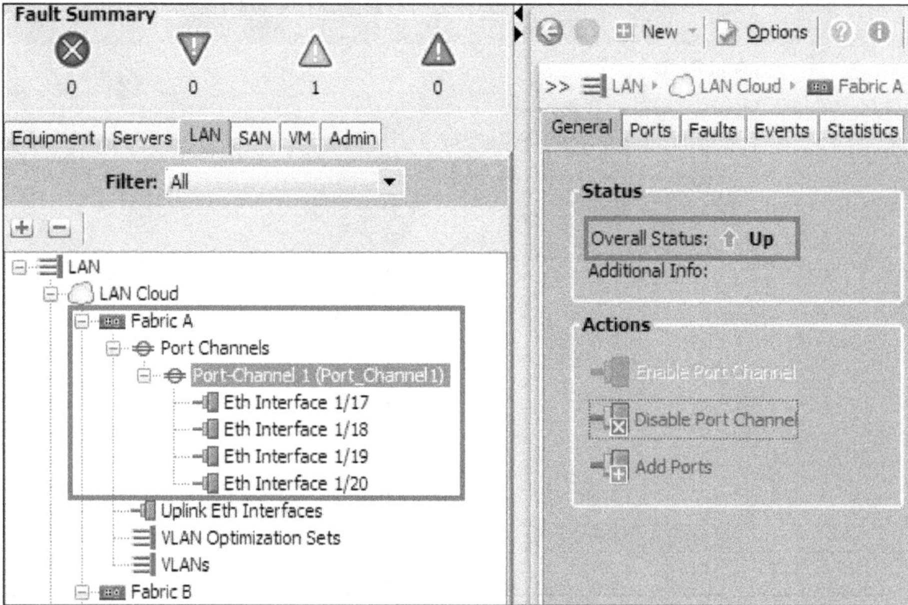

Repeat the preceding procedure to verify the other Port channel group on **Fabric B**.

There's more...

If the FI uplink Ethernet Switches support vPC (such as, N5K or N7K) or VSS (such as some Catalyst models), then the physical connections from each FI can be dual-homed to both Switches.

If the FI uplink Ethernet Switches do not support vPC or VSS, then FI-A must connect to Switch-A, and FI-B to Switch-B—that is, without dual-homing. The connections can still be LACP-teamed:

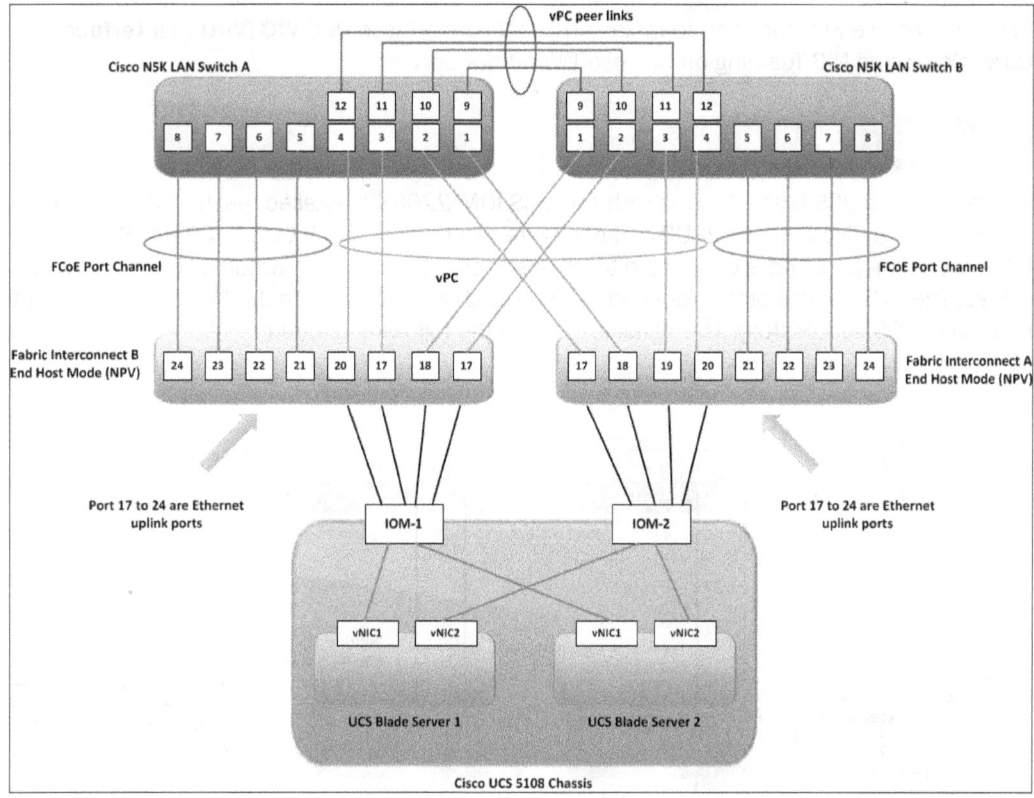

Installing and configuring the NIC Teaming on Microsoft Windows

In this recipe, we will learn how to install and configure a Cisco UCS **VIC** (**Virtual Interface Card**) Driver and NIC Teaming on Microsoft Windows Server.

Getting ready

Prepare a Cisco UCS 5108 Chassis with two UCS IOM 2208XP installed, each UCS IOM is connected to a Cisco UCS 6428UP and configure two ports on each Cisco UCS 6428UP as an Ethernet uplink port that is connected to an upstream Ethernet LAN Switch by Fibre Channel cables. The UCS service profile (defined two vNIC1/2) is associated to the UCS Server and can boot up the OS successfully. The detail is listed in the following diagram:

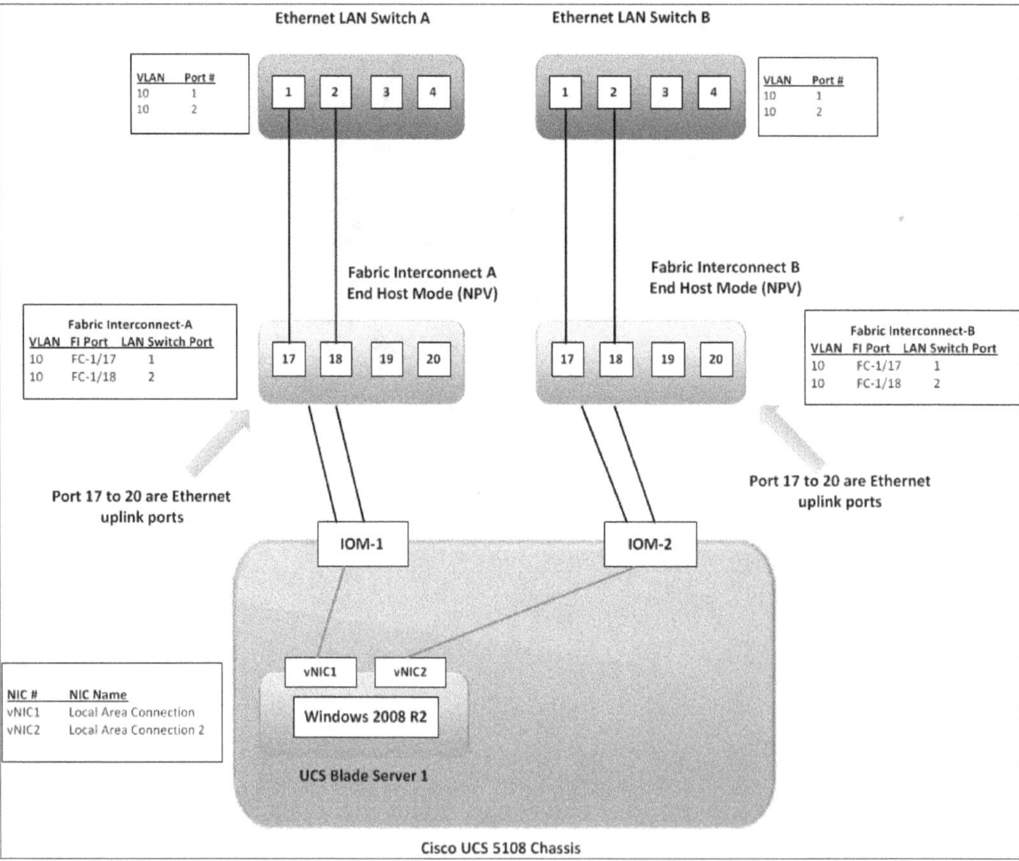

How to do it...

In this recipe, we will learn how to download Cisco VIC driver and NIC Teaming driver on the Cisco support website, then install and configure a VIC driver and NIC Teaming driver on Microsoft Windows Server 2008 R2.

Download the Cisco VIC driver with the following steps:

1. Navigate to `https://software.cisco.com/download/navigator.html` and login to the **My Cisco** account. Select **Products**; the details are shown in the following screenshot:

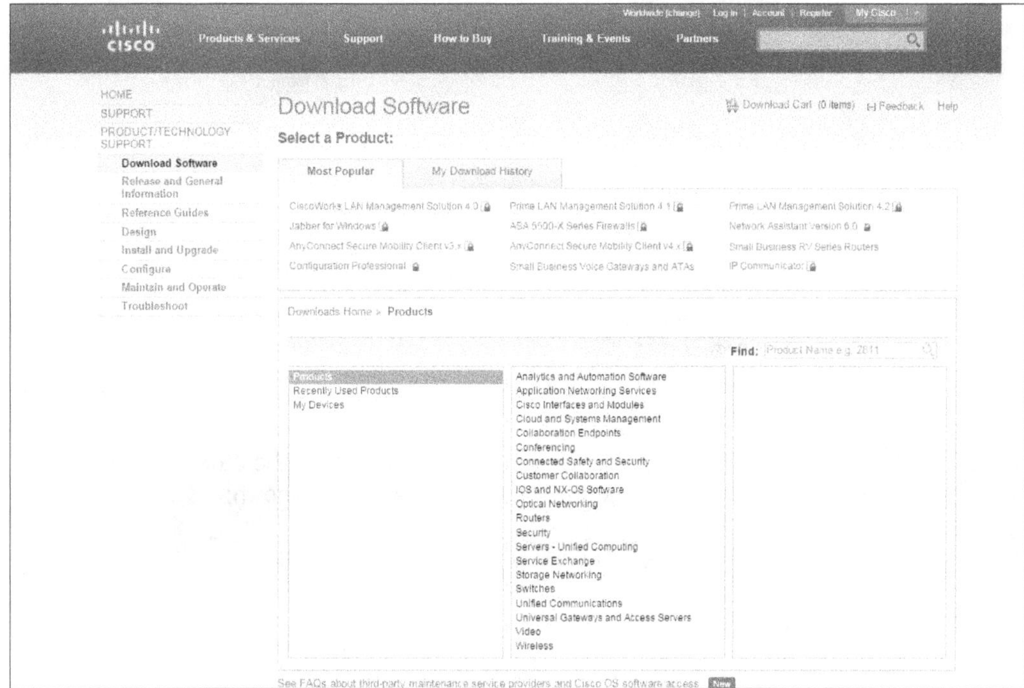

Note: Access to downloading the UCS driver is limited to users with an active Technical Support contract with Cisco.

2. Select **2.2(5b)** and download **ucs-bxxx-drivers.2.2.5b.iso**, as shown:

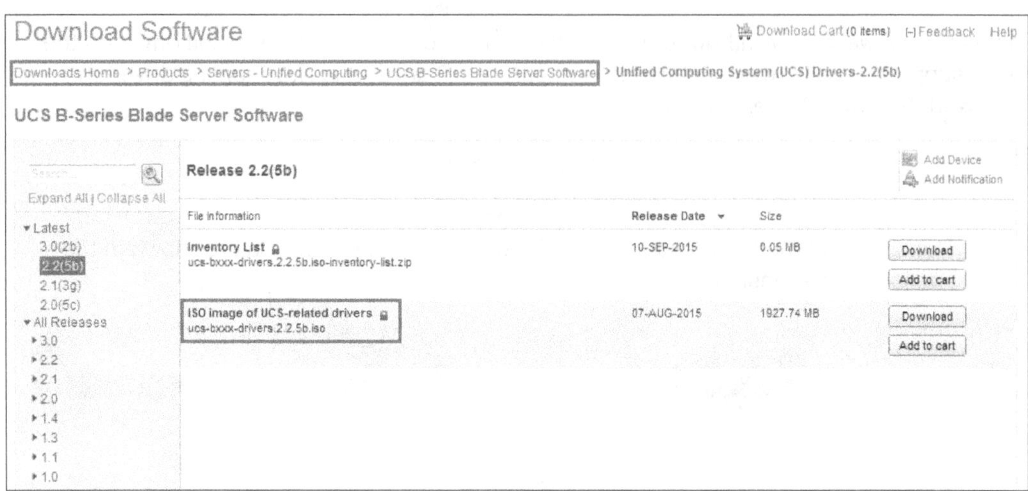

Install Cisco VIC driver

Assume that the model of VIC (Virtual Interface Card) is 1340 and is ready to be installed into the UCS Blade Server. Windows Server 2008 R2 is already installed into the UCS Blade Server; the Cisco VIC driver is not installed.

3. Go to the Windows **Device Manager** and then right-click on the Ethernet or Fibre Channel device and choose **Update Driver Software...**, as shown:

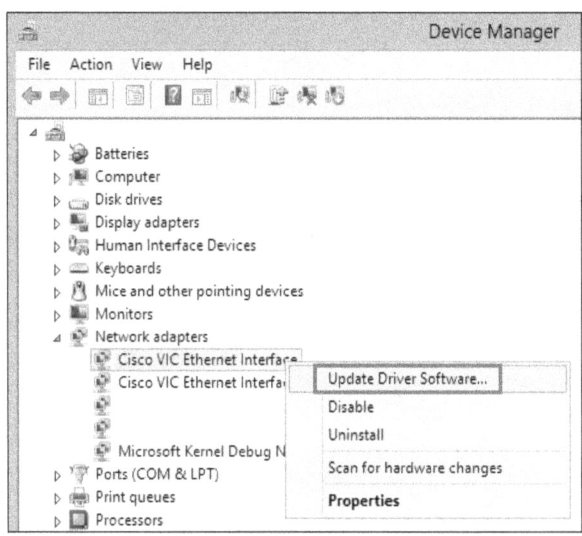

4. Click on **Browse in my computer for driver software.**

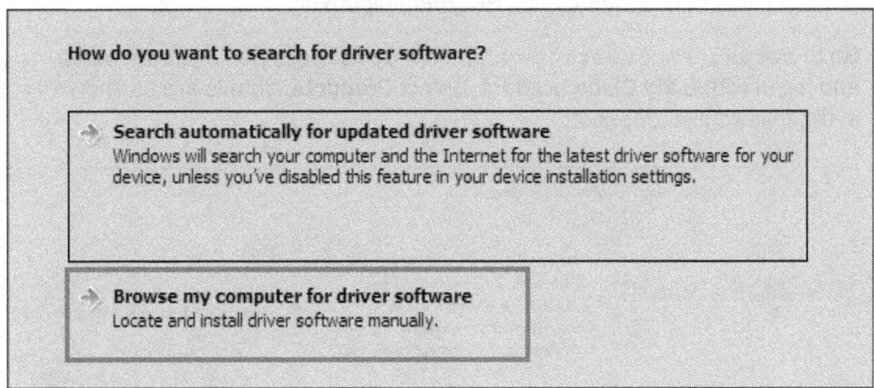

How do you want to search for driver software?
Search automatically for updated driver software
Windows will search your computer and the Internet for the latest driver software for your device, unless you've disabled this feature in your device installation settings.
Browse my computer for driver software
Locate and install driver software manually.

5. Click on **Let me pick from a list of device drivers on my computer**.
6. In the **Select your drivers type list below** window, make sure that **Show All Network Adapter** is selected and click on **Next**.
7. In the **Select the device driver you want to install for this hardware** window, click on **Have Disk**.
8. In the **Install from Disk** window, **Browse...** for the driver and click on **OK**.
9. Click **Next** on the **Select the device driver you want to install for this hardware** screen.
10. Click on **Close** to exit the wizard.

Downloading the Cisco NIC Teaming driver

Follow the steps listed to download Cisco NIC Teaming driver:

1. Go to `https://software.cisco.com/download/navigator.html` and log in with a **My Cisco** account. Select **Products**; details are as shown in the following screenshot:

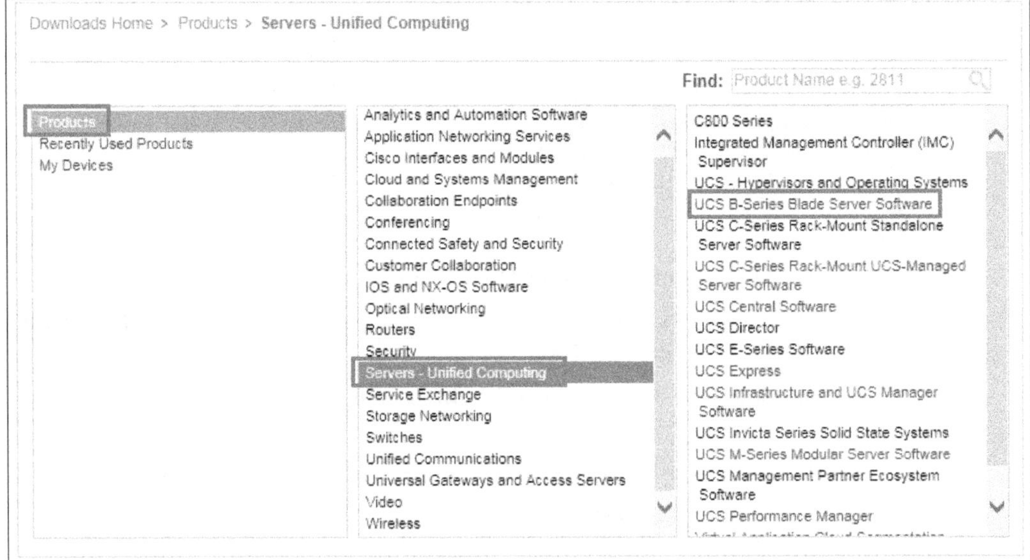

Note: Access to downloading UCS VIC Teaming is limited to users with an active Technical Support contract with Cisco.

2. Select the **Windows** platform:

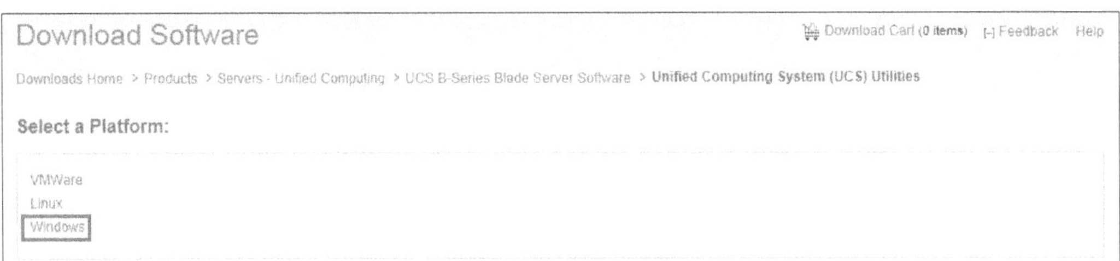

3. Download **ucs-bxxx-utils-windows.2.2.5.iso**, as shown:

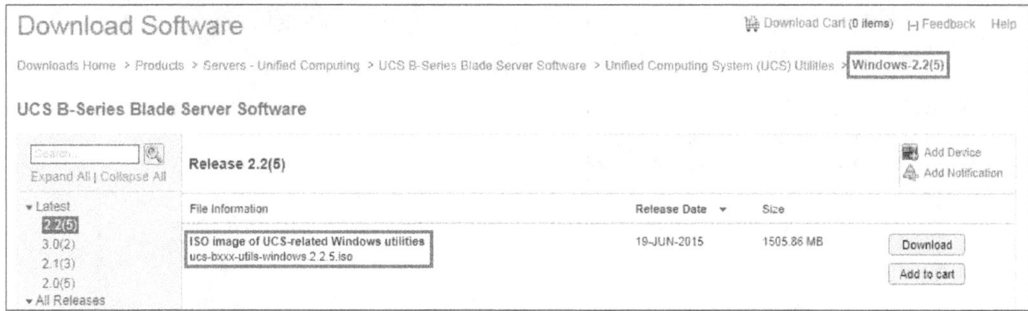

Installing and configuring the Cisco NIC Teaming driver

Assume that the UCS-related Windows Utilities ISO is stored on `c:\temp\` and perform the following steps:

1. Extract the UCS-related Windows Utilities; you can see **enictool.exe**, which is used to install and configure a Cisco NIC Teaming driver:

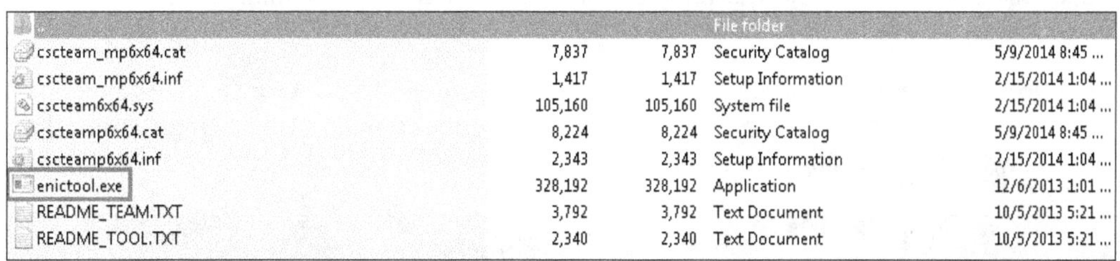

Name			Type	Date
..			File folder	
cscteam_mp6x64.cat	7,837	7,837	Security Catalog	5/9/2014 8:45 ...
cscteam_mp6x64.inf	1,417	1,417	Setup Information	2/15/2014 1:04 ...
cscteam6x64.sys	105,160	105,160	System file	2/15/2014 1:04 ...
cscteamp6x64.cat	8,224	8,224	Security Catalog	5/9/2014 8:45 ...
cscteamp6x64.inf	2,343	2,343	Setup Information	2/15/2014 1:04 ...
enictool.exe	328,192	328,192	Application	12/6/2013 1:01 ...
README_TEAM.TXT	3,792	3,792	Text Document	10/5/2013 5:21 ...
README_TOOL.TXT	2,340	2,340	Text Document	10/5/2013 5:21 ...

2. Open a Command Prompt with administrator privileges on a Windows platform:

   In the Command Prompt, execute `enictool.exe` to install Cisco NIC Teaming Driver. The following is a sample installation:

```
c:\temp> enictool.exe -p "c:\temp"
```

> The Cisco NIC Teaming Driver is installed using the `.inf` files located in the specified directory.

3. Once the driver is installed, you can start configuring the teaming on the desired NICs.

4. In the **Network Connections** window, assume that the device names of the two NICs are **Local Area Connection** and **Local Area Connection 2**. Execute `enictool.exe` to configure the NIC Teaming mode. The following example lists how to configure NIC Teaming in mode 1:

```
c:\temp> enictool -c "Local Area Connection" "Local Area
Connection 2" -m 1
```

Cisco NIC Teaming has four modes; the options are as follows:

1 - Active Backup

2 - Active Backup with failback to Active mode

3 - Active Active (transmit load balancing)

4 - 802.3ad LACP

How it works...

In this recipe, we will learn how to verify the state of the Cisco NIC Teaming driver on Microsoft Windows Server 2008 R2.

In the **Network Connections** window, it appears as a new NIC **Local Area Connection 3** connection, which is the NIC Teaming of **Local Area Connection** and **Local Area Connection 2**, as shown in the following screenshot:

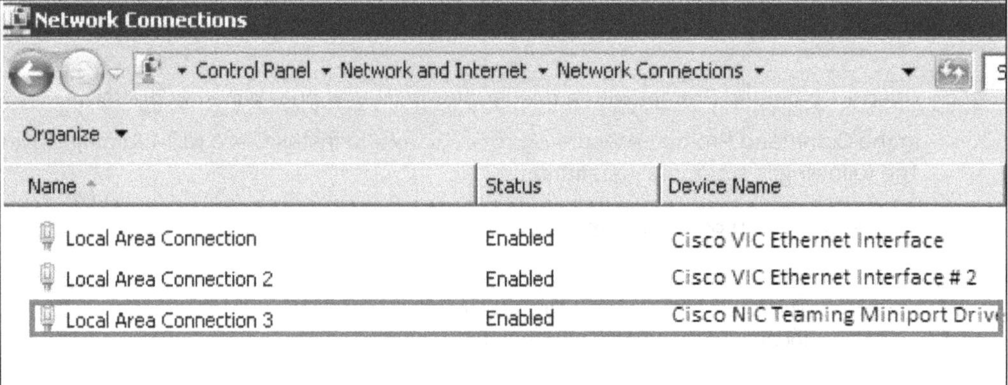

There's more...

If you are installing Microsoft Windows 2008/2012 on a SAN LUN, you must install Cisco VIC drivers for Windows during the OS installation. If you do not provide the drivers during the OS installation, the system will not be able to detect the SAN LUN. The following is the procedure to install a Cisco VIC driver:

1. When you install Microsoft Windows, click on **Load Driver** on the Windows installation screen.
2. Browse to the driver and click on **OK**. The driver appears in the **Select the driver to be installed** window.
3. Confirm that the correct VIC driver is displayed on the **Select the driver to be installed** screen and click on **Next**.
4. Once the VIC driver is installed, you can continue to install Microsoft Windows on the selected SAN LUN.

Configuring the load-balancing and failover on VMware vSphere

In this recipe, we will learn how to configure load-balancing and failover on VMware vSphere Server.

Getting ready

Prepare a **Cisco UCS 5108 Chassis** with two UCS IOM 2208XP installed, each UCS IOM connected to a Cisco UCS 6428UP and configure two ports on each Cisco UCS 6428UP as an Ethernet uplink port that is connected to an upstream Ethernet LAN Switch by Fibre Channel cables. The UCS service profile (defined four vNIC1/2/3/4) is associated to a UCS Server and can boot up the OS successfully. The details are listed in the following diagram:

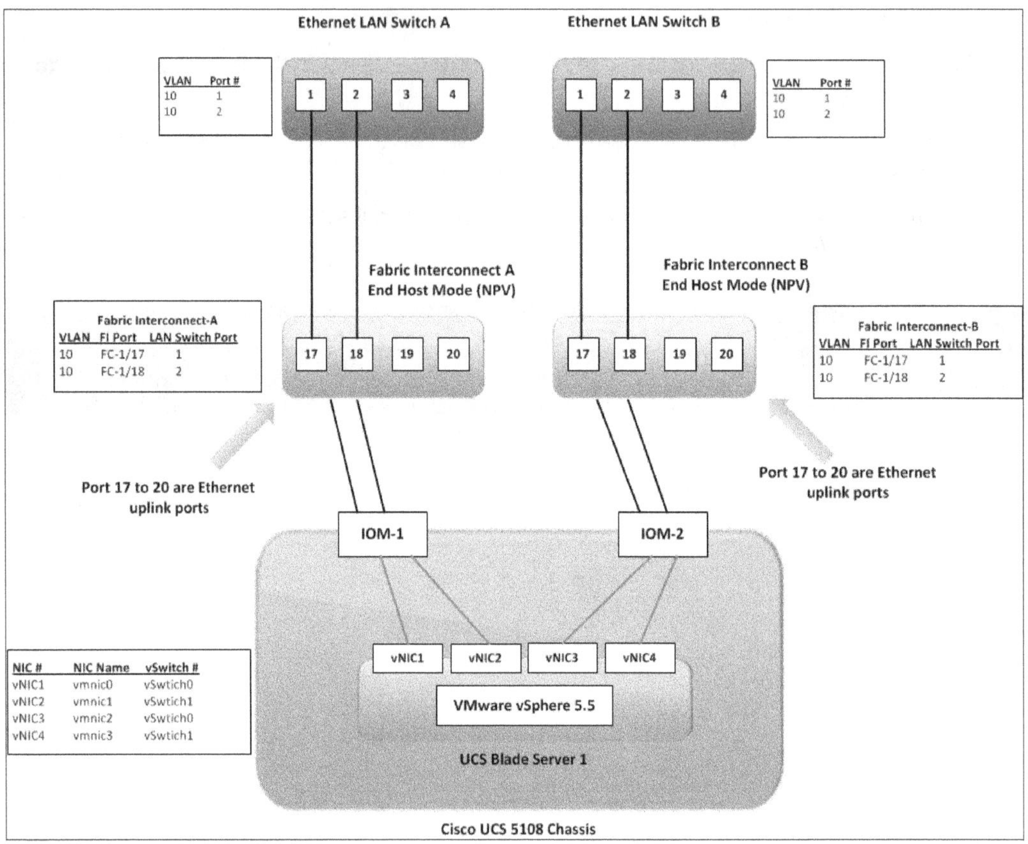

How to do it...

In this recipe, we will learn how to set up **VMware Standard Switch** (**VSS**) and configure the failover policy on a VMware vSphere Server.

We assume that we have created one UCS service profile as `ESXi5.5_Service_Profile` on Cisco UCS Manager, the following table lists the details of each virtual network adapter on the service profile:

vNIC #	**vNIC Name**	**Fabric ID**	**Enable Failover**
vNIC1	vNIC_FIA_P17	A	Disable
vNIC2	vNIC_FIA_P18	A	Disable
vNIC3	vNIC_FIB_P17	B	Disable
vNIC4	vNIC_FIB_P18	B	Disable

Follow these steps to set up VSS and configure the failover policy on a VMware vSphere Server:

1. Go to the **Servers** tab on the UCS Manager, verify the **Fabric ID** of the service profile (**ESXi5.5_Service_Profile**) on the **Network** tab:

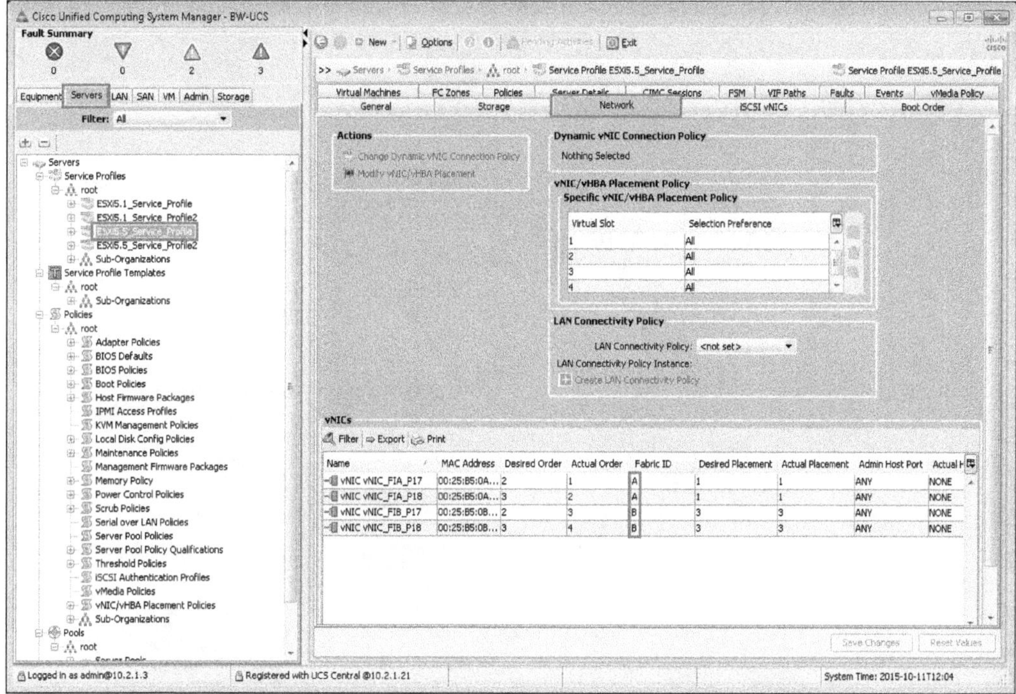

For VMware ESXi, since the hypervisor manages load-balancing and failover using the vNICs attached to each vSwitch, vNIC failover should also be disabled. For detail, you can reference the following link:

`https://supportforums.cisco.com/sites/default/files/attachments/discussion/fabric_failover_on_ucs_white_paper_0.pdf`

2. Log in to the VMware vSphere host with a vSphere Client, then create 2 VSS on vSphere using the following 4 vmnic; details are as given in the following table:

vSwitch #	ESXi vNIC Name	Cisco vNIC Name	vSwitch active uplink
vSwitch0	vmnic0	vNIC_FIA_P17	Active
vSwitch0	vmnic2	vNIC_FIB_P17	Active
vSwitch1	vmnic1	vNIC_FIA_P18	Active
vSwitch1	vmnic3	vNIC_FIB_P18	Active

3. Go to **Networking** on the **Configuration** tab of a vSphere host, and then create a vSwitch using **Add Network Wizard**. Select **vmnic1** and **vmnic3** and the **Create a vSphere standard switch** option, as shown:

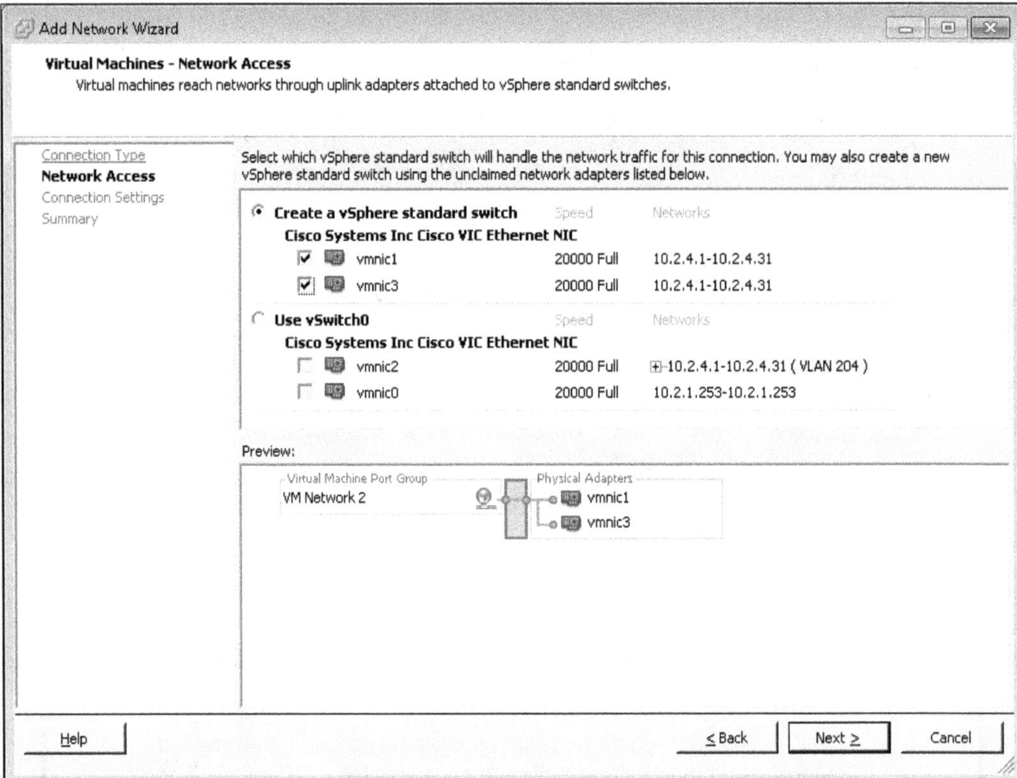

4. Once the vSwitch is created, you can see a 2 vSwitches being displayed in **Networking** on the **Configuration** tab of a vSphere host:

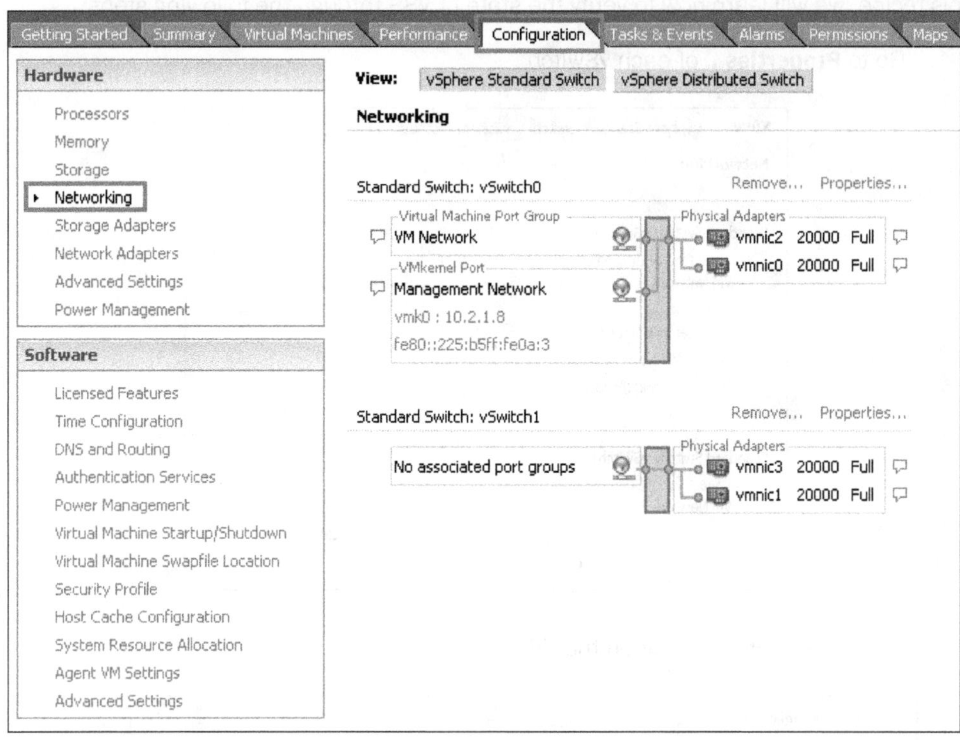

How it works...

In this recipe, we will learn how to verify the state of VSS through the following steps:

1. Go to **Properties...** of each vSwitch:

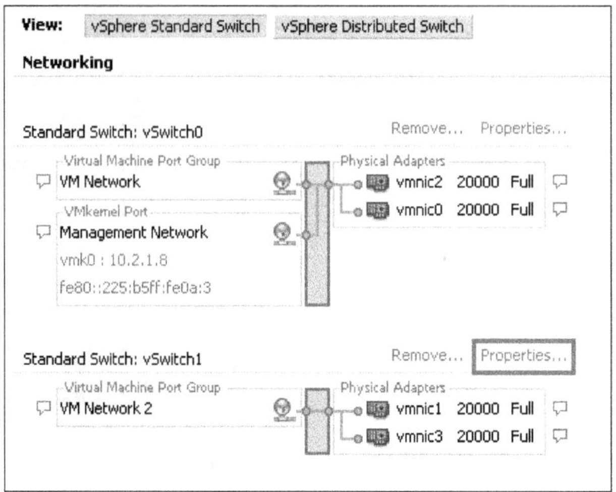

2. Select **vSwitch** and click on the **Edit...** button:

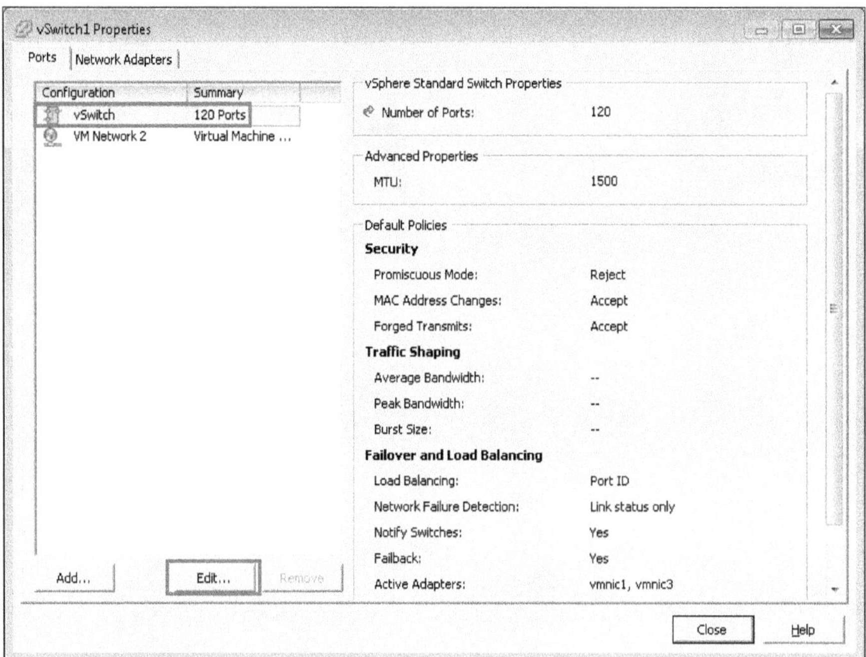

3. Go to the **NIC Teaming** tab and make sure that **Load Balancing** is selected as **Route based on the originating virtual port ID** and **Active Adapters** are selected displays **vnmic1** and **vnmic3**:

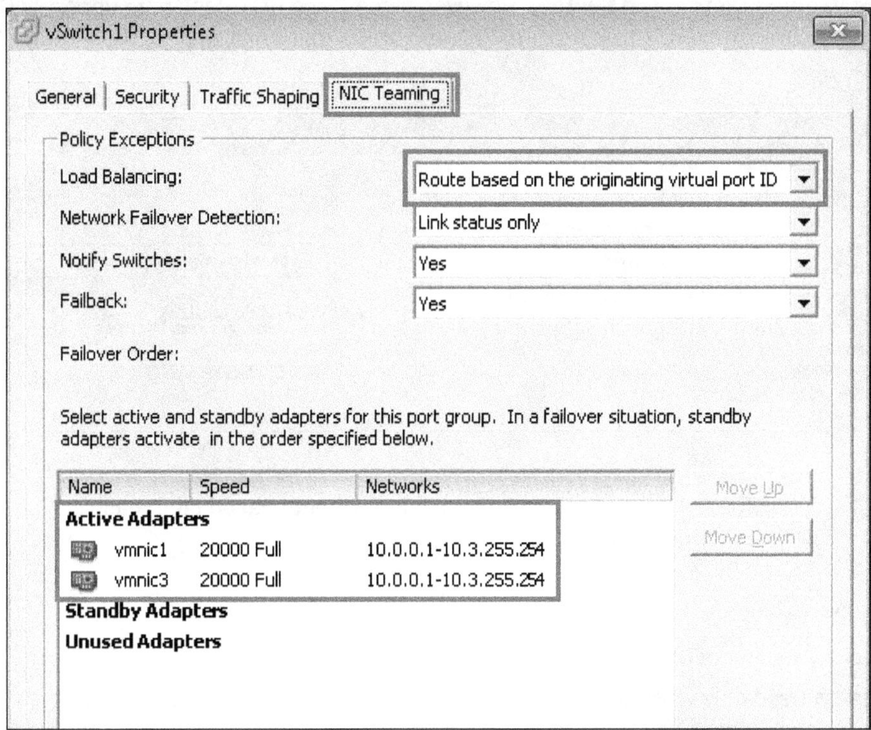

Use the default Load Balancing policy route based on the originating virtual port for the vmnics that come from vNICs pointing to FI-A and FI-B.

There's more...

For VMware ESXi, VMware only supports **LACP** (**Link Aggregation Control Protocol**) on **vDS** (**VMware vSphere Distributed Switch**). However, since Cisco UCS does not support LACP port channels between the vNICs that point to FI-A and vNICs that point to FI-B, the VMware LACP cannot be used:

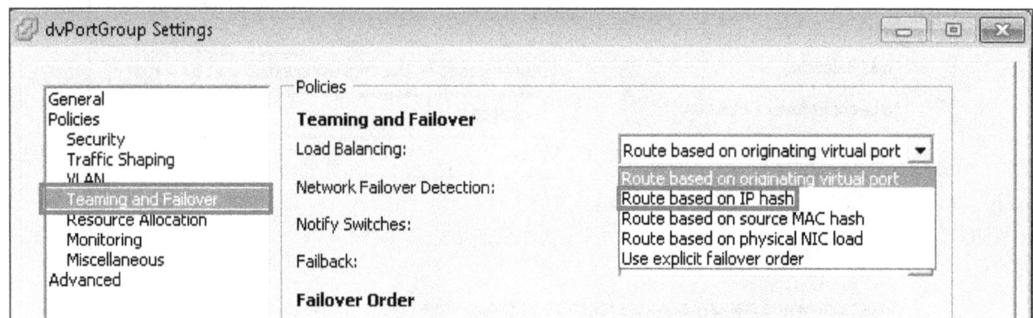

The VMware vDS Load Balancing policy **Route based on IP hash** is the LACP mode.

See also

IP hashing is used only when you have both the pnics (vmnics) ports channeled, which you don't. UCS does not port-channel the A and B fabric uplinks (vNICs) together. For details, you can refer to the following link:

`https://supportforums.cisco.com/discussion/11827911/vswitch-load-balancing-ucs`

Configuring LAN pin groups on UCS Fabric Interconnect

In this recipe, we will learn how to create a LAN pin group on UCS Fabric Interconnect.

Getting ready

Prepare a **Cisco UCS 5108 Chassis** with two UCS IOM 2208XP installed; each UCS IOM is connected to a Cisco UCS 6428UP. Configure four ports on each Cisco UCS 6428UP as an Ethernet uplink port (port 17/18), which is connected to the Cisco LAN Switch by Fibre Channel cables. The UCS service profile (defined by two vNIC1/2) is associated to the UCS Server and can boot up the OS successfully. The details are listed in the following diagram:

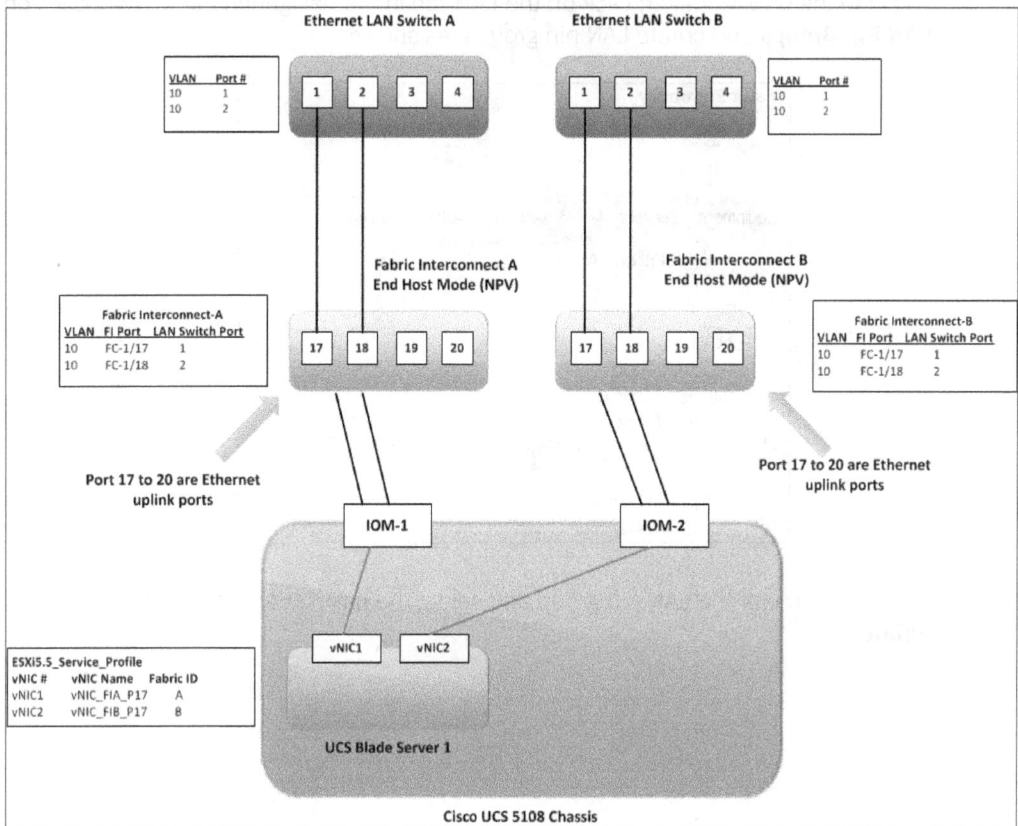

How to do it...

In this recipe, we will learn how to create a static LAN pin group by an FI-A uplink and FI-B uplink on Fabric Interconnect.

We assume that the two defined vNICs can be added into the service profile detail, as shown in the following table:

Service profile Name	vNIC #	vNIC Name	Fabric ID	Enable Failover
ESXi5.5_Service_Profile	vNIC1	vNIC_FIA_P17	A	Disable
	vNIC2	vNIC_FIB_P17	B	Disable

1. Log in to the UCS Manager; click on the **LAN** tab in the navigation pane. Right-click on **LAN Pin Groups** and create LAN pin groups, as shown:

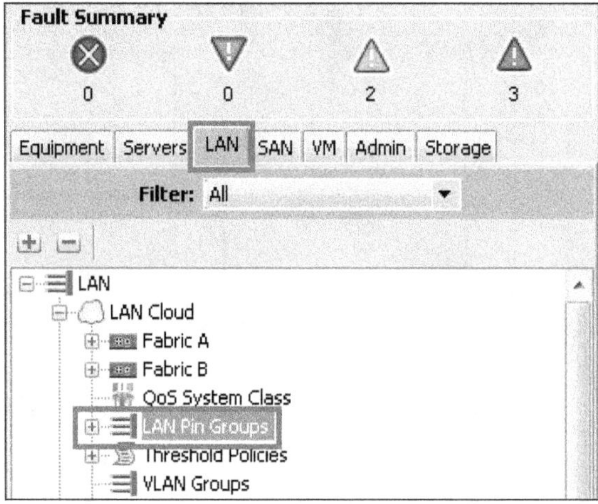

2. Input the name of the LAN pin group and select the **Interface** of **Fabric A** and **Fabric B**:

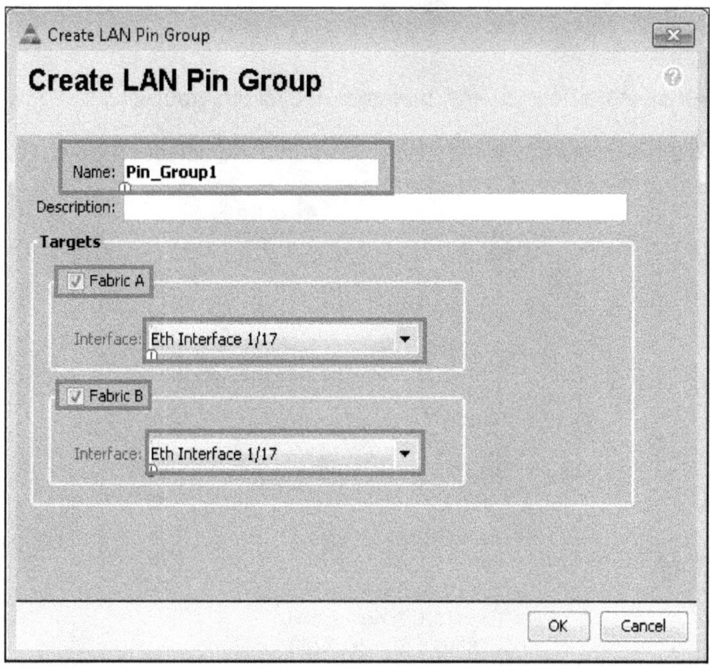

3. Once the **LAN Pin Group PIN_Group1** is created, it has two uplink Interfaces, which are FI-A Ethernet Interface 1/17 and FI-B Ethernet Interface 1/17, as shown in the following screenshot:

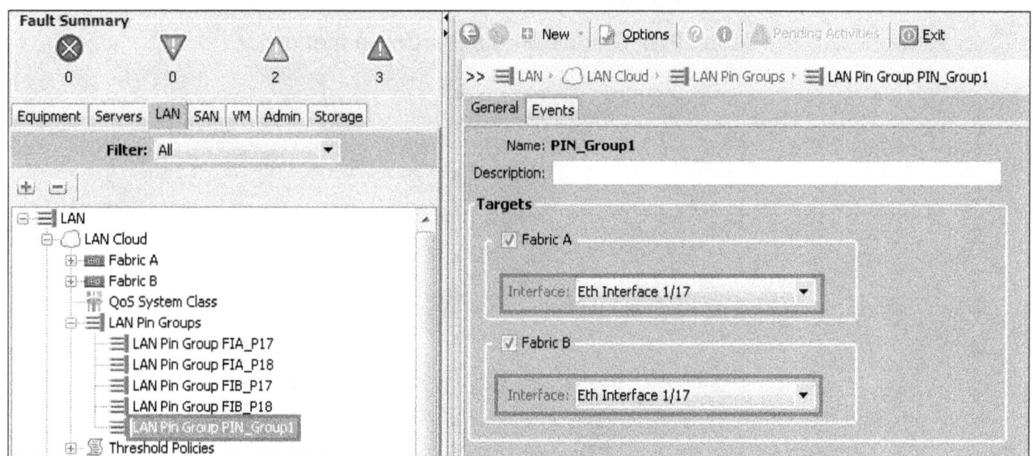

How it works...

In this recipe, we will learn how to verify the state of LAN pin group on FI.

1. Click on the **Servers** tab in the navigation pane and select **vNICs** on the **ESXi5.5_Service_Profile** on the **Service Profiles**:

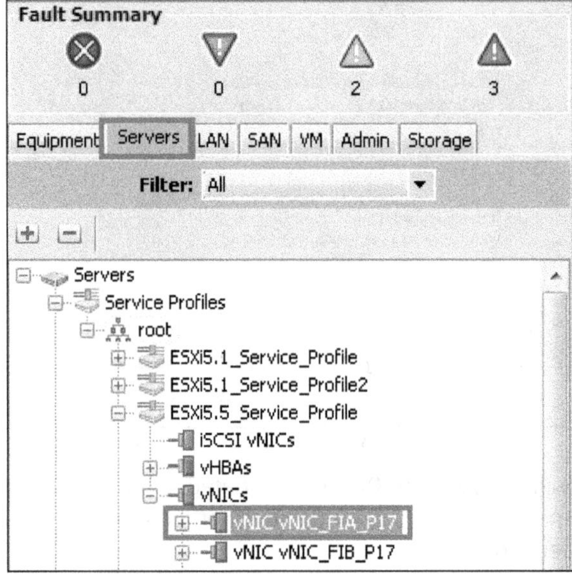

2. Choose **LAN Pin Group PIN_Group1** on the **Pin Group** menu:

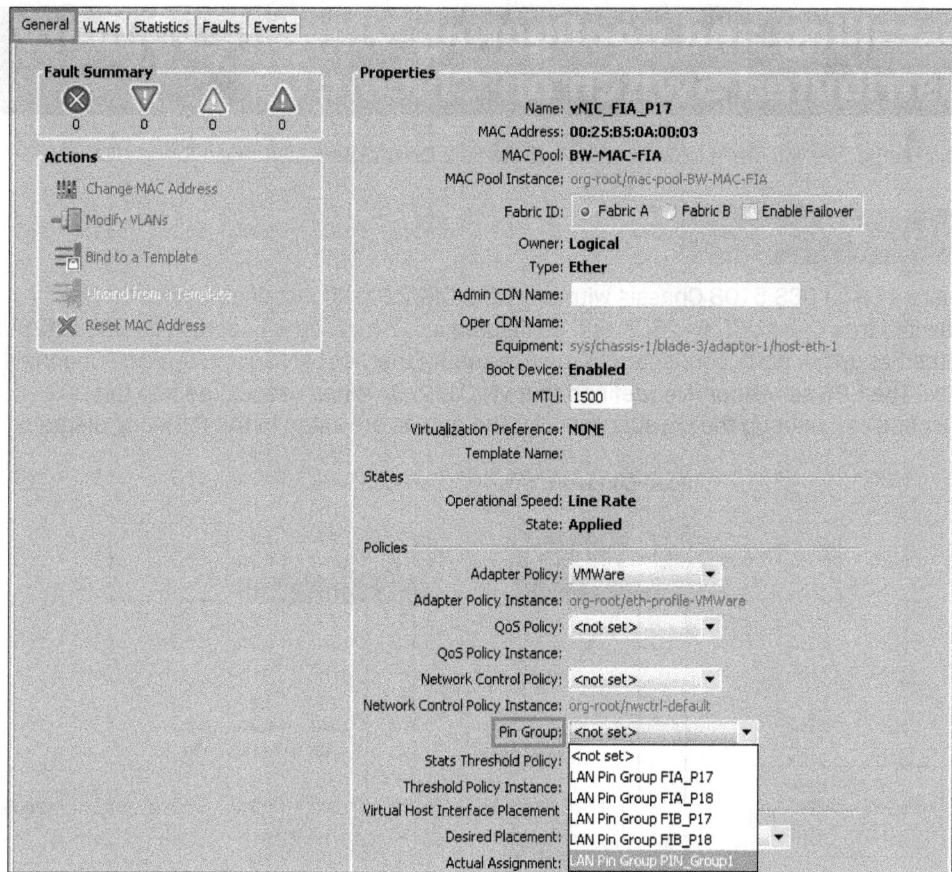

Repeat the preceding procedure to configure the pin group on other vNIC.

There's more...

LAN pin groups can be configured as static or dynamic pin groups. By default, the configuration is a dynamic pin group. In dynamic pinning, Fabric Interconnect automatically binds Server vNICs to uplink FI ports. The mapping of UCS vNICs to uplink FI ports depends upon the total number of active uplinks configured, which can be 1, 2, 4, or 8.

Installing and configuring VMware vSphere Distributed Switch on Cisco UCS

In this recipe, we will learn how to create vSphere's Distributed Switch on Cisco UCS.

Getting ready

Prepare a Cisco UCS 5108 Chassis with two UCS IOM 2208XP installed; each UCS IOM is connected to a Cisco UCS 6428UP and configured into two ports on each Cisco UCS 6428UP as Ethernet uplink ports connected to the upstream Ethernet LAN Switch by Fibre Channel cables. The UCS service profile (defined four vNIC1/2/3/4) has associated into the UCS Server and can boot up the OS successfully. The details are listed in the following diagram:

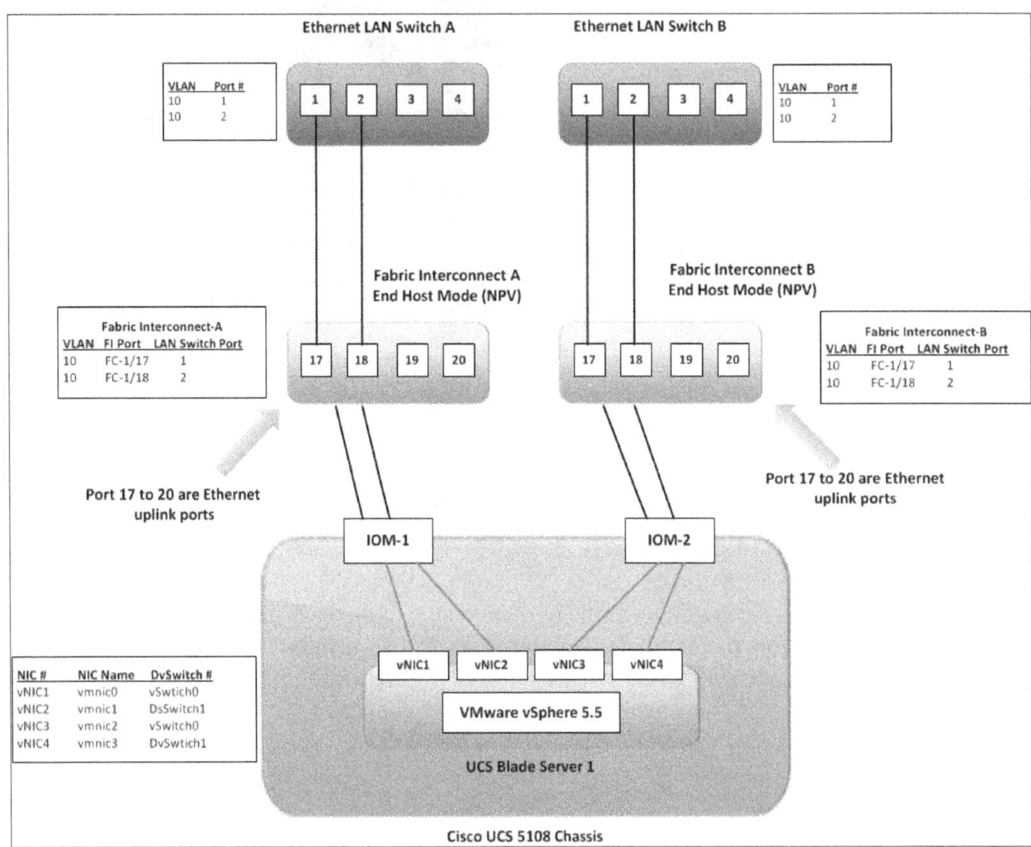

How to do it...

In this recipe, we will learn how to set up vDS on VMware vSphere Server.

We assume that the we have created a service profile `ESXi5.5_Service_Profile` on Cisco UCS Manager, the details are in the following table:

vNIC #	vNIC Name	Fabric ID	Enable Failover
vNIC1	vNIC_FIA_P17	A	Disable
vNIC2	vNIC_FIA_P18	A	Disable
vNIC3	vNIC_FIB_P17	B	Disable
vNIC4	vNIC_FIB_P18	B	Disable

Follow these steps to set up vDS on VMware vSphere Server:

1. Go to the **Servers** tab on the UCS Manager, verify the **Fabric ID** of the service profile **ESXi5.5_Service_Profile** on the **Network** tab:

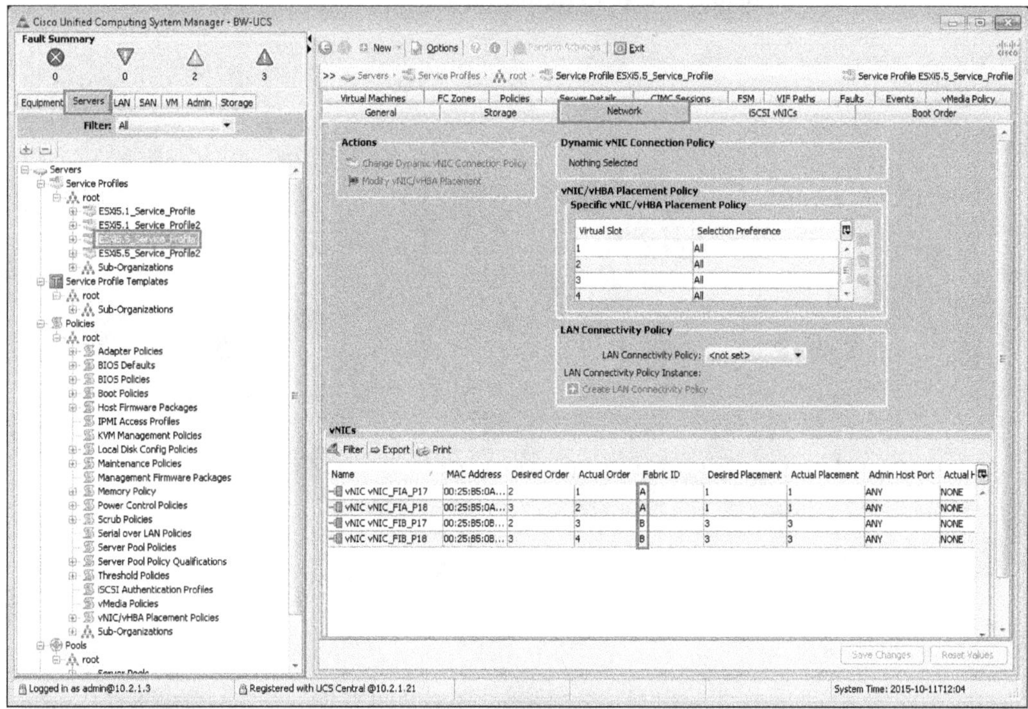

For VMware ESXi, since the hypervisor manages load-balancing and failover using the vNICs attached to each vSwitch, the vNIC failover should also be disabled.

`https://supportforums.cisco.com/sites/default/files/attachments/discussion/fabric_failover_on_ucs_white_paper_0.pdf`

2. Log in to the VMware vSphere host as a vSphere Client and then create 1 DvSwitch on vSphere using the following two vmnics (vmnic1 and vmnic3); the details are given in the following table:

vSwitch #	ESXi vNIC Name	Cisco vNIC Name	vSwitch active uplink
vSwitch0	vmnic0	vNIC_FIA_P17	Active
vSwitch0	vmnic2	vNIC_FIB_P17	Active
DvSwitch1	vmnic1	vNIC_FIA_P18	Active
DvSwitch1	vmnic3	vNIC_FIB_P18	Active

3. Click the **Home** button and go to **Networking**:

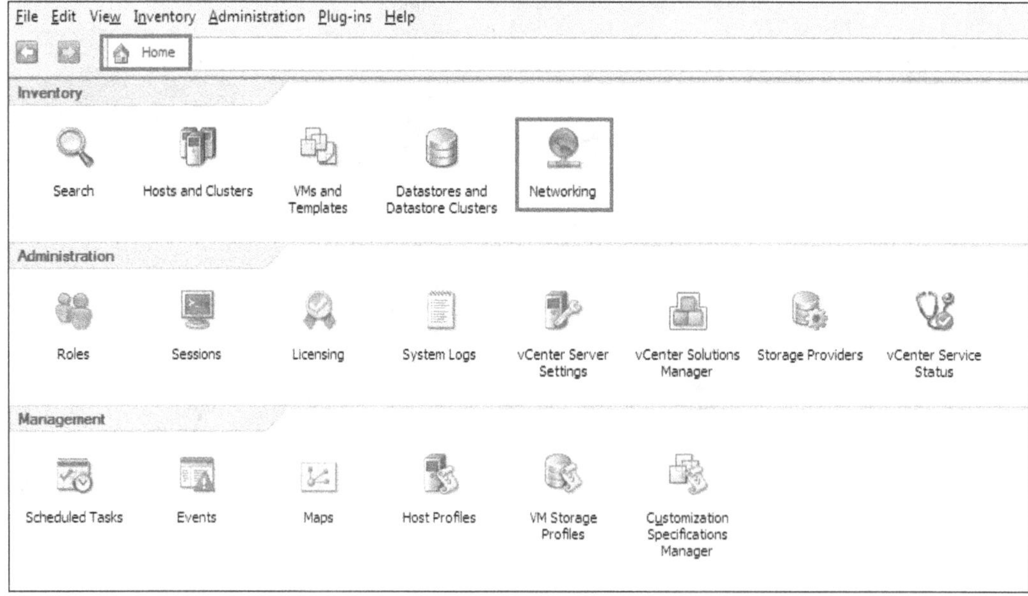

4. Right-click on the datacenter and select **New vSphere Distributed Switch...** on the menu, as shown:

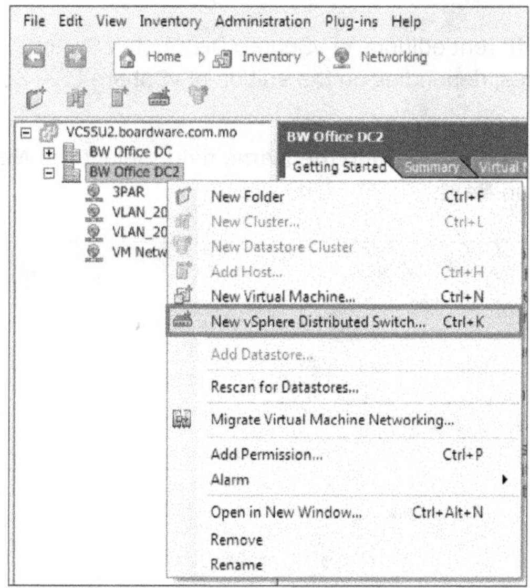

5. Choose **vSphere Distributed Switch Version 5.5.0** and then click on **Next**:

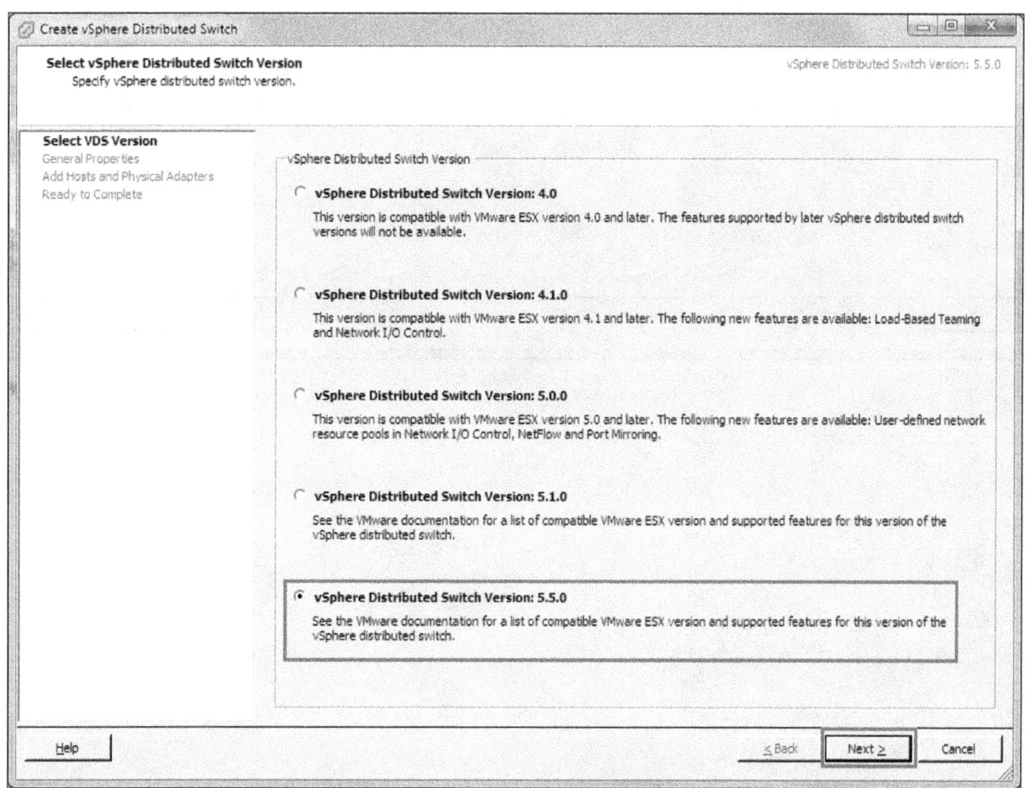

The different editions of vSphere Distributed Switch have different features, depending on the edition of vSphere ESXi Server.

6. Input the name as `dvSwitch` in the **Name** field. Select the **Number of uplink ports** as **2**, then click on **Next**:

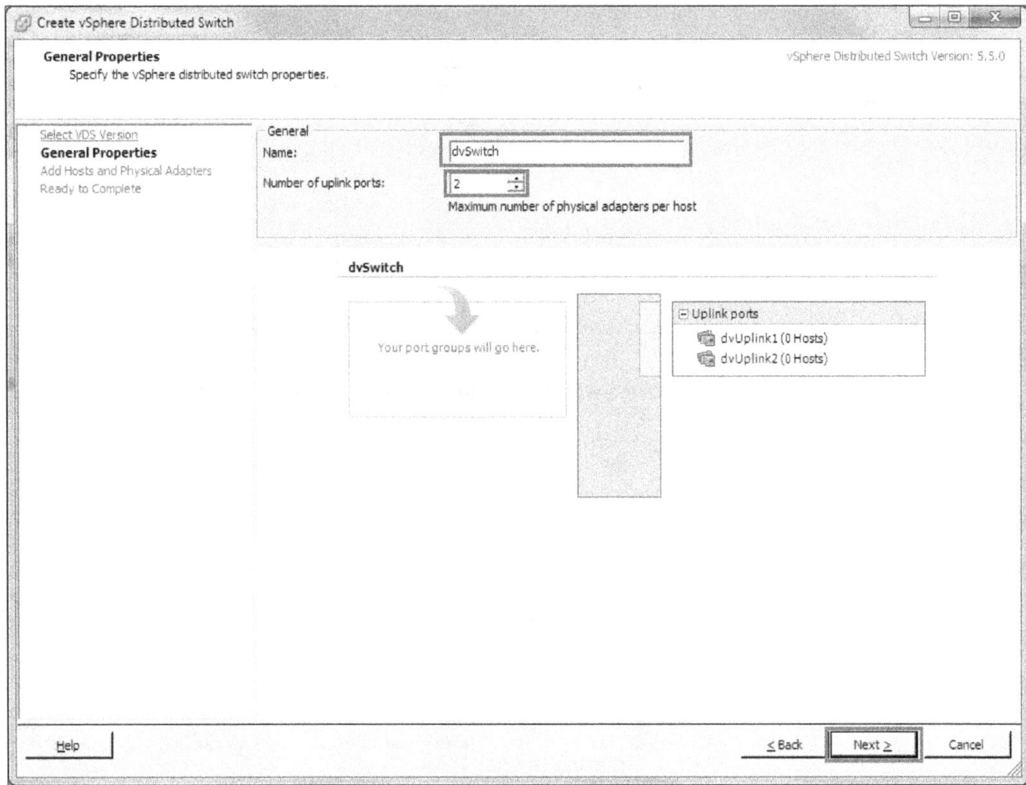

7. Select the **vmnic1** and **vmnic3 physical adapters** for the dvSwitch on the ESXi host and then click on **Next**:

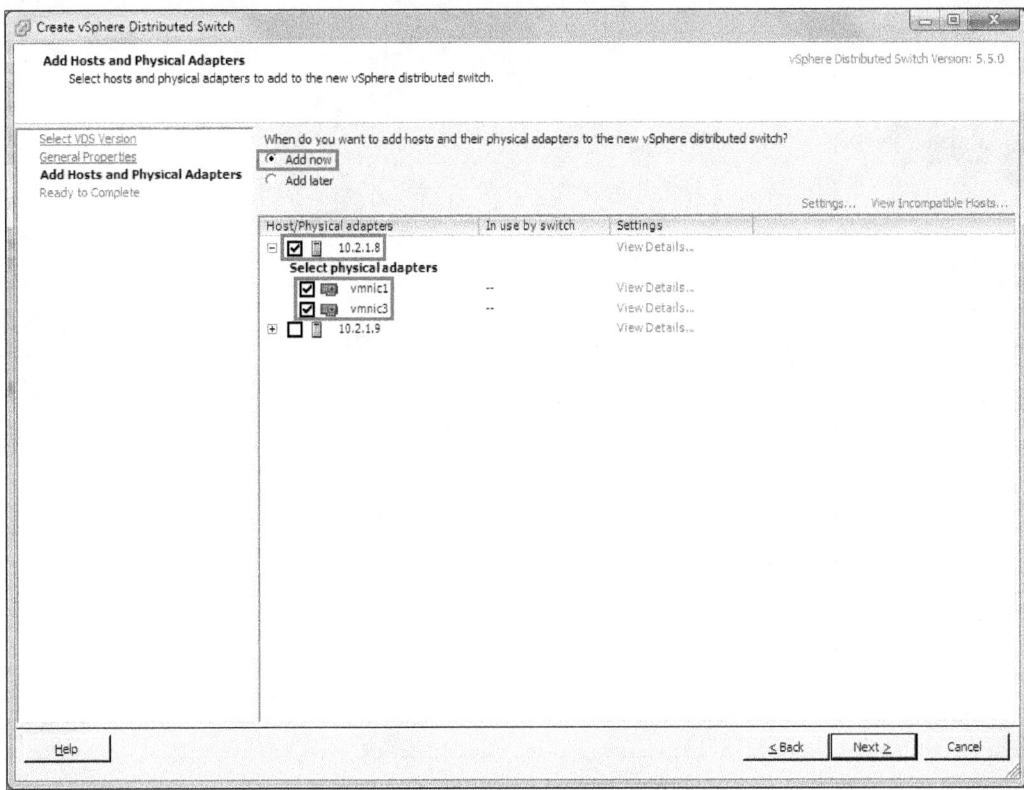

8. Now, you can see two **Uplink ports** under **dvSwitch**. Click on **Finish**:

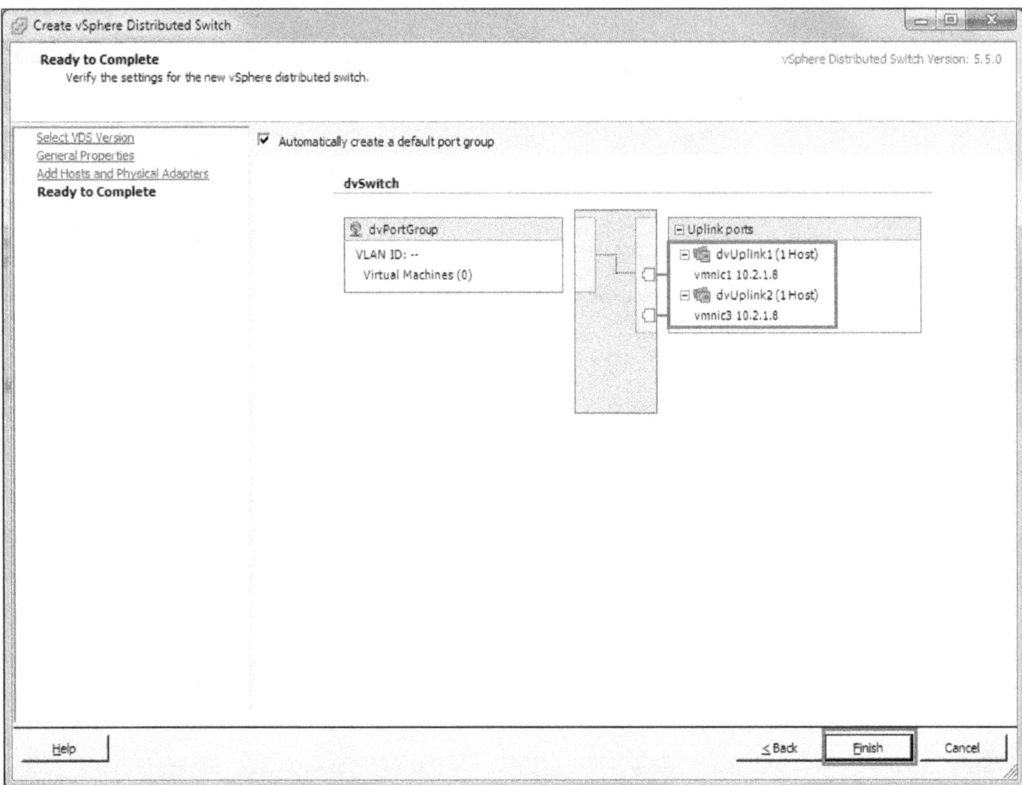

9. The dvSwitch is created.

How it works...

In this recipe, we will learn how to verify the state of the VMware Distributed Switch.

1. When dvSwitch is created, you can start creating a dvPortGroup. Right-click on the **dvSwitch** and choose **New Port Group...** on the **dvSwitch** menu:

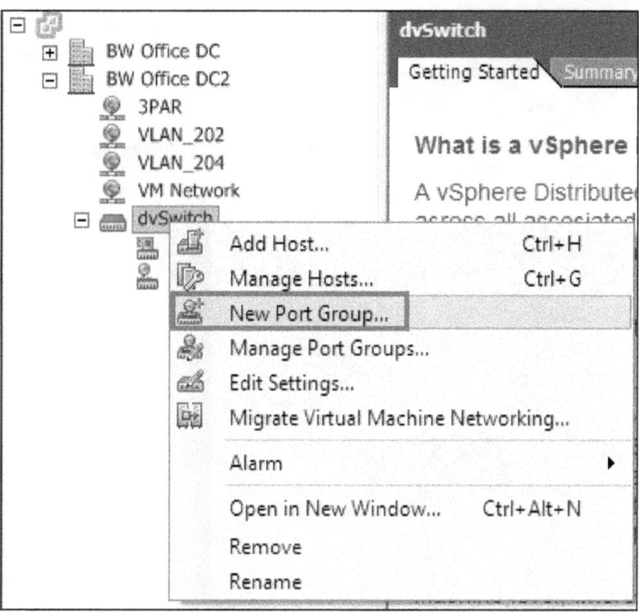

2. Input the **Name** of the port group and select **None** as the **VLAN type** for the dvSwitch. Click on **Next**:

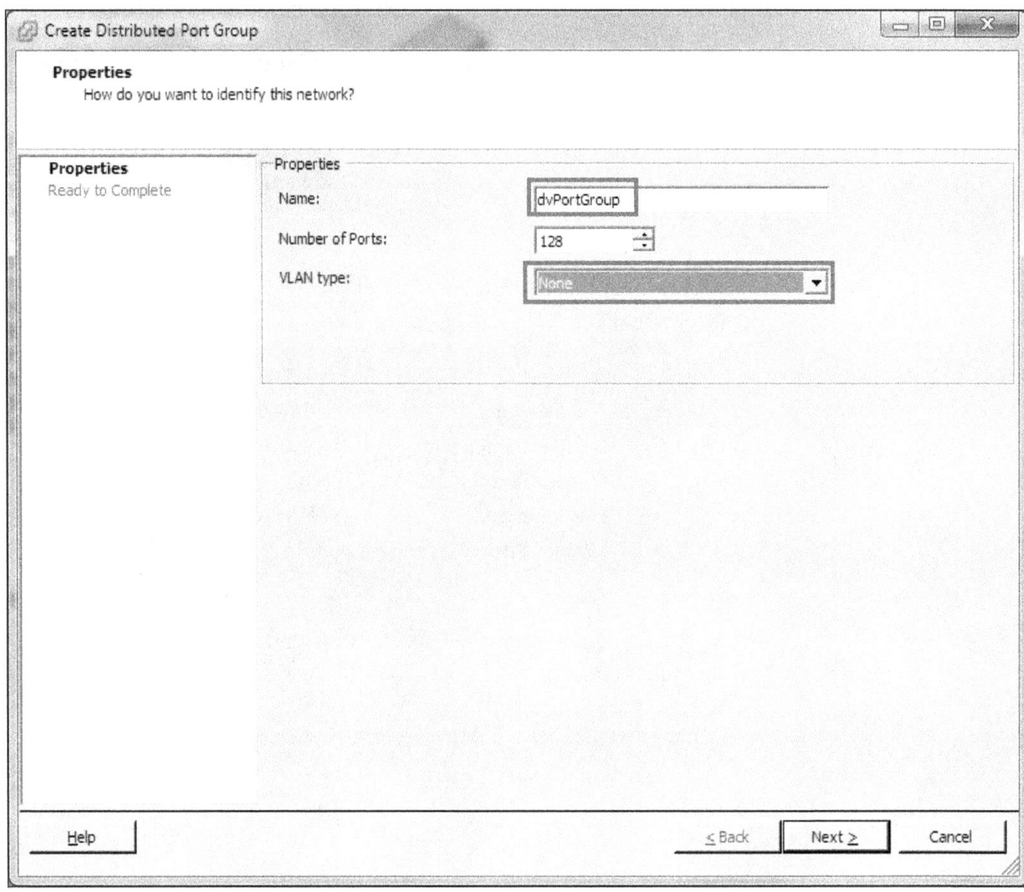

It has four options of VLAN type on distributed port group:

- **None**: port is assigned to a native VLAN (untagged traffic on uplinks when using VST mode) or same as uplinks ports (when in EST mode) indicating no VLAN tagging (uplinks are connected to access ports on physical switches
- **VLAN**: ports are assigned to that specific VLAN when virtual switch is in VST mode (VLAN tagged traffic on uplinks)
- **VLAN Trunking**: the traffic is passed through to Guest VM with VLAN tags intact
- **Private VLAN**: Private VLANs are a new feature of vDS that permit per Guest VM isolation on a shared IP subnet

3. Once the **dvPortGroup** is created, go to the **Configuration** tab of vSphere and select **Networking**. Click on **vSphere Distributed Switch**; you can see that the **dvSwitch** has one **dvPortGroup** and two uplinks:

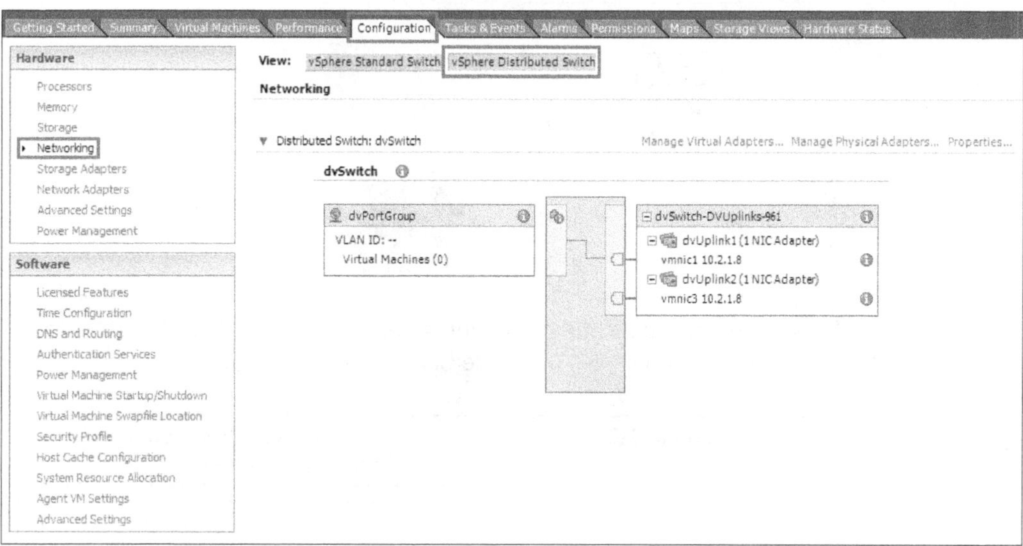

There's more...

The Cisco VM-FEX technology allows the VMs to bypass the hypervisor networking stack and access the network directly. Cisco VM-FEX utilizes the capability to create multiple vNICs in combination with VMware VMDirectPath and Intel ® VT-d technologies. The Cisco VM-FEX uses the Cisco UCS VIC (Virtual Interface Card) for hardware connectivity.
The following diagram shows VM Network Connectivity with Cisco VM-FEX.

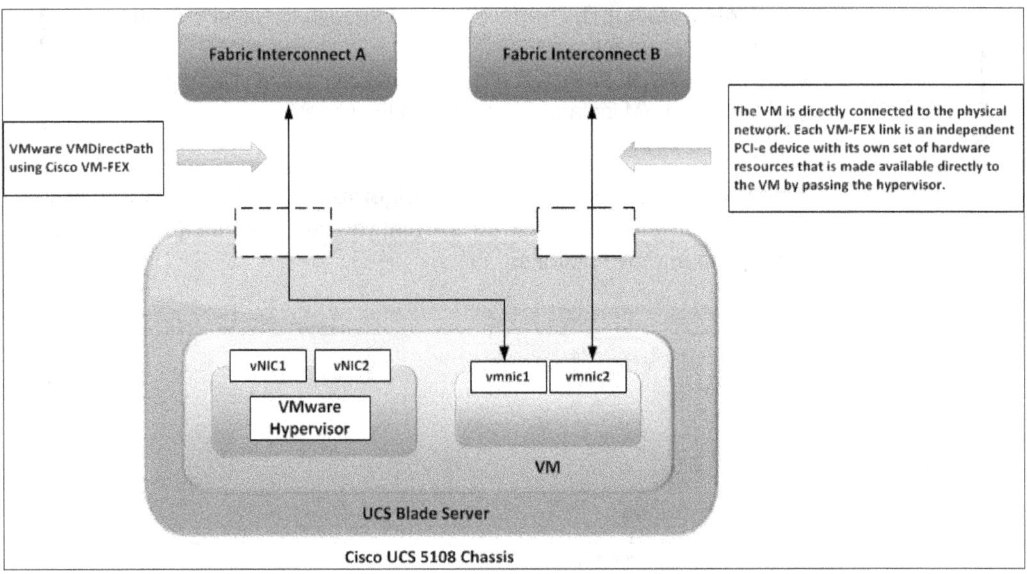

The following table lists the advantage and disadvantage of the Cisco VM-FEX and VMware vSwitch network connectivity technologies using the Cisco UCS

	Cisco VM-FEX	**VM Network Connectivity with VMware vSwitch**
Bypass the hypervisor	Supported	Not Supported
CPU Utilization	Low	High
VMDirectPath with vMotion	Supported Note: VMDirectPath with vMotion supported with ESX 5.0 or above	Not Supported

The following diagram represents VM Network Connectivity with VMware vSwitch:

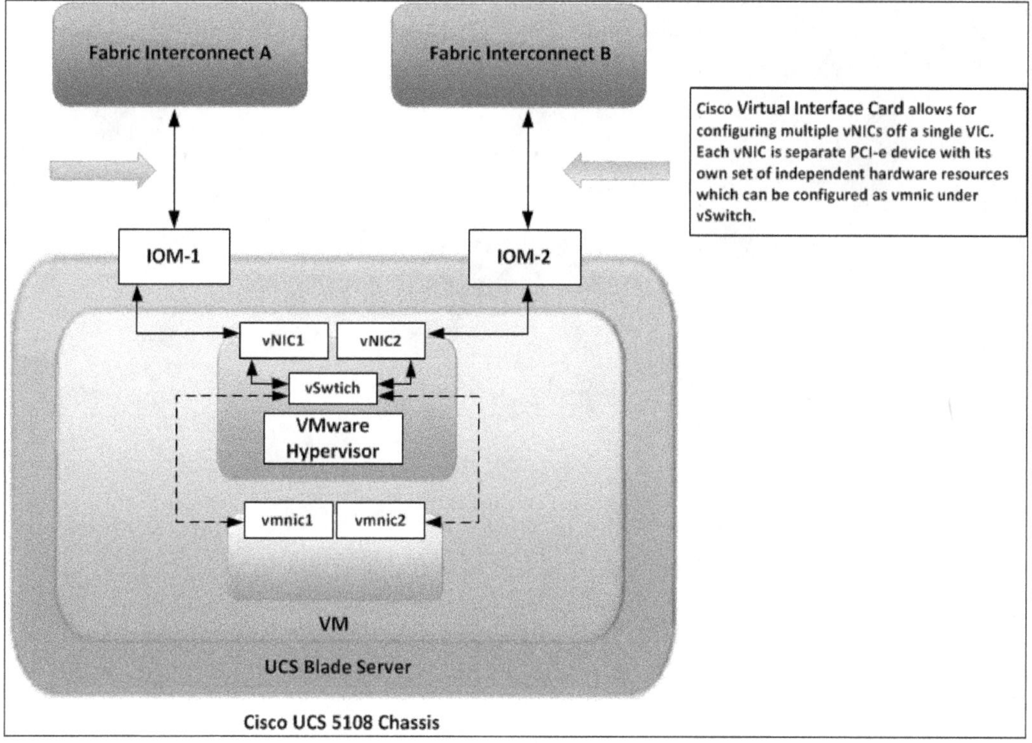

3

Installing an Operating System on Cisco UCS

In this chapter, we will cover the following topics:

- Microsoft Windows 2008 R2 local boot installation and configuration
- Microsoft Windows 2012 R2 local boot installation and configuration
- VMware vSphere 5.5 local boot installation and configuration
- VMware vSphere SAN boot configuration in EMC Storage
- VMware vSphere SAN boot configuration in HP 3PAR Storage
- Microsoft Windows 2008 R2 SAN boot configuration in EMC Storage
- Microsoft Windows 2008 R2 SAN boot configuration in HP 3PAR Storage

Introduction

In this chapter, you will learn how to accomplish tasks related to an OS platform installation on Cisco UCS 2.2; it includes both Microsoft Windows 2008/2012 local boot and SAN boot installation and configuration and VMware vSphere Server local and SAN boot installation and configuration.

Microsoft Windows 2008 R2 local boot installation and configuration

In this recipe, we will learn how to install and configure Microsoft Windows 2008 R2 local boot.

Getting ready

Prepare a Cisco **UCS 5108 Chassis** with two UCS IOM 2208XP installed; each UCS IOM is connected to a Cisco UCS 6248UP. There is a UCS B200 M3 with a VIC 1240 installed into the chassis. Configure four ports on each Cisco UCS 6248UP as an Ethernet uplink port and FC uplink port, which is connected to SAN Switches and LAN Switches by Fibre Channel cables. Due to each port being a unified port, you can configure it for different roles. For a chassis uplink, it is connected by Twinax copper (SFP-H10GB-CU1M); for a SAN uplink, it is connected by an 8 GB SFP (DS-SFP-FC8G-SW); for an Ethernet uplink, it is connected by a 10 GB SFP (SFP-10G-SR). Prepare a UCS service profile, it includes two vNICs, two vHBAs, and local drive with mirror mode (RAID 1). The details are listed in the following service profile:

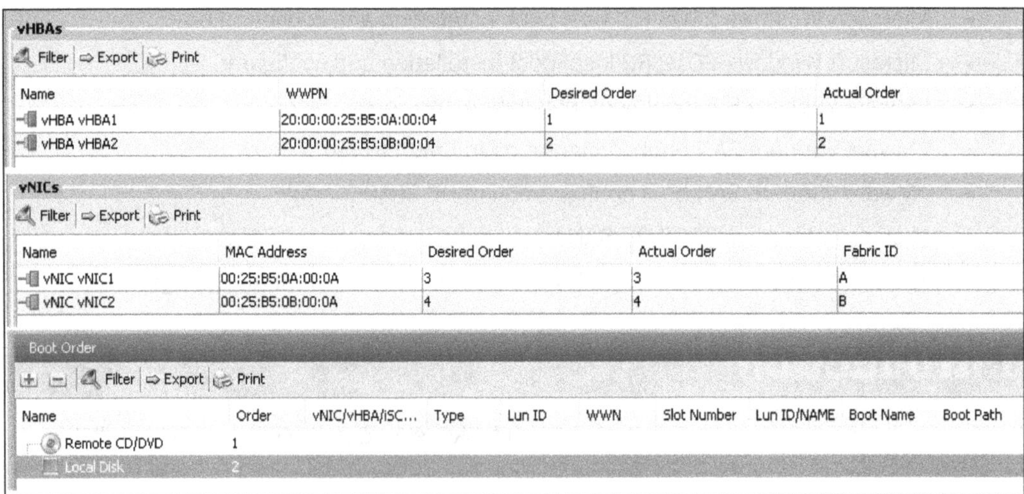

vHBAs
Filter | Export | Print
Name | WWPN | Desired Order | Actual Order
vHBA vHBA1 | 20:00:00:25:B5:0A:00:04 | 1 | 1
vHBA vHBA2 | 20:00:00:25:B5:0B:00:04 | 2 | 2
vNICs
Filter | Export | Print
Name | MAC Address | Desired Order | Actual Order | Fabric ID
vNIC vNIC1 | 00:25:B5:0A:00:0A | 3 | 3 | A
vNIC vNIC2 | 00:25:B5:0B:00:0A | 4 | 4 | B
Boot Order
Filter | Export | Print
Name | Order | vNIC/vHBA/iSC... | Type | Lun ID | WWN | Slot Number | Lun ID/NAME | Boot Name | Boot Path
Remote CD/DVD | 1
Local Disk | 2

How to do it...

In this recipe, we will learn how to prepare a boot policy on the UCS for Microsoft Server 2008 local boot installation.

Assume that there are two 300 GB SAS local disks and a LSI MegaRAID SAS 2004 installed on a Blade Server and you have prepared a service profile `WIN08_Local_Boot`, which is defined as two vNICs and two vHBAs:

1. Log in to a UCS Manager; click on the **Servers** tab in the navigation pane and right-click on **Local Disk Config Policies** and select **Create Local Disk Configuration Policy**.
2. Now, define the local disk policy in Raid 1. Input the **Name** of the local disk as `localdisk_raid1` and **Mode** in **RAID 1 Mirrored**:
3. Go to the **Servers** tab and select a service profile **WIN08_Local_Boot**, select **Change Local Disk Configuration Policy** on **Storage** tab and select the **localdisk_raid1** on the **Select the Local Disk Configuration Policy** menu:

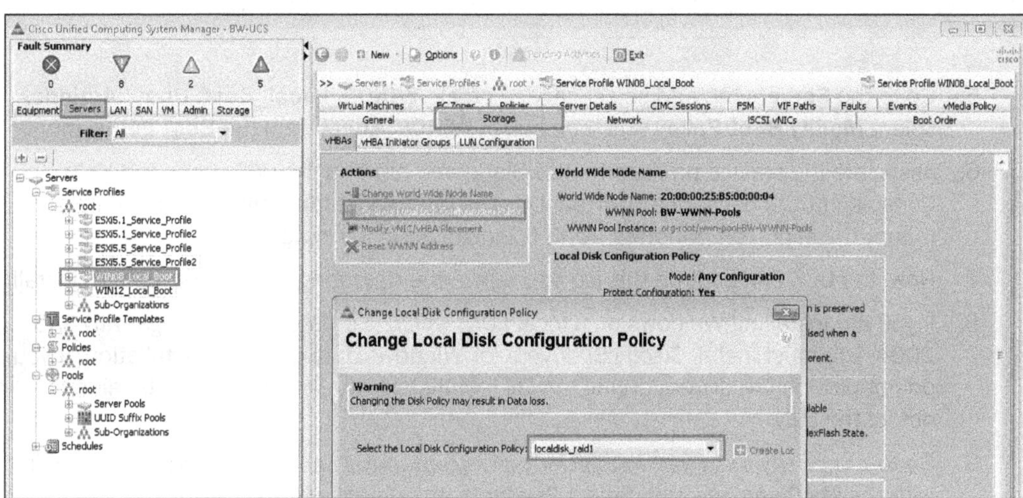

4. Right-click on **Boot Policies** and select **Create Boot Policy**. Input the **Name** of the boot policy and add **Remote CD/DVD** in **Order 1**, and **Local Disk** in **Order 2**, as shown in the screenshot:

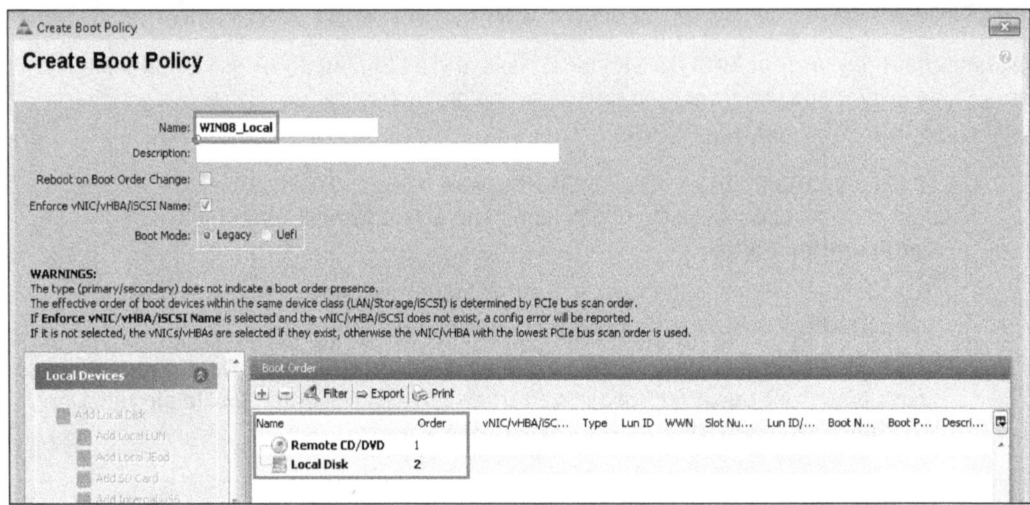

5. Go to the **Servers** tab and select service profile **WIN08_Local_Boot**. Under **Actions**, select **Modify Boot Policy** and then select **WIN08_Local** from the **Boot Policy** menu.

6. Associate the service profile into UCS Blade and boot up the UCS. Open the KVM Console of UCS, activate the Virtual Devices on the **Virtual Media** tab, and then mount the Microsoft Windows 2008 R2 installation iso image.

7. Now, the UCS can boot up this iso and select the operating system you want to install.

8. If you are installing Windows on a local LUN, which is created by LSI MegaRAID SAS 2004, you must install Cisco LSI drivers for Windows during the OS installation. If you do not provide the drivers during the OS installation, the system will not be able to detect the LUN.

9. Go to `https://software.cisco.com/download/navigator.html` and log in with the **My Cisco** account. Select **Products**, the details are as shown:

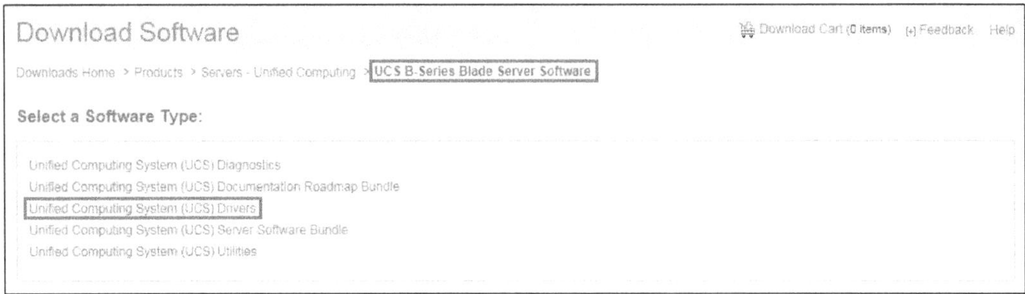

Note: Access to the download UCS driver is limited to users with an active Technical Support contract with Cisco.

10. Select **2.2(5b)** and download **ucs-bxxx-drivers.2.2.5b.iso**:

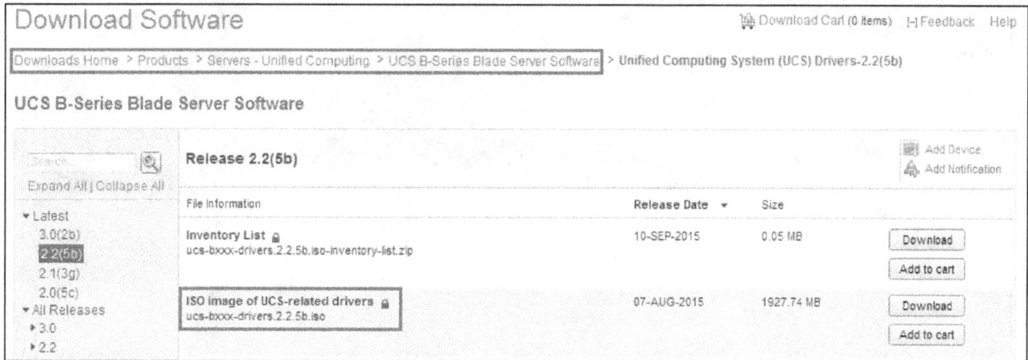

11. Load the LSI driver during the OS installation.

You need to un-mount Microsoft Windows 2008 installation iso first and mount the UCS driver iso to load the driver into UCS.

12. After loading the driver, you can see the local drive and click on **Next** to install the OS.
13. It starts to install Microsoft Windows 2008 and will reboot automatically when it finishes the installation.

How it works...

In this recipe, we will learn how to verify that Microsoft Windows 2008 can local boot successfully and install the Cisco VIC driver into Windows 2008 R2.

Follow these steps to local boot the Windows 2008 and install the Cisco VIC driver into Windows 2008 R2:

1. After booting up Windows 2008 R2, you wont be able to view the **Storage adapter** and **Network adapter** that were listed in the **Device Manager**.
2. Mount the `ucs-bxxx-drivers.2.2.5b.iso` and install the Cisco VIC driver into Windows 2008 R2 by Cisco VIO Installer.

3. After installing the Cisco VIC driver, you can check that the **Cisco VIC Ethernet Interface** and **Cisco VIC FCoE Storport Miniport** are listed in the **Device Manager**, as shown:

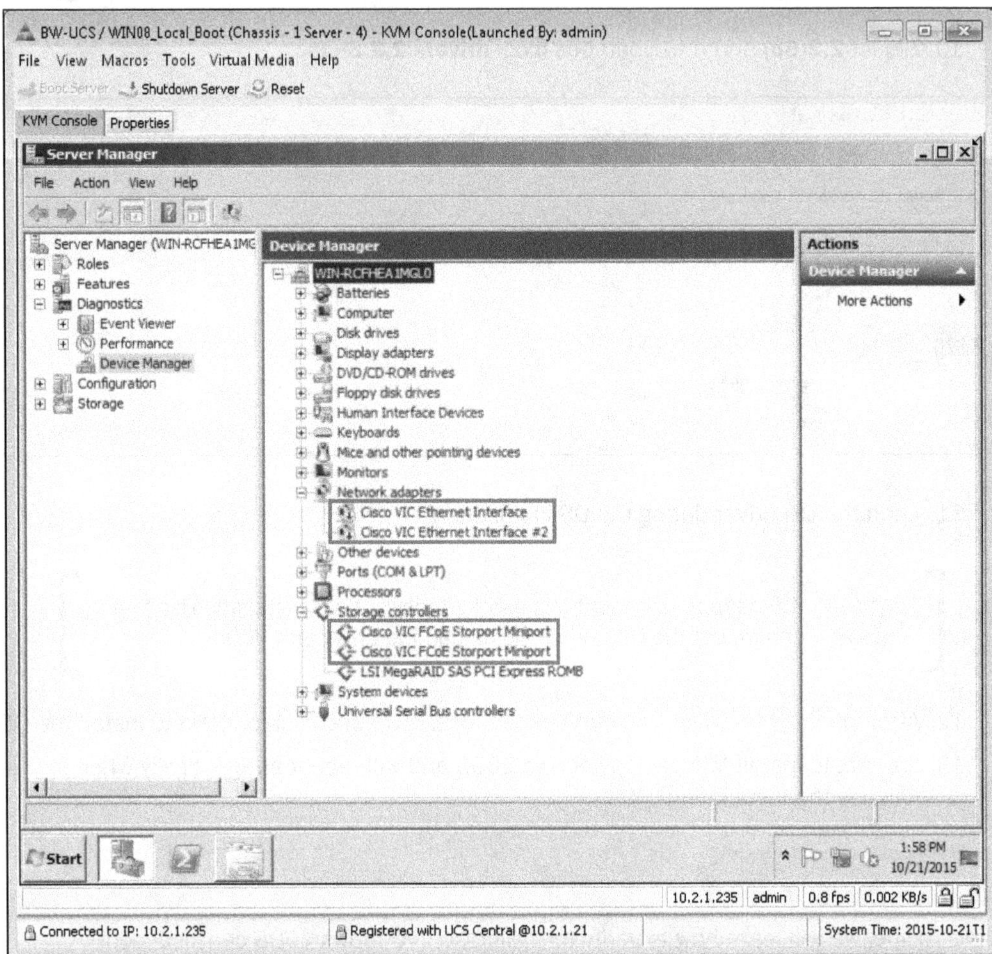

Microsoft Windows 2012 R2 local boot installation and configuration

In this recipe, we will learn how to install and configure Microsoft Windows 2012 R2 local boot.

Getting ready

Prepare a Cisco UCS 5108 Chassis with two UCS IOM 2204XP installed, each UCS IOM is connected to a Cisco UCS 6248UP. There is a UCS B200 M4 with one VIC 1340 installed into this chassis and configure four ports on each Cisco UCS 6248UP as an Ethernet uplink port and an FC uplink port, which is connected to SAN Switches and LAN Switches by Fibre Channel cables.

Due to each port being a unified port, you can configure it as different roles. For chassis, the uplink is connected by Twinax copper (SFP-H10GB-CU1M); for SAN uplink, it is connected by an 8 GB SFP (DS-SFP-FC8G-SW); for Ethernet uplink, it is connected by a 10 GB SFP (SFP-10G-SR). Prepare a UCS service profile, it includes two vNICs, two vHBAs, and a local drive with mirror mode (RAID 1). The details are listed in the following service profile:

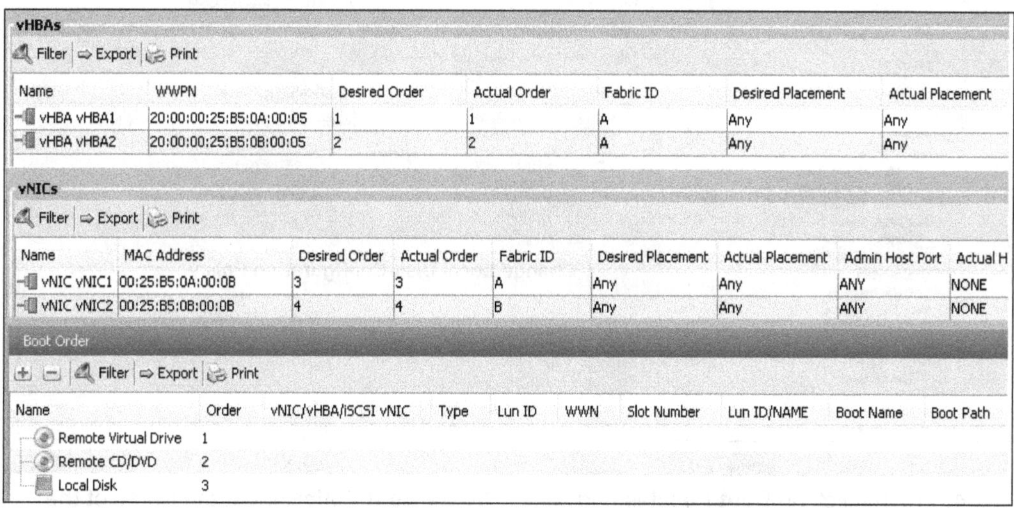

vHBAs

Name	WWPN	Desired Order	Actual Order	Fabric ID	Desired Placement	Actual Placement
vHBA vHBA1	20:00:00:25:B5:0A:00:05	1	1	A	Any	Any
vHBA vHBA2	20:00:00:25:B5:0B:00:05	2	2	A	Any	Any

vNICs

Name	MAC Address	Desired Order	Actual Order	Fabric ID	Desired Placement	Actual Placement	Admin Host Port	Actual H
vNIC vNIC1	00:25:B5:0A:00:0B	3	3	A	Any	Any	ANY	NONE
vNIC vNIC2	00:25:B5:0B:00:0B	4	4	B	Any	Any	ANY	NONE

Boot Order

Name	Order	vNIC/vHBA/iSCSI vNIC	Type	Lun ID	WWN	Slot Number	Lun ID/NAME	Boot Name	Boot Path
Remote Virtual Drive	1								
Remote CD/DVD	2								
Local Disk	3								

How to do it...

In this recipe, we will learn how to prepare a boot policy on UCS for Microsoft Server 2012 local boot installation.

Assume that there are two 300 GB SAS local disks and LSI MegaRAID SAS 2004 installed on Blade Server and you have prepared one service profile `WIN12_Local_Boot`, which is defined by two vNICs and two vHBAs:

1. Log in to UCS Manager, click on the **Servers** tab in the navigation pane, and then right-click on **Local Disk Config Policies** and select **Create Local Disk Configuration Policy**.
2. Now define the local disk policy in Raid 1. Input the **Name** of the local disk as `localdisk_raid1` and **Mode** in **RAID 1 Mirrored**.
3. Go to the **Servers** tab and select service profile **WIN12_Local_Boot**, select **Change Local Disk Configuration Policy** on the **Storage** tab. Select the **localdisk_raid1** on the **Select the Local Disk Configuration Policy** menu:

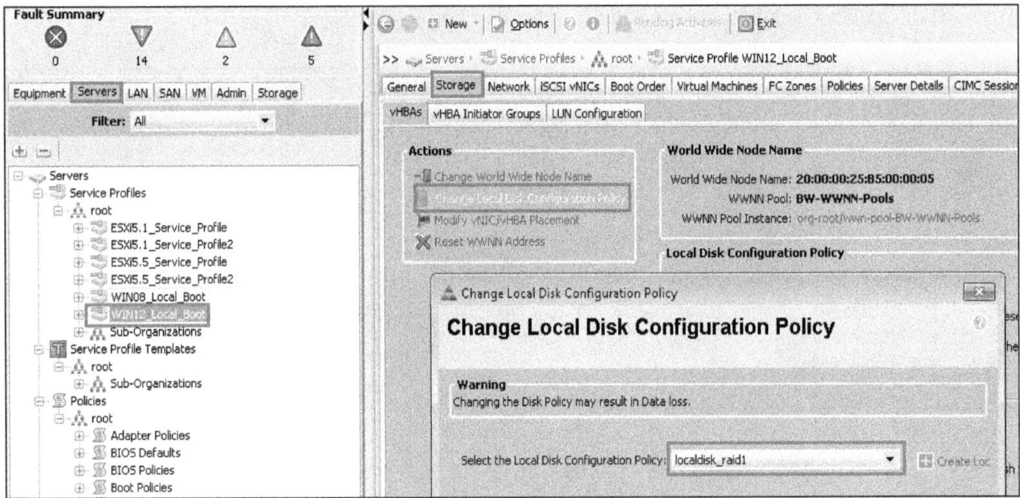

4. Right-click on **Boot Policies** and select **Create Boot Policy**. Input the Name of the boot policy and add **Remote CD/DVD** in **Order 1**, and **Local Disk** in **Order 2**:

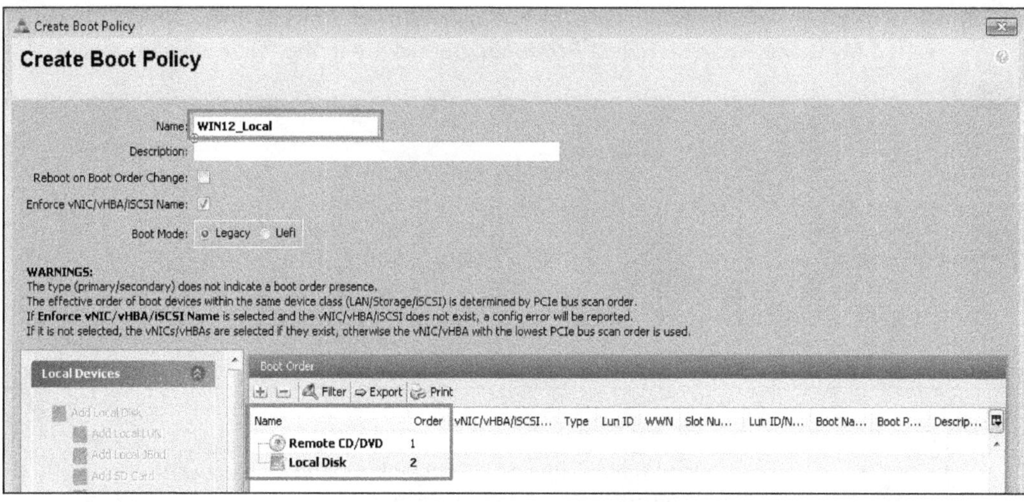

5. Go to the **Servers** tab and select service profile **WIN12_Local_Boot**. Under **Actions**, select **Modify Boot Policy**, also select **WIN12_Local** on the **Boot Policy** menu.
6. Associate the service profile to the UCS Blade and boot up the UCS. Open KVM Console of UCS and activate the Virtual Devices on the **Virtual Media** tab. Mount the Microsoft Windows 2012 R2 installation iso image.
7. The UCS can now boot up by this iso, select the operating system you want to install.
8. You can then see the local drive and click on **Next** to install the OS.
9. It starts to install Microsoft Windows 2012 and it will reboot automatically when it finishes the installation.

How it works...

In this recipe, we will learn how to verify that Microsoft Windows 2012 can local boot successfully and install the Cisco VIC driver into the Windows 2012 R2, by the following steps:

1. After booting up Windows 2012 R2, you cannot see the **Storage adapter** and **Network adapter**, which were listed in the **Device Manager**.

2. Go to `https://software.cisco.com/download/navigator.html` and login with a **My Cisco** account. Select **Products**, details are in the following screenshot:

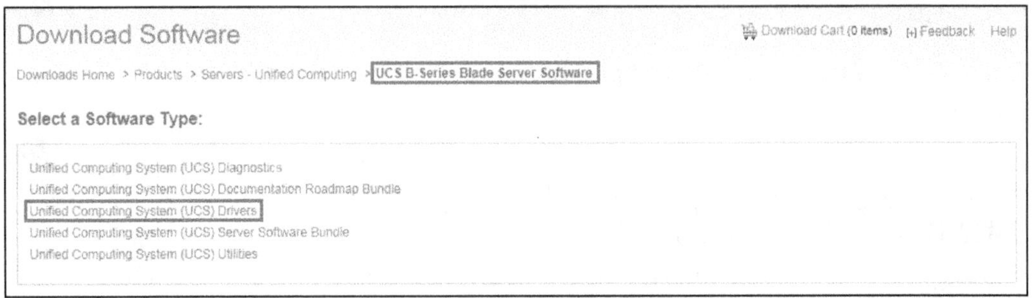

Note: Access to the download UCS driver is limited to users with an active Technical Support contract with Cisco.

3. Select **2.2(5b)** and download **ucs-bxxx-drivers.2.2.5b.iso**:

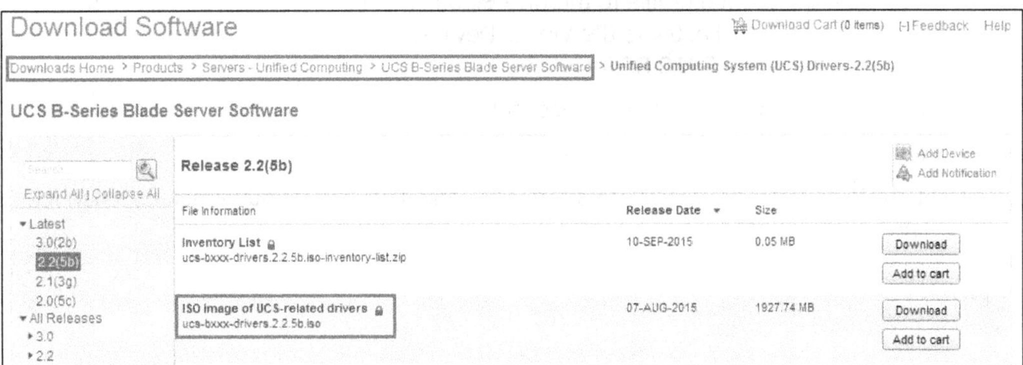

4. Mount `ucs-bxxx-drivers.2.2.5b.iso` by virtual media and install Cisco VIC driver into Windows 2012 R2 by Cisco VIO Installer.
5. After installing Cisco VIC driver, you can check that the **Cisco VIC Ethernet Interface** and **Cisco VIC-FCoE Storport Miniport** are listed in the **Device Manager**:

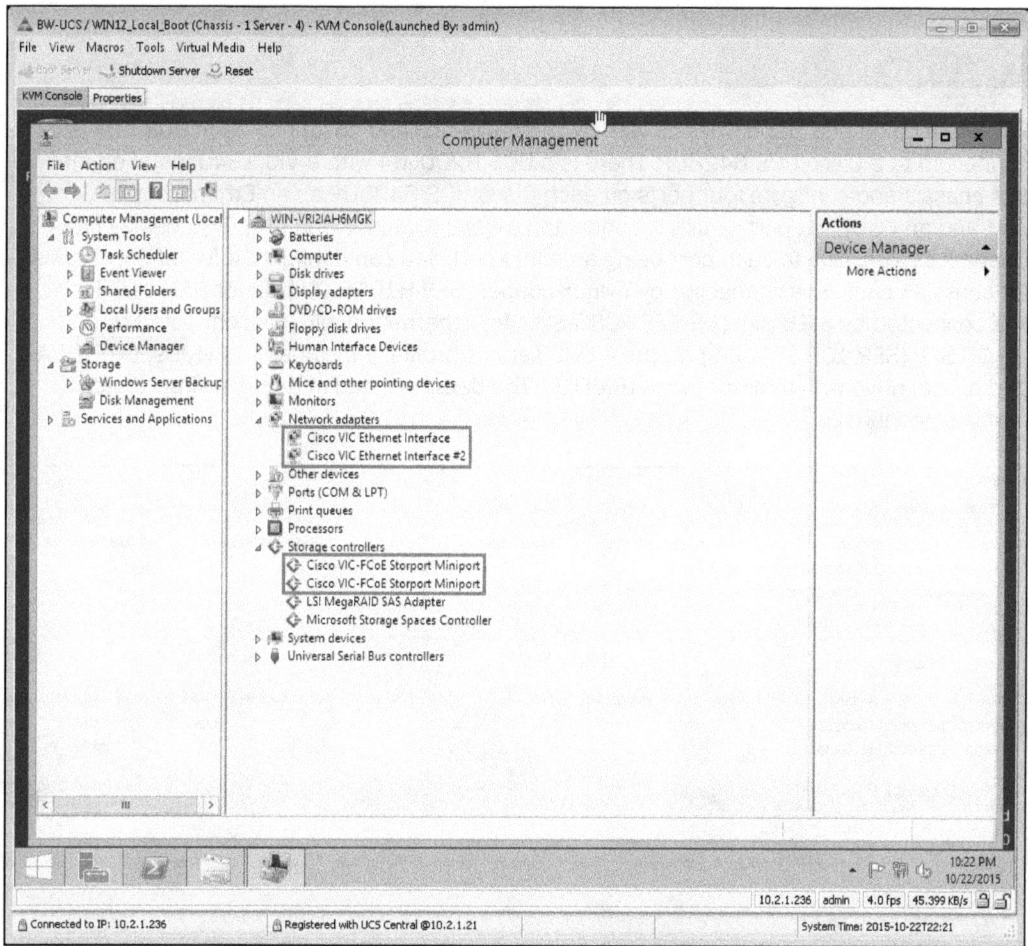

VMware vSphere 5.5 local boot installation and configuration

In this recipe, we will learn how to install and configure VMware vSphere 5.5 local boot.

Getting ready

Prepare a Cisco UCS 5108 Chassis with two UCS IOM 2208XP installed, each UCS IOM is connected to a Cisco UCS 6428UP. There is a UCS B200 M4 with a VIC 1340 installed into this chassis and configure four ports on each Cisco UCS 6428UP as an Ethernet uplink port and an FC uplink port, which is connected to SAN Switches and LAN Switches by Fibre Channel cables. Due to each port being a unified port, you can configure it for different roles; for chassis uplink, it is connected by Twinax copper (SFP-H10GB-CU1M); for SAN uplink, it is connected by 8 GB SFP (DS-SFP-FC8G-SW); for Ethernet uplink, it is connected by a 10 GB SFP (SFP-10G-SR) and prepare a UCS service profile. It includes two vNICs, two vHBAs, and a local drive with a mirror mode (RAID 1). The detail is listed in the following service profile screenshot:

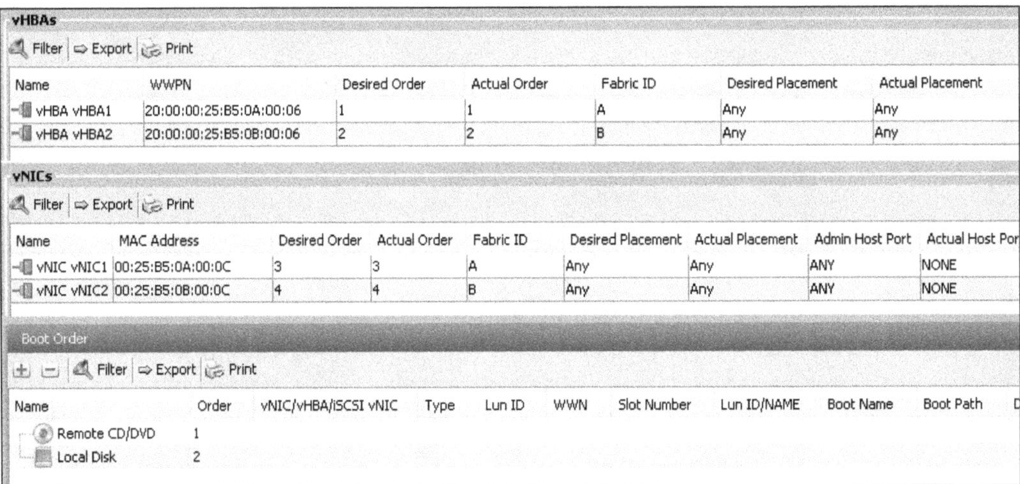

vHBAs

Filter | Export | Print

Name	WWPN	Desired Order	Actual Order	Fabric ID	Desired Placement	Actual Placement
vHBA vHBA1	20:00:00:25:B5:0A:00:06	1	1	A	Any	Any
vHBA vHBA2	20:00:00:25:B5:0B:00:06	2	2	B	Any	Any

vNICs

Filter | Export | Print

Name	MAC Address	Desired Order	Actual Order	Fabric ID	Desired Placement	Actual Placement	Admin Host Port	Actual Host Por
vNIC vNIC1	00:25:B5:0A:00:0C	3	3	A	Any	Any	ANY	NONE
vNIC vNIC2	00:25:B5:0B:00:0C	4	4	B	Any	Any	ANY	NONE

Boot Order

Filter | Export | Print

Name	Order	vNIC/vHBA/iSCSI vNIC	Type	Lun ID	WWN	Slot Number	Lun ID/NAME	Boot Name	Boot Path
Remote CD/DVD	1								
Local Disk	2								

How to do it...

In this recipe, we will learn how to prepare a boot policy on UCS for VMware vSphere 5.5 local boot installation.

Assume there are two 300 GB SAS local disks and a LSI MegaRAID SAS 2004 installed on a Blade Server, and you have prepared one service profile `ESXi5.5_Local_Boot`, which is defined by two vNICs and two vHBAs:

1. Log in to UCS Manager, click on the **Servers** tab in the navigation pane and right-click on **Local Disk Config Policies**, and select **Create Local Disk Configuration Policy**.
2. Now, define the local disk policy in Raid 1. Input the **Name** of local disk as `localdisk_raid1` and **Mode** in **RAID 1 Mirrored**.
3. Go to the **Servers** tab and select a service profile **ESXi5.5_Local_Boot**, and also select the **Change Local Disk Configuration Policy** on the **Storage** tab. Select the **localdisk_raid1** on the **policy** menu:

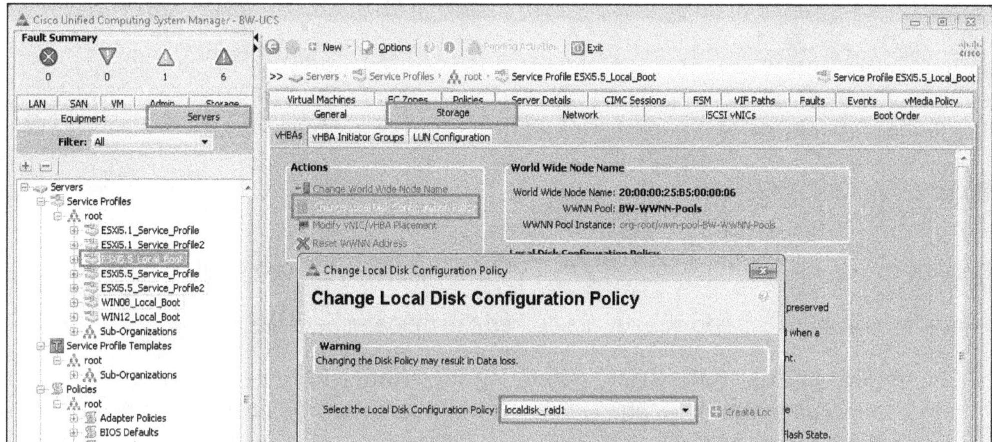

4. Right-click on **Boot Policies** and select **Create Boot Policy**. Input the **Name** of the boot policy and add a **Remote CD/DVD** in **Order 1**, and **Local Disk** in **Order 2**:

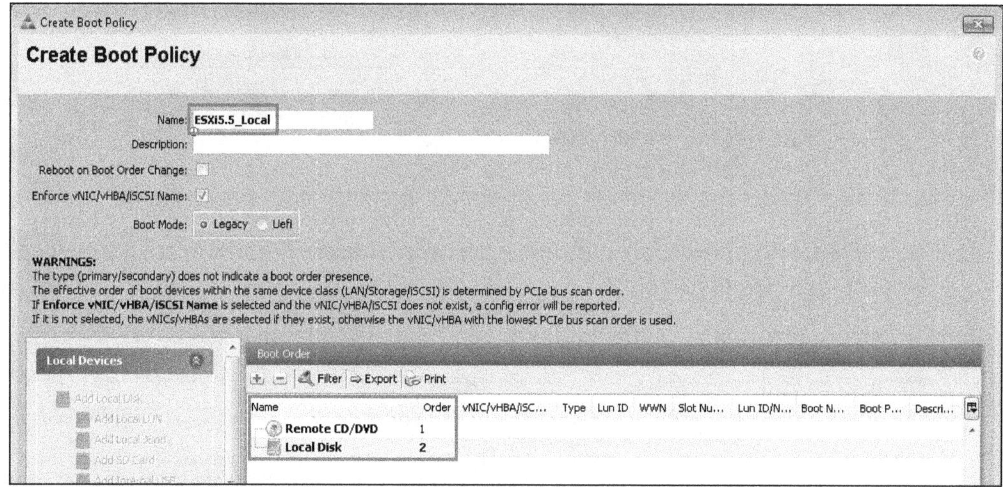

5. Go to the **Servers** tab and select a service profile **ESXi5.5_Local_Boot**. Under **Actions**, select **Modify Boot Policy**, and select **ESXi5.5_Local** from the **Boot Policy** menu.

6. Associate service profile into the UCS Blade and boot up the UCS. Open the KVM Console of UCS, you can see the Active Virtual Devices on **Virtual Media** tab. Mount the VMware vSphere 5.5 installation iso image.

> According to Cisco best practice, install ESXi using Cisco Custom Image for ESXi 5.5 iso.

7. The UCS can boot up by this iso, start installing ESXi 5.5.
8. Now, you can see the local drive and click on **Next** to install the OS.
9. It starts to install ESXi 5.5 and will reboot automatically when it finishes the installation.

How it works...

In this recipe, we will learn how to verify that VMware vSphere 5.5 can local boot successfully.

Assume that vSphere 5.5 has already configured the management IP:

1. After booting up vSphere 5.5 and logging into it with a VMware vSphere Client. Go to the **Configuration** tab and choose **Storage Adapters**. You can see **vmhba1** and **vmhba2** drivers on **Cisco VIC FCoE HBA Driver**:

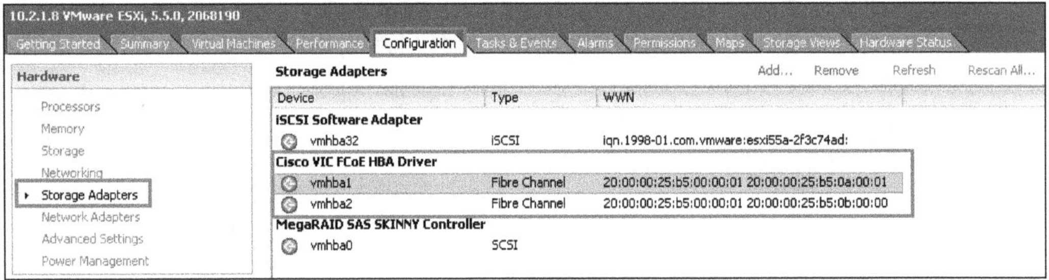

2. Go to the **Configuration** tab and choose **Network Adapters**. You can see **vmnic0** and **vmnic1** on **Network Adapters**:

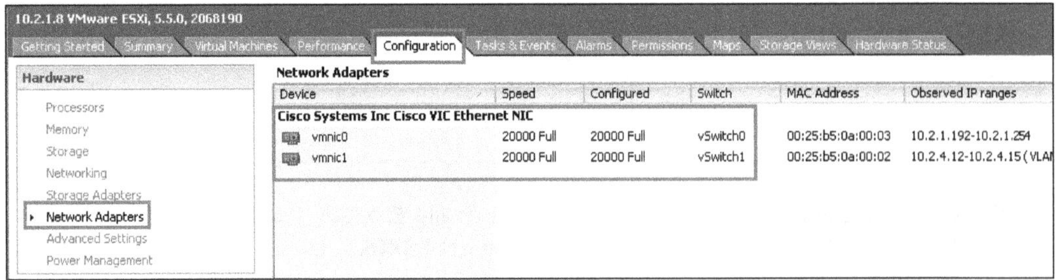

VMware vSphere SAN boot configuration in EMC Storage

In this recipe, we will learn how to install and configure VMware vSphere 5.5 SAN boot in EMC Storage.

Getting ready

Prepare a Cisco UCS 5108 Chassis with two UCS IOM 2208XP installed; each UCS IOM is connected to a Cisco UCS 6428UP. There is one UCS B200 M3, with one VIC 1240 installed into the Chassis. Configure four ports on each Cisco UCS 6428UP as an Ethernet uplink port (port 17/18) and FC uplink port (port 6/7), which is connected to SAN Switches and LAN Switches by Fibre Channel cables. The EMC SAN Storage has two controllers, and each controller has two FC ports, which are connected to SAN Switches. Prepare a UCS service profile, it includes two vNICs, and two vHBAs. The detail is listed in the following diagram:

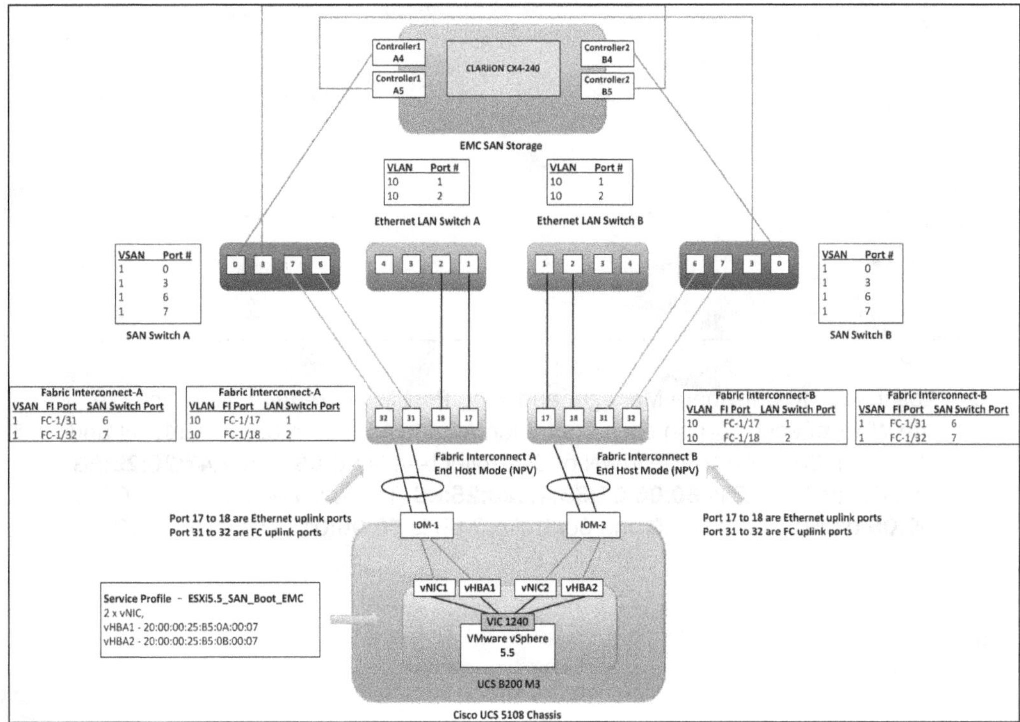

How to do it...

In this recipe, we will learn how to prepare a boot policy on UCS for VMware ESXi 5.5 SAN boot installation. Assume that the name of the service profile is `ESXi5.5_SAN_Boot_EMC` and the EMC SAN Storage is CLARiiON CX4-240.

Follow these steps to prepare a boot policy on UCS for VMware ESXi 5.5 SAN boot installation:

1. First, you note the WWPN of each vHBA on the **Storage** tab of this service profile **ESXi5.5_SAN_Boot_EMC**, as shown in the following screenshot. The **WWPN** of **vHBA1** is **20:00:00:25:B5:0A:00:07** and **vHBA2** is **20:00:00:25:B5:0B:00:07**:

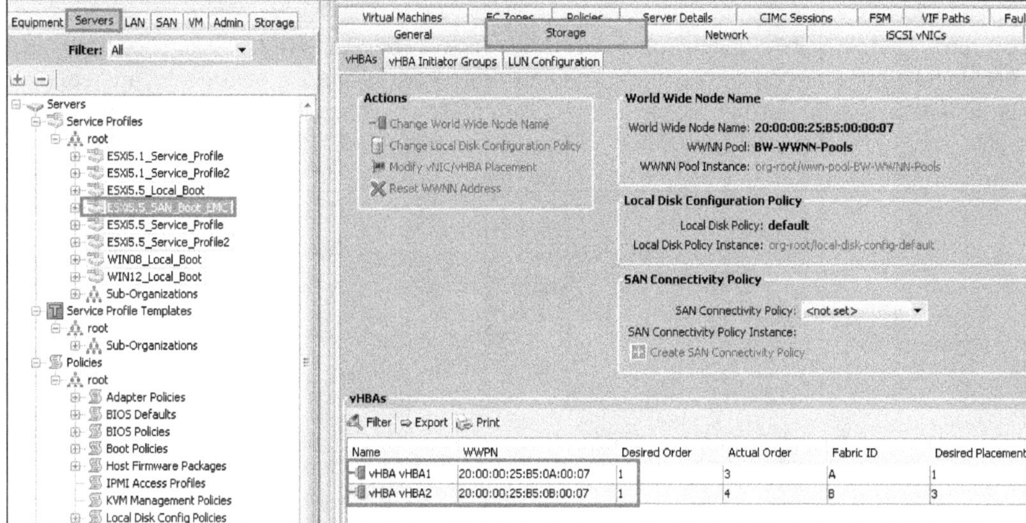

2. Log in to EMC Unisphere Manager and go to **Port Management**, you can note the WWN of each port on each Controller; A4 and A5 are on Controller1, B4 and B5 are on Controller2. The WWN of Controller1-A4 is **50:06:01:64:47:20:25:EB** and Controller1-A5 is **50:06:01:65:47:20:25:EB**. The WWN of Controller2-B4 is **50:06:01:6C:47:20:25:EB** and Controller2-B5 is **50:06:01:6D:47:20:25:EB**:

Physical Location	SP-Port △	Type	Speed	IP Addresses	IQN/WWN
Slot A0, Port 2	A-0	Fibre	N/A	N/A	50:06:01:60:C7:20:25:EB:50:06:01:60:47:20:25:EB
Slot A0, Port 3	A-1	Fibre	N/A	N/A	50:06:01:60:C7:20:25:EB:50:06:01:61:47:20:25:EB
Slot A1, Port 0	A-2	iSCSI	N/A	N/A	iqn.1992-04.com.emc:cx.apm00120503654.a2
Slot A1, Port 1	A-3 (MirrorView)	iSCSI	N/A	N/A	iqn.1992-04.com.emc:cx.apm00120503654.a3
Slot A2, Port 0	A-4	Fibre	4Gbps	N/A	50:06:01:60:C7:20:25:EB:50:06:01:64:47:20:25:EB
Slot A2, Port 1	A-5	Fibre	4Gbps	N/A	50:06:01:60:C7:20:25:EB:50:06:01:65:47:20:25:EB
Slot A2, Port 2	A-6	Fibre	N/A	N/A	50:06:01:60:C7:20:25:EB:50:06:01:66:47:20:25:EB
Slot A2, Port 3	A-7 (MirrorView)	Fibre	N/A	N/A	50:06:01:60:C7:20:25:EB:50:06:01:67:47:20:25:EB
Slot A0, Port 0	A-Bus 0	Fibre	4Gbps	N/A	N/A
Slot A0, Port 1	A-Bus 1	Fibre	N/A	N/A	N/A
Slot B0, Port 2	B-0	Fibre	N/A	N/A	50:06:01:60:C7:20:25:EB:50:06:01:68:47:20:25:EB
Slot B0, Port 3	B-1	Fibre	N/A	N/A	50:06:01:60:C7:20:25:EB:50:06:01:69:47:20:25:EB
Slot B2, Port 0	B-4	Fibre	4Gbps	N/A	50:06:01:60:C7:20:25:EB:50:06:01:6C:47:20:25:EB
Slot B2, Port 1	B-5	Fibre	4Gbps	N/A	50:06:01:60:C7:20:25:EB:50:06:01:6D:47:20:25:EB
Slot B2, Port 2	B-6	Fibre	N/A	N/A	50:06:01:60:C7:20:25:EB:50:06:01:6E:47:20:25:EB
Slot B2, Port 3	B-7 (MirrorView)	Fibre	N/A	N/A	50:06:01:60:C7:20:25:EB:50:06:01:6F:47:20:25:EB
Slot B0, Port 0	B-Bus 0	Fibre	4Gbps	N/A	N/A
Slot B0, Port 1	B-Bus 1	Fibre	N/A	N/A	N/A

EMC Unisphere Manager is the Web-based tool to manage and monitor EMC CLARiiON/VNX SAN Storage.

3. Associate this service profile to a Blade Server and power up the Server.
4. You must power on the UCS otherwise the WWPN of each vHBA will not be able to log in to SAN Switches; then, log in to SAN Switch-A by SSH and verify that the WWPN of each Controller's FC port and WWN of each vHBA can successfully log in to the SAN switch. According to the following screenshot, you can see that port 0 and 3 are the WWPN of Controller1-SPA4 and Controller2-SPB5, by executing the `switchshow` command. Ports 6 and 7 are FI's FC uplinks:

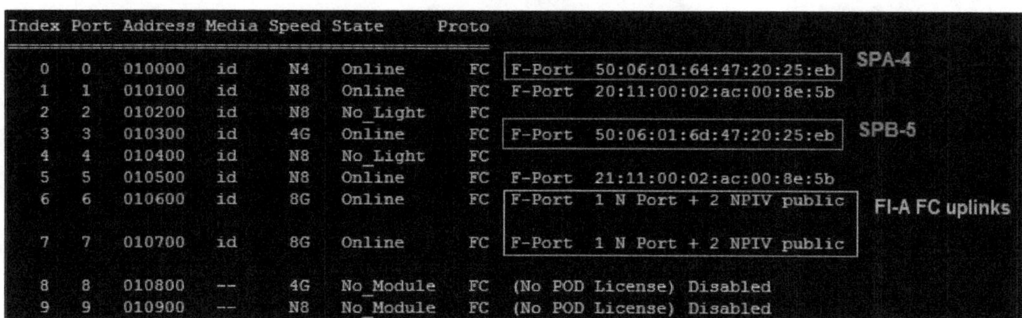

Index	Port	Address	Media	Speed	State	Proto	
0	0	010000	id	N4	Online	FC	F-Port 50:06:01:64:47:20:25:eb
1	1	010100	id	N8	Online	FC	F-Port 20:11:00:02:ac:00:8e:5b
2	2	010200	id	N8	No_Light	FC	
3	3	010300	id	4G	Online	FC	F-Port 50:06:01:6d:47:20:25:eb
4	4	010400	id	N8	No_Light	FC	
5	5	010500	id	N8	Online	FC	F-Port 21:11:00:02:ac:00:8e:5b
6	6	010600	id	8G	Online	FC	F-Port 1 N Port + 2 NPIV public
7	7	010700	id	8G	Online	FC	F-Port 1 N Port + 2 NPIV public
8	8	010800	--	4G	No_Module	FC	(No POD License) Disabled
9	9	010900	--	N8	No_Module	FC	(No POD License) Disabled

Due to ports 6 and 7 being **N_Port ID Virtualization** (**NPIV**), you need to perform a `portloginshow <port number>` command to verify that the WWN of vHBA can be successfully logged on to the SAN Switch; you can see the WWN of **vHBA1** can log in to port 6 as shown in the following screenshot:

```
Type  PID     World Wide Name          credit df_sz cos
=======================================================
 fe   010701 20:00:00:25:b5:0a:00:07    16   2112   8  scr=0x3
 fe   010700 20:20:00:2a:6a:ea:b3:80    16   2112   8  scr=0x0
 ff   010701  20:00:00:25:b5:0a:00:07    0      0   8  d_id=FFFFFC
 ff   010700  20:20:00:2a:6a:ea:b3:80    8   2112   c  d_id=FFFFFA
 ff   010700  20:20:00:2a:6a:ea:b3:80    8   2112   c  d_id=FFFFFC
```

vHBA1

Finally, you can see that all WWNs can log in to SAN Switch-A successfully, the details are shown in the following table:

SAN Switch	Port Number	WWPN/WWN	Devices
SAN Switch-A	0	50:06:01:64:47:20:25:EB	Controller1-A4
	3	50:06:01:6D:47:20:25:EB	Controller2-B5
	6	20:00:00:25:B5:0A:00:07	vHBA1

5. Repeat the procedure of Step 4 to verify all WWPN/WWN on SAN Switch-B; you can see that all WWN can log in to SAN Switch-B successfully, as shown in the following screenshot:

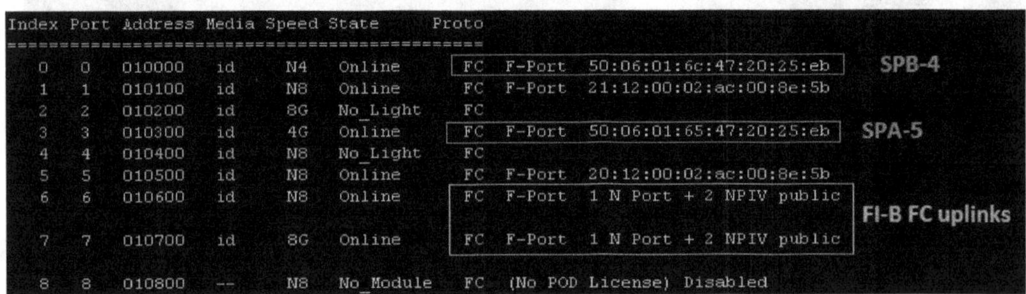

```
Index Port Address Media Speed State     Proto
==============================================
  0   0   010000   id    N4   Online      FC  F-Port  50:06:01:6c:47:20:25:eb
  1   1   010100   id    N8   Online      FC  F-Port  21:12:00:02:ac:00:8e:5b
  2   2   010200   id    8G   No_Light    FC
  3   3   010300   id    4G   Online      FC  F-Port  50:06:01:65:47:20:25:eb
  4   4   010400   id    N8   No_Light    FC
  5   5   010500   id    N8   Online      FC  F-Port  20:12:00:02:ac:00:8e:5b
  6   6   010600   id    N8   Online      FC  F-Port  1 N Port + 2 NPIV public

  7   7   010700   id    8G   Online      FC  F-Port  1 N Port + 2 NPIV public

  8   8   010800   --    N8   No_Module   FC  (No POD License) Disabled
```


The following table lists the summary of all WWPN/WWN on SAN Switch-B:

SAN Switch	Port Number	WWPN/WWN	Devices
SAN Switch-B	0	50:06:01:6c:47:20:25:EB	Controller2-B4
	3	50:06:01:65:47:20:25:EB	Controller1-A5
	6	20:00:00:25:B5:0B:00:07	vHBA2

Finally, create two zones on each SAN Switch and enable all zones, the following table lists the summary of each FC zone:

SAN Switch	Zone Name	Zone Member1	Zone Member2
SAN Switch-A	vHBA1_Controll1-A4	vHBA1-	Controller1-A4
	vHBA1_Controll2-B5	vHBA1	Controller2-B5
SAN Switch-B	vHBA2_Controll1-A5	vHBA2	Controller1-A5
	vHBA2_Controll2-B4	vHBA2	Controller2-B4

According to the best practice of FC zoning, single initiator zoning is recommended (one initiator to one target).

6. When the FC zoning is created on both SAN Switches, log in to EMC Unisphere Manager, right-click on the system, and choose **Connectivity Status**, as shown in the following screenshot. Then you can see all the UCS's initiators (WWN of each vHBA) on **Host Initiators**, manually register two initiators **20:00:00:25:B5:0A:00:07** and two initiators **20:00:00:25:B5:0B:00:07** into one host **esxi55.testlab.com**:

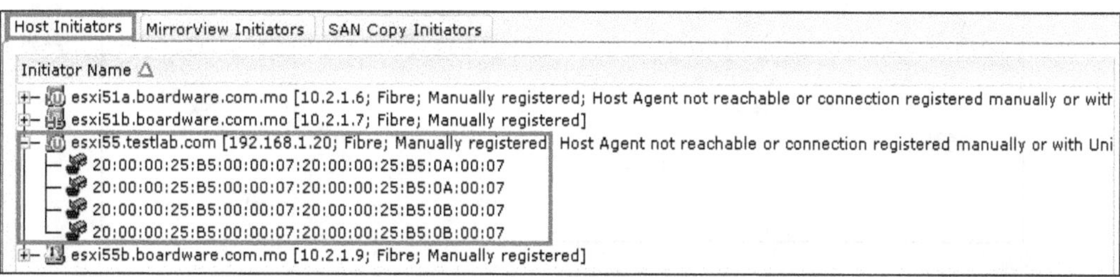

7. Go to **Storage** tab and create a new storage group on the **Storage** menu, enter the name of the **Storage Group**.

8. After creating the storage group, select the **Hosts** tab and move the host initiator group **esxi55.testlab.com** to the right-hand side and click on the **Apply** button. Finally, the EMC Storage connectivity of Cisco UCS is complete:

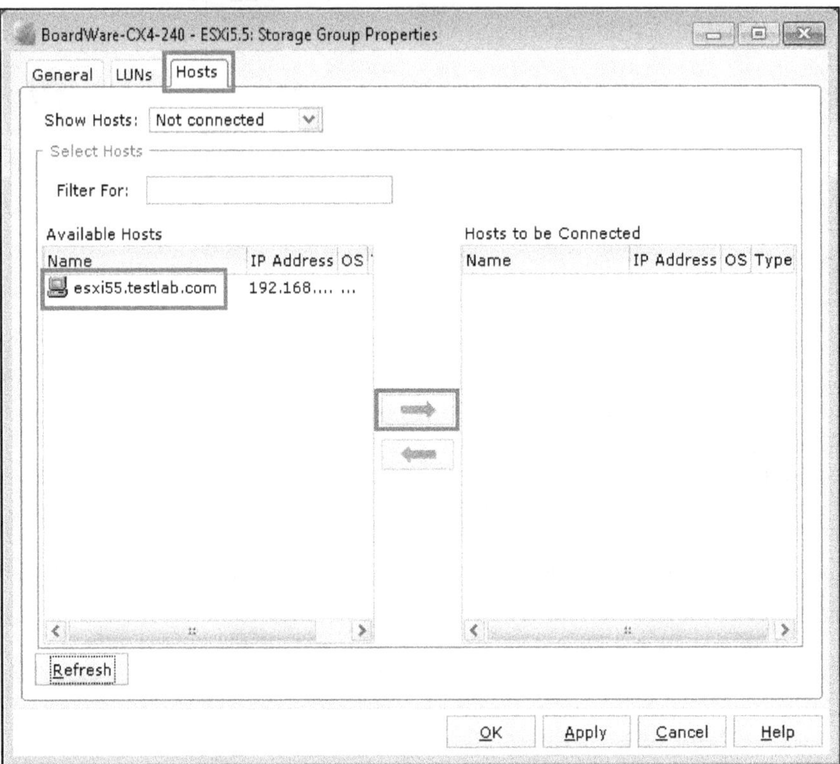

9. Assume that the OS LUN is prepared and its capacity is 20 GB. Select the **LUNs** tab, add ESX's OS LUN into **Selected LUNs**, and then press **OK**:

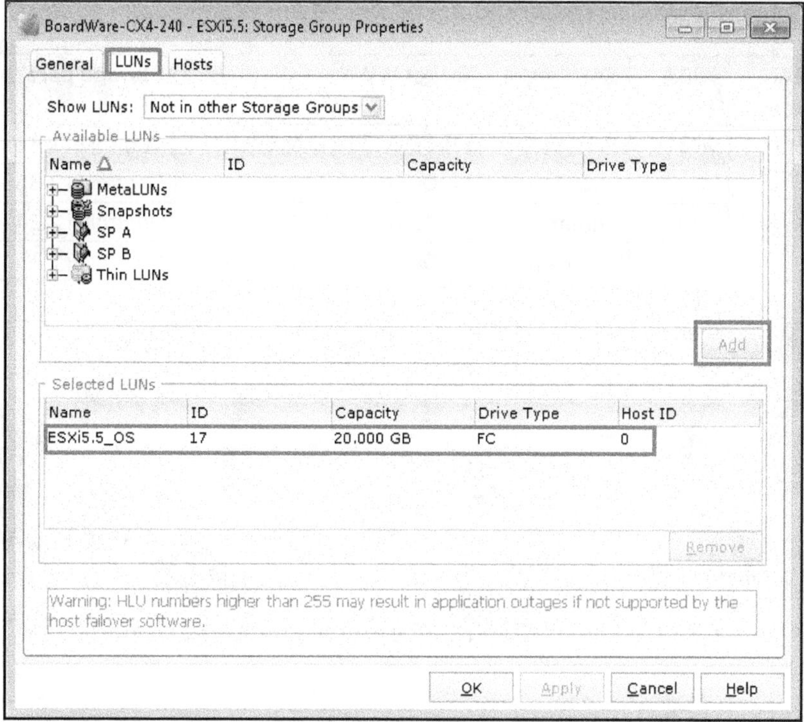

10. Go to UCS Manager, right-click on **Boot Policies** and select **Create Boot Policy** on **Servers** tab:

11. Input the **Name** of the boot policy and move **Remote CD/DVD** in **Order 1**, and **SAN Boot** in **Order 2**. Each SAN boot has two boot targets, you need to input the vHBA name and WWN of the SAN target. The name of vHBA must be same as the name of the UCS's vHBA, otherwise the boot target cannot work.

The table lists the summary of the SAN boot target:

SAN boot	vHBA	SAN target	Target WWN	Storage port
SAN boot	vHBA1	Primary	50:06:01:64:47:20:25:EB	Controller1-A4
		Secondary	50:06:01:6D:47:20:25:EB	Controller2-B5
	vHBA2	Primary	50:06:01:6c:47:20:25:EB	Controller2-B4
		Secondary	50:06:01:65:47:20:25:EB	Controller1-A5

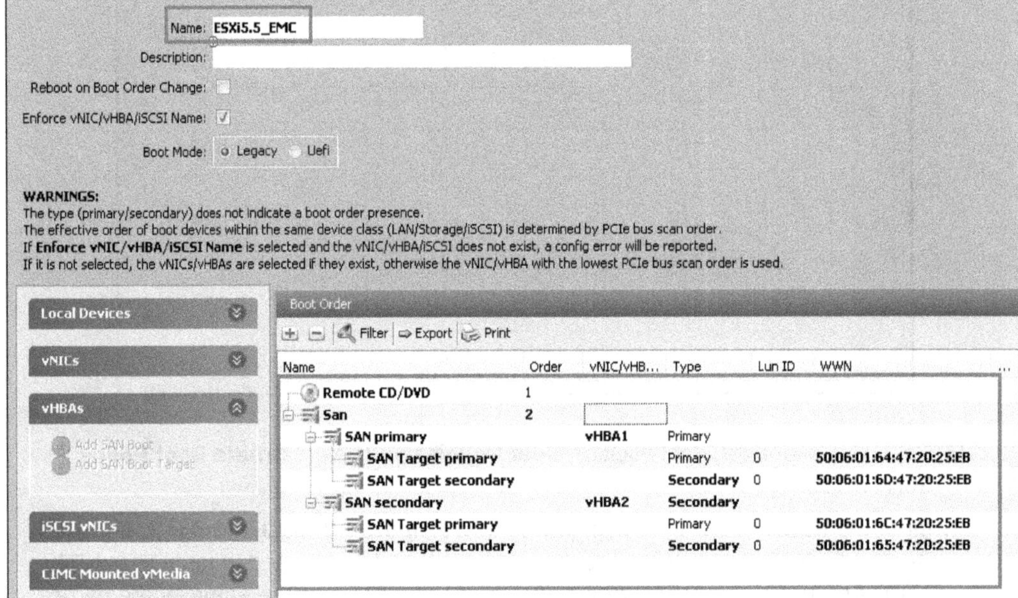

12. Go to the **Servers** tab and select service profile **ESXi5.5_SAN_Boot_EMC**, and select **Modify Boot Policy** on **Boot Order** tab. Select **ESXi5.5_EMC** on the **Boot Policy** menu.
13. Power down UCS and re-associate this service profile into UCS again. Then, power on UCS and open the KVM Console, you can see four paths appear during UCS boot up, these are the WWN of the SAN boot target:

```
Cisco VIC FC, Boot Driver Version 4.0(1d)
(C) 2010 Cisco Systems, Inc.
 DGC         50060164472025eb:000
 DGC         5006016d472025eb:000
Option ROM installed successfully

Cisco VIC FC, Boot Driver Version 4.0(1d)
(C) 2010 Cisco Systems, Inc.
 DGC         5006016c472025eb:000
 DGC         50060165472025eb:000
Option ROM installed successfully
_
```

14. Activate the **Virtual Devices** on the **Virtual Media** tab. Mount the VMware vSphere 5.5 installation iso.

[According to Cisco best practice, please install ESXi using the Cisco Custom Image for ESXi 5.5 iso.]

15. The UCS can boot up by this iso, start to install ESXi 5.5.
16. You can select **EMC's 20GB LUN** and click on **Next** to install the OS.
17. It starts to install ESXi 5.5 and it will reboot automatically when it finishes the installation.

How it works...

In this recipe, we will learn how to verify that VMware vSphere 5.5 can SAN boot successfully.

Assume that vSphere 5.5 has already configured the management IP:

1. After booting up vSphere 5.5 and logging into it by VMware vSphere Client. Go to the **Configuration** tab and choose **Storage Adapters**. You can see **vmhba1** and **vmhba2** on **Cisco VIC FCoE HBA Driver**:

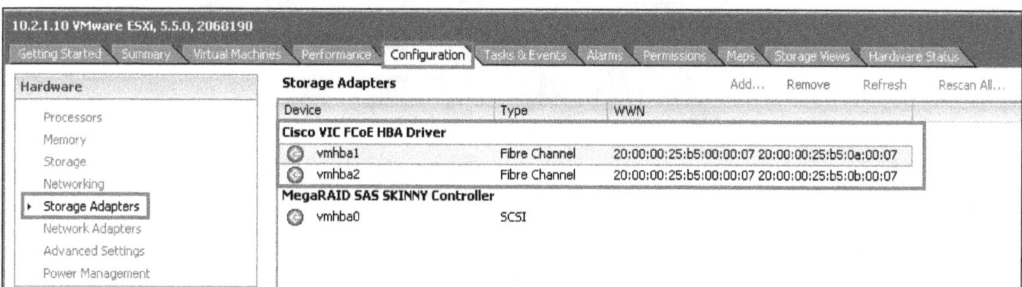

2. Go to the **Configuration** tab and choose **Network Adapters**. You can see **vmnic0** and **vmnic1** on **Network Adapters**:

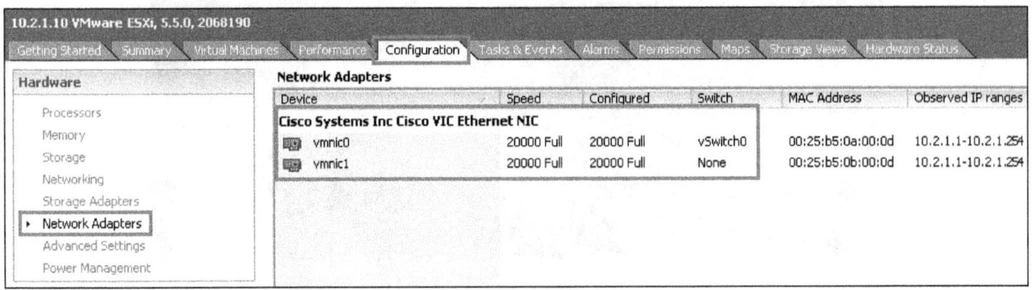

There's more...

Assume that **Server 4** is the ESXi host. Choose the UCS Server on **Equipment** tab and go to the **General** tab. You can also see all the SAN boot targets on the **Actual Boot Order** tab:

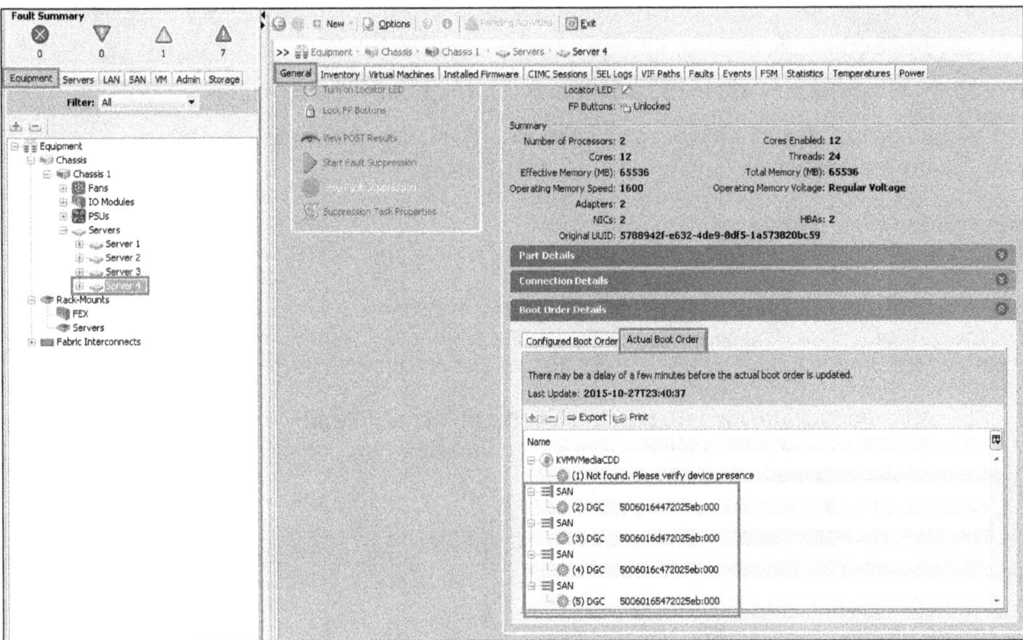

VMware vSphere SAN boot configuration in HP 3PAR Storage

In this recipe, we will learn how to install and configure VMware vSphere 5.5 SAN boot in HP 3PAR Storage.

Getting ready

Prepare a Cisco UCS 5108 Chassis with two UCS IOM 2208XP installed, each UCS IOM is connected to a Cisco UCS 6428UP. There is one UCS B200 M3 with one VIC 1240 installed into the chassis and configure four ports on each Cisco UCS 6428UP as an Ethernet uplink port (port 17/18) and an FC uplink port (port 6/7), which is connected to SAN Switches and LAN Switches by Fibre Channel cables. The EMC SAN Storage has two controllers and each controller has two FC ports that are connected to each SAN Switch. Prepare a UCS service profile, it includes two vNICs, two vHBAs. The details are listed in the following diagram:

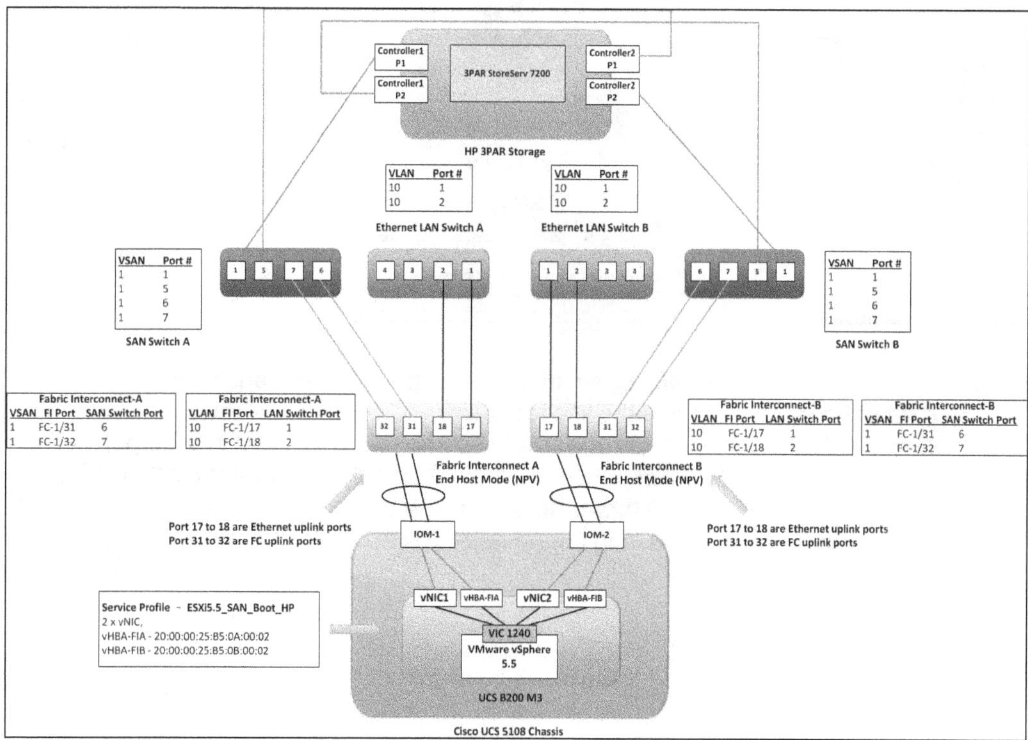

How to do it...

In this recipe, we will learn how to prepare a boot policy on UCS for VMware ESXi 5.5 SAN boot installation.

Assume that the name of service profile is `ESXi5.5_SAN_Boot_HP` and the HP 3PAR Storage is StoreServ 7200:

1. First, you will note the WWPN of each vHBA on the **Storage** tab of this service profile **ESXi5.5_SAN_Boot_HP**, as shown in the following screenshot. The **WWPN** of **vHBA-FIA** is **20:00:00:25:B5:0A:00:02** and **vHBA-FIB** is **20:00:00:25:B5:0B:00:02**:

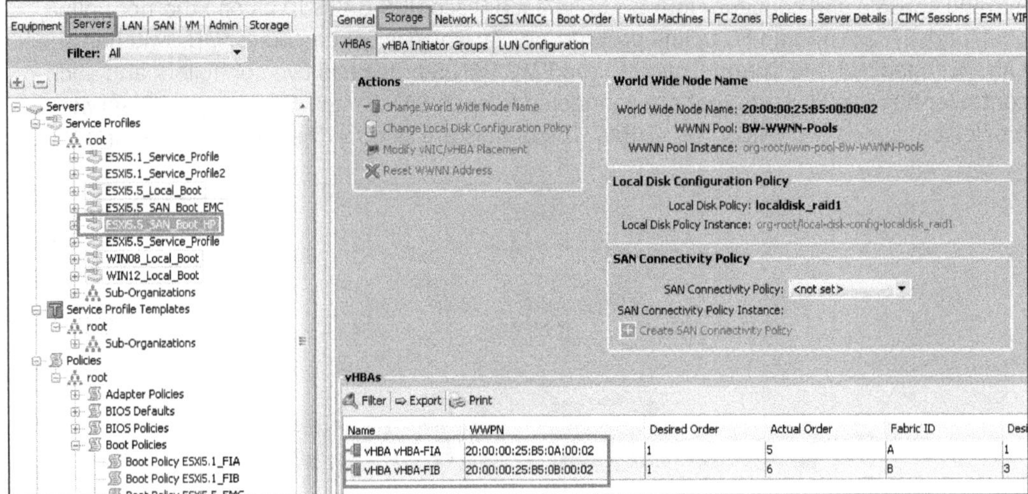

2. Log in to the **HP 3PAR Management Console**, go to **Systems** and choose **Host** of **Ports**, you can note the **WWN** of each port on each Controller. On Controller1, **0:1:1** is port1 and **0:1:2** is port2; **1:1:1** is port1, and **1:1:2** is port2 on Controller2. The **WWN** of Controller1-P1 is **20:11:00:02:AC:00:8E:5B**, and Controller1-P2 is **20:12:00:02:AC:00:8E:5B**. The **WWN** of Controller2-P1 is **21:11:00:02:AC:00:8E:5B**, and Controller2-P2 is **21:12:00:02:AC:00:8E:5B**:

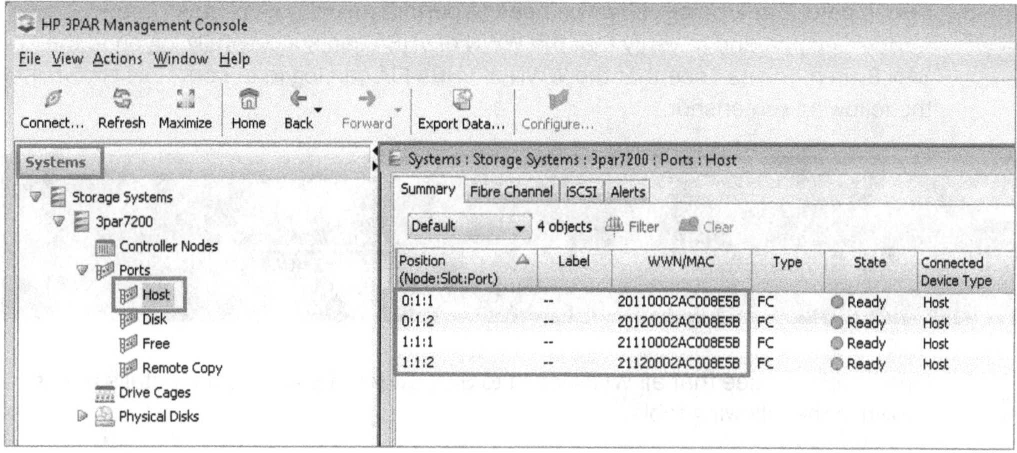

3PAR Management Console is a management tool that is used to manage HP 3PAR Storage.

3. Associate this service profile into UCS and then power on the UCS.
4. You must power on the UCS, otherwise the WWPN of each vHBA cannot log in to each SAN Switches. Then log in to SAN Switch-A by SSH and verify that the WWPN of each 3PAR Controller's FC port and WWN of each vHBA can successfully log on to the SAN switch. According to the following screenshot, you can see that port 1 and 5 are the WWPN of Controller1-P1 and Controller2-P1 by executing the `switchshow` command. Ports 6 and 7 are FI's FC uplinks:

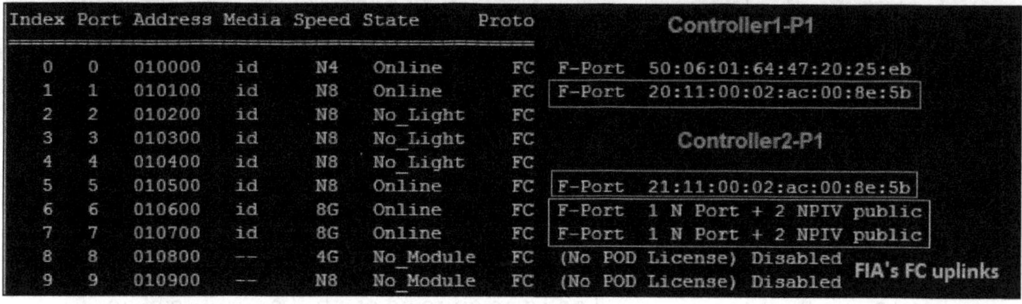

Index	Port	Address	Media	Speed	State	Proto	
0	0	010000	id	N4	Online	FC	F-Port 50:06:01:64:47:20:25:eb
1	1	010100	id	N8	Online	FC	F-Port 20:11:00:02:ac:00:8e:5b
2	2	010200	id	N8	No_Light	FC	
3	3	010300	id	N8	No_Light	FC	
4	4	010400	id	N8	No_Light	FC	
5	5	010500	id	N8	Online	FC	F-Port 21:11:00:02:ac:00:8e:5b
6	6	010600	id	8G	Online	FC	F-Port 1 N Port + 2 NPIV public
7	7	010700	id	8G	Online	FC	F-Port 1 N Port + 2 NPIV public
8	8	010800	--	4G	No_Module	FC	(No POD License) Disabled
9	9	010900	--	N8	No_Module	FC	(No POD License) Disabled

5. Due to ports 6 & 7 being NPIV. You need to perform `portloginshow <port number>` command to verify that the WWN of vHBA can successfully log on to the SAN Switch, you can see that the WWN of vHBA-FIA can log in to port 7, as shown in the following screenshot:

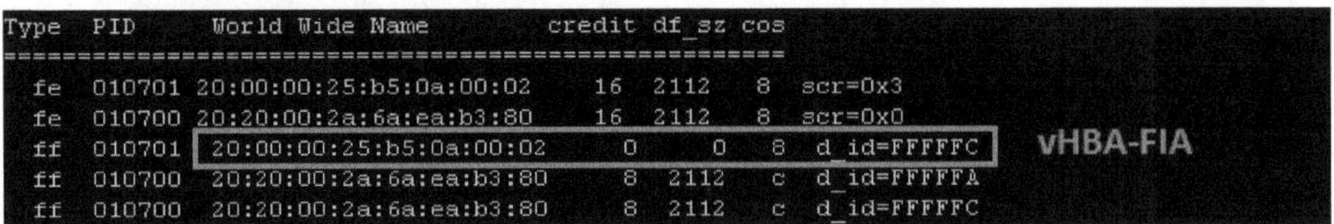

Finally, you can see that all WWN log in to SAN Switch-A successfully, details are as shown in the following table:

SAN Switch	Port Number	WWPN/WWN	Devices
SAN Switch-A	1	20:11:00:02:AC:00:8E:5B	Controller1 Port1
	5	21:11:00:02:AC:00:8E:5B	Controller2 Port1
	7	20:00:00:25:B5:0A:00:02	vHBA-FIA

6. Repeat the procedure in Step 3 to verify all WWPN/WWN on SAN Switch-B, you can see all WWN can log in to SAN Switch-B successfully; refer to the following screenshot for reference:

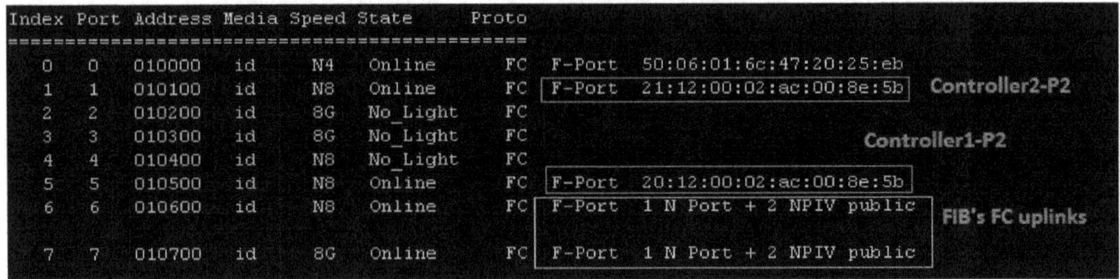

The following table lists a summary of all WWPN/WWN on SAN Switch-B:

SAN Switch	Port Number	WWPN/WWN	Devices
SAN Switch-B	1	21:12:00:02:AC:00:8E:5B	Controller2 Port2
	5	20:12:00:02:AC:00:8E:5B	Controller1 Port2
	7	20:00:00:25:B5:0B:00:02	vHBA-FIB

Finally, create two zones on each SAN Switch and enable all zones, the following table lists the summary of each FC zone:

SAN Switch	Zone Name	Zone Member1	Zone Member2
SAN Switch-A	vHBA-FIA_Controll1-P1	vHBA-FIA	Controller1 Port1
	vHBA-FIA_Controll1-P2	vHBA-FIA	Controller2 Port1
SAN Switch-B	vHBA-FIB_Controll1-P2	vHBA-FIB	Controller1 Port2
	vHBA-FIB_Controll1-P2	vHBA-FIB	Controller2 Port2

According to the best practice of FC zoning, single initiator zoning is recommended (one initiator to one target).

7. When all the FC zoning is created on both the SAN Switches, log in to **HP 3PAR Management Console**, go to **Hosts**, and create a host group.
8. Input the **Name** for this host group and select **Host OS** as **ESX 4.x/5.x**, as shown in the following screenshot:

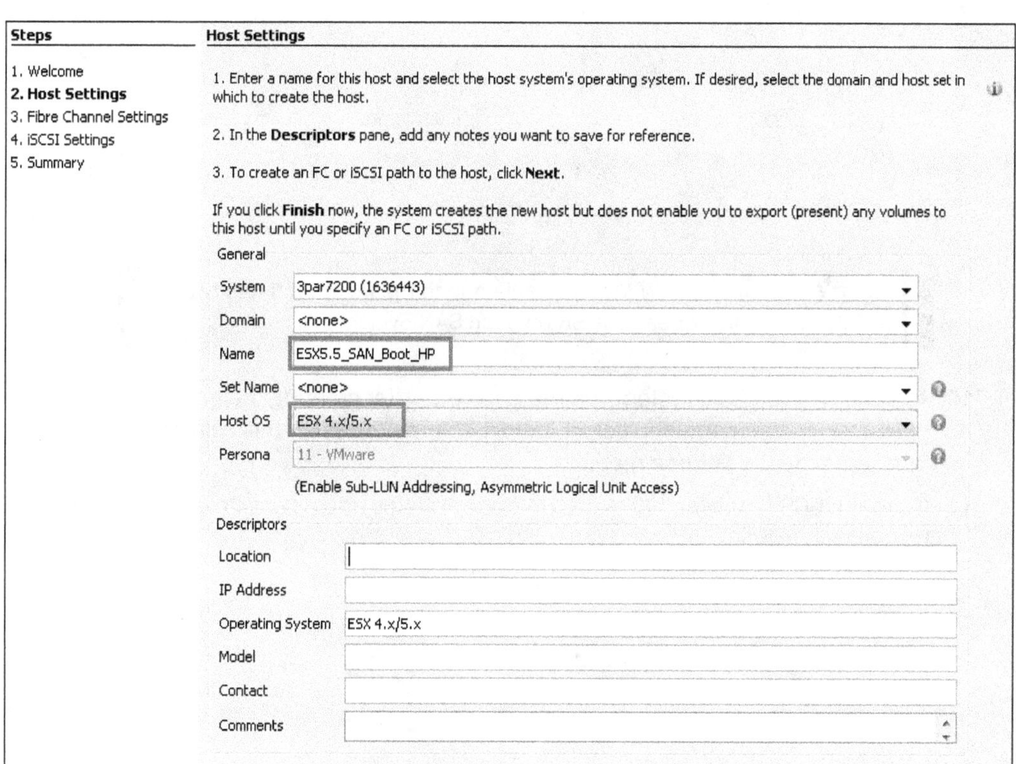

9. Move all the **Available WWNs** that are related to UCS's vHBA-FIA and vHBA-FIB, that is, **20:00:00:25:B5:0A:00:02** and **20:00:00:25:B5:0B:00:02**, to **Assigned WWNs**, as shown in the following screenshot:

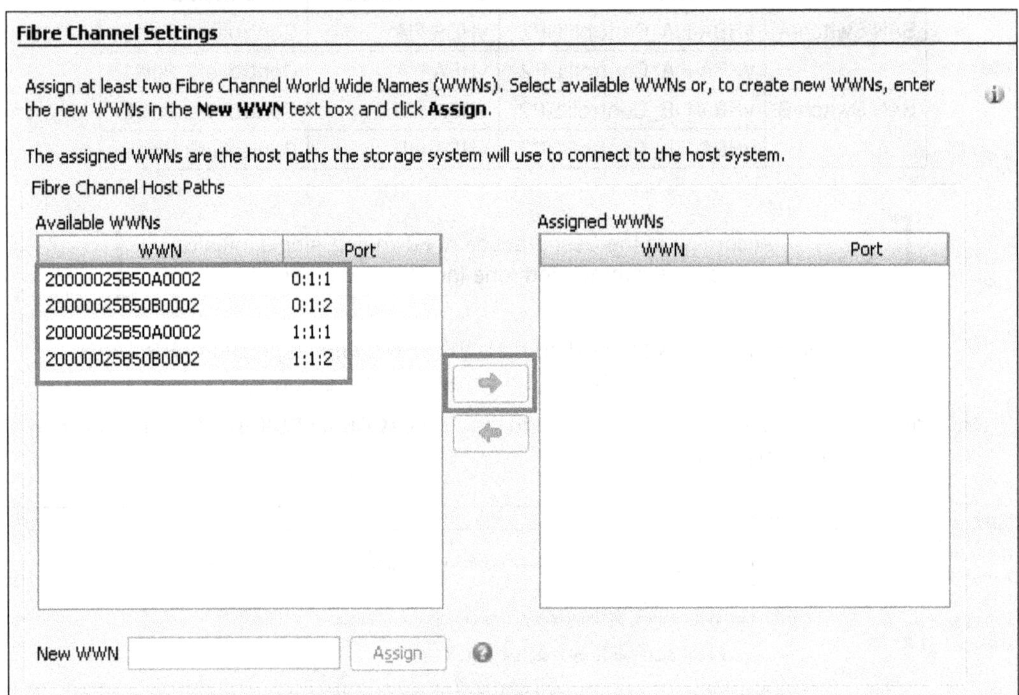

It has four WWNs available due to the fact that it has two zones for each vHBA on each SAN Switch.

10. Assume that the ESXi system volume is 10 GB. After creating the host group, right-click on the menu and select **Export Volume** to assign this volume to the host group on the **Volume** menu.
11. Go to the UCS Manager, right-click on **Boot Policies** and select **Create Boot Policy** on the **Servers** tab.

12. Input the **Name** of the boot policy and move the **Remote CD/DVD** in **Order 1** and **SAN Boot** in **Order 2**. Each SAN boot has two boot targets, you need to input the vHBA Name and WWN of the SAN target. The name of the vHBA must be same as the name of UCS's vHBA, otherwise, the boot target cannot work.

    The following table lists the summary of the SAN boot target:

SAN boot	vHBA	SAN target	Target WWN	Storage Port
SAN boot	vHBA-FIA	Primary	20:11:00:02:AC:00:8E:5B	Controller1 Port1
		Secondary	21:11:00:02:AC:00:8E:5B	Controller2 Port1
	vHBA-FIB	Primary	21:12:00:02:AC:00:8E:5B	Controller2 Port2
		Secondary	20:12:00:02:AC:00:8E:5B	Controller1 Port2

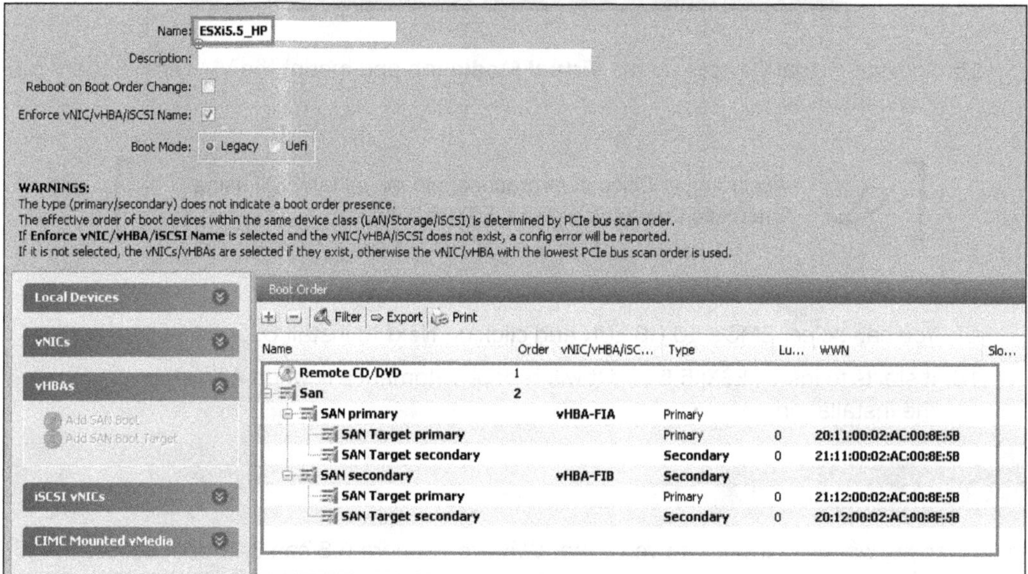

13. Go to the **Servers** tab and select the service profile **ESXi5.5_SAN_Boot_HP**, modify **Boot Policy** on the **Boot Order tab**. Select **ESXi5.5_HP** on the **Boot Policy** menu.

14. Power down UCS and re-associate this service profile into the UCS. Then power on the UCS and open the KVM Console; you can see the four paths appear during UCS boot up, these are the WWN of SAN boot target:

```
Cisco VIC FC, Boot Driver Version 4.0(1d)
(C) 2010 Cisco Systems, Inc.
 3PARdata 20110002ac008e5b:000
 3PARdata 21110002ac008e5b:000
Option ROM installed successfully

Cisco VIC FC, Boot Driver Version 4.0(1d)
(C) 2010 Cisco Systems, Inc.
 3PARdata 21120002ac008e5b:000
 3PARdata 20120002ac008e5b:000
Option ROM installed successfully
_
```

15. Activate Virtual Devices on the **Virtual Media** tab and mount the VMware vSphere 5.5 installation iso.

According to Cisco best practice, please install ESXi using the Cisco Custom Image for ESXi 5.5 iso.

16. The UCS can boot up this iso. Start to install ESXi 5.5.
17. You can select EMC's 10 GB LUN and click on **Next** to install OS.
18. It starts to install ESXi 5.5 and it will reboot automatically when it finishes the installation.

How it works...

In this recipe, we will learn how to verify that VMware vSphere 5.5 can SAN boot successfully.

Assume that vSphere 5.5 is already configured in the management IP:

1. After booting up vSphere 5.5 and logging in to it as a VMware vSphere Client. Go to the **Configuration** tab and choose **Storage Adapters**. You can see **vmhba1** and **vmhba2** on **Cisco VIC FCoE HBA Driver**:

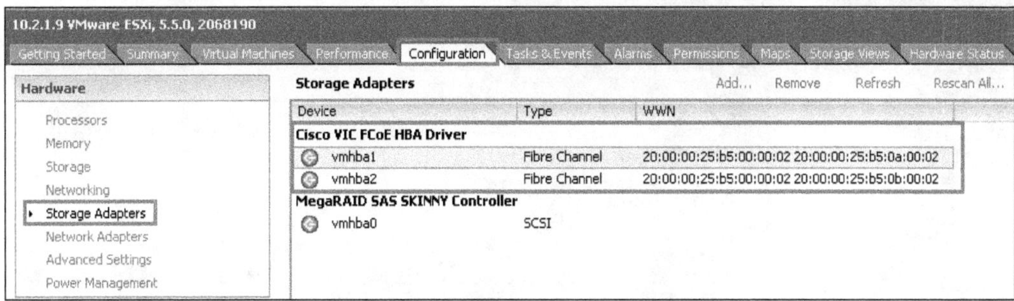

2. Go to the **Configuration** tab and choose **Network Adapters**. You can see **vmnic0** and **vmnic1** on **Network Adapters**:

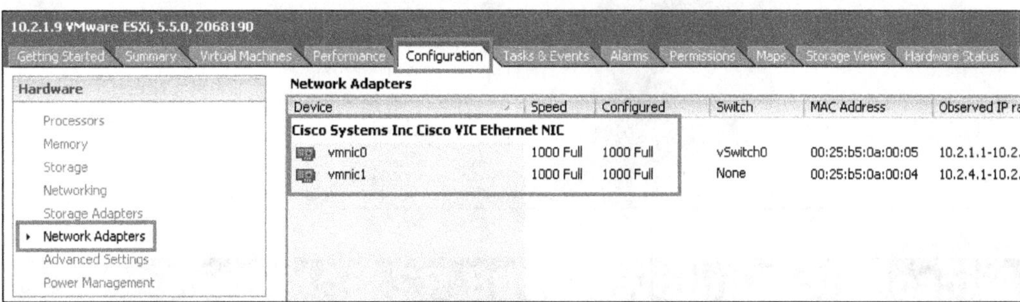

There's more...

Assume that **Server 4** is an ESXi host. Choose the UCS Server on the **Equipment** tab and go to the **General** tab; you can also see all the SAN boot targets on the **Actual Boot Order** tab:

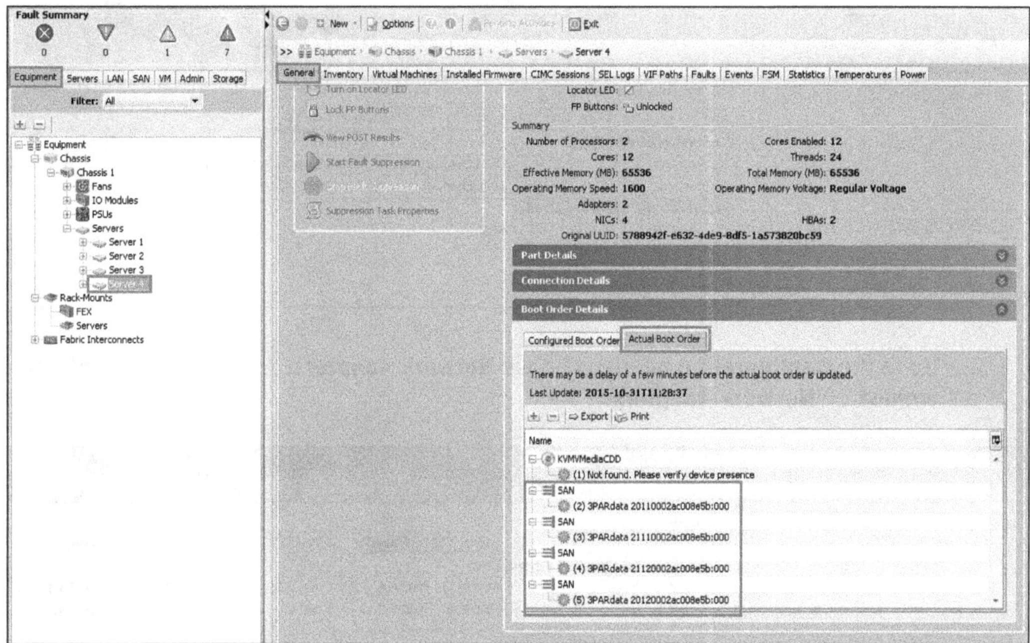

Microsoft Windows 2008 R2 SAN boot configuration in EMC Storage

In this recipe, we will learn how to install and configure Microsoft Windows 2008 R2 SAN boot in EMC Storage.

Getting ready

Prepare a Cisco UCS 5108 Chassis with two UCS IOM 2208XP installed, each UCS IOM is connected to a Cisco UCS 6428UP. There is a UCS B200 M3 with a VIC 1240 installed into this chassis. Configure four ports on each Cisco UCS 6428UP as an Ethernet uplink port (port 17/18) and an FC uplink port (port 6/7), which is connected to SAN Switches and LAN Switches by Fibre Channel cables. EMC SAN Storage has two controllers and each controller has two FC ports, which are connected to each SAN Switch. Prepare a UCS service profile, it includes two vNICs, two vHBAs. The details are listed in the following diagram:

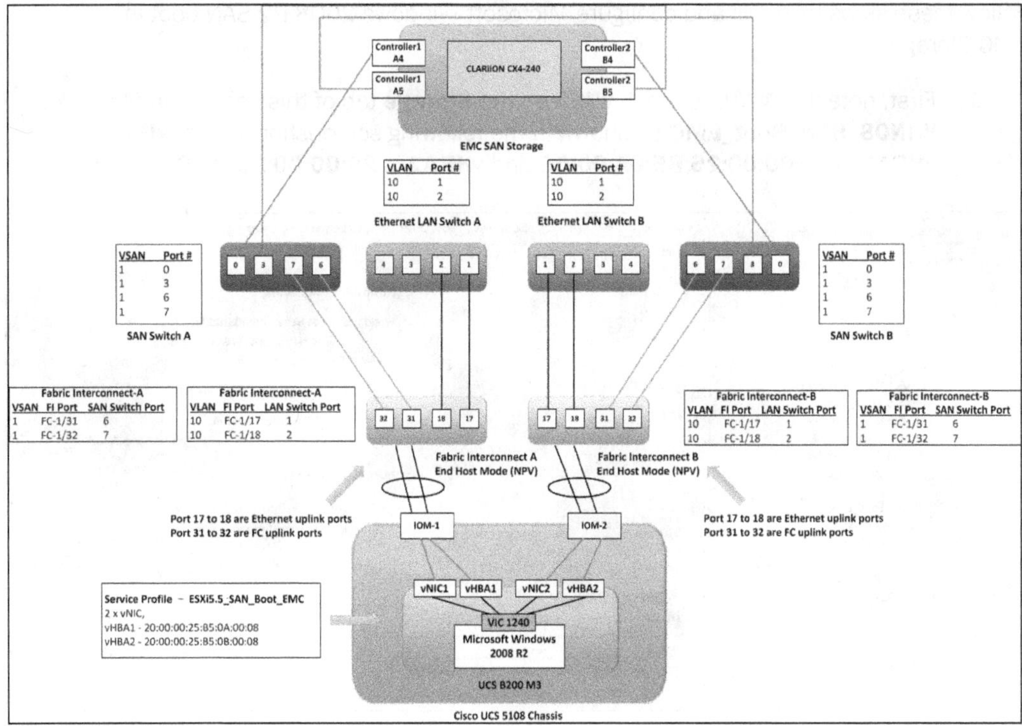

How to do it...

In this recipe, we will learn how to prepare a boot policy on UCS for Microsoft Windows 2008 R2 SAN boot installation. Assume that the name of the service profile is `WIN08_SAN_Boot_EMC` and the EMC SAN Storage is CLARiiON CX4-240.

Follow these steps to install and configure Microsoft Windows 2008 R2 SAN boot in EMC Storage:

1. First, note the WWPN of each vHBA on the **Storage** tab of this service profile **WIN08_SAN_Boot_EMC** as shown in the following screenshot. The **WWPN** of **vHBA1** is **20:00:00:25:B5:0A:00:08** and **vHBA2** is **20:00:00:25:B5:0B:00:08**:

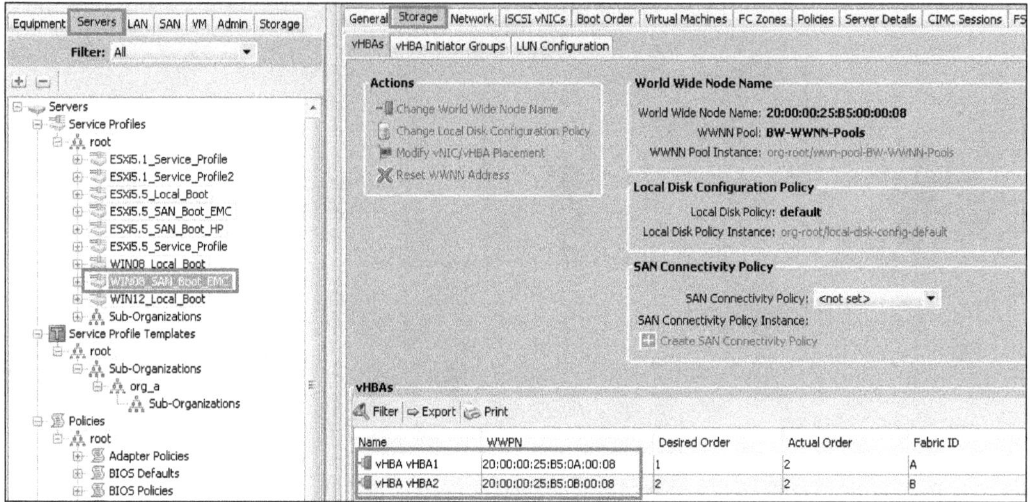

2. Log in to EMC Unisphere Manager and go to **Port Management**, you can note the WWN of each port on each Controller. A4 & A5 are on Controller1, with B4 and B5 on Controller2. The **WWN** of Controller1-A4 is **50:06:01:64:47:20:25:EB**, and Controller1-A5 is **50:06:01:65:47:20:25:EB**. The **WWN** of Controller2-B4 is **50:06:01:6C:47:20:25:EB**, and Controller2-B5 **is 50:06:01:6D:47:20:25:EB**:

Physical Location	SP-Port	Type	Speed	IP Addresses	IQN/WWN
Slot A0, Port 2	A-0	Fibre	N/A	N/A	50:06:01:60:C7:20:25:EB:50:06:01:60:47:20:25:EB
Slot A0, Port 3	A-1	Fibre	N/A	N/A	50:06:01:60:C7:20:25:EB:50:06:01:61:47:20:25:EB
Slot A1, Port 0	A-2	iSCSI	N/A	N/A	iqn.1992-04.com.emc:cx.apm00120503654.a2
Slot A1, Port 1	A-3 (MirrorView)	iSCSI	N/A	N/A	iqn.1992-04.com.emc:cx.apm00120503654.a3
Slot A2, Port 0	A-4	Fibre	4Gbps	N/A	50:06:01:60:C7:20:25:EB:50:06:01:64:47:20:25:EB
Slot A2, Port 1	A-5	Fibre	4Gbps	N/A	50:06:01:60:C7:20:25:EB:50:06:01:65:47:20:25:EB
Slot A2, Port 2	A-6	Fibre	N/A	N/A	50:06:01:60:C7:20:25:EB:50:06:01:66:47:20:25:EB
Slot A2, Port 3	A-7 (MirrorView)	Fibre	N/A	N/A	50:06:01:60:C7:20:25:EB:50:06:01:67:47:20:25:EB
Slot A0, Port 0	A-Bus 0	Fibre	4Gbps	N/A	N/A
Slot A0, Port 1	A-Bus 1	Fibre	N/A	N/A	N/A
Slot B0, Port 2	B-0	Fibre	N/A	N/A	50:06:01:60:C7:20:25:EB:50:06:01:68:47:20:25:EB
Slot B0, Port 3	B-1	Fibre	N/A	N/A	50:06:01:60:C7:20:25:EB:50:06:01:69:47:20:25:EB
Slot B2, Port 0	B-4	Fibre	4Gbps	N/A	50:06:01:60:C7:20:25:EB:50:06:01:6C:47:20:25:EB
Slot B2, Port 1	B-5	Fibre	4Gbps	N/A	50:06:01:60:C7:20:25:EB:50:06:01:6D:47:20:25:EB
Slot B2, Port 2	B-6	Fibre	N/A	N/A	50:06:01:60:C7:20:25:EB:50:06:01:6E:47:20:25:EB
Slot B2, Port 3	B-7 (MirrorView)	Fibre	N/A	N/A	50:06:01:60:C7:20:25:EB:50:06:01:6F:47:20:25:EB
Slot B0, Port 0	B-Bus 0	Fibre	4Gbps	N/A	N/A
Slot B0, Port 1	B-Bus 1	Fibre	N/A	N/A	N/A

EMC Unisphere Manager is a Web-based tool to manage and monitor EMC CLARiiON/VNX SAN Storage.

3. Associate this service profile into UCS and then power on the UCS.
4. You must power on the UCS, otherwise the WWPN of each vHBA cannot log in to each SAN Switch; then, log in to SAN Switch-A by SSH and verify that the WWPN of each Controller's FC port and WWN of each vHBA can successfully log in to the SAN switch. According to the following screenshot, you can see that ports 0 and 3 are the WWPN of Controller1-SPA4 and Controller2-SPB5, by executing the `switchshow` command. Ports 6 and 7 are the FI's FC uplink:

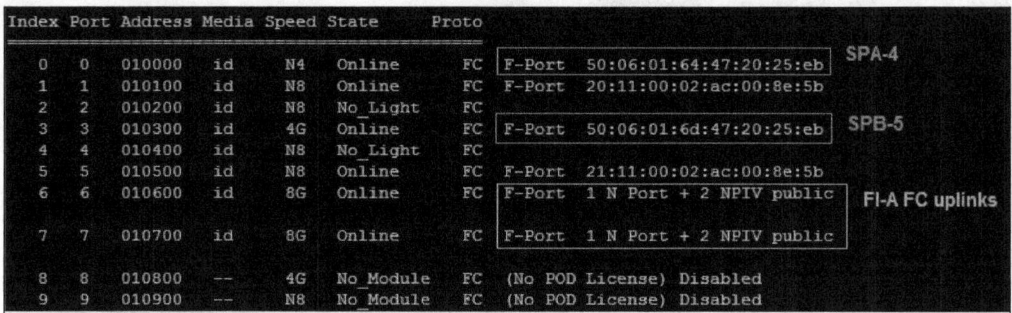

```
Index Port Address Media Speed State      Proto
===============================================
  0    0   010000   id    N4   Online       FC  F-Port  50:06:01:64:47:20:25:eb
  1    1   010100   id    N8   Online       FC  F-Port  20:11:00:02:ac:00:8e:5b
  2    2   010200   id    N8   No_Light     FC
  3    3   010300   id    4G   Online       FC  F-Port  50:06:01:6d:47:20:25:eb
  4    4   010400   id    N8   No_Light     FC
  5    5   010500   id    N8   Online       FC  F-Port  21:11:00:02:ac:00:8e:5b
  6    6   010600   id    8G   Online       FC  F-Port  1 N Port + 2 NPIV public

  7    7   010700   id    8G   Online       FC  F-Port  1 N Port + 2 NPIV public

  8    8   010800   --    4G   No_Module    FC  (No POD License) Disabled
  9    9   010900   --    N8   No_Module    FC  (No POD License) Disabled
```


Due to ports 6 and 7 being NPIV, you need to perform `portloginshow <port number>` command to verify that the WWN of vHBA can successfully log on to the SAN switch; you can see that the WWN of vHBA-FIA can log in to port 6, as shown in the following screenshot:

```
Type  PID     World Wide Name          credit df_sz cos
=======================================================
 fe  010701 20:00:00:25:b5:0a:00:08     16   2112   8   scr=0x3
 fe  010700 20:20:00:2a:6a:ea:b3:80     16   2112   8   scr=0x0
 ff  010701  20:00:00:25:b5:0a:00:08     0      0   8   d_id=FFFFFA
 ff  010701  20:00:00:25:b5:0a:00:08     0      0   8   d_id=FFFFFC
 ff  010700  20:20:00:2a:6a:ea:b3:80     8   2112   c   d_id=FFFFFA
 ff  010700  20:20:00:2a:6a:ea:b3:80     8   2112   c   d_id=FFFFFC
```

vHBA1

Finally, you can see that the WWN can log in to SAN Switch-A successfully, the details are as shown in the following table:

SAN Switch	Port Number	WWPN/WWN	Devices
SAN Switch-A	0	50:06:01:64:47:20:25:EB	Controller1-A4
	3	50:06:01:6D:47:20:25:EB	Controller2-B5
	7	20:00:00:25:B5:0A:00:08	vHBA1

5. Repeat the procedure for Step 4 to verify all WWPN/WWN on SAN Switch-B, you can see that all WWN can log in to SAN Switch-B successfully, the following screenshot can be used for reference:

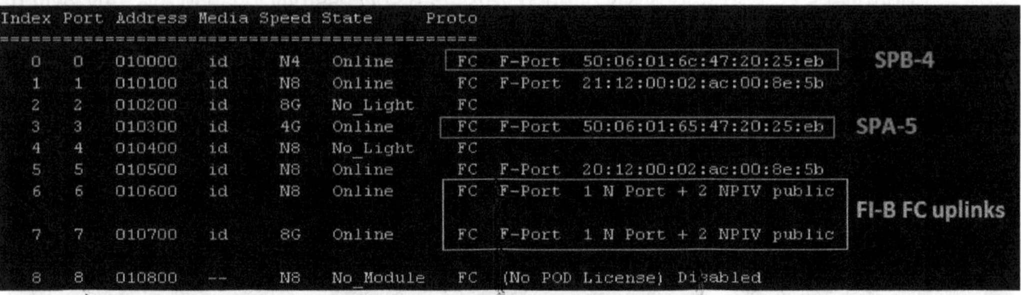

The following table lists the summary of all WWPN/WWN on SAN Switch-B:

SAN Switch	Port Number	WWPN/WWN	Devices
SAN Switch-B	0	50:06:01:6c:47:20:25:EB	Controller2-B4
	3	50:06:01:65:47:20:25:EB	Controller1-A5
	7	20:00:00:25:B5:0B:00:08	vHBA2

6. Finally, create two zones on each SAN Switch. In this moment, you only enable one zone to install Microsoft Windows on SAN LUN. The Windows will detect four same SAN disks, if you enable four zones during Windows installation. It is because the Microsoft default doesn't install any multipath software, so that Windows cannot combine the paths of four SAN disks into one logical drive. We suggest that you enable a zone, then it can detect one SAN disk during Windows installation, you can enable the other zones again after Windows installation.

   The following table lists the summary of each FC zone:

SAN Switch	Zone Name	Zone Member1	Zone Member2	Remark
SAN Switch-A	vHBA1_ Controll1-A4	vHBA1-	Controller1-A4	Enable this zone before installing Windows on SAN LUN
	vHBA1_ Controll2-B5	vHBA1	Controller2-B5	Enable this zone after installing Windows on SAN LUN

SAN Switch	Zone Name	Zone Member1	Zone Member2	Remark
SAN Switch-B	vHBA2_ Controll1-A5	vHBA2	Controller1-A5	Enable this zone after installing Windows on SAN LUN
	vHBA2_ Controll2-B4	vHBA2	Controller2-B4	Enable this zone after installing Windows on SAN LUN

According to the best practice of FC zoning, single initiator zoning is recommended (one initiator to one target).

7. After all FC zones are created on both SAN Switch and enabled one of four zones, then log in to EMC Unisphere Manager, right-click on the System, and choose a **Connectivity Status**. Since you only enable one zone on SAN Switch, you can see only one UCS's initiators (WWN of each vHBA) display on **Host Initiators**, you need to manually register one initiators, **20:00:00:25:B5:0A:00:08**, into one host, **win08.testlab.com**:

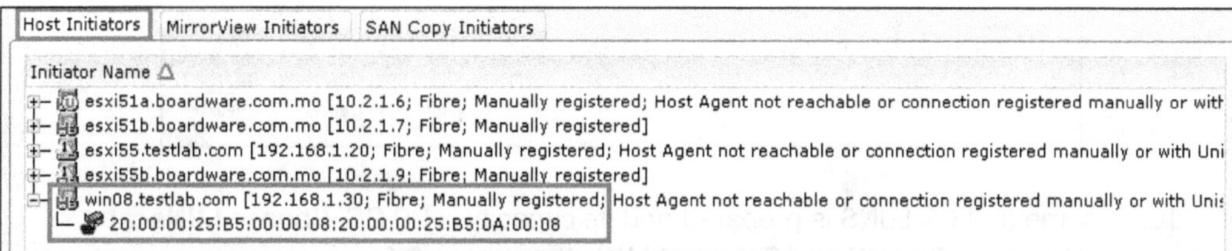

8. Go to **Storage** and create a new storage group on the **Storage** menu and enter the name of the storage group.

9. After creating the storage group, select the **Hosts** tab and move the host initiator group **win08.testlab.com** to the right-hand side, and click on **Apply**, as shown in the following screenshot.

   Finally, the EMC Storage connectivity of Cisco UCS is complete:

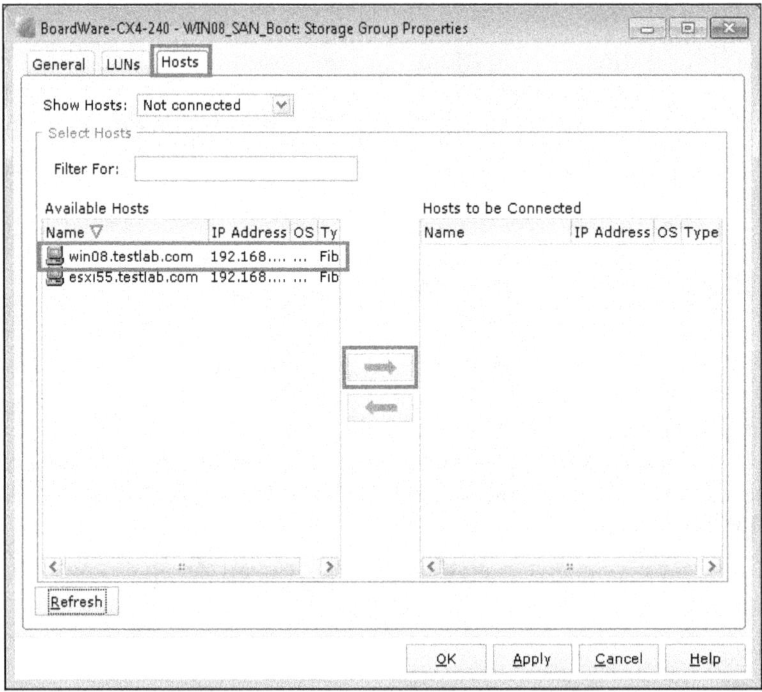

10. Assume that OS LUNS is prepared and its capacity is 90 GB. Choose **LUNs** tab, add Windows OS LUN into **Selected LUNs** then press **OK**:

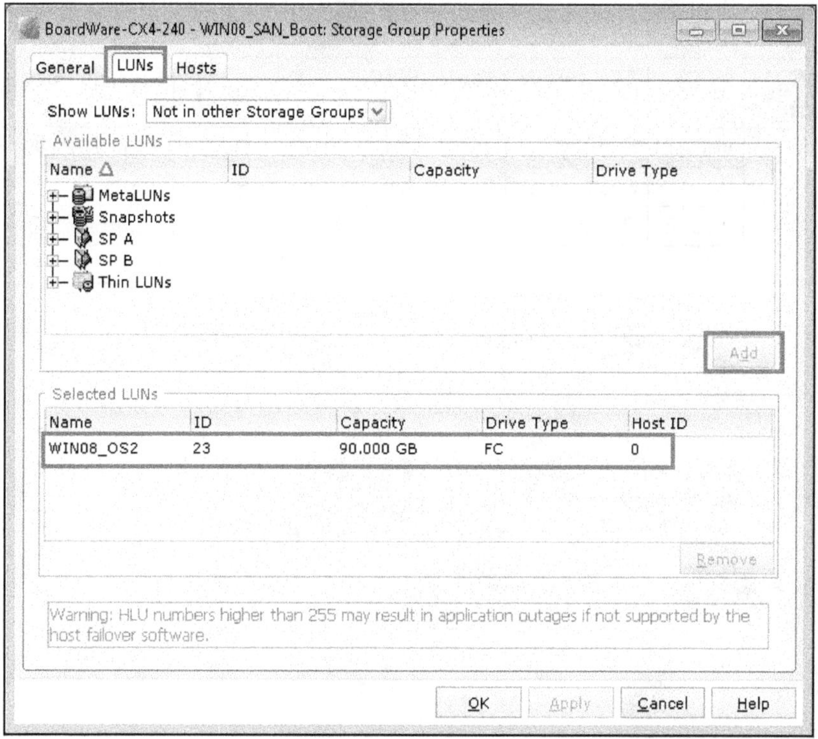

11. Go to UCS Manager, right-click on **Boot Policies**, and select **Create Boot Policy** on the **Servers** tab.
12. Input the **Name** of the boot policy and move **Remote CD/DVD** in **Order 1** and **SAN Boot** in **Order 2**. Each SAN boot has two boot targets, you need to input the vHBA name and WWN of the SAN target. The name of vHBA must be same as the name of UCS's vHBA, otherwise the boot target cannot work. Make sure that Windows can detect only one SAN disk with one logical path during Windows installation, now add only one SAN boot target into this boot policy. Then, add an other boot target into the policy after finishing the Windows installation.

The following table lists a summary of the SAN boot target:

SAN boot	vHBA	SAN target	Target WWN	Storage Port
SAN boot	vHBA1	Primary	50:06:01:64:47:20:25:EB	Controller1-A4
		Secondary	50:06:01:6D:47:20:25:EB	Controller2-B5
	vHBA2	Primary	50:06:01:6c:47:20:25:EB	Controller2-B4
		Secondary	50:06:01:65:47:20:25:EB	Controller1-A5

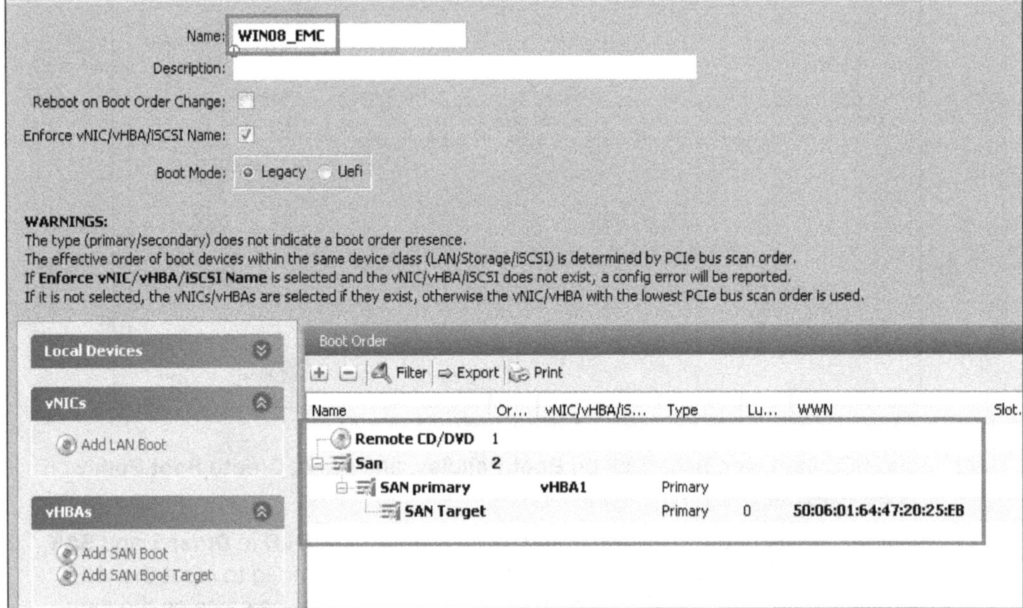

13. Go to the **Servers** tab and select service profile **WIN08_SAN_Boot_EMC** and select **Modify the Boot Policy** on the **Boot Order** tab. Select **WIN08_EMC** on the **Boot Policy** menu.
14. Power down UCS and re-associate this service profile into UCS again. Then power on UCS and open the KVM Console, you can see one path appearing during the UCS boot up; these are the WWN of SAN boot target:

```
Cisco VIC FC, Boot Driver Version 4.0(1d)
(C) 2010 Cisco Systems, Inc.
 DGC        50060164472025eb:000
Option ROM installed successfully
```

15. Open the KVM Console of UCS, activate the Virtual Devices on **Virtual Media** tab and mount the Microsoft Windows 2008 R2 installation iso image.
16. The UCS can boot up by this iso and select the operating system you want to install.
17. If you are installing Windows on SAN LUN, you must install Cisco VIC drivers for Windows during the OS installation. If you do not provide the drivers during the OS installation, the system will not be able to detect the SAN LUN.
18. Go to `https://software.cisco.com/download/navigator.html` and log in with a **My Cisco** account. Select **Products**, as shown:

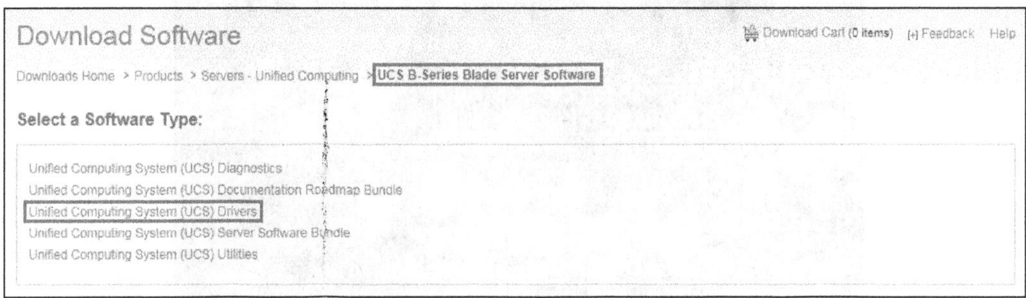

Note: Access to download UCS driver is limited to users with an active Technical Support contract with Cisco.

19. Select **2.2(5b)** and download **ucs-bxxx-drivers.2.2.5b.iso**:

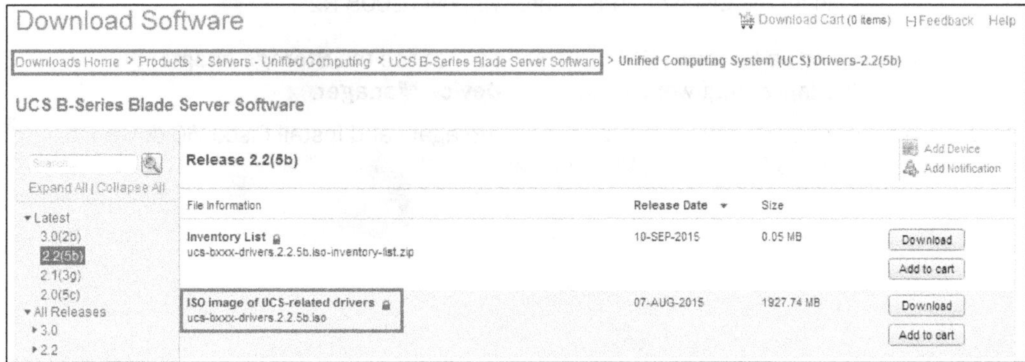

20. Load the VIC driver during OS installation.

You need to un-mount Microsoft Windows 2008 installation iso first, and mount UCS driver iso, to load the driver into UCS.

21. After loading the driver, you can see the local drive, click on **Next** to install OS.
22. It starts to install Microsoft Windows 2008 and it will reboot automatically when it finishes the installation.
23. After finishing the installation, you can boot up Microsoft Windows 2008 and shut down UCS. Enable the other zone from Step 6 and add the other SAN boot target into boot policy as in Step 12. After that, power on the UCS again, you can see four paths that appear during a UCS boot up. Now Windows 2008 can boot up successfully by four paths:

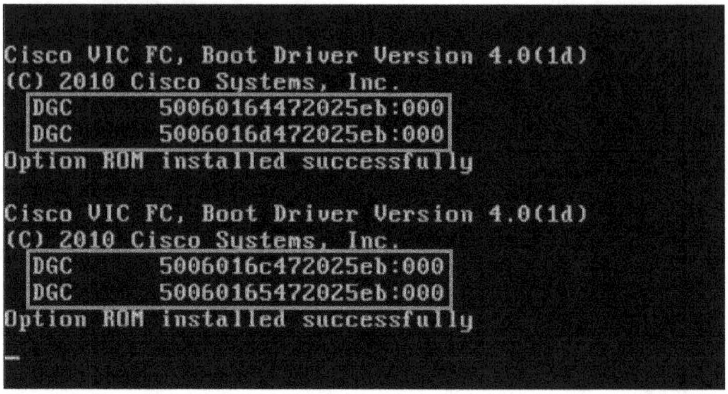

```
Cisco VIC FC, Boot Driver Version 4.0(1d)
(C) 2010 Cisco Systems, Inc.
 DGC        50060164472025eb:000
 DGC        5006016d472025eb:000
Option ROM installed successfully

Cisco VIC FC, Boot Driver Version 4.0(1d)
(C) 2010 Cisco Systems, Inc.
 DGC        5006016c472025eb:000
 DGC        50060165472025eb:000
Option ROM installed successfully
```

How it works...

In this recipe, we will learn how to verify that Microsoft Windows 2008 can SAN boot successfully and install the Cisco VIC driver into Windows 2008 R2:

1. After booting up Windows 2008 R2, you cannot see the **Storage adapter** and **Network adapter** that were listed in the **Device Manager**.
2. Mount `ucs-bxxx-drivers.2.2.5b.iso` again and install Cisco VIC driver into Windows 2008 R2 by Cisco VIO Installer.

3. After installing Cisco VIC driver, you can see that the **Cisco VIC Ethernet Interface** and **Cisco VIC FCoE Storport Miniport** is listed on the **Device Manager**:

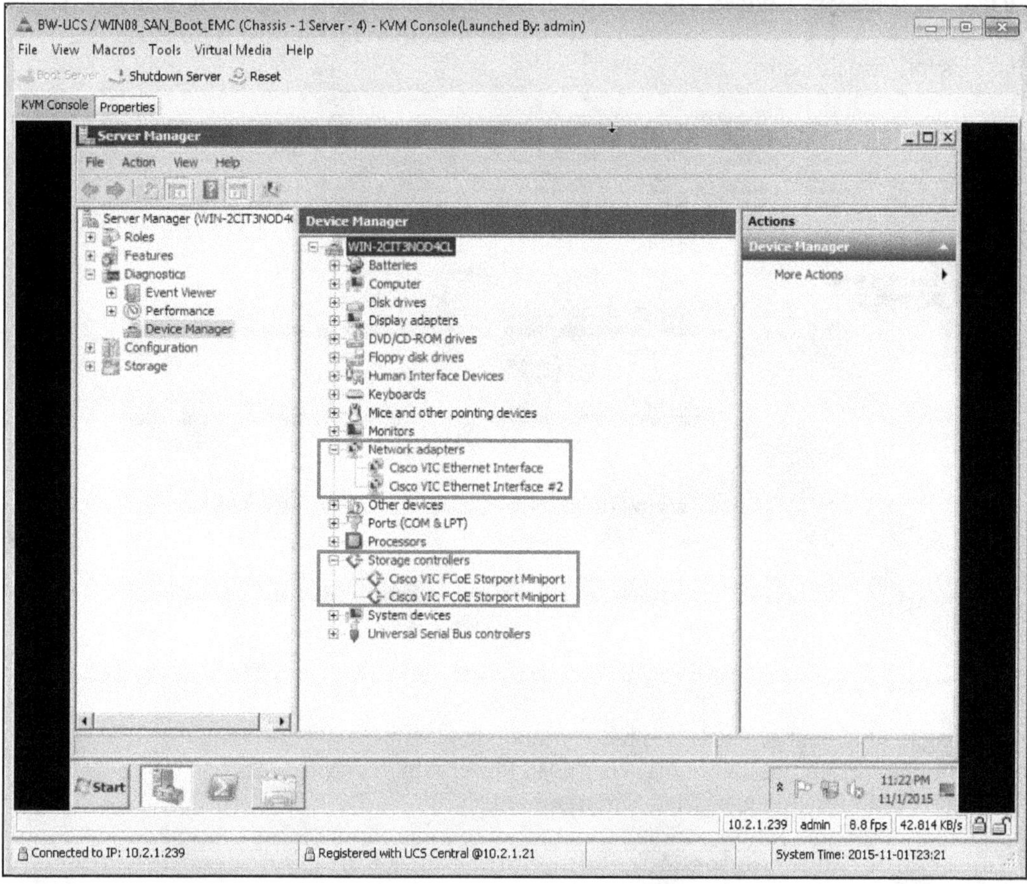

There's more...

By default, Microsoft Windows 2008 R2 does not install any multipath software, so it detects four SAN disks with the same capacity on Windows **Disk Management**. It is because this SAN disk has four logical paths:

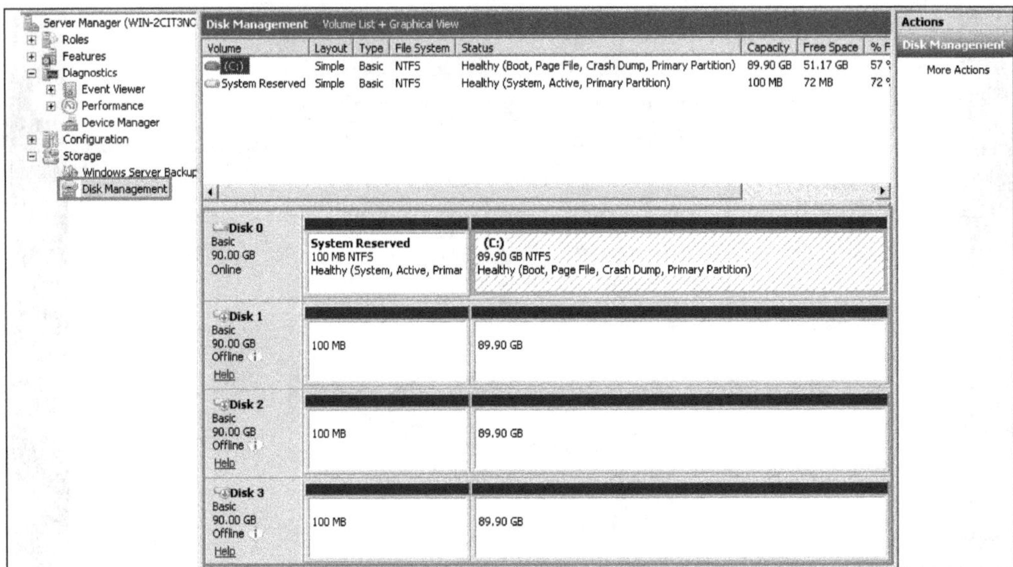

According to EMC best practice, it is recommended to install EMC Powerpath for Windows to enable multipath features. After installing EMC Powerpath, it only detects one SAN disk with four logical paths on Windows **Disk Management**:

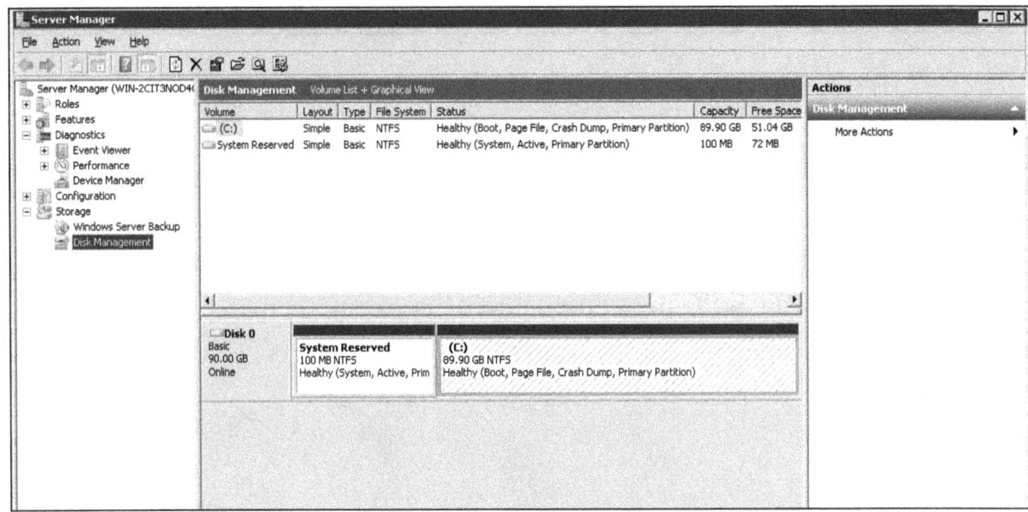

EMC Powerpath for Windows is a software that is used to enable multipath features with EMC Storage. This software requires the license to enable the multipath feature.

When you open an **EMC_Powerpath_Console**, you can see four logical paths for this disk:

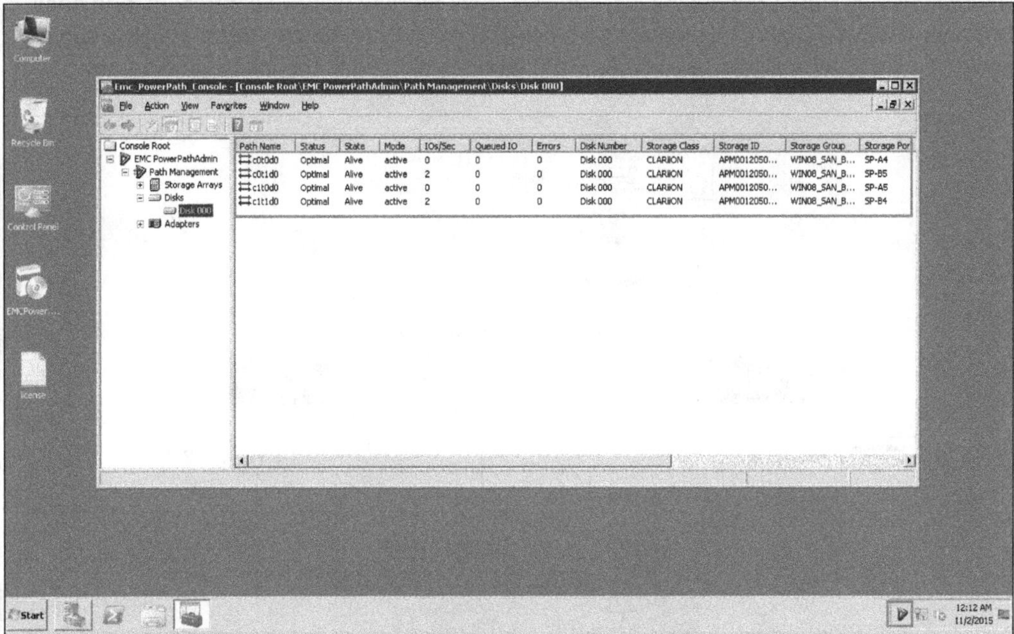

Microsoft Windows 2008 R2 SAN boot configuration in HP 3PAR Storage

In this recipe, we will learn how to install and configure Microsoft Windows 2008 R2 SAN boot in HP 3PAR Storage.

Getting ready

Prepare a Cisco UCS 5108 Chassis with two UCS IOM 2208XP installed, each UCS IOM is connected to one Cisco UCS 6428UP. There is one UCS B200 M3 with one VIC 1240 installed into this chassis; configure four ports on each Cisco UCS 6428UP as an Ethernet uplink port (port 17/18) and an FC uplink port (port 6/7), which is connected to SAN Switches and LAN Switches by Fibre Channel cables. The EMC SAN Storage has two controllers, and each controller has two FC ports, which are connected to each SAN Switch. Prepare a UCS service profile, it includes two vNICs, two vHBAs. The details are listed in the following diagram:

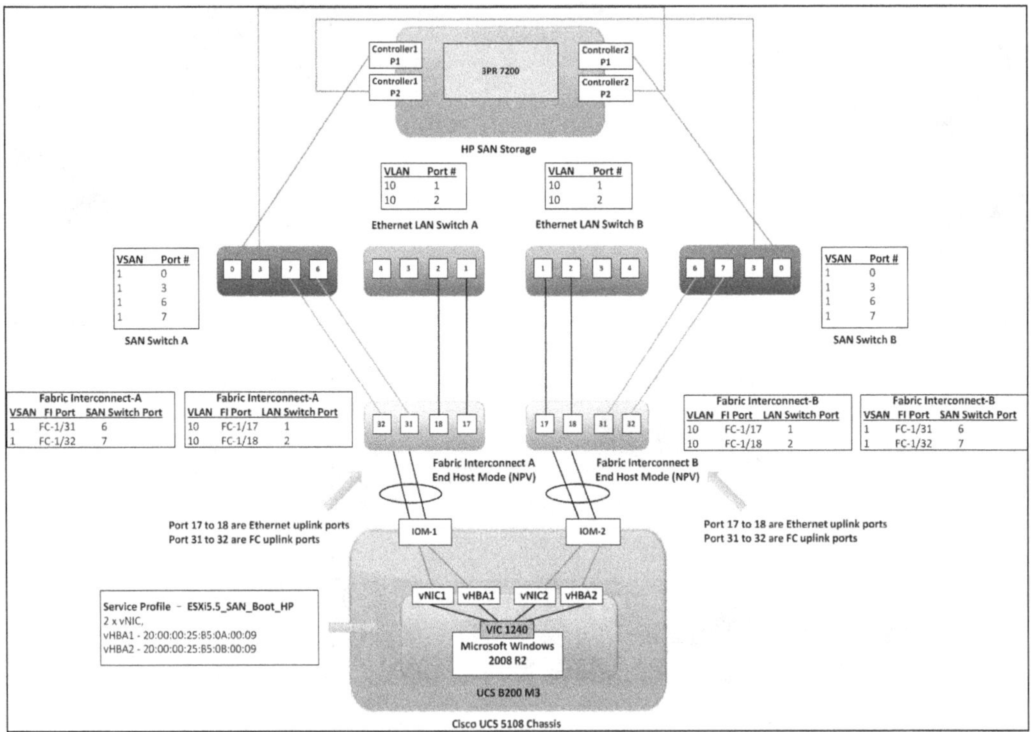

How to do it...

In this recipe, we will learn how to prepare a boot policy on UCS for Microsoft Windows 2008 R2 SAN boot installation. Assume that the name of the service profile is `WIN08_SAN_Boot_HP`, and the HP SAN Storage is 3PAR StoreServ 7200:

1. First, note the WWPN of each vHBA on **Storage** tab of this service profile **WIN08_SAN_Boot_HP** as shown in the following screenshot. The **WWPN** of **vHBA1** is **20:00:00:25:B5:0A:00:09**, and vHBA2 is **20:00:00:25:B5:0B:00:09**:

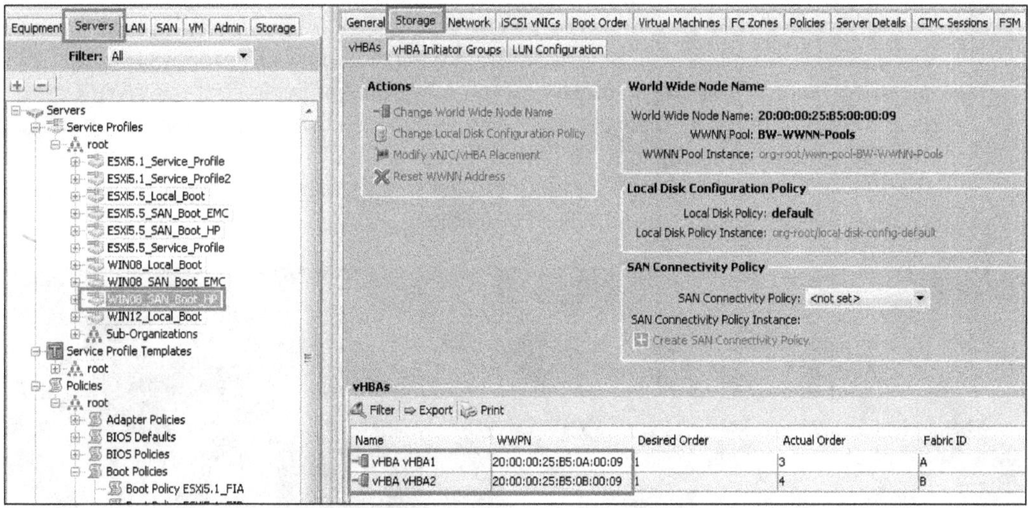

2. Log in to **HP 3PAR Management Console**, go to **Systems** and choose **Host** of **Ports**, you can see the WWN of each port on each Controller. On Controller1, **0:1:1** is port1 & **0:1:2** is port2; **1:1:1** is port1 & **1:1:2** is port2 on Controller2. The **WWN** of Controller1-P1 is **20:11:00:02:AC:00:8E:5B**, Controller1-P2 is **20:12:00:02:AC:00:8E:5B**. The **WWN** of Controller2-P1 is **21:11:00:02:AC:00:8E:5B**, and Controller2-P2 is **21:12:00:02:AC:00:8E:5B**:

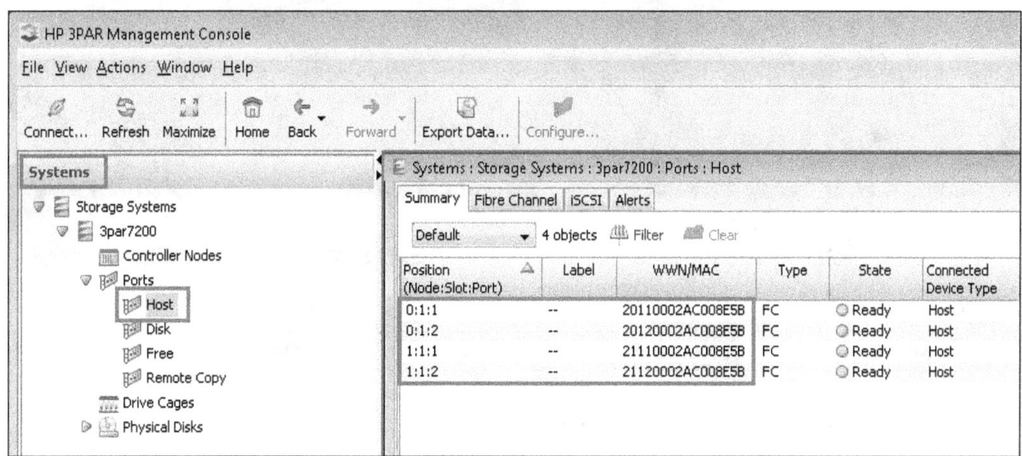

3PAR Management Console is a management tool which is used to manage HP 3PAR Storage.

3. Associate this service profile into UCS and then power on the UCS.
4. You must power on the UCS, otherwise the WWPN of each vHBA cannot log in to each SAN Switch; then, log in to SAN Switch-A by SSH and verify that the WWPN of each 3PAR Controller's FC port and WWN of each vHBA can successfully log on to the SAN switch. According to the following screenshot, you can see ports 1 and 5 are the WWPN of Controller1-P1 and Controller2-P1 by executing the `switchshow` command. Ports 6 and 7 are the FI's FC uplinks:

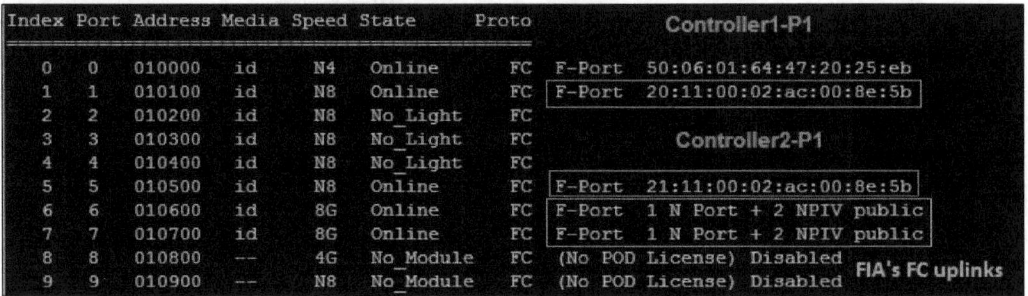


```
Index Port Address Media Speed State      Proto
==================================================
  0    0   010000   id    N4   Online      FC  F-Port  50:06:01:64:47:20:25:eb
  1    1   010100   id    N8   Online      FC  F-Port  20:11:00:02:ac:00:8e:5b
  2    2   010200   id    N8   No_Light    FC
  3    3   010300   id    N8   No_Light    FC
  4    4   010400   id    N8   No_Light    FC
  5    5   010500   id    N8   Online      FC  F-Port  21:11:00:02:ac:00:8e:5b
  6    6   010600   id    8G   Online      FC  F-Port  1 N Port + 2 NPIV public
  7    7   010700   id    8G   Online      FC  F-Port  1 N Port + 2 NPIV public
  8    8   010800   --    4G   No_Module   FC  (No POD License) Disabled
  9    9   010900   --    N8   No_Module   FC  (No POD License) Disabled
```

Due to ports 6 and 7 being NPIV, You need to perform `portloginshow <port number>` command to verify that the WWN of vHBA can successfully log on to the SAN switch; you can see that the WWN of vHBA1 can log in to port 7 as shown:

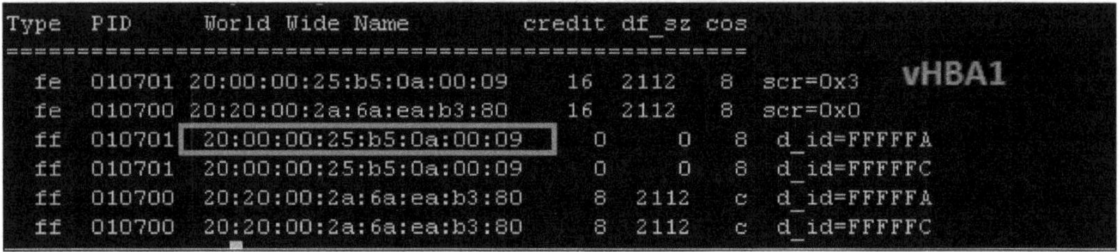


```
Type  PID     World Wide Name          credit df_sz cos
=======================================================
 fe   010701 20:00:00:25:b5:0a:00:09    16   2112   8  scr=0x3
 fe   010700 20:20:00:2a:6a:ea:b3:80    16   2112   8  scr=0x0
 ff   010701  20:00:00:25:b5:0a:00:09    0      0   8  d_id=FFFFFA
 ff   010701  20:00:00:25:b5:0a:00:09    0      0   8  d_id=FFFFFC
 ff   010700  20:20:00:2a:6a:ea:b3:80    8   2112   c  d_id=FFFFFA
 ff   010700  20:20:00:2a:6a:ea:b3:80    8   2112   c  d_id=FFFFFC
```

Finally, you can see that the WWN can log in to SAN Switch-A successfully; the details are as shown in the following table:

SAN Switch	Port Number	WWPN/WWN	Devices
SAN Switch-A	1	20:11:00:02:AC:00:8E:5B	Controller1 Port1
	5	21:11:00:02:AC:00:8E:5B	Controller2 Port1
	7	20:00:00:25:B5:0A:00:02	vHBA1

5. Repeat the procedure from Step 3 to verify all WWPN/WWN on SAN Switch-B; you can see that WWN can log in to SAN Switch-B successfully. Take a look at the following screenshot for reference:

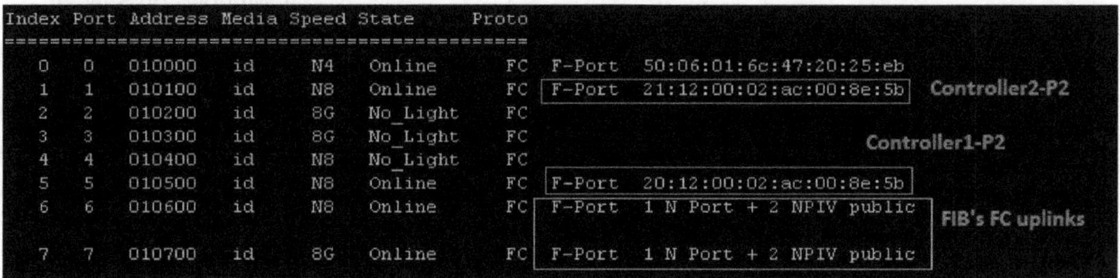

The following is the listed summary of all WWPN/WWN on SAN Switch-B:

SAN Switch	Port Number	WWPN/WWN	Devices
SAN Switch-B	1	21:12:00:02:AC:00:8E:5B	Controller2 Port2
	5	20:12:00:02:AC:00:8E:5B	Controller1 Port2
	7	20:00:00:25:B5:0B:00:02	vHBA2

6. Finally, create two zones on each SAN Switch. In this moment, you only enable one zone for the installation of Microsoft Windows on SAN LUN, Windows will detect four same SAN disks if you enable four zones during the Windows installation. This is because Microsoft Windows' default doesn't install any multipath software, so that Windows cannot combine the paths of four SAN disks into one logical drive. We suggest that you enable one zone, then it can detect one SAN disk during the Windows installation, you can enable the other zones again after Windows installation.

   The following table lists the summary of each FC zone:

SAN Switch	Zone Name	Zone Member1	Zone Member2	Remark
SAN Switch-A	vHBA1_ Controll1-P1	vHBA1	Controller1 Port1	Enable this zone before installing Windows on SAN LUN
	vHBA1_ Controll1-P2	vHBA1	Controller2 Port1	Enable this zone after installing Windows on SAN LUN

SAN Switch	Zone Name	Zone Member1	Zone Member2	Remark
SAN Switch-B	vHBA2_ Controll1-P2	vHBA2	Controller1 Port2	Enable this zone after installing Windows on SAN LUN
	vHBA2_ Controll1-P2	vHBA2	Controller2 Port2	Enable this zone after installing Windows on SAN LUN

According to the best practice of FC zoning, single initiator zoning is recommended (one initiator to one target).

7. After all the FC zones are created on both the SAN Switch and enabled on one of the four zones, log in to 3PAR Management and create a new host group. Due to the fact that you only enable one zone, you can see one UCS's initiator (WWN of each vHBA) on a **Host Initiators**, manually register one initiators **20000025B50A0009** into this host group:

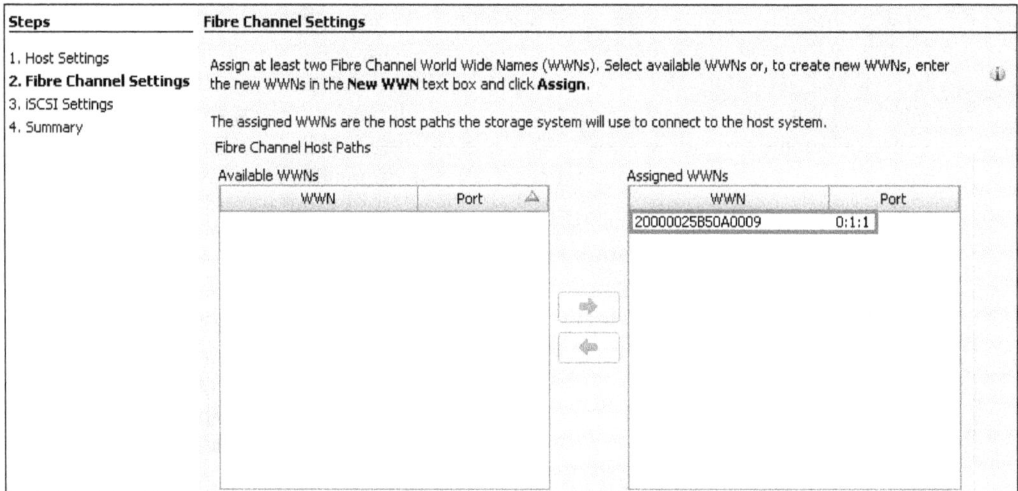

8. Assume that the Windows system volume is 100 GB. After creating the host group, right-click on the menu and select **Export Volume** to assign this volume to this host group on the **Volume** menu.
9. Go to UCS Manager, right-click on **Boot Policies** and select **Create Boot Policy** on the **Servers** tab.

10. Input the **Name** of boot policy and move the **Remote CD/DVD** in **Order 1**, and **SAN Boot** in **Order 2**. Each SAN boot has two boot targets; you need to input the name of the vHBA, and WWN of the SAN target. The name of the vHBA must be the same as the name of UCS's vHBA otherwise the boot target cannot work. Make sure that Windows can detect only one SAN disk with one logical path during Windows installation; now only add one SAN boot target into this boot policy. Then add the other boot target into the policy after finishing the Windows installation.

    This table lists the summary of the SAN boot target:

SAN boot	vHBA	SAN target	Target WWN	Storage Port
SAN boot	vHBA1	Primary	20:11:00:02:AC:00:8E:5B	Controller1 Port1
		Secondary	21:11:00:02:AC:00:8E:5B	Controller2 Port1
	vHBA2	Primary	21:12:00:02:AC:00:8E:5B	Controller2 Port2
		Secondary	20:12:00:02:AC:00:8E:5B	Controller1 Port2

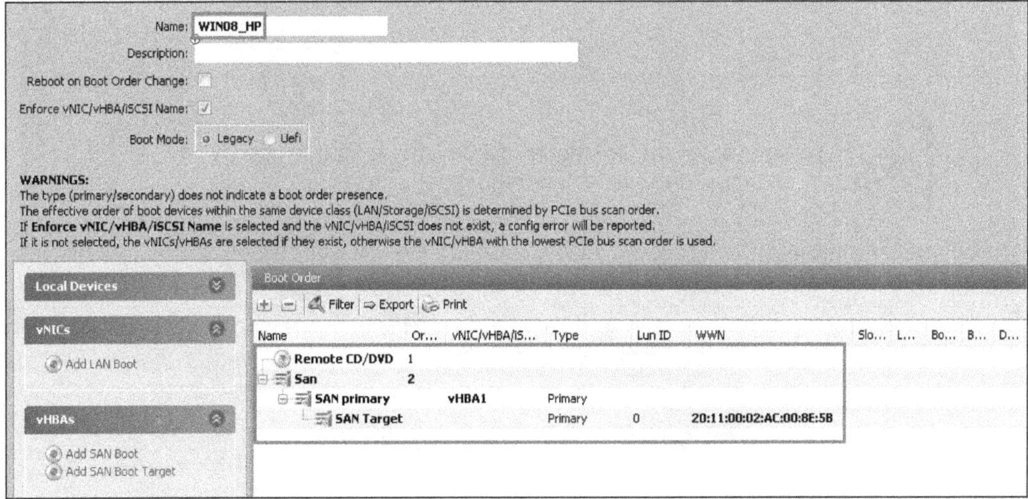

11. Go to the **Servers** tab and select service profile **WIN08_SAN_Boot_HP**, **Modify Boot Policy** on the **Boot Order** tab. Select **WIN08_EMC** on the **Boot Policy** menu.
12. Power down the UCS and re-associate this service profile into the UCS again. Then power on the UCS and open a KVM Console, you can see a path appear during UCS boot up, these are the WWN of the SAN boot target:

```
Cisco VIC FC, Boot Driver Version 4.0(1d)
(C) 2010 Cisco Systems, Inc.
 3PARdata 20110002ac008e5b:000
Option ROM installed successfully
```

13. Open the KVM Console of UCS, activate the Virtual Devices on **Virtual Media** tab, and then mount the Microsoft Windows 2008 R2 installation iso image.
14. The UCS can boot up by this iso; select the operating system you want to install. If you are installing Windows on SAN LUN, you must install Cisco VIC drivers for Windows during the OS installation. If you do not provide the drivers during the OS installation, the system is not able to detect the SAN LUN.
15. Navigate to `https://software.cisco.com/download/navigator.html` and log in with a **My Cisco** account. Select **Products**, the details are as shown in the following screenshot:

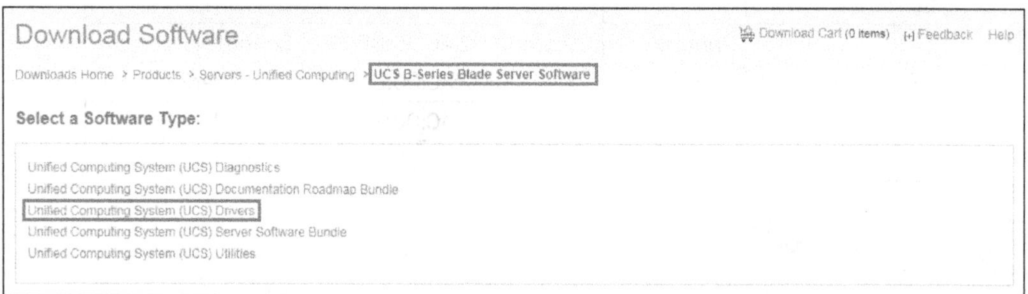

Note: Access to download UCS driver is limited to users with an active Technical Support contract with Cisco.

16. Select **2.2(5b)** and download **ucs-bxxx-drivers.2.2.5b.iso**:

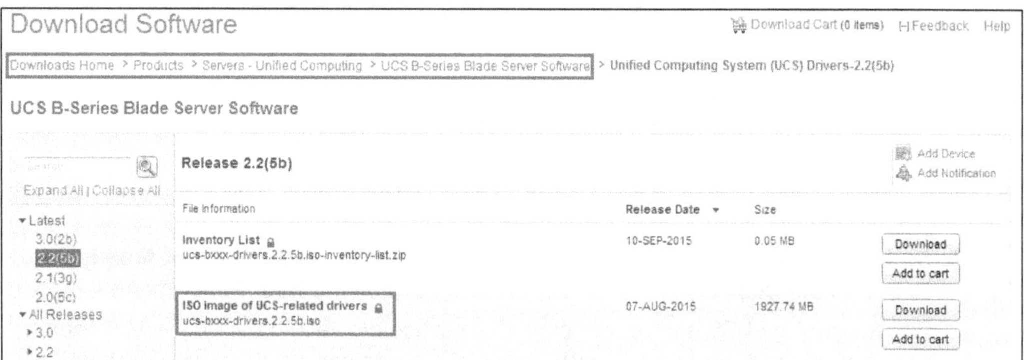

17. Load the VIC driver during OS installation.

You need to un-mount Microsoft Windows 2008 installation iso first and mount UCS driver iso to load the driver into UCS.

18. After loading the driver, you can see the local drive and press **Next** to install the OS.
19. It starts to install Microsoft Windows 2008 and it will reboot automatically when it finishes the installation.
20. After finishing the installation, we can boot up Microsoft Windows 2008. Shut down UCS. Enable the other zone in Step 6 and add the other SAN boot target into boot policy in Step 12. After that, power on UCS again; you can see four paths appear during UCS boot up. Now, Windows 2008 can boot up successfully by four paths:

```
Cisco VIC FC, Boot Driver Version 4.0(1d)
(C) 2010 Cisco Systems, Inc.
  3PARdata 20110002ac008e5b:000
  3PARdata 21110002ac008e5b:000
Option ROM installed successfully

Cisco VIC FC, Boot Driver Version 4.0(1d)
(C) 2010 Cisco Systems, Inc.
  3PARdata 21120002ac008e5b:000
  3PARdata 20120002ac008e5b:000
Option ROM installed successfully
_
```

How it works...

In this recipe, we will learn how to verify that Microsoft Windows 2008 can SAN boot successfully and install the Cisco VIC driver into Windows 2008 R2:

1. After booting up Windows 2008 R2, you cannot see the **Storage adapter** and **Network adapter** that were listed in the **Device Manager**.
2. Mount the `ucs-bxxx-drivers.2.2.5b.iso` again and install Cisco VIC driver into Windows 2008 R2 with the Cisco VIO Installer.

3. After installing the Cisco VIC driver, you can see that **Cisco VIC Ethernet Interface** and **Cisco VIC FCoE Storport Miniport** are listed in the **Device Manager**:

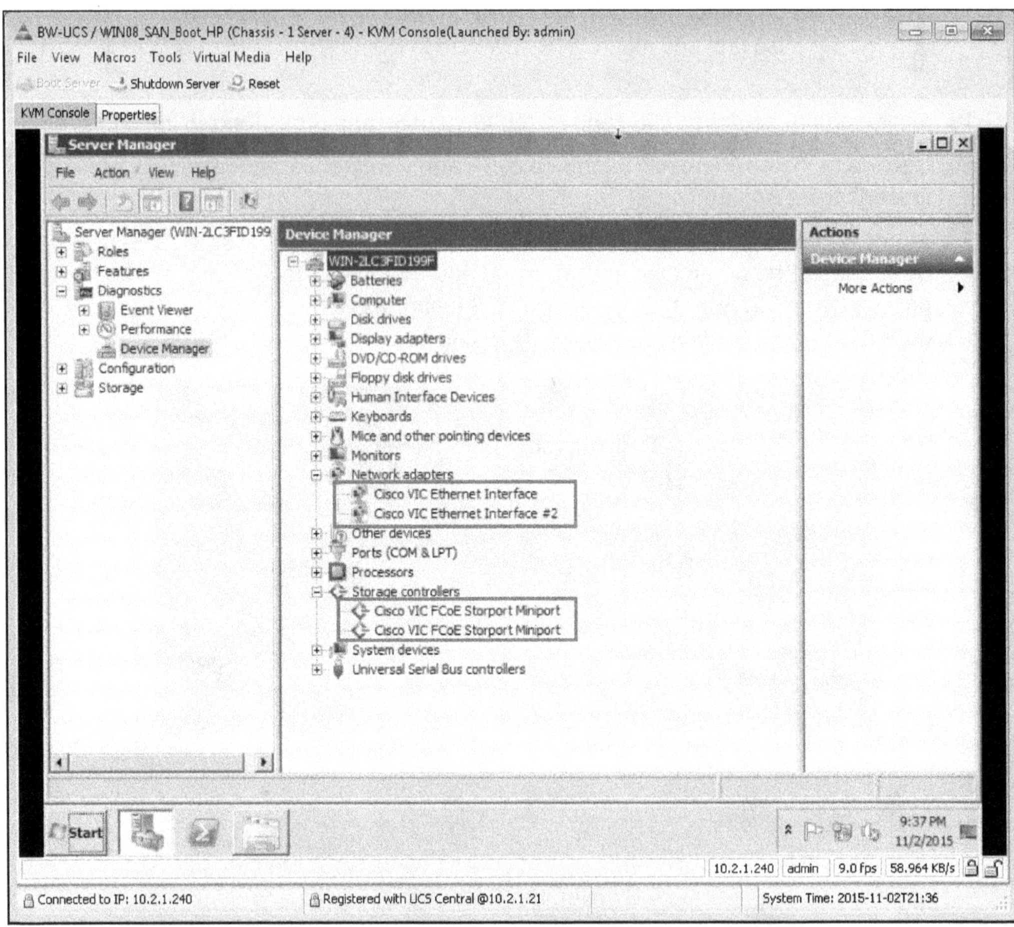

There's more...

By default, Microsoft Windows 2008 R2 doesn't install any multipath software; so it detects four SAN disk with same capacity on Windows **Disk Management**. It is because this SAN disk has four logical paths:

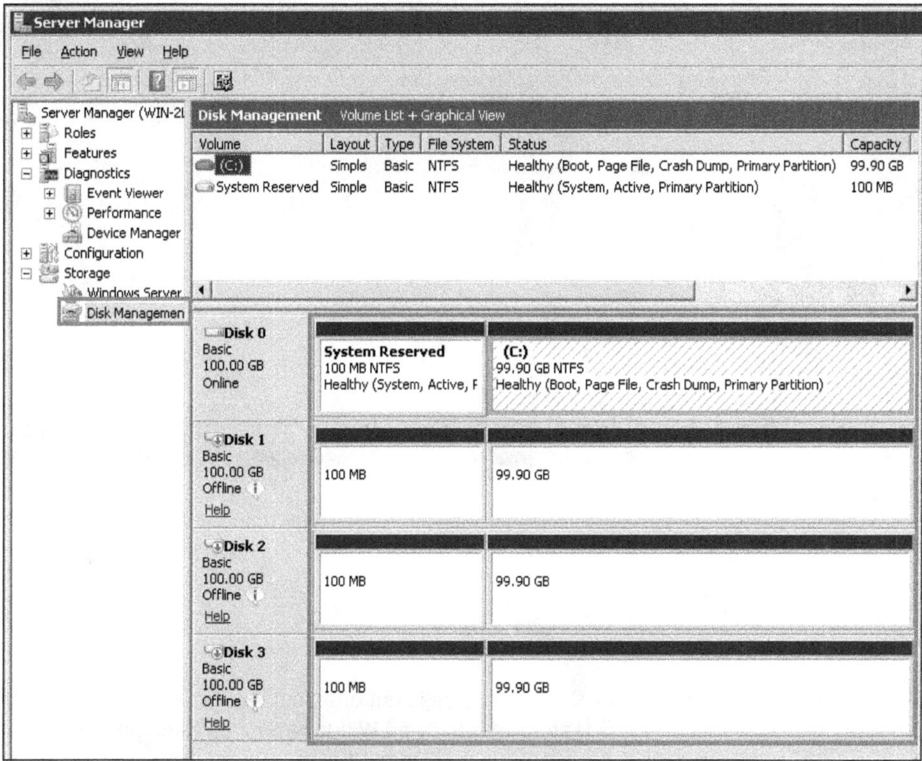

According to HP best practice, it is recommended to enable Windows MPIO multipath features for HP 3PAR StoreServ 7200. After enabling the Windows MPIO feature, it only detects one SAN disk with four logical paths on Windows **Disk Management**:

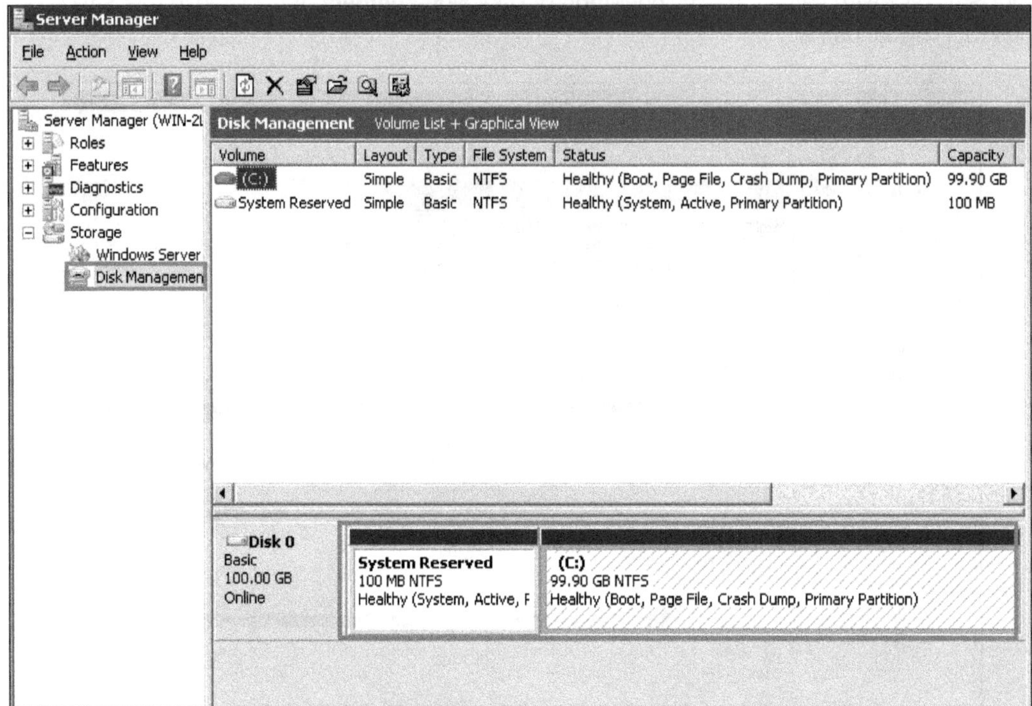

By default, Windows MPIO feature is not enabled; it is necessary to add Multipath I/O feature manually on Windows Server Manager. It is required to host reboot after enabled Multipath I/O feature.

Go to **Disk drives** on Windows **Device Manager**, you also can see one **3PARdata VV Multi-Path Disk Device**:

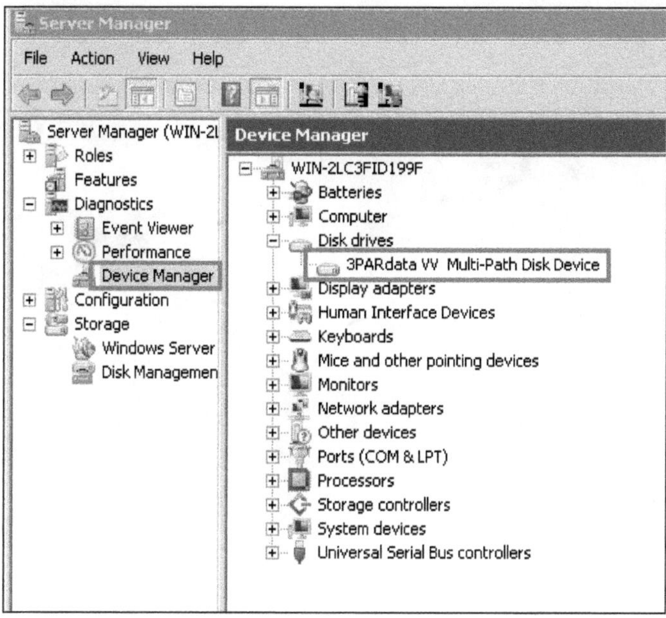

Right-click on 3PAR disk and choose the **MPIO** tab, you can see the state of all paths of the disk:

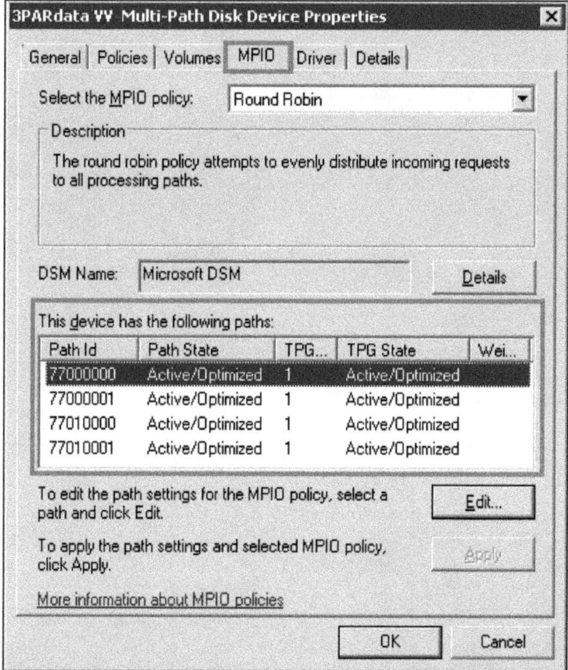

4

Data Migration to Cisco UCS

In this chapter, we will cover the following topics:

- Migrating VMware vSphere on HP C7000 to Cisco UCS
- P2V migration of HP C7000 to Cisco UCS
- Migrating the MSCS 2008 virtual machine to Cisco UCS
- Migrating the MSCS 2008 physical machine to Cisco UCS

Introduction

In this chapter, you will learn how to accomplish tasks related to data migration to Cisco UCS, how to migrate the physical machine and the virtual machine from the HP Server (C7000 Blade Server/Proliant Sever) to Cisco UCS, the platform including VMware vSphere Server, Microsoft Windows Server and Microsoft Windows Cluster Server, as well as Physical to Virtual (P2V) conversion to Cisco UCS.

Migrating VMware vSphere on HP C7000 to Cisco UCS

In this recipe, we will learn how to migrate VMware vSphere on HP C7000 to Cisco UCS.

Getting ready

The source ESXi host is running on an HP BL460c Blade Server, which is installed on an HP C7000 chassis. There are two Brocade 8 GB FC modules and two HP Flex-10 GB Ethernet modules installed on this chassis. The source ESXi host is connected to one EMC CX4-240 SAN storage unit through SAN Switches and one EMC LUN (ESXi datastore) is assigned to this ESXi host. Some virtual machines are running on this EMC LUN. To do the data migration, prepare one Cisco UCS 5108 Chassis with two UCS IOM 2208XPs installed, each UCS IOM being connected to one Cisco UCS 6248UP. There is one UCS B200 M3 Blade Server 0 installed on this chassis. This blade is configured with one VIC 1240 adapter. Configure four ports on each Cisco UCS 6428UP as an Ethernet uplink port (port 17/18) and an FC uplink port (port 6/7), which is connected to SAN Switches and LAN Switches by Fibre Channel cables. EMC SAN storage has two controllers and each controller has two FC ports that are connected to each SAN Switch. Create one UCS service profile defined by four vNICs with two vHBAs and associate this service with UCS B200 M3. VMware ESXi 5.5 is already installed on this UCS B200 M3 (local boot) and boots up successfully. The UCS B200 M3 is the target ESXi host.

The following table gives a summary of the hardware and software specifications for the source and target ESXi hosts:

Machine	HP C7000 Chassis	FC Interface	Network Interface
Source ESXi host	▸ QLogic QMH2572 8 GB FC HBA x 1 ▸ HP FlexFabric 10 GB 2-port 554FLB Adapter x 1 ▸ Intel(R) Xeon(R) CPU E5-2640 x 2 ▸ 64 GB Memory	Brocade 8 GB SAN Module x 2	HP Flex-10 GB VC Module x 2
	System Platform	**Number of vmnic/ vSwitch**	**Number of vHBA/ Datastore**
	VMware ESXi 5.5	4 x vmnic vSwitch0 (vmnic0, vmnic2) vSwitch1 (vmnic1, vmnic3)	2 x vmhba 1 x ESXi Datastore

Machine	HP C7000 Chassis	FC Interface	Network Interface
Target ESXi host	**Cisco 5108 Chassis**	**FC Interface**	**Network Interface**
	UCS B200 M3 x 1 installed with ▸ Cisco VIC 1240 x 1 ▸ Intel(R) Xeon(R) CPU E5-2640 x 2 ▸ 64 GB Memory	Fabric Interconnect 6248UP x 2	Fabric Interconnect 6248UP x 2
	System Platform	**Number of vmnic**	**Number of vHBA**
	VMware ESXi 5.5	4 x vmnic vSwitch0 (vmnic0, vmnic2) vSwitch1 (vmnic1, vmnic3)	2 x vmhba 1 x ESXi Datastore

The details are illustrated in the following diagram:

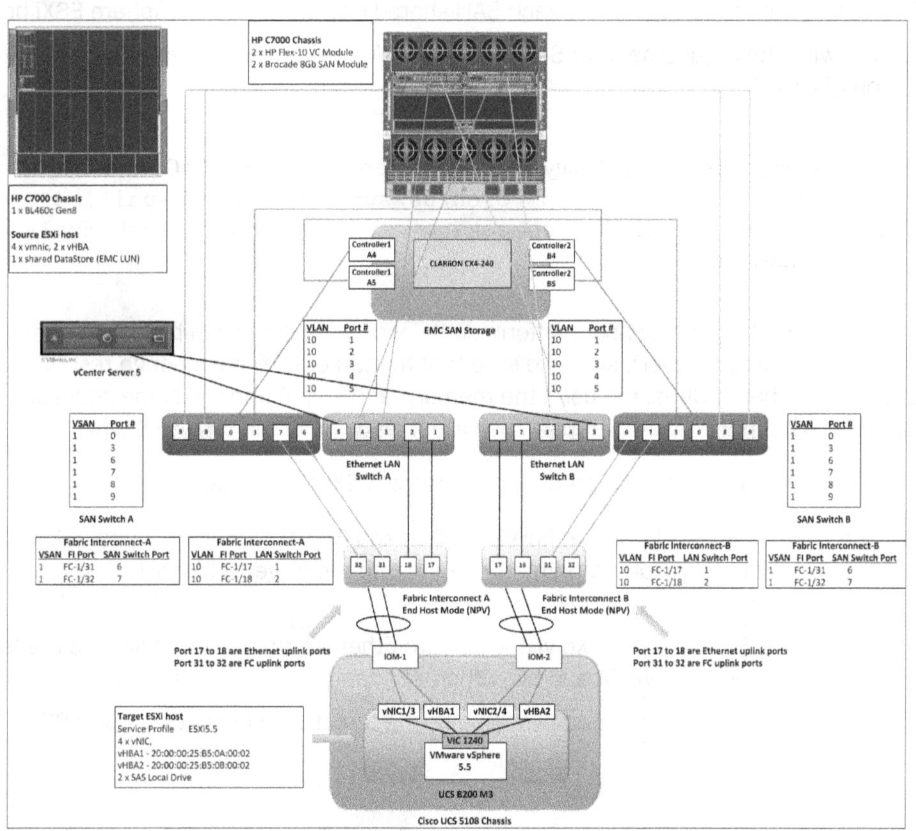

How to do it...

In this recipe, we will learn how to prepare the ESXi 5.5 on Cisco UCS for data migration from the HP C7000.

Assume that the ESXi on the source machine (HP DL460c) is version 5.5. It has two **Host Bus Adapters** (**HBA**), which are connected to one EMC storage unit with a Brocade 8 GB SAN module. This ESXi host has four Ethernet adapters which are connected to Ethernet Switches. This ESXi host has already been incorporated into one VMware vCenter 5.5.

Before data migration, you need the following prerequisites on the source ESXi host:

1. The licensed edition of vSphere ESXi host.
2. Knowledge of the physical CPU and memory installed on the vSphere ESXi host.
3. The number of HBAs and network adapters installed on the vSphere ESXi host.
4. The type of virtual network Switches being used on the vSphere ESXi host: **vNetwork Standard Switch** (**vSS**) or **vNetwork Distributed Switch** (**vDS**). You also need to know how many port groups and uplinks there are on each virtual Switch.
5. Knowledge of the capacity of each SAN-shared datastore on the vSphere ESXi host.
6. Knowing the requirement for SAN storage, HBA drivers, and firmware for the ESXi host on Cisco UCS.

To check UCS compatibility, go to UCSM Managed UCS Server Compatibility at `http://www.cisco.com/c/en/us/support/servers-unified-computing/unified-computing-system/products-technical-reference-list.html`

Due to VMware, ESXi is a hypervisor platform so the virtual machine can bypass the backend hardware (the HP Blade Server), so make sure that the target ESXi has enough resources (for example, the number of CPUs, the core, the memory, and so on) and the same configuration and features. We can then easily migrate the virtual machine to the target ESXi host.

Following are the prerequisites for preparing the target ESXi host on UCS:

1. The source ESXi host has two physical CPUs and 64 GB of memory installed, its VMware license is vSphere 5 Enterprise Plus, so the target ESXi host must meet all requirements.
2. The source ESXi host has two vHBA and two Ethernet adapters installed so the target ESXi host needs two vHBA and two Ethernet adapters installed on UCS.
3. The source ESXi host created two vSSs so the target ESXi host needs two vSSs.

4. The source ESXi host is connected to one EMC CLARiiON CX4-240 storage unit and has one datastore mounted so the target ESXi host needs two EMC CLARiiON CX4-240 storage units and one datastore mounted.
5. If you follow the preceding table for the target ESXi host, you can create one UCS service profile and define the number of vHBAs and vNICs, then associate this service profile with the target UCS Blade Server. Then, install vSphere 5.5 on this Blade Server.
6. After finishing the installation on the target vSphere ESXi, you can add the target ESXi host to the same ESXi host cluster group with the vSphere Web Client. Firstly, open a web browser, for example IE or Firefox, and then input the IP address of the vCenter Server:

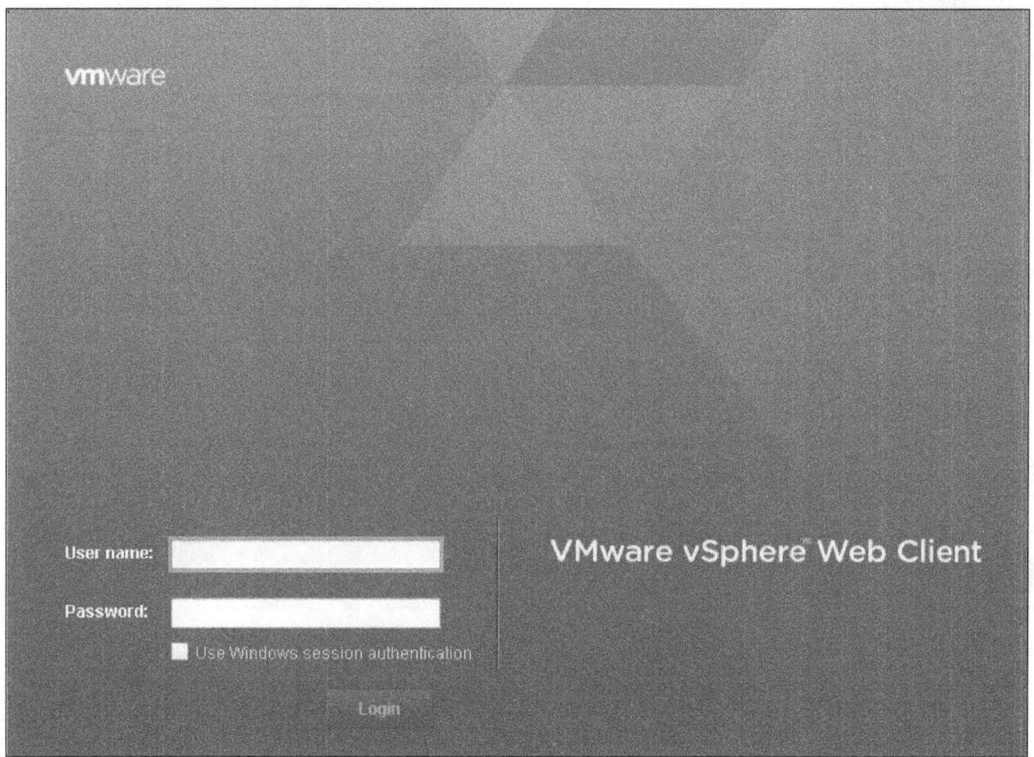

7. Log in to the vCenter Server using the vSphere Web Client. Assume that the existing ESXi cluster group is **Cluster 5.5**. Make sure that **VMware EVC** (**VMware Enhanced vMotion Compatibility**) is enabled before adding the target ESXi host to the cluster group. If the model of the CPU on the source ESXi host and the target ESXi host is different, the virtual machine cannot migrate online between the ESXi host with VMware vMotion. Select **Cluster 5.5** and go to the **Manage** tab, then click the **Edit** button on **VMware EVC** in the **Configuration** menu, as shown in the following screenshot:

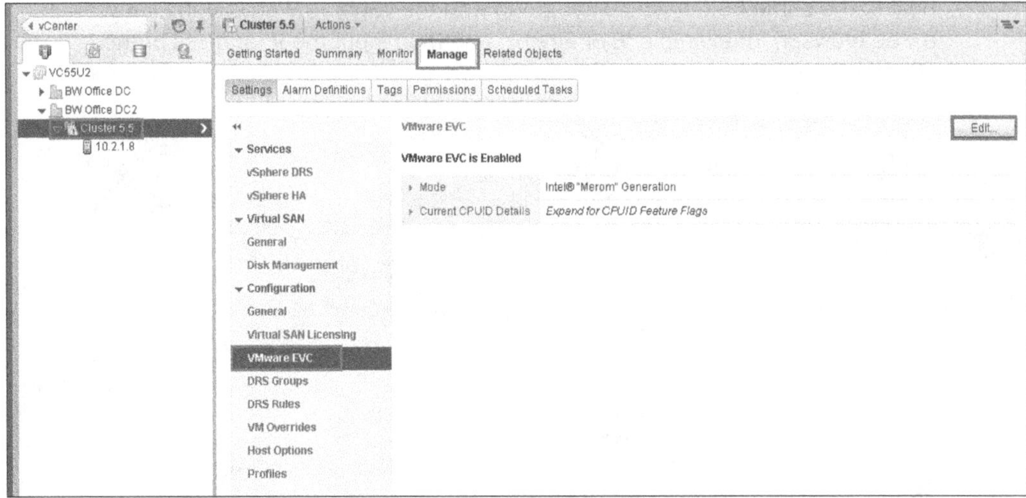

8. Click **Enable EVC for Intel Hosts** and select **Intel "Merom" Generation** from the **VMware EVC Mode** menu and click **OK**:

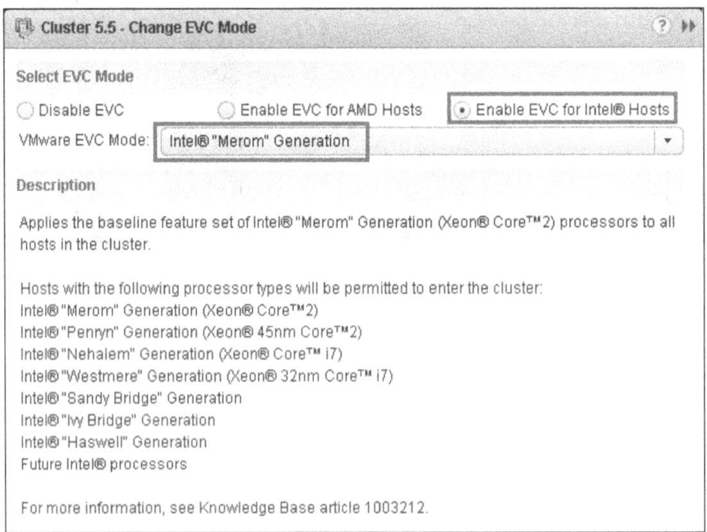

When EVC is disabled in the ESX cluster group, the virtual machine is required to shut down and it can then migrate if the source ESXi host and the target ESXi host have different CPU models.

For EVC compatibility checking, you can go to the VMware Compatibility Guide at `http://www.vmware.com/resources/compatibility/search.php?deviceCategory=cpu`.

9. After that, right-click the ESX cluster group and select **Add Host...** to add the target ESXi host to the cluster group.
10. After adding the target ESXi host, you can see the source ESXi host and the target ESXi host in the same cluster group: **Cluster 5.5**. Then, add the required VMware license to the target ESXi host. Go to the **Manage** tab of the ESXi host and select **Settings**, select **Licensing** on **System** and then click the **Assign License Key...** button to add the vSphere license to the licensing:

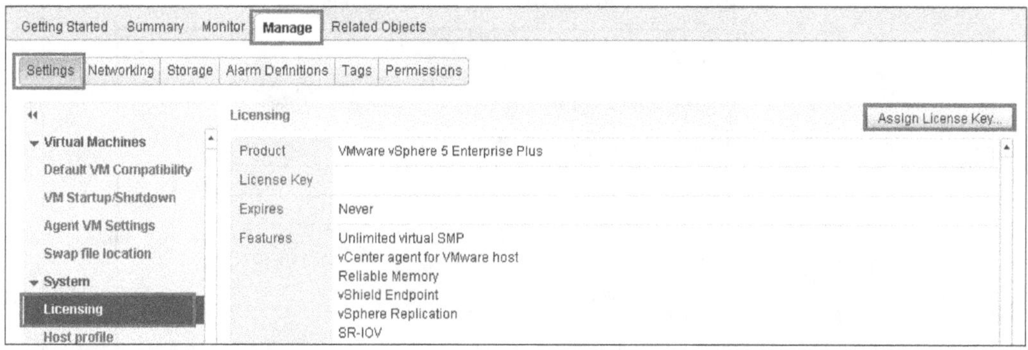

11. Go to the **Manage** tab of the source ESXi host and choose **Networking** where you can see two virtual Switches: **vSwitch0** and **vSwitch1**. Please note that all of the information about each vSwitch; for example, the name of the port group, the **VLAN ID** of each port group, and the number of **Physical Adapters**, can be found there.

    The information for **vSwitch0** is shown in the following screenshot:

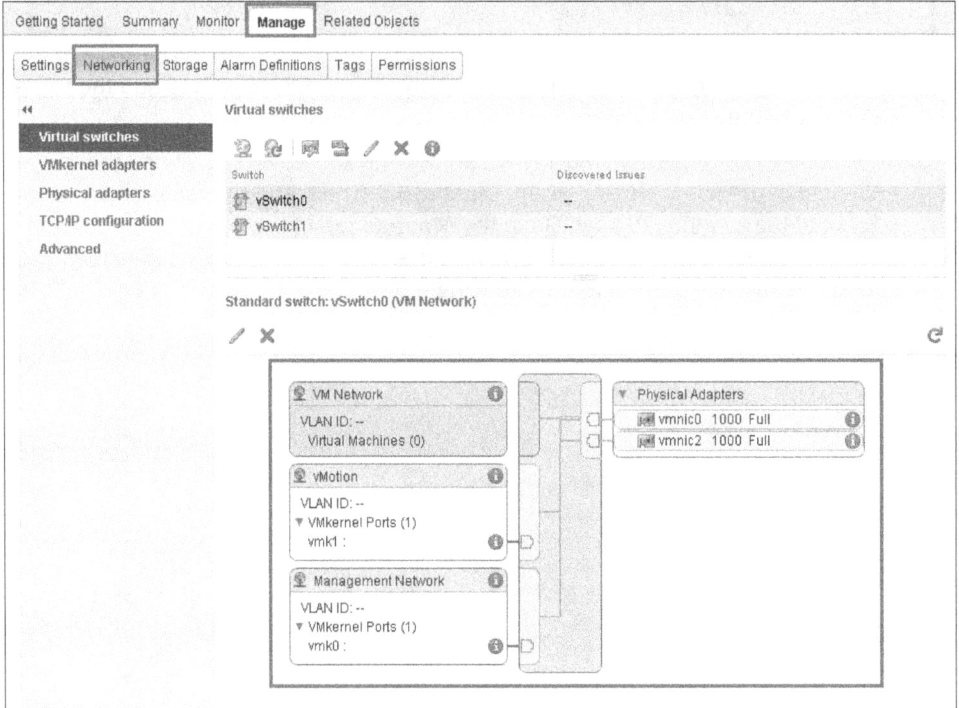

12. After collecting all of the information about each virtual Switch on the source ESXi host, you can create a virtual Switch on the target ESXi host based on the information from the source ESXi host:

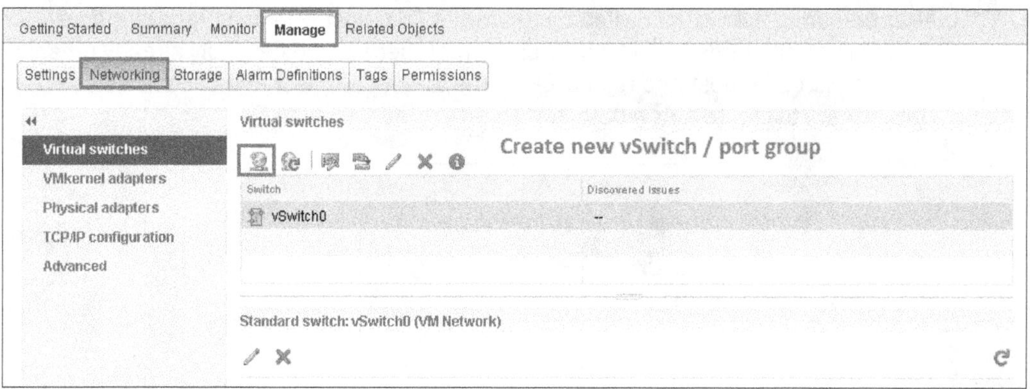

The following table gives a summary of virtual Switches for both source and target ESXi hosts:

ESXi host	Virtual Switch	Port Group Name	VLAN ID	Uplinks	Teaming
Source ESXi host - 10.2.1.8	vSwitch0	VM Network		vmnic0	Active
		vMotion		vmnic2	Active
		Management Network			
	vSwitch1	VLAN_204	204	vmnic1	Active
		VLAN_202	202	vmnic3	Active
Target ESXi host - 10.2.1.9	vSwitch0	VM Network		vmnic0	Active
		vMotion		vmnic2	Active
		Management Network			
	vSwitch1	VLAN_204	204	vmnic1	Active
		VLAN_202	202	vmnic3	Active

All of the port group names for the target ESXi host must be the same as the source ESXi host, otherwise the virtual machine cannot migrate into the target ESXi host with vMotion.

13. After preparing the virtual Switch on the target ESXi host, you can prepare the new datastore on the target ESXi host. Assume that there is one new LUN already present on the target ESXi host and right-click on the target ESXi host and choose **New Datastore...** to create a new datastore:

14. Click on **Next**:

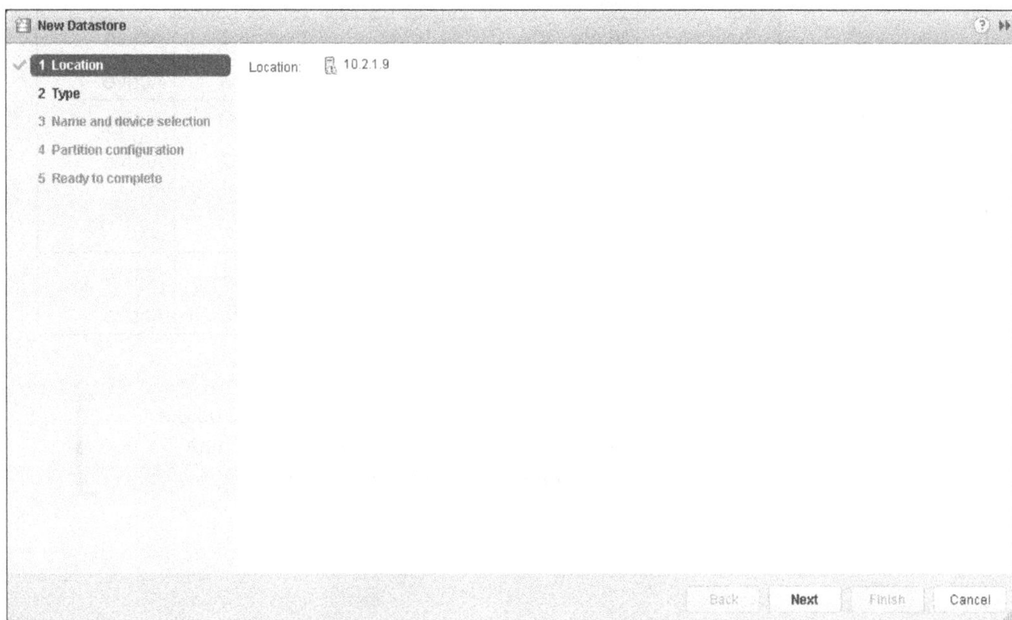

15. Select **VMFS**, and click on **Next**:

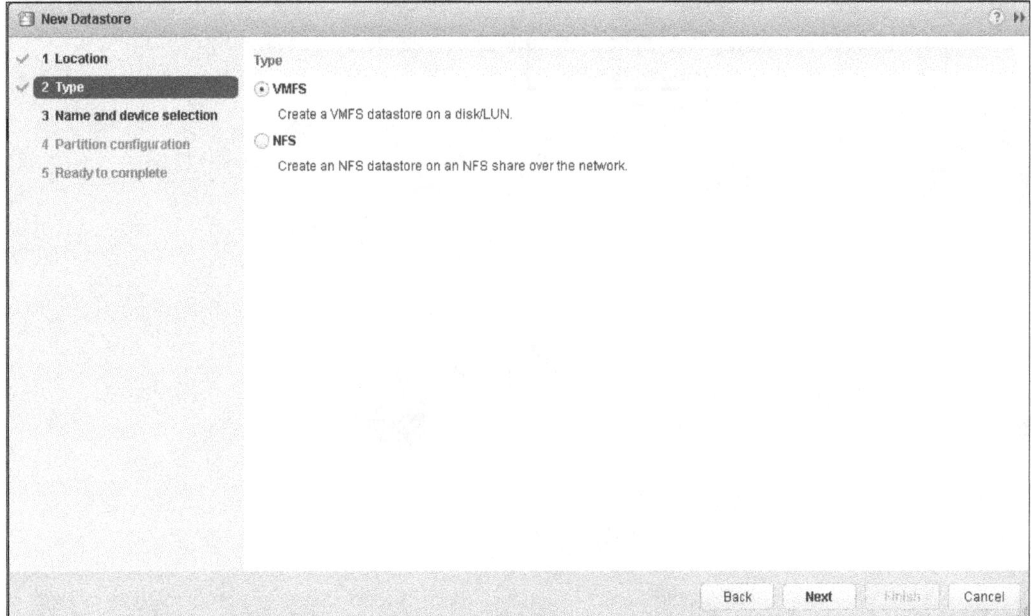

16. In the **DataStore name:** field, type `EMC_DS3` and select the target LUN, and then click on **Next**:

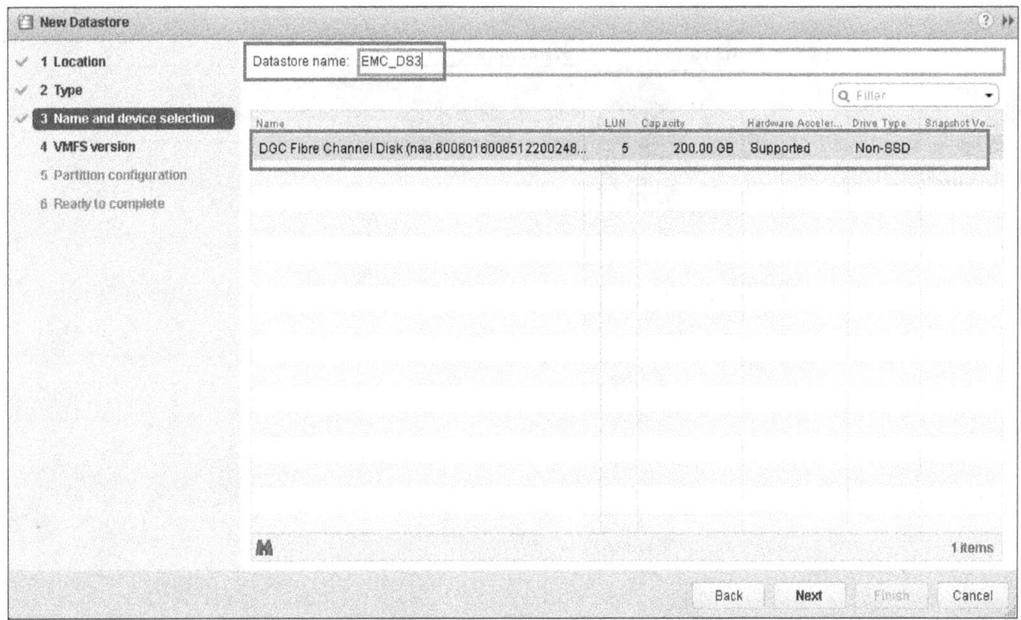

17. Select **VMFS 5** and click on **Next**:

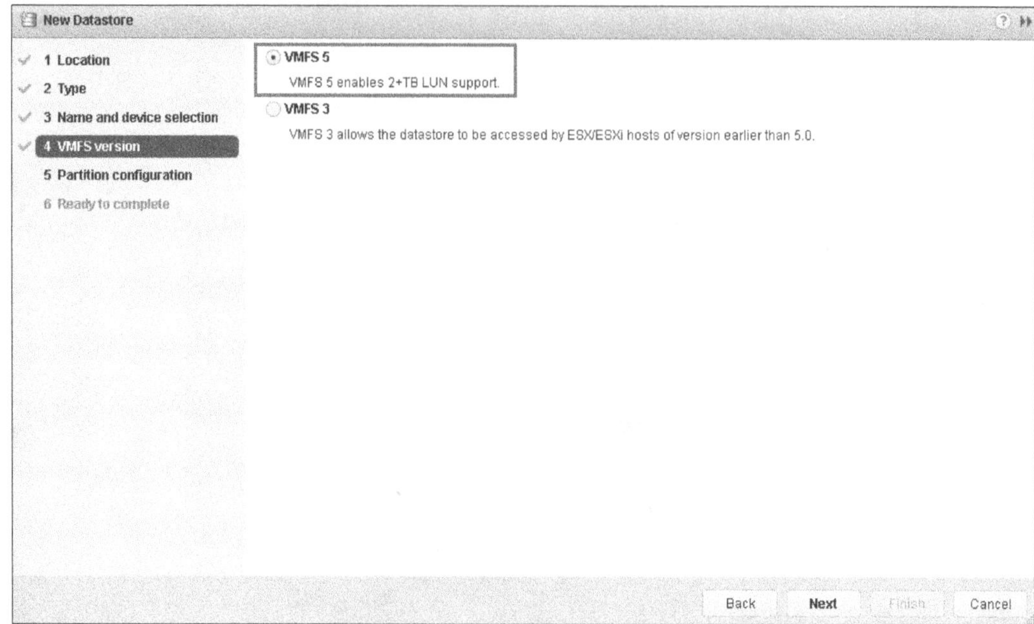

18. Select **Use all available partitions** on the **Partition Configuration** menu, then click on **Next**:

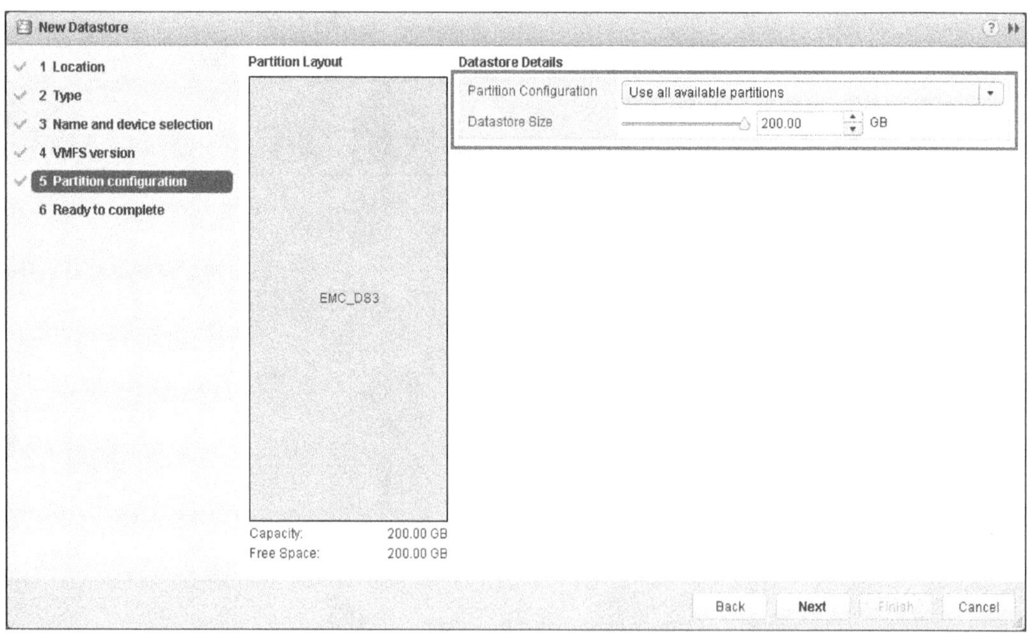

19. This displays general information about the datastore. Click on **Finish**:

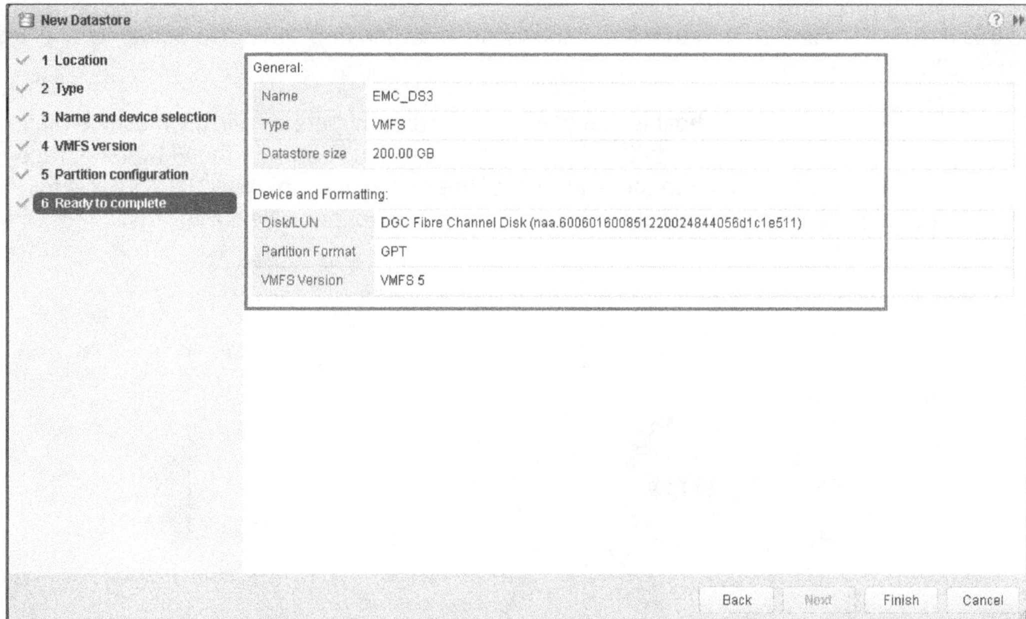

20. After creating the datastore, you should see one new datastore on the **Datastores** tab in **Related Objects**, assuming its name is **EMC_DS3**:

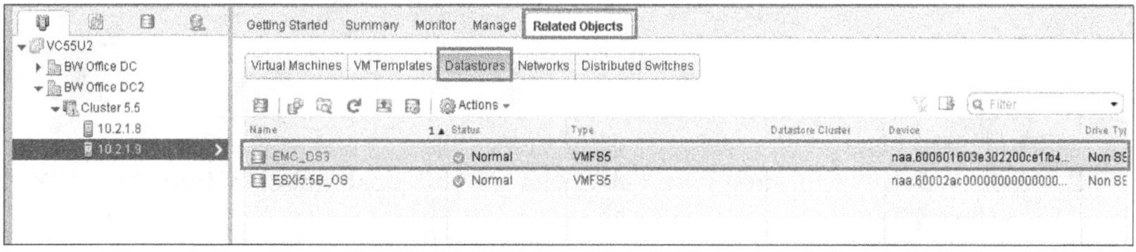

How it works...

In this recipe, we will learn how to migrate the virtual machine from HP Blade Server to Cisco UCS.

1. When the target ESXi host is ready, you can start to migrate the virtual machine that runs on HP Blade Server to Cisco UCS (the target ESXi host) with the VMware storage feature, vMotion. Assume the migration of the virtual machine **WIN2012_Test** is to the target ESXi host, right-click on the virtual machine, and select **Migrate...**:

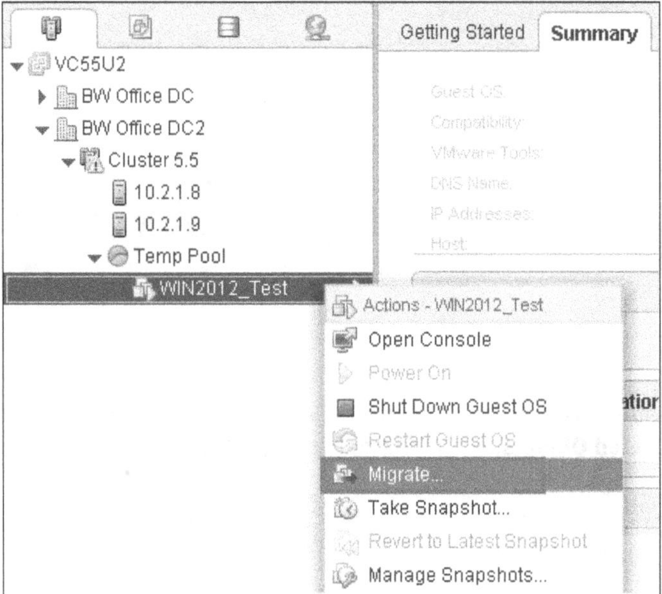

2. Click on **Select Migration Type**, select **Change both host and datastore**, then click on **Next**:

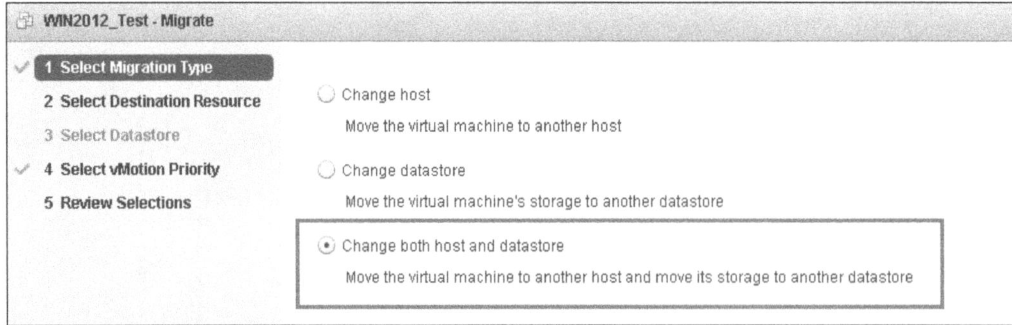

3. Click on **Select Destination Resource**, assume that the target resource is **Temp Pool**, then click on **Next**:

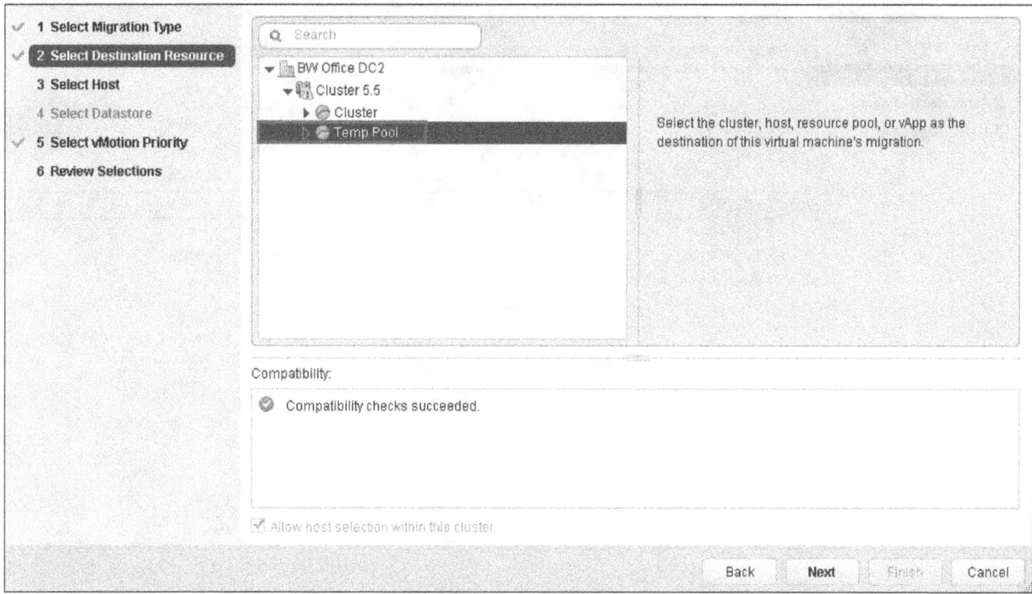

4. Select the target host, which is **10.2.1.9**, then click on **Next**:

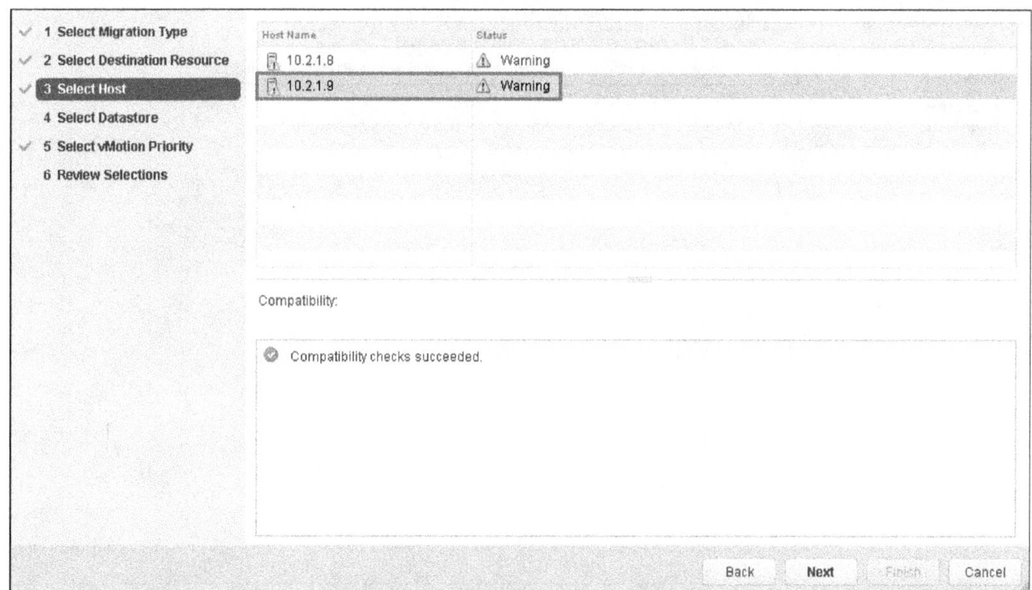

5. Select the target datastore, **EMC_DS3**, then click on **Next**:

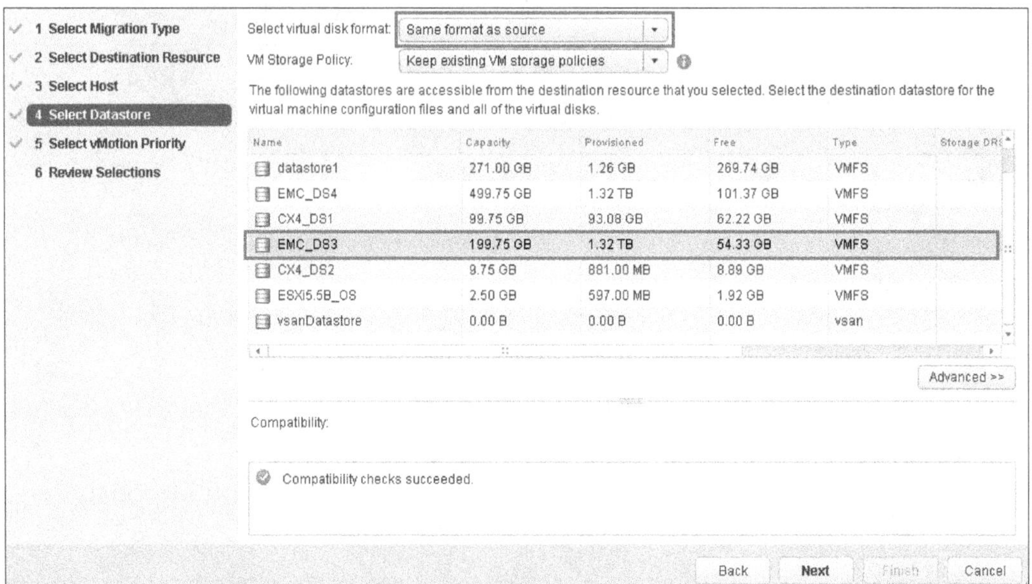

6. Select **Reserve CPU for optimal vMotion performance (Recommended)** on **Select vMotion Priority**, then click on **Next**:

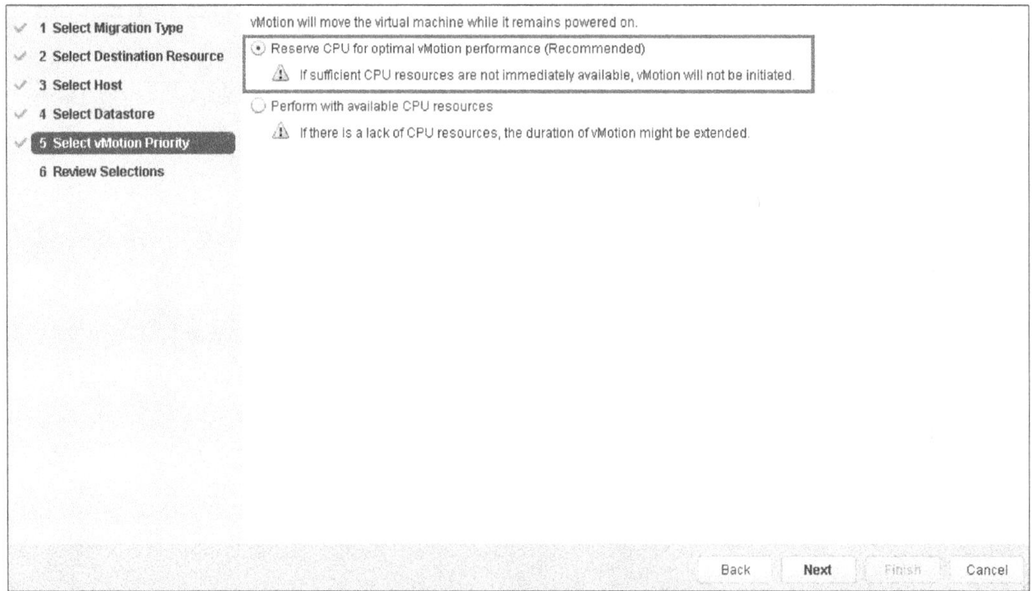

7. Review the selections under **Review Selections**, then click **Finish**:

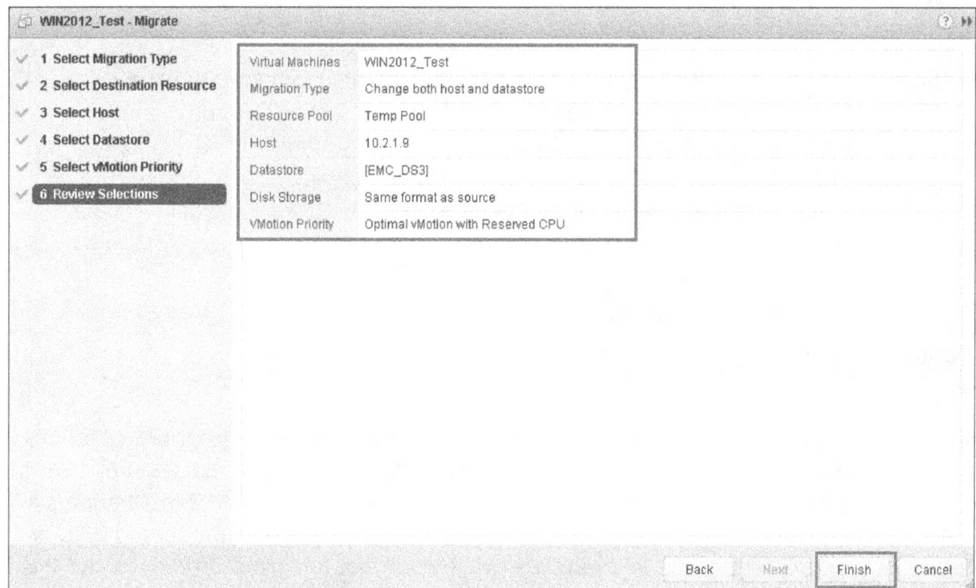

8. The storage vMotion task of VM **WIN2012_Test** starts automatically:

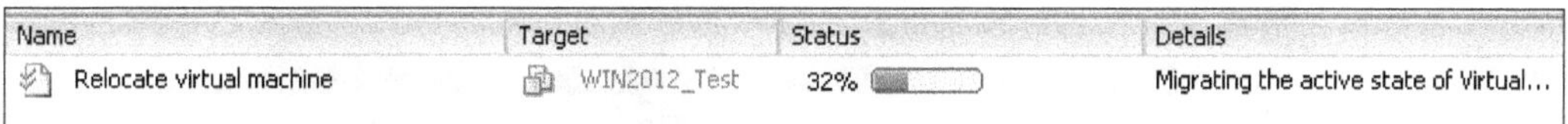

9. After finishing **WIN2012_Test** with vMotion storage, you should see the owner of the host change to the target ESXi host **10.2.1.9**:

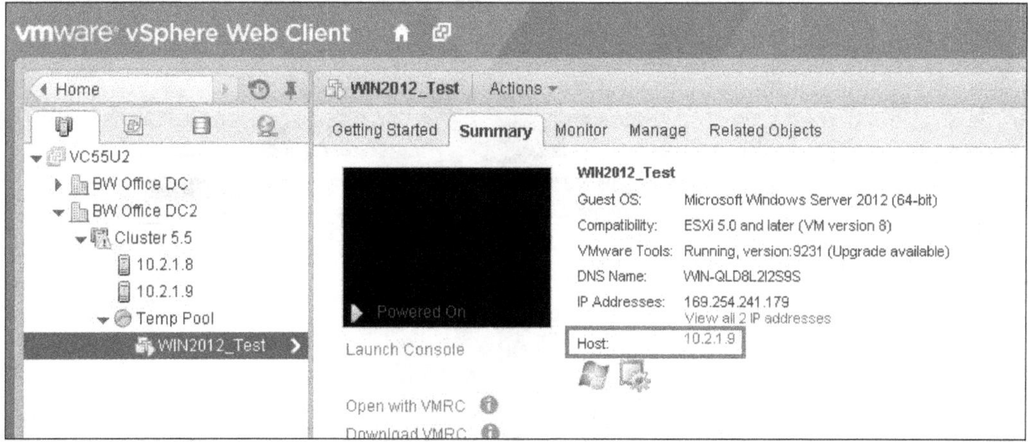

10. Repeat the preceding steps to migrate the other virtual machines to UCS using Storage vMotion.

> ESX/ESXi 4 and later version can perform migration with Storage vMotion. For Storage vMotion requirements and limitations, check `https://pubs.vmware.com/vsphere-55/index.jsp?topic=%2Fcom.vmware.vsphere.vcenterhost.doc%2FGUID-A16BA12`.
>
> If the virtual machine has **Raw Device Mappings** (**RDMs**), migrating can be performed in three ways; you can check this out at: `http://kb.vmware.com/kb/1005241`.

There's more...

When considering a hardware upgrade, the memory configuration is very important for the Server. The UCS Blade Server contains 24 DIMM slots, 12 for each CPU. Each set of 12 DIMM slots are arranged into four channels in which each channel has three DIMMs. Channels A to D are for CPU1, and channels E to H are for CPU2. Each DIMM slot is numbered 0, 1, or 2. Note that each DIMM slot 0 is colored blue, while each slot 1 is black, and each slot 2 is white. The following diagram is a physical representation of the DIMMs and channels:

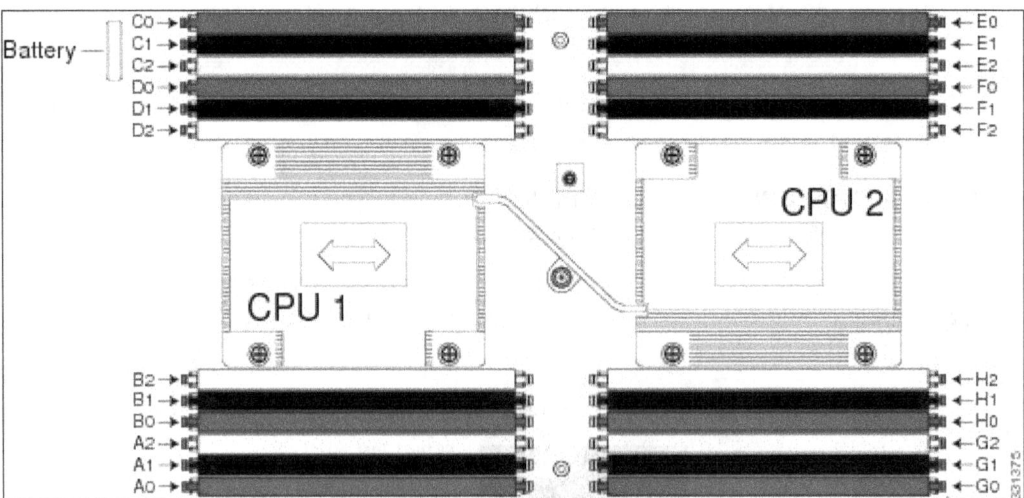

The following diagram is a logical representation of the DIMMs and channels:

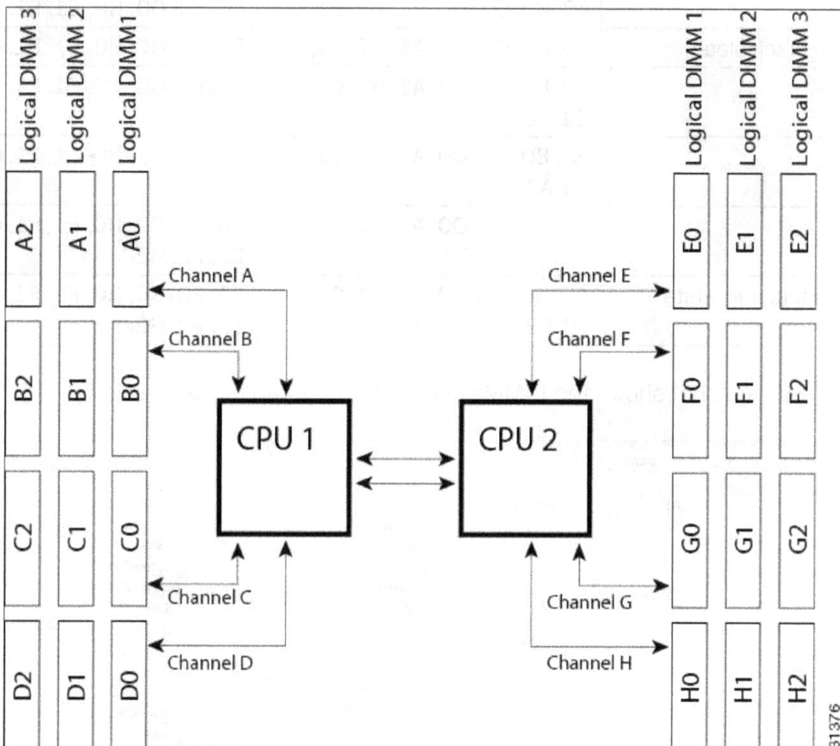

DIMMs can be used in the Blade Server in a **one DIMM per channel** (**1DPC**) configuration, in a **two DIMMs per channel** (**2DPC**) configuration, or a **three DIMMs per channel** (**3DPC**) configuration.

Each CPU in a Cisco UCS B200 M3 Blade Server supports four channels with three memory slots each. In a 1DPC configuration, DIMMs are in slot 0 only. In a 2DPC configuration, DIMMs are in both slot 0 and slot 1. In a 3DPC configuration, DIMMs are in slot 0, slot 1, and slot 2.

The following table shows the supported DIMM population order:

DIMMs per CPU	CPU1 installed slots	CPU2 installed slots
1	A0	E0
2	A0, B0	E0, F0
3	A0, B0, C0	E0, F0, G0
4 (Blue slots)	**A0, B0, C0, D0**	**E0, F0, G0, H0**
5	A0, B0, C0, D0, A1	E0, F0, G0, H0, E1
6	A0, B0, C0, D0, A1, B1	E0, F0, G0, H0, E1, F1

DIMMs per CPU	CPU1 installed slots	CPU2 installed slots
7	A0, B0, C0, D0, A1, B1, C1	E0, F0, G0, H0, E1, F1, G1
8 (Blue and black slots)	A0, B0, C0, D0, A1, B1, C1, D1	E0, F0, G0, H0, E1, F1, G1, H1
9	A0, B0, C0, D0, A1, B1, C1, D1,A2	E0, F0, G0, H0, E1, F1, G1, H1, E2
10	A0, B0, C0, D0, A1, B1, C1, D1,A2, B2	E0, F0, G0, H0, E1, F1, G1, H1, E2, F2
11	A0, B0, C0, D0, A1, B1, C1, D1,A2, B2, C2	E0, F0, G0, H0, E1, F1, G1, H1, E2, F2, G2
12 (Blue, black, and white slots)	A0, B0, C0, D0, A1, B1, C1, D1,A2, B2, C2, D2	E0, F0, G0, H0, E1, F1, G1, H1, E2, F2, G2, H2

The following screenshot shows the DIMMs installed on the target ESXi host:

Name	Location	Capacity(GB)	Clock(MHz)
Memory 1	A0	8.00	1866
Memory 2	A1	Unspecified	Unspecified
Memory 3	A2	Unspecified	Unspecified
Memory 4	B0	8.00	1866
Memory 5	B1	Unspecified	Unspecified
Memory 6	B2	Unspecified	Unspecified
Memory 7	C0	8.00	1866
Memory 8	C1	Unspecified	Unspecified
Memory 9	C2	Unspecified	Unspecified
Memory 10	D0	8.00	1866
Memory 11	D1	Unspecified	Unspecified
Memory 12	D2	Unspecified	Unspecified
Memory 13	E0	8.00	1866
Memory 14	E1	Unspecified	Unspecified
Memory 15	E2	Unspecified	Unspecified
Memory 16	F0	8.00	1866
Memory 17	F1	Unspecified	Unspecified
Memory 18	F2	Unspecified	Unspecified
Memory 19	G0	8.00	1866
Memory 20	G1	Unspecified	Unspecified
Memory 21	G2	Unspecified	Unspecified
Memory 22	H0	8.00	1866
Memory 23	H1	Unspecified	Unspecified
Memory 24	H2	Unspecified	Unspecified

According to the preceding data migration (HP Blade to UCS), the target ESXi host installed 64 GB memory (8 x 8 GB DIMM). The memory configuration of the target ESXi host is based on the configuration in Bold text in a preceding table. When considering the memory configuration of the UCS Blade Server, there are several things you need to consider:

1. When mixing DIMMs of different densities, the highest density DIMM goes in slot 1 and others follow in descending density.
2. The selected CPU(s) may have some effect on performance.
3. DIMMs can be run in a 1DPC, a 2DPC, or a 3DPC configuration. 1 DPC and 2DPC provide the maximum rated speed that the CPU and DIMMs are rated for while 3DPC causes the DIMMs to run at a slower speed.

See also

According to the preceding hardware refreshment (HP C7000 to Cisco UCS), HP BL460c Blade Server installed two different types of adapters: the HP Qlogic 8 GB FC adapter and a HP FlexFabric 10 GB adapter. The UCS Blade Server B200 M3 installed one Cisco UCS virtual interface card 1240, which is a 4-port 10 Gigabit Ethernet, **Fibre Channel over Ethernet** (**FCoE**), and **modular LAN On Motherboard** (**mLOM**). It offers up to 256 PCIe standard-compliant interfaces to the host (ESXi) that can be dynamically configured as either NICs or HBAs.

If the source machine is the rackmount server, the table below shows a typical configuration for this server. You can also migrate the virtual machine to Cisco UCS by using the preceding procedures:

HP Proliant DL380e Gen8	**FC Interface**	**Network Interface**
▸ 8 GB FC 2 ports HBA x 2 ▸ 1 GB 4 ports Ethernet Adapter x 1 ▸ Intel(R) Xeon(R) CPU E5-2640 x 2 ▸ 64 GB Memory	8 GB HBA Adapter x 2	1 GB Ethernet Adapter x 1
System Platform	**Number of vmnic**	**Number of vHBA**
VMware ESXi 5.5	4 x vmnic vSwitch0 (vmnic0, vmnic2) vSwitch1 (vmnic1, vmnic3)	2 x vmhba 1 x ESXi Datastore

P2V migration of HP C7000 to Cisco UCS

In this recipe, we will learn how to use P2V migration from the HP C7000 Blade Server to Cisco UCS.

Getting ready

Microsoft Windows 2008 R2 is running on the source HP BL460c Blade Server, which is installed on the HP C7000 Chassis (Slot1). The chassis has two Brocade 8 GB FC modules and two HP Flex-10 GB Ethernet modules. The source machine is connected to one EMC CX4-240 SAN Storage through SAN Switches and one EMC LUN is assigned to the Windows 2008 host. For P2V migration, prepare one Cisco UCS 5108 Chassis with two UCS IOM 2208XPs installed, each UCS IOM being connected to one Cisco UCS 6428UP. There is one UCS B200 M3 with one VIC 1240 installed on this chassis. Configure four ports on each Cisco UCS 6428UP as an Ethernet uplink port (port 17/18) and an FC uplink port (port 6/7), connected to SAN Switches and LAN Switches with Fibre Channel cables. EMC SAN Storage has two controllers and each controller has two FC ports connected to each SAN Switch. Prepare one UCS service profile; it should include four vNICs and two vHBAs and be associated with UCS B200 M3. VMware ESXi 5.5 is already installed on this UCS (local boot) and should boot up successfully. The UCS is the target ESXi host. Before the P2V conversion, we should also prepare another HP BL460c installed on the C7000 Chassis (Slot2) as a VMware convertor Server.

The following table gives a summary of the hardware and software specifications for the source ESXi host and the target ESXi host:

HP C7000 Chassis	FC Interface	Network Interface
Slot1 - BL460c Gen8 x 1 installed with ▸ QLogic QMH2572 8 GB FC HBA x 1 ▸ HP FlexFabric 10 GB 2-port 554FLB Adapter x 1 ▸ Intel(R) Xeon(R) CPU E5-2640 x 2 ▸ 64 GB Memory	Brocade 8 GB SAN Module x 2	HP Flex-10 GB VC Module x 2

System Platform	**Number of NIC**	**Number of HBA**
Microsoft Windows 2008 R2	4 x NIC	2 x HBA
Slot2 - BL460c Gen8 x 1 installed with ▸ QLogic QMH2572 8 GB FC HBA x 1 ▸ HP FlexFabric 10 GB 2-port 554FLB Adapter x 1 ▸ Intel(R) Xeon(R) CPU E5-2640 x 2 ▸ 64 GB Memory		1 x EMC LUN
System Platform	**Number of NIC**	**Number of HBA**
Microsoft Windows 2008 R2 VMware vCenter Convertor Standalone 5.5	4 x NIC	2 x HBA

Source: Microsoft Windows 2008 and VMware vCenter Converter

Cisco 5108 Chassis	**FC Interface**	**Network Interface**
UCS B200 M3 x 1 installed with ▸ Cisco VIC 1240 x 1 ▸ Intel(R) Xeon(R) CPU E5-2640 x 2 ▸ 64 GB Memory	Fabric Interconnect 6248UP x 2	Fabric Interconnect 6248UP x 2
System Platform	**Number of vmnic**	**Number of HBA**
VMware ESXi 5.5	4 x vmnic	2 x HBA 1 x ESXi Datastore

Target ESXi host

The details are shown in the following diagram:

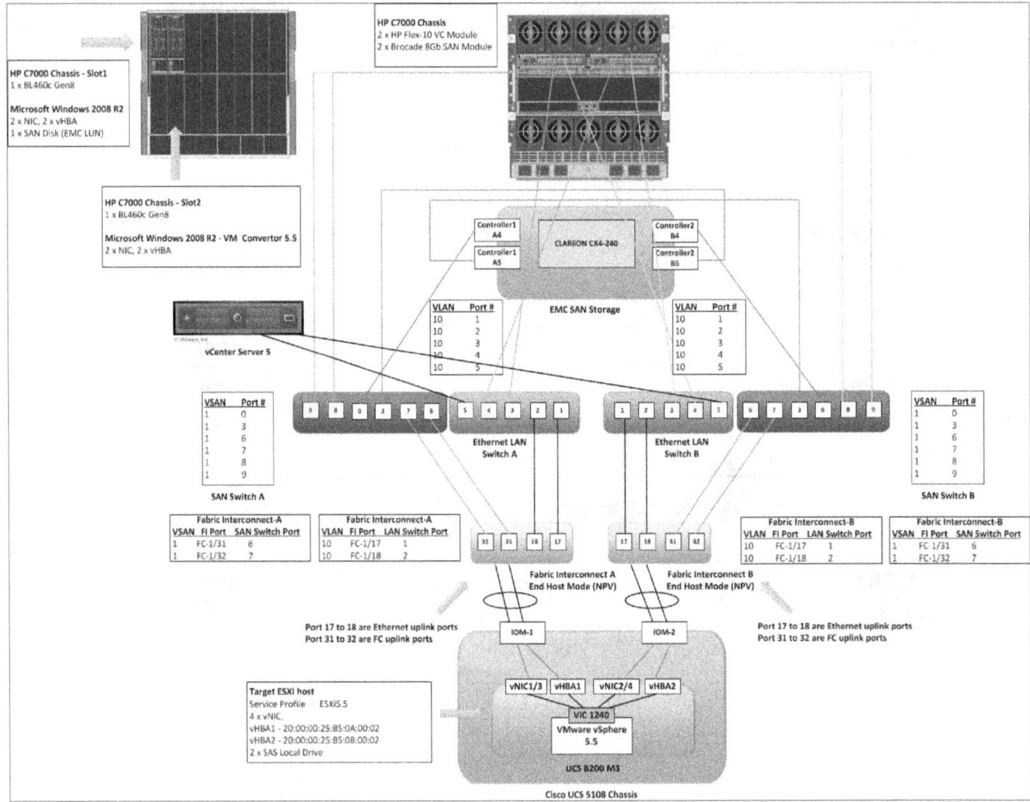

How to do it...

In this recipe, we will learn how to prepare the VMware vCenter convertor for standalone and physical migration from Virtual (P2V) Microsoft Windows 2008 R2 to Cisco UCS.

1. Firstly, we need to prepare **VMware vCenter Convertor Standalone** 5.5, which you can download from: `https://my.vmware.com/web/vmware/info/slug/infrastructure_operations_management/vmware_vcenter_converter_standalone/5_5`. It is freeware and is used to convert the physical machine to a virtual machine.

You can check the release notes for **VMware vCenter Convertor Standalone** for P2V compatibility at: `https://www.vmware.com/support/pubs/converter_pubs.html`.

2. Microsoft Windows 2008 R2 should already be installed on HP DL460c (Slot2). Then, you can install vCenter Convertor 5.5 on this Blade Server:

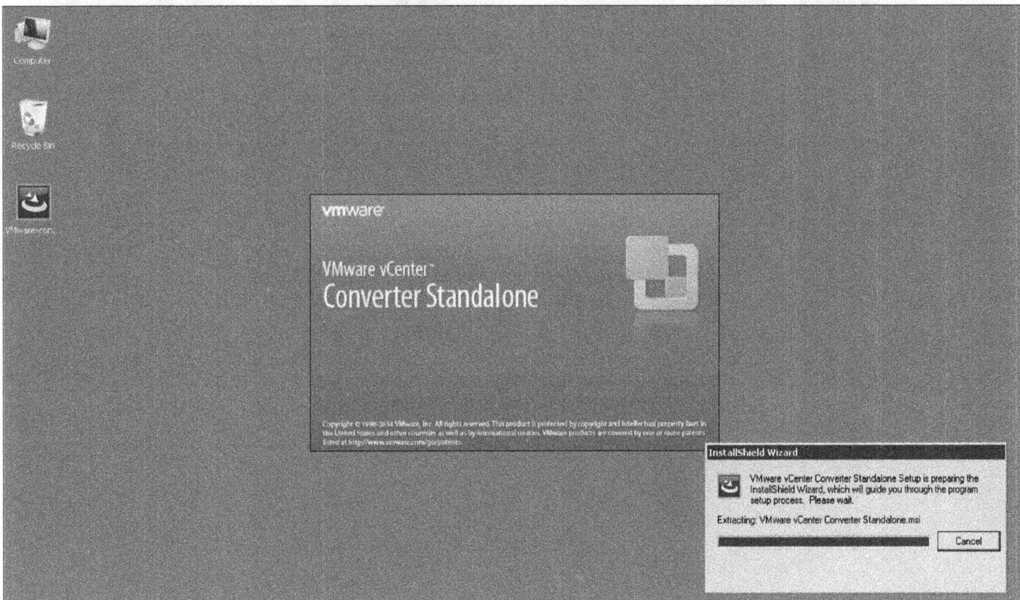

3. Choose **Local installation**, then click **Next**:

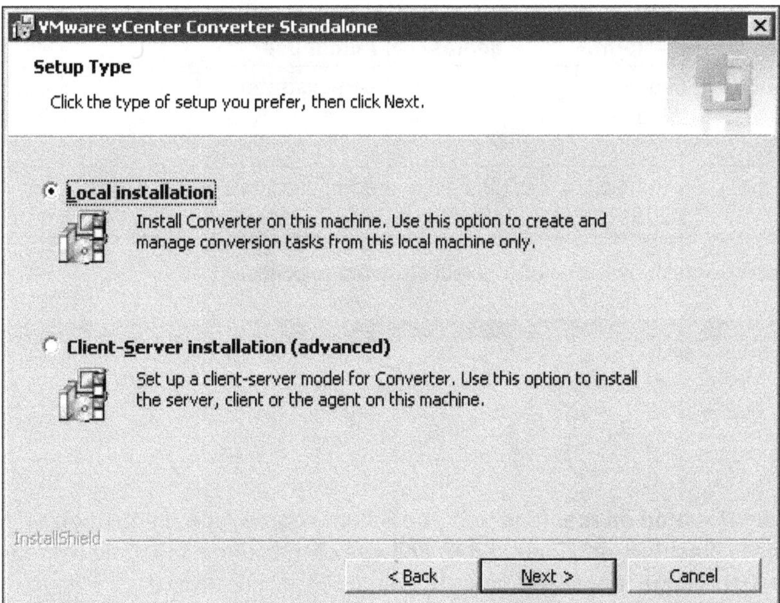

4. Complete the vCenter Convertor installation, then click on **Finish**:

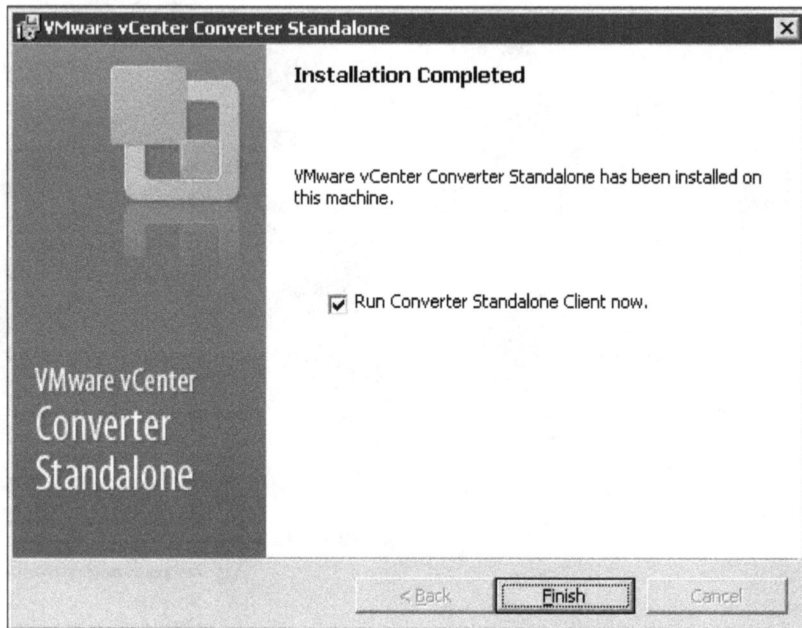

5. After completing the installation, you can create P2V sessions for Microsoft Windows 2008. Before creating a session, you should find out about the systems:

System	Platform	IP address	Admin User	Password
HP DL460c	Source - Windows 2008 R2	10.2.1.90	administrator	--
vCenter 5.5	Windows 2008 R2	10.2.1.4	administrator@vsphere.local	---

6. Open vCenter Convertor and select **Convert machine**:

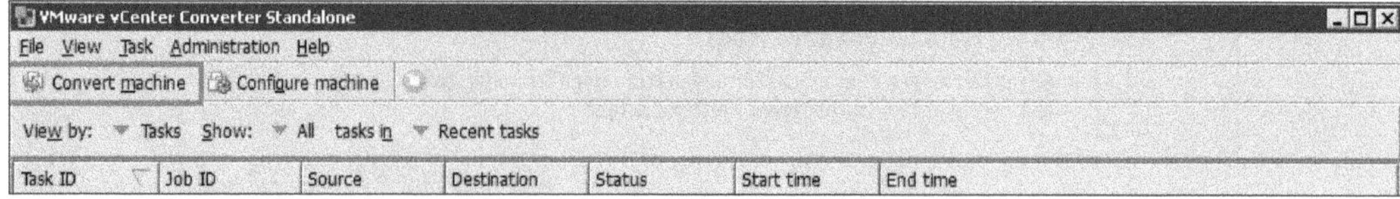

7. Select **Powered-on machine** from the **Select source type** menu, then select **A remote machine**, and input the **IP address** of the source machine (Windows 2008 R2), **User name**, **Password**, and **OS Family**. Then, click **Next**:

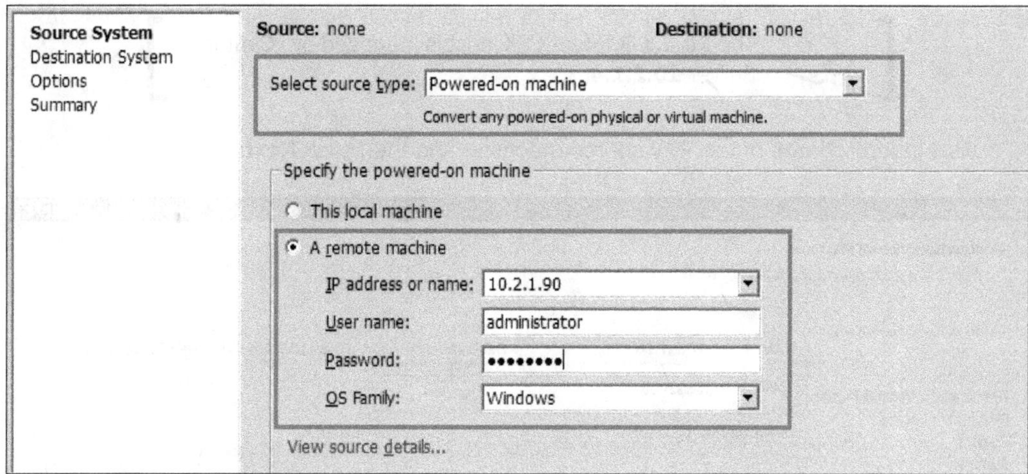

8. The VMware vCenter Converter agent needs to be temporarily installed on the remote source machine so select **Automatically uninstall the files when import succeeds**. Then, click **Yes**.

The VMware vCenter Converter agent uninstalls automatically from the source machine after finishing the P2V conversion.

9. After deploying the vCenter Converter agent on the source machine, select **VMware Infrastructure virtual machine** on the **Select destination type** menu. Input the IP address of the vCenter Server, **User name**, and **Password**. Then, click **Next**:

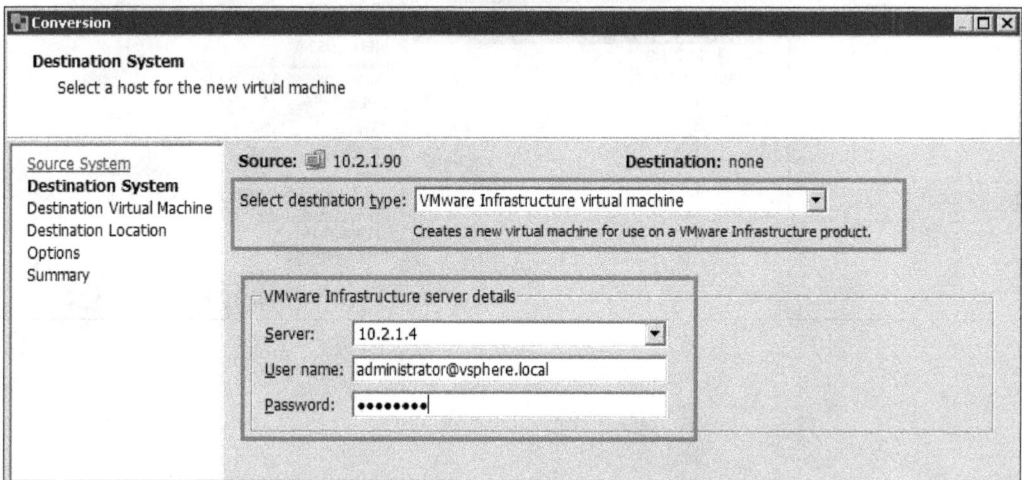

The **10.2.1.9** target ESXi host is managed by vCenter Server **10.2.1.4**.

10. Input the **Name** of the P2V source machine, and then click **Next**:

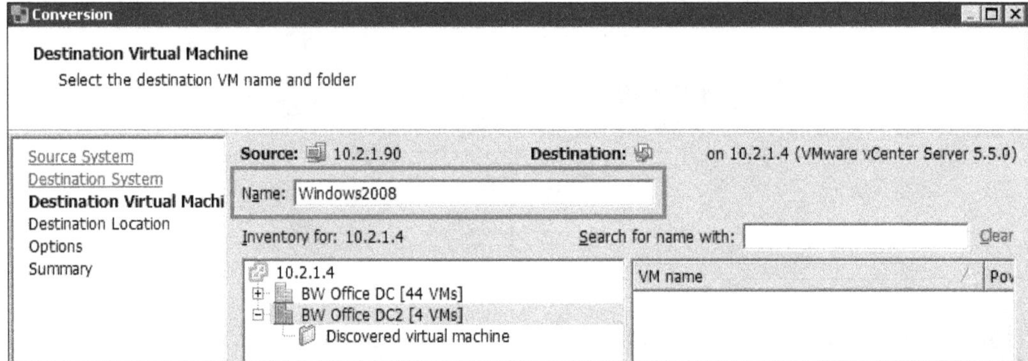

11. Select **EMC_DS3** from the **Datastore** menu and select **Version 10** on the **Virtual machine version** menu. Then, click **Next**:

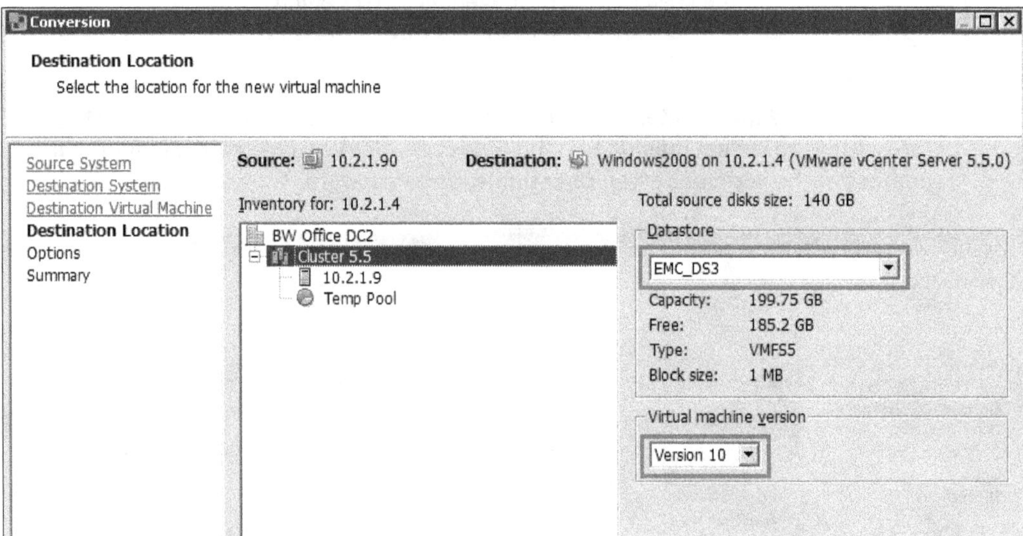

12. Go to **Options**, then click on **Next**:

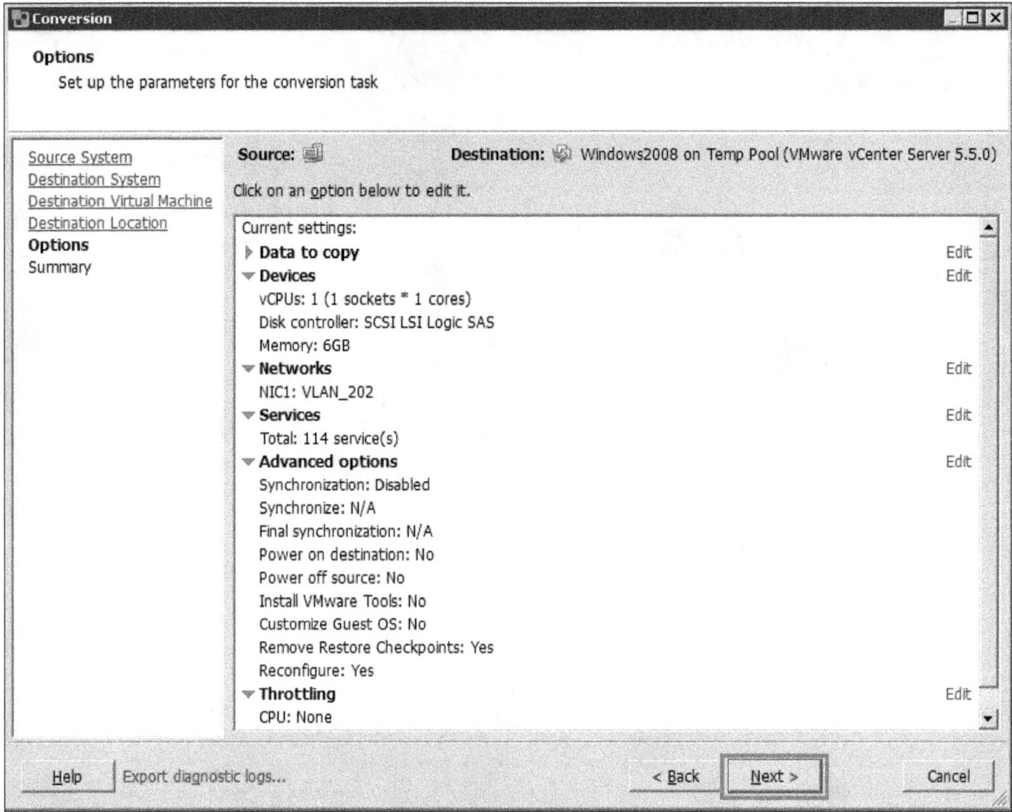

It will display the summary of the P2V session.

13. Click on **Finish**:

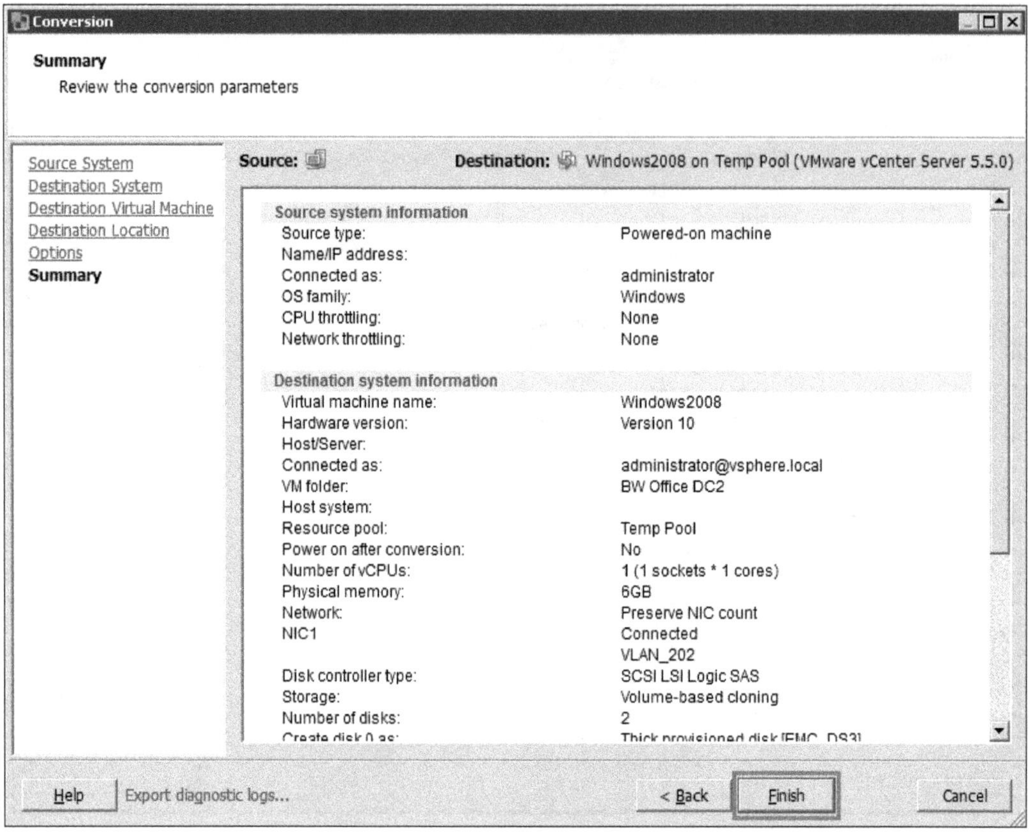

Conversion
Summary
Review the conversion parameters
Source System
Destination System
Destination Virtual Machine
Destination Location
Options
Summary
Source:
Destination: Windows2008 on Temp Pool (VMware vCenter Server 5.5.0)
Source system information
Source type: Powered-on machine
Name/IP address:
Connected as: administrator
OS family: Windows
CPU throttling: None
Network throttling: None
Destination system information
Virtual machine name: Windows2008
Hardware version: Version 10
Host/Server:
Connected as: administrator@vsphere.local
VM folder: BW Office DC2
Host system:
Resource pool: Temp Pool
Power on after conversion: No
Number of vCPUs: 1 (1 sockets * 1 cores)
Physical memory: 6GB
Network: Preserve NIC count
NIC1 Connected
VLAN_202
Disk controller type: SCSI LSI Logic SAS
Storage: Volume-based cloning
Number of disks: 2
Help
Export diagnostic logs...
< Back
Finish
Cancel

14. After that, the P2V task is created and starts automatically. The P2V conversion of the source machine starts to convert the physical machine into the virtual machine on the target ESXi host:

VMware vCenter Converter Standalone
File View Task Administration Help
Convert machine
Configure machine
View by: Tasks Show: All tasks in Recent tasks
Task ID
Job ID
Source
Destination
Status
Start time
End time
1
1
10.2.1.90
10.2.1.4/Wind...
35%
11/12/2015 11:32:35 ...
Estimated time remaining: 11 minutes

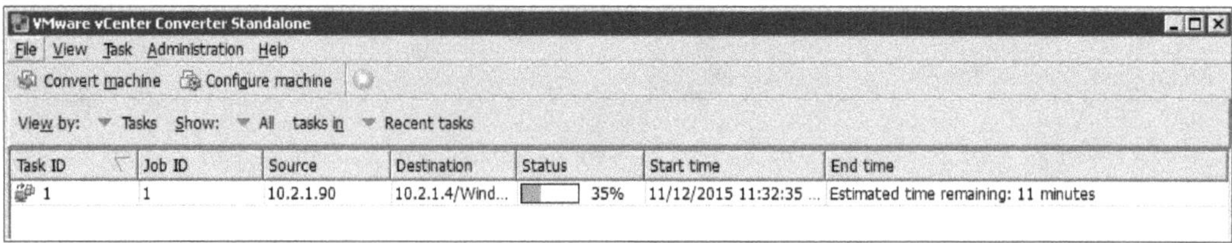

15. When the **Status** of the task shows **Completed**, the P2V conversion has completed successfully:

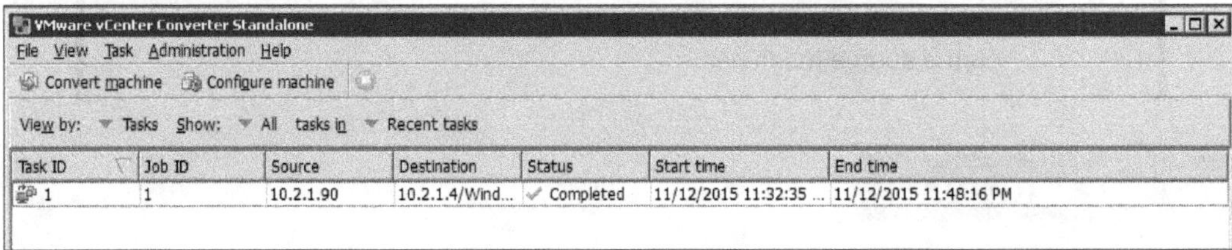

16. When a P2V session has been completed, you log in into vCenter and can see the Windows2008 virtual machine stored on the 10.2.1.9 ESXi host:

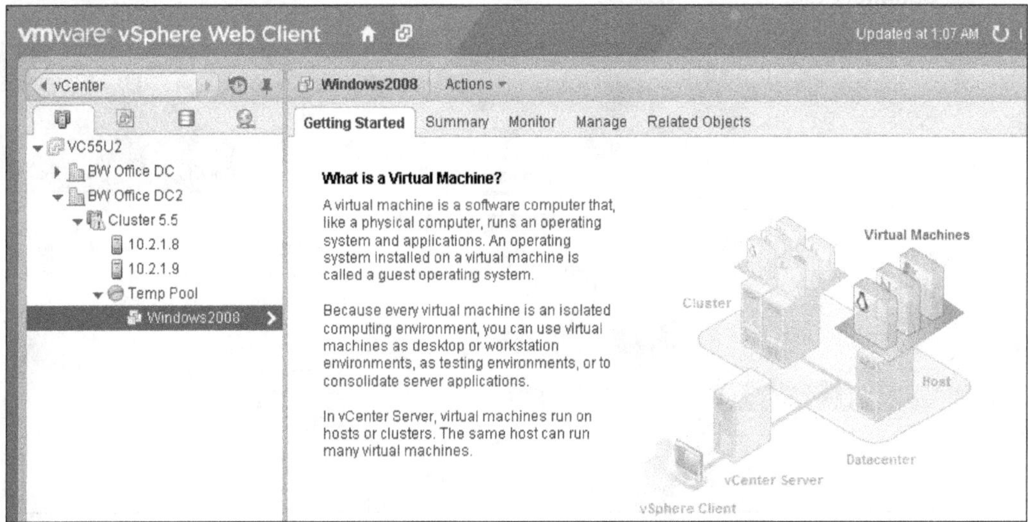

If you follow VMware best practice, it is recommended to stop all application services on the source machine during P2V conversion. The P2V conversion time is dependent on the capacity of the system on the source machine.

How it works...

In this recipe, we will learn how to verify that the virtual machine is healthy on the ESXi host after the P2V conversion.

1. Power on the Windows2008 virtual machine and select **Launch Console** on the **Summary** tab:

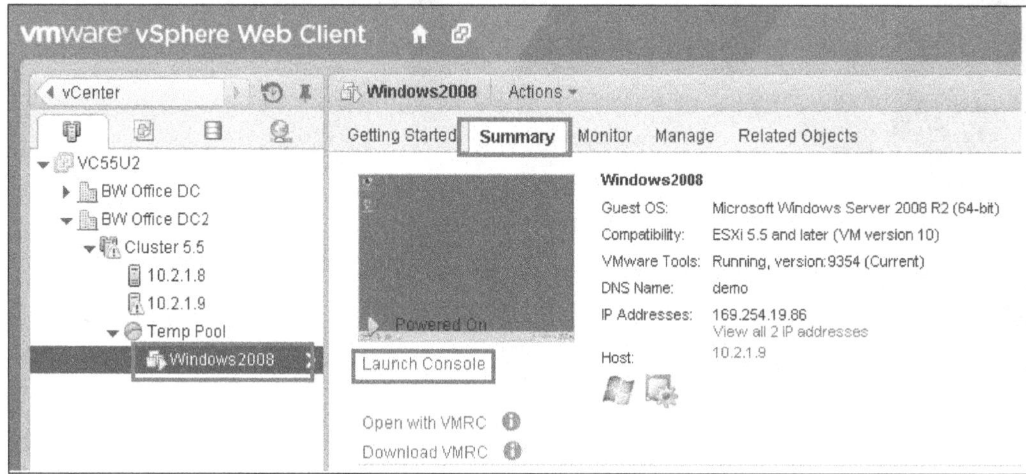

2. Log in to the virtual machine, Windows 2008, and go to the Windows **Control Panel**, and uninstall the **HP driver** and **HP monitor tools**. Then, install VMware Tools and reboot the virtual machine after the VMware Tools installation. Right-click the virtual machine and select **All vCenter Actions** and choose **Install VMware Tools** on the **Guest OS** menu:

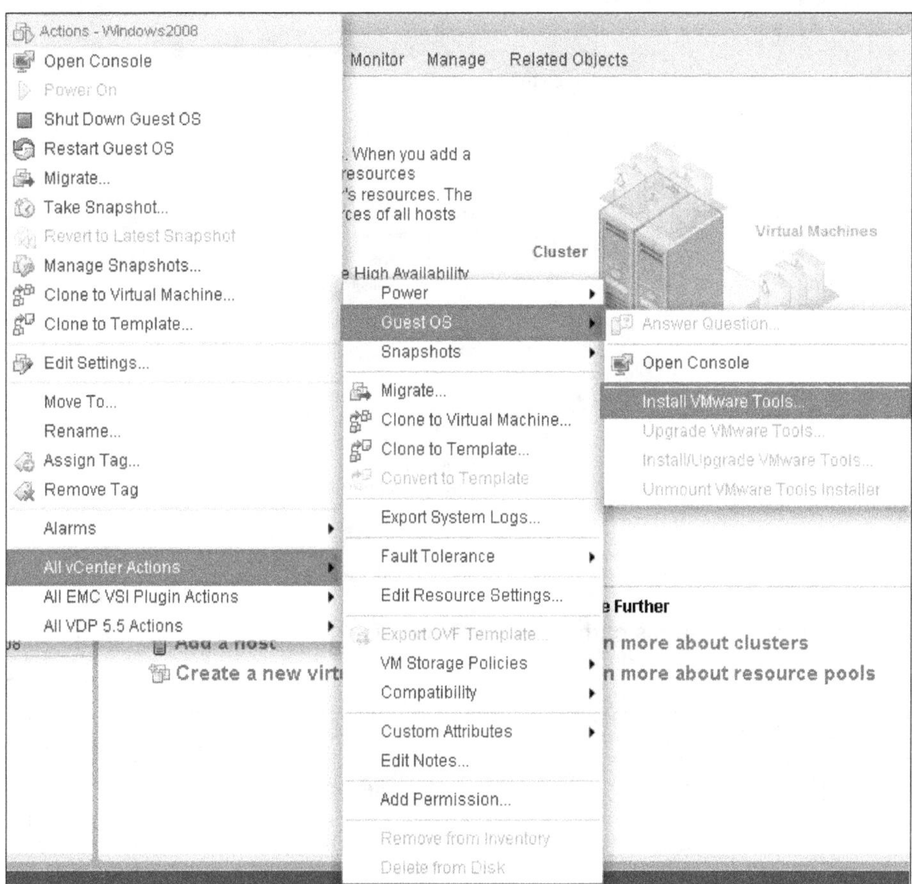

3. After rebooting the virtual machine, you should see all of the virtual device drivers installed on this virtual machine by **Server Manager**:

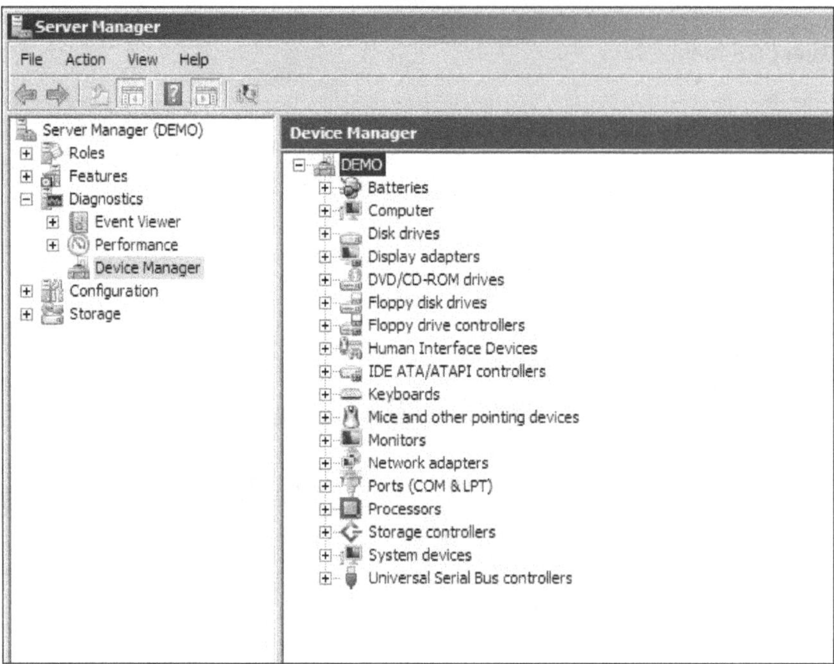

4. You can see the status of the **VMware Tools** display running on the **Summary** tab, as shown:

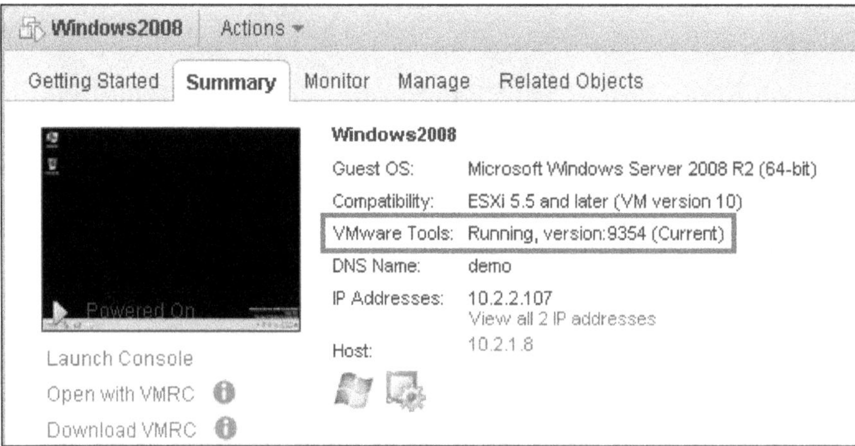

There's more...

If the customer cannot schedule a long downtime for P2V conversion, you can use the VMware incremental synchronization feature for P2V conversion. It minimizes service downtime for P2V conversion. You can enable this feature with **Advanced options** while creating a P2V session.

The following is the procedure to enable the incremental synchronization feature:

1. Choose **Edit** on **Advanced options** while creating the P2V session:

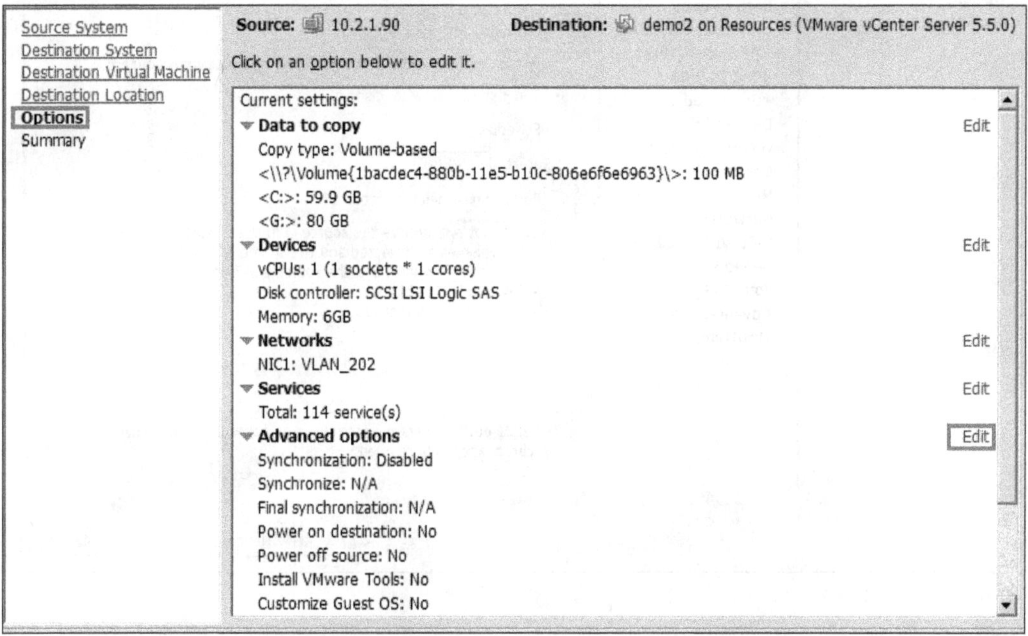

2. Check the **Synchronize changes** checkbox but do not check **Perform final synchronization**:

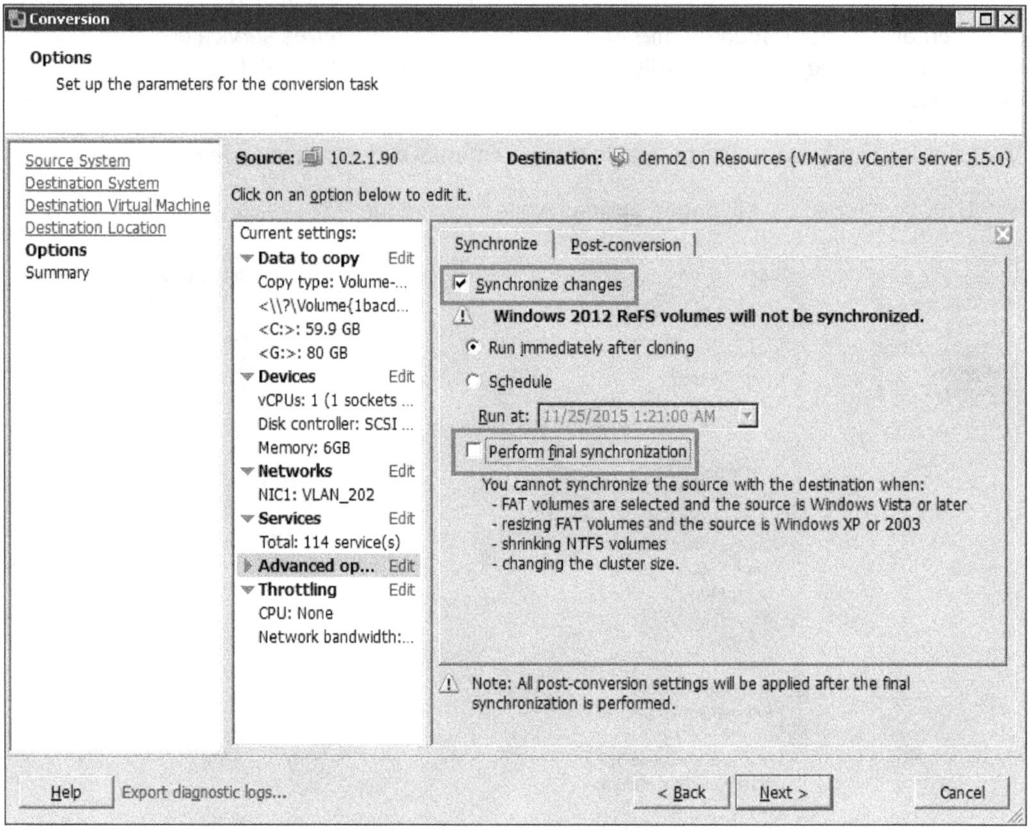

Synchronizing changes between the source and the destination virtual machine is only supported on the Windows platform; Linux is not supported.

See also

If the source machine is the rackmount Server, the table below gives a typical configuration for this Server. You can also migrate the virtual machine to Cisco UCS by using the same procedures:

HP Proliant DL380e Gen8	FC Interface	Network Interface
▸ 8 GB FC 2 ports HBA x 2 ▸ 1 GB 4 ports Ethernet Adapter x 1 ▸ Intel(R) Xeon(R) CPU E5-2640 x 2 ▸ 64 GB Memory	8 GB HBA Adapter x 2	1 GB Ethernet Adapter x 1
System Platform	**Number of NIC**	**Number of HBA**
Microsoft Windows 2008 R2	4 x NIC	2 x HBA

Migrating the MSCS 2008 virtual machine to Cisco UCS

In this recipe, we will learn how to migrate the Microsoft Clustering 2008 virtual machine from the HP Proliant Server to Cisco UCS.

Getting ready

There are two ESXi 5.5 hosts running on a HP DL380e Gen8 that has two 8 GB FC dual port bus host adapters and a 1 x 1 GB qual ports Ethernet adapter. Both source machines are connected to one EMC CX4-240 SAN Storage through SAN Switches and one shared EMC LUN is assigned to these two ESXi hosts. There are two Microsoft Windows 2008 Clustering virtual machines (Cluster-Node1 and Cluster-Node2) and both are running on both ESXi hosts. For data migration, prepare one Cisco UCS 5108 Chassis with two UCS IOM 2208XPs installed, each UCS IOM being connected to one Cisco UCS 6428UP. There is one UCS B200 M3 with one VIC 1240 installed on this chassis. Configure four ports on each Cisco UCS 6428UP as an Ethernet uplink port (port 17/18) and an FC uplink port (port 6/7), connected to SAN Switches and LAN Switches with Fibre Channel cables. EMC SAN Storage has two controllers and each controller has two FC ports that are connected to each SAN Switches. Prepare two UCS service profiles (ESXi 5.5A/ESXi 5.5B), which include four vNICs and two vHBAs and associated into each UCS B200 M3. VMware ESXi 5.5 is already installed on each UCS (local boot) and should boot up successfully. The UCS is the target ESXi host.

The following table gives a summary of the hardware and software specification for the source ESXi host and the target ESXi host.

HP Proliant DL380e Gen8	**FC Interface**	**Network Interface**
▸ 8 GB FC 2 ports HBA x 2 ▸ 1 GB 4 ports Ethernet Adapter x 1 ▸ Intel(R) Xeon(R) CPU E5-2640 x 2 ▸ 64 GB Memory	8 GB HBA Adapter x 2	1 GB Ethernet Adapter x 1
System Platform	**Number of vmnic/ vSwitch/PortGroup**	**Number of vHBA/ Datastore**
VMware ESXi 5.5 IP address: 10.2.1.6	▸ 4 x vmnic ▸ vSwitch0 (vmnic0, vmnic2) ▸ PortGroup1 ▸ vSwitch1 (vmnic1, vmnic3) ▸ PortGroup1 (VLAN 10)	2 x vHBA EMC_DS1 (DataStore)
Virtual Machine	**Number of VMDK**	**Number of RDM**
Cluster-Node1	1 x VMDK (system drive)	1 x RDM (cluster quorum) 1 x RDM (cluster shared drive)

Source: ESXi host A

HP Proliant DL380e Gen8	FC Interface	Network Interface
▸ 8 GB FC 2 ports HBA x 2 ▸ 1 GB 4 ports Ethernet Adapter x 1 ▸ Intel(R) Xeon(R) CPU E5-2640 x 2 ▸ 64 GB Memory	8 GB HBA Adapter x 2	1 GB Ethernet Adapter x 1
System Platform	**Number of vmnic/ vSwitch/PortGroup**	**Number of vHBA/ Datastore**
VMware ESXi 5.5 IP address: 10.2.1.7	▸ 4 x vmnic ▸ vSwitch0 (vmnic0, vmnic2) ▸ PortGroup1 ▸ vSwitch1 (vmnic1, vmnic3) ▸ PortGroup1 (VLAN 10)	2 x vHBA EMC_DS1 (Datastore)
Virtual Machine	**Number of VMDK**	**Number of RDM**
Cluster-Node2	1 x VMDK (system drive)	1 x RDM (cluster quorum) 1 x RDM (cluster shared drive)

Source ESXi host B

Cisco 5108 Chassis	FC Interface	Network Interface
UCS B200 M3 x 1 installed with ▸ Cisco VIC 1240 x 1 ▸ Intel(R) Xeon(R) CPU E5-2640 x 2 ▸ 64 GB Memory	Fabric Interconnect 6248UP x 2	Fabric Interconnect 6248UP x 2

Cisco 5108 Chassis	FC Interface	Network Interface
System Platform	**Number of vmnic/vSwitch/ PortGroup**	**Number of vHBA/ Datastore/RDM**
VMware ESXi 5.5 IP address: 10.2.1.8	▸ 4 x vmnic ▸ vSwitch0 (vmnic0, vmnic2) ▸ PortGroup1 ▸ vSwitch1 (vmnic1, vmnic3) ▸ PortGroup1 (VLAN 10)	2 x vHBA EMC_DS1 (Datastore) 1 x RDM (cluster quorum) 1 x RDM (cluster shared drive)

Target ESXi host A

Cisco 5108 Chassis	FC Interface	Network Interface
UCS B200 M3 x 1 installed with ▸ Cisco VIC 1240 x 1 ▸ Intel(R) Xeon(R) CPU E5-2640 x 2 ▸ 64 GB Memory	Fabric Interconnect 6248UP x 2	Fabric Interconnect 6248UP x 2
System Platform	**Number of vmnic/vSwitch/ PortGroup**	**Number of vHBA/ Datastore/RDM**
VMware ESXi 5.5 IP address: 10.2.1.9	▸ 4 x vmnic ▸ vSwitch0 (vmnic0, vmnic2) ▸ PortGroup1 ▸ vSwitch1 (vmnic1, vmnic3) ▸ PortGroup1 (VLAN 10)	2 x vHBA EMC_DS1 (Datastore) 1 x RDM (cluster quorum) 1 x RDM (cluster shared drive)

Target ESXi host B

The details are shown in the following diagram:

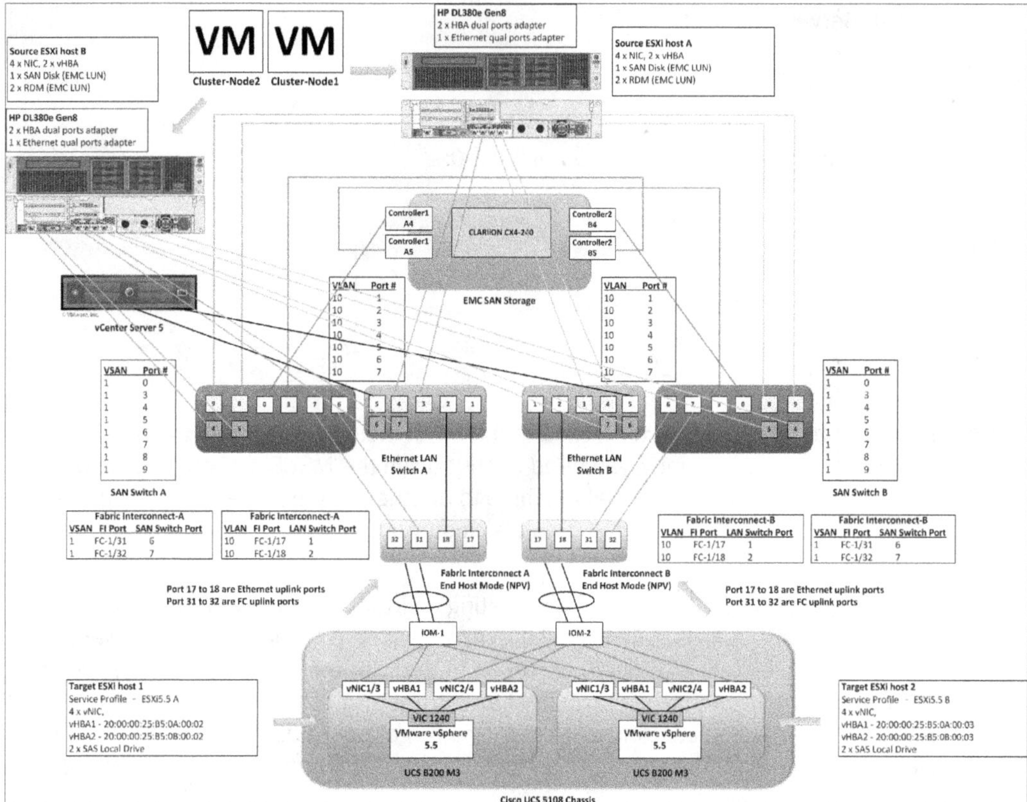

How to do it...

In this recipe, we will learn how to prepare for the migration of the Microsoft Clustering 2008 virtual machine from the HP Proliant Server to Cisco UCS.

1. The two target ESXi hosts should already be installed on UCS B200 M3 and will add these two ESXi hosts into one ESXi cluster group, which already has two ESXi members (the source ESXi host).
2. After adding these two ESXi hosts to the ESXi cluster group in the vSphere Web Client, there will now be four members in the ESXi cluster group (2 HP Server + 2 Cisco UCS). By following the preceding tables showing the configuration for the source ESXi host A and the ESXi host B, you can create the virtual Switch and ESXi datastore on each target ESXi host. Make sure that the target ESXi host vSwitch name, Port Group name and VLAN ID are the same as for the source ESXi host. Then, share all of the datastore and RDM from the source ESXi host to each target ESXi host.

3. After finishing the configuration on each target ESXi host, you can use the VMware Storage vMotion feature to migrate the Microsoft MSCS 2008 virtual machine from the HP Server to Cisco UCS:

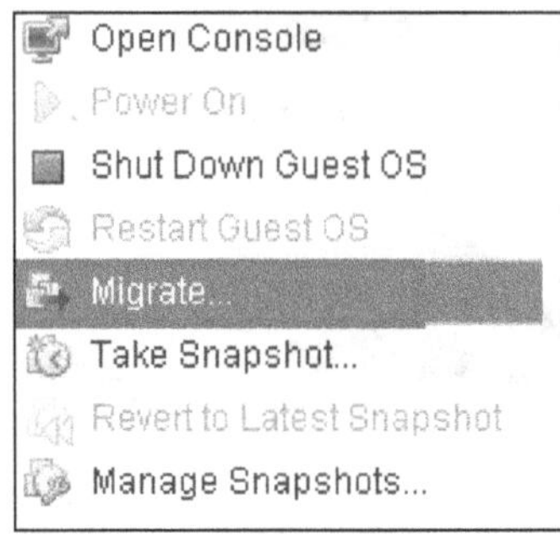

4. If the virtual machine **Cluster-Node1** is the MSCS active node, **Cluster-Node2** is the MSCS standby node. Firstly, you need to shut down the MSCS standby node, so that then you can migrate this virtual machine to another ESXi host because each MSCS node virtual machine has two RDMs, it is cluster quorum and cluster shared drive in MSCS.
5. According to VMware best practice, migrating a virtual machine with RDM can be performed in three ways. One is cold migration, with the virtual machine powered off. When you migrate MSCS standby node in the vSphere Web Client, choose **Select Migration Type** from **Change both host and datastore**. Select the destination resource in the default setting and select the target host **10.2.1.9**, select **Datastore** in the default settings and then click on **Finish**.
6. Since all of the ESXi datastores and RDMs from the source ESXi host are already shared to the target ESXi host, you can cold-migrate the virtual machine with RDM to another ESXi host.

   The following table gives a summary of MSCS migration:

Source ESXi host	**Virtual Machine**		**Target ESXi host**
10.2.1.6 (HP Server)	Cluster-Node1	**Migrate to**	10.2.1.8 (UCS B200 M3)
10.2.1.7 (HP Server)	Cluster-Node2		10.2.1.9 (UCS B200 M3)

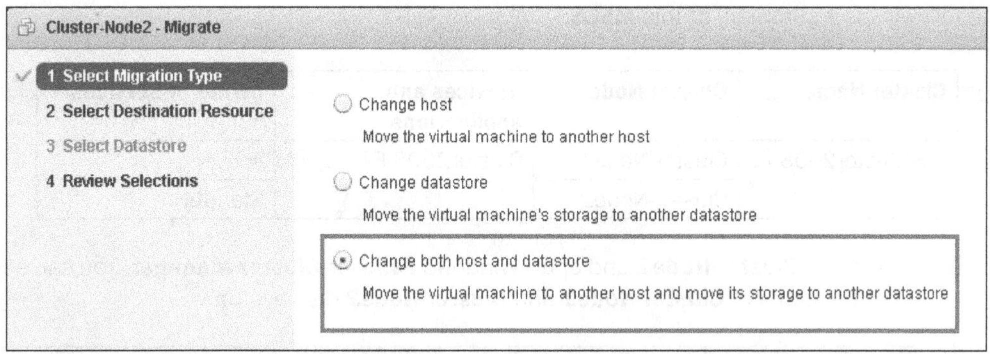

7. After finishing migrating **Cluster-Node2** to the target ESXi host **10.2.1.9**, you can power on this virtual machine, then verify that the cluster service is active again in Windows **Failover Cluster Manager**. Change **Cluster-Node2** to active node and **Cluster-Node1** to standby node in Windows **Failover Cluster Manager** and then shut down the **Cluster-Node1** virtual machine.
8. Follow Step 3 again to migrate **Cluster-Node1** to another target ESXi host **10.2.1.8** by using VMware Storage vMotion. After finishing the process of Storage vMotion on **Cluster-Node1**, power it on and verify that the cluster service in Windows **Failover Cluster Manager** is working again. Finally, both **Cluster-Node1** and **Cluster-Node2** virtual machines can migrate to UCS B200 M3.

For more on the VMware virtual machine with RDM migration, you can reference this knowledge base: `http://kb.vmware.com/kb/1005241`.

How it works...

In this recipe, we will learn how to verify that the MSCS virtual machine is healthy and passes the failover test after the migration.

It should have the configured file Server service Cluster2008-FS in MSCS.

The following is a summary of this MSCS:

Cluster Name	Cluster Node	Services and applications	Owner of Services
MS-Cluster2008	Cluster-Node1	Cluster2008-FS	Active
	Cluster-Node2		Standby

1. Log in into **Cluster-Node1** and open Windows **Failover Cluster Manager**. You can see that the status of **Cluster-Node1** and **Cluster-Node2** displays **Up**:

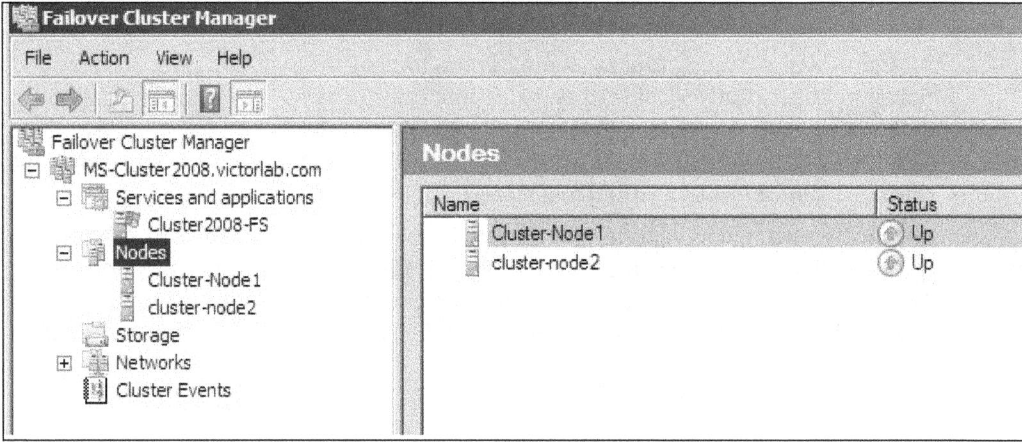

2. Select **Cluster2008-FS** in **Failover Cluster Manager** and you should see that the current owner of this service is **Cluster-Node1**:

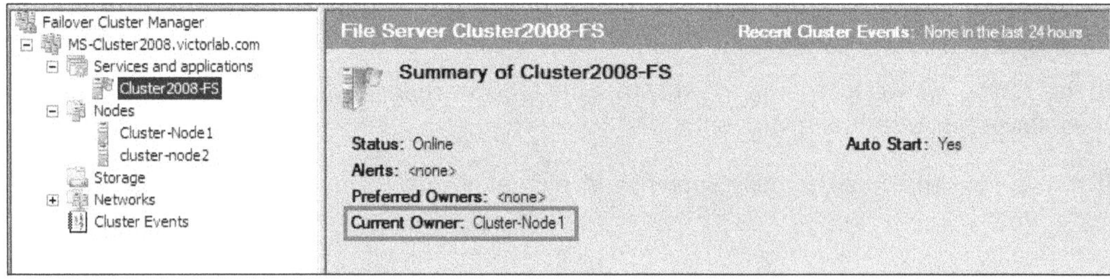

3. Right-click **Cluster2008-FS** and choose **Move this service or application to another node** | **1 - Move to the node cluster-node2**:

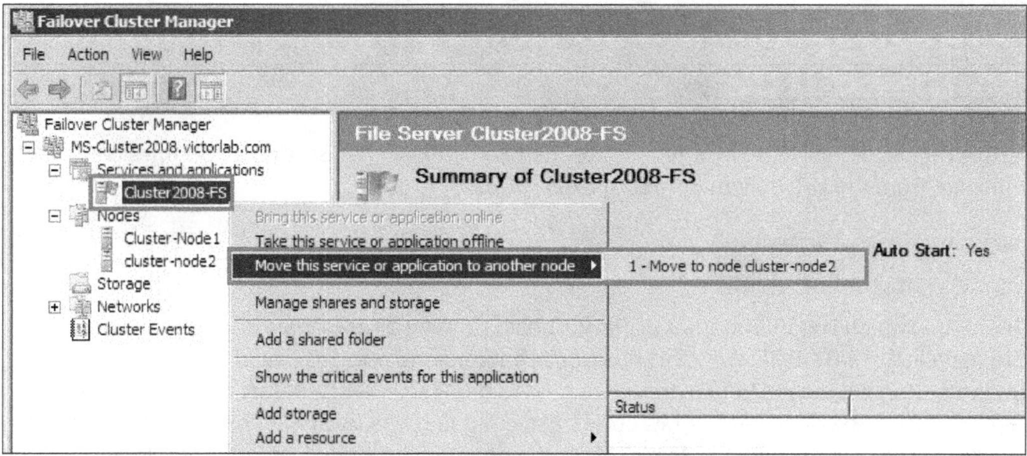

4. After that, you should see that the current owner of **Cluster2008-FS** has been changed to **cluster-node2**. The MSCS failover has been completed successfully:

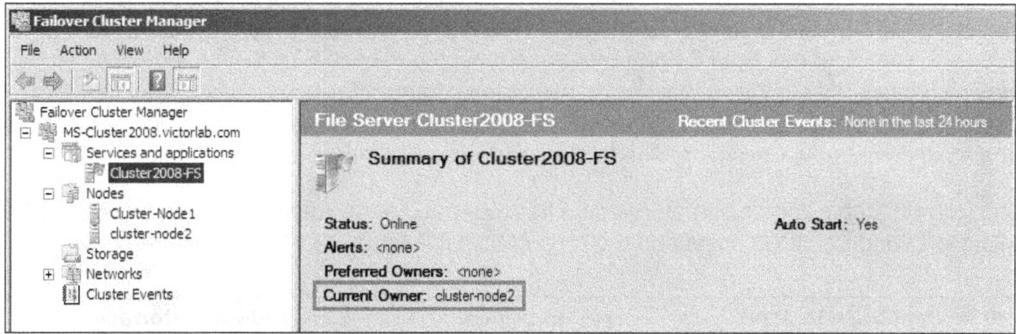

There's more...

The preceding scenario was focused on Server migration, it didn't include SAN migration. According to the preceding scenario, all ESXi datastores and RDMs keep the same configuration and just share it to a new ESXi host (Cisco UCS). If you also plan to migrate VMDK and RMD into other ESXi datastores or a new RDM, for VMDK migration, you can also migrate all VMDK into the new ESXi datastore with VMware Storage vMotion. RDM migration cannot be performed by VMware Storage vMotion. You can migrate a physical or virutal RDM to one new RDM by using VMware `vmkfstools`; you can find the details at: `http://kb.vmware.com/kb/3443266/`.

Migrating the MSCS 2008 physical machine to Cisco UCS

In this recipe, we will learn how to migrate the Microsoft Cluster Service 2008 physical machine from the HP Proliant Server to Cisco UCS.

Getting ready

There are two Microsoft Windows 2008 R2 hosts running on HP DL380e Gen8, on which are installed two 8 GB FC dual port bus host adapters and one 1 GB qual ports Ethernet adapter. Both source machines are connected to one EMC CX4-240 SAN Storage through SAN Switches and one shared EMC LUN is assigned to these two ESXi hosts. Windows 2008 R2 is running on two nodes for Microsoft Clustering (Cluster-Node1 and Cluster-Node2). For data migration, prepare one Cisco UCS 5108 Chassis with two UCS IOM 2208XP installed, each UCS IOM being connected to one Cisco UCS 6428UP. There is one UCS B200 M3 with one VIC 1240 installed on this chassis. Configure four ports on each Cisco UCS 6428UP as an Ethernet uplink port (port 17/18) and an FC uplink port (port 6/7), connected to SAN Switches and LAN Switches with Fibre Channel cables. EMC SAN Storage has two controllers and each controller has two FC ports that are connected to each SAN Switch. Prepare two UCS service profiles (`ESXi 5.5A/ESXi 5.5B`), including four vNICs, two vHBAs associated into each UCS B200 M3. Microsoft Windows 2008 R2 is already installed on each UCS (local boot) and should boot up successfully. The UCS is the target ESXi host.

The following table gives a summary of the hardware and software specification for the source Microsoft Windows 2008 hosts and the target Microsoft Windows 2008 host.

HP Proliant DL380e Gen8	**FC Interface**	**Network Interface**
▸ 8 GB FC 2 ports HBA x 2 ▸ 1 GB 4 ports Ethernet Adapter x 1 ▸ Intel(R) Xeon(R) CPU E5-2640 x 2 ▸ 64 GB Memory	8 GB HBA Adapter x 2	1 GB Ethernet Adapter x 1
System Platform	**Number of NIC/Network adapter Name**	**Number of HBA/EMC LUN**
Microsoft Windows 2008 R2 Ent SP1 Node IP address: 10.2.2.101 Heat Bit IP address: 192.168.1.20 Cluster IP address: 10.2.2.100	4 x NIC Data_Network - NIC1 HB_Network - NIC2	2 x HBA 1 x quorum (EMC LUN) 1 x FS_LUN (EMC LUN)

Windows Cluster Name	Services and Applications	Cluster Node
MS-Cluster2008	Cluster2008-FS Service IP address: 10.2.2.105	Cluster-Node1

Source: Microsoft Windows 2008 R2 A

HP Proliant DL380e Gen8	FC Interface	Network Interface
8 GB FC 2 ports HBA x 2 1 GB 4 ports Ethernet Adapter x 1 Intel(R) Xeon(R) CPU E5-2640 x 2 64 GB Memory	8 GB HBA Adapter x 2	1 GB Ethernet Adapter x 1
System Platform	**Number of NIC/Network adapter Name**	**Number of HBA/EMC LUN**
▸ Microsoft Windows 2008 R2 Ent SP1 ▸ Node IP address: 10.2.2.103 ▸ Heat Bit IP address: 192.168.1.21 ▸ Cluster IP address: 10.2.2.100	4 x NIC Data_Network - NIC1 HB_Network - NIC2	2 x HBA 1 x quorum (EMC LUN) 1 x FS_LUN (EMC LUN)
Windows Cluster Name	**Services and Applications**	**Cluster Node**
MS-Cluster2008	Cluster2008-FS Service IP address: 10.2.2.105	Cluster-Node2

Source Microsoft Windows 2008 R2 B

Cisco 5108 Chassis	FC Interface	Network Interface
UCS B200 M3 x 1 installed with ▸ Cisco VIC 1240 x 1 ▸ Intel(R) Xeon(R) CPU E5-2640 x 2 ▸ 64 GB Memory	Fabric Interconnect 6248UP x 2	Fabric Interconnect 6248UP x 2

Cisco 5108 Chassis	**FC Interface**	**Network Interface**
System Platform	**Number of NIC/Network adapter Name**	**Number of HBA/EMC LUN**
Microsoft Windows 2008 R2 Ent SP1 Node IP address: 10.2.2.106 Heat Bit IP address: 192.168.1.22 Cluster IP address: 10.2.2.100	2 x NIC Data_Network - NIC1 HB_Network - NIC2	2 x HBA 1 x quorum (EMC LUN) 1 x FS_LUN (EMC LUN)
Windows Cluster Name	**Services and Applications**	**Cluster Node**
MS-Cluster2008	Cluster2008-FS Service IP address: 10.2.2.105	Cluster-Node3

Target Microsoft Windows 2008 R2 A

Cisco 5108 Chassis	**FC Interface**	**Network Interface**
UCS B200 M3 x 1 installed with ▸ Cisco VIC 1240 x 1 ▸ Intel(R) Xeon(R) CPU E5-2640 x 2 ▸ 64 GB Memory	Fabric Interconnect 6248UP x 2	Fabric Interconnect 6248UP x 2
System Platform	**Number of NIC/Network adapter Name**	**Number of HBA/EMC LUN**
Microsoft Windows 2008 R2 Ent SP1 Node IP address: 10.2.2.107 Heat Bit IP address: 192.168.1.23 Cluster IP address: 10.2.2.100	2 x NIC Data_Network - NIC1 HB_Network - NIC2	2 x HBA 1 x quorum (EMC LUN) 1 x FS_LUN (EMC LUN)
Windows Cluster Name	**Services and Applications**	**Cluster Node**
MS-Cluster2008	Cluster2008-FS Service IP address: 10.2.2.105	Cluster-Node4

Target Microsoft Windows 2008 R2 B

The details are shown in the following diagram:

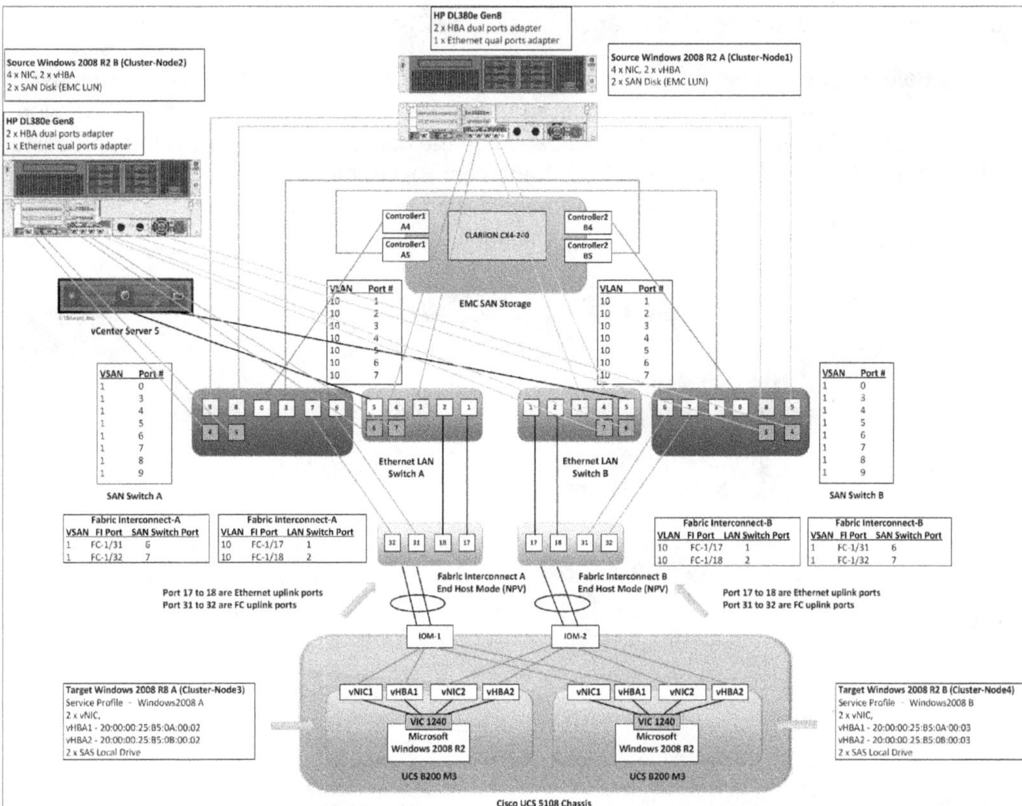

How to do it...

In this recipe, we will learn how to prepare for the migration of the Microsoft Clustering 2008 physical machine from the HP Proliant Server to Cisco UCS.

The two target Microsoft Windows 2008 hosts are already installed on both UCS B200 M3 and we will add these two Microsoft Windows 2008 hosts onto two nodes from Microsoft Cluster Service 2008 (Cluster-Node1 and Cluster-Node2).

1. Before adding these two target Windows 2008 hosts to two nodes MSCS, you must manually enable the **Failover Clustering** feature in **Server Manager** on each version of the target Windows 2008. And, based on the configuration shown in the preceding tables (target Windows 2008 host A and host B), create the cluster data network and the heartbeat network, share the quorum and cluster, and share the disk of the source Windows host to each target Windows host:

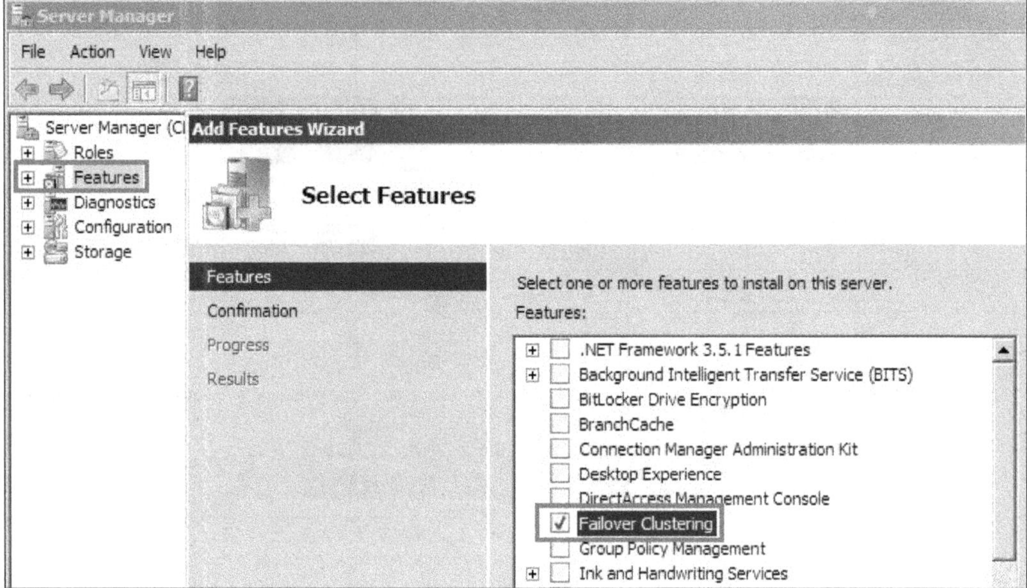

2. After performing the preceding step, you can add these two Windows 2008 hosts into the two nodes MSCS 2008 **MS-Cluster2008** in **Failover Cluster Manager**, so that it becomes four nodes MSCS 2008 (two HP Servers and two Cisco UCS). Now you can start to migrate the cluster services and the application **Cluster2008-FS** to the target Windows 2008 host (Cisco UCS B200):

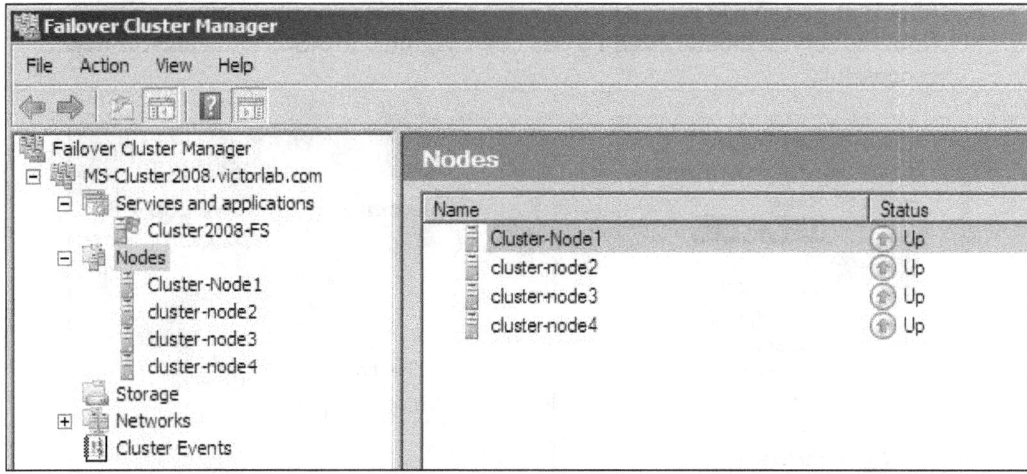

3. Go to **Services and applications** and you can see that the current owner of **Cluster2008-FS** is **Cluster-Node1**:

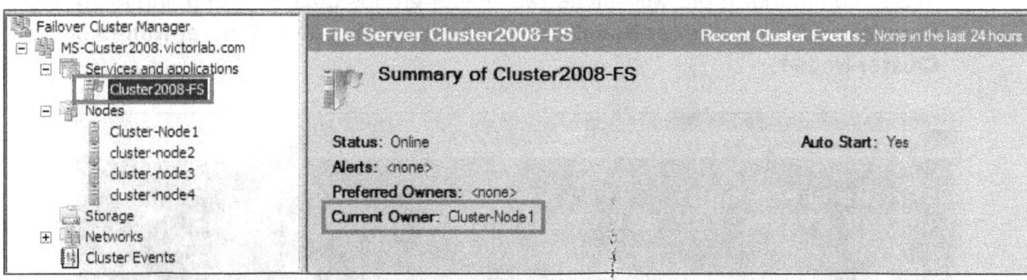

4. Right-click on **Cluster2008-FS** and select **Move this service or application to another node** | **3 - Move to node cluster-node3**:

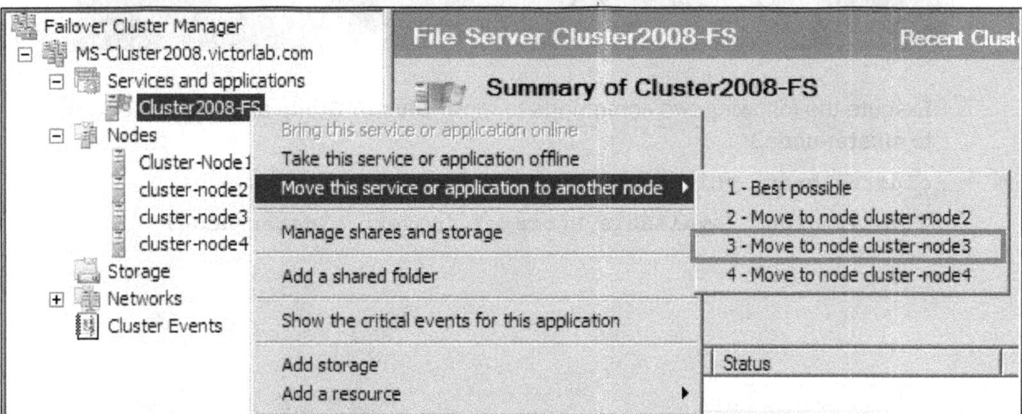

5. After that, you should see that the current owner has changed to **cluster-node3**. Now, the service **Cluster2008-FS** has been migrated to MSCS node **cluster-node3** successfully:

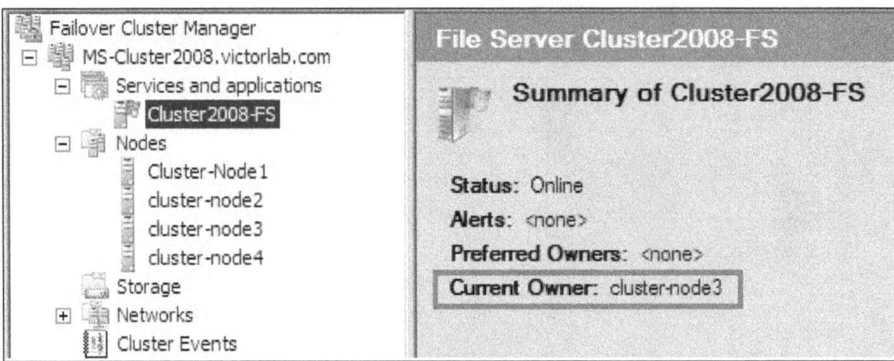

6. There is still one quorum disk that needs to migrate to the target Windows 2008, but you can check on the current owner of all the cluster groups by using the `cluster group` command. There will still be two cluster groups **Cluster Group** and **Available Storage** running in **Cluster-Node1**, which you must migrate to **Cluster-Node3** or **Cluster-Node4**:

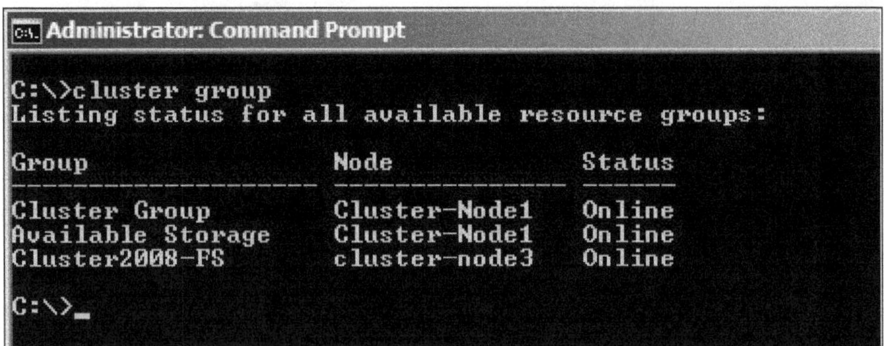

7. Execute the following two commands to move **Cluster Group** and **Available Storage** to **cluster-node3**:

```
cluster group "Cluster Group" /moveto:cluster-node3
cluster group "Available Storage" /moveto:cluster-node3
```

```
Administrator: Command Prompt

C:\>cluster group
Listing status for all available resource groups:

Group                 Node            Status
--------------------  --------------  ------
Cluster Group         Cluster-Node1   Online
Available Storage     Cluster-Node1   Online
Cluster2008-FS        cluster-node3   Online

C:\>cluster group "Cluster Group" /moveto:cluster-node3

Moving resource group 'Cluster Group'...

Group                 Node            Status
--------------------  --------------  ------
Cluster Group         cluster-node3   Online


C:\>
```

8. After executing these commands, you can see all of the cluster groups change to **cluster-node3**. Now, all of the cluster services have migrated to UCS successfully:

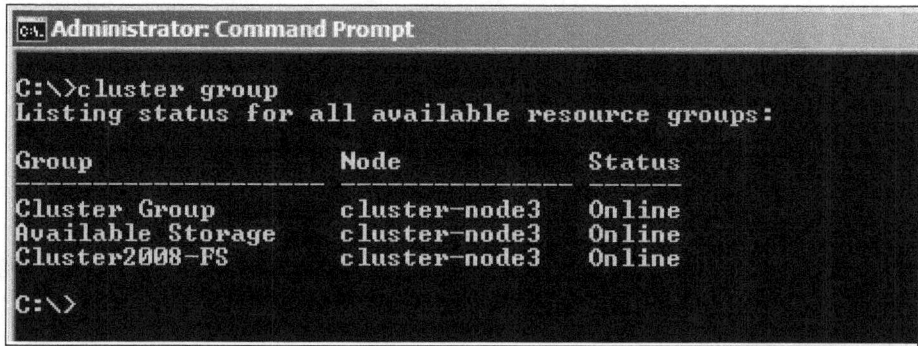

```
Administrator: Command Prompt

C:\>cluster group
Listing status for all available resource groups:

Group                 Node            Status
--------------------  --------------  ------
Cluster Group         cluster-node3   Online
Available Storage     cluster-node3   Online
Cluster2008-FS        cluster-node3   Online

C:\>
```

How it works...

In this recipe, we will learn how to verify that the MSCS virtual machine is healthy and that it passes the failover test after the migration.

The following shows a summary of this MSCS:

Cluster Name	Cluster Node	Services and applications	Owner of Services
MS-Cluster2008	Cluster-Node1	Cluster2008-FS	Standby
	Cluster-Node2		Standby
	Cluster-Node3		Active
	Cluster-Node4		Standby

1. Select **Cluster2008-FS** in **Failover Cluster Manager**, and you should see that the current owner of this service is **cluster-node3**:

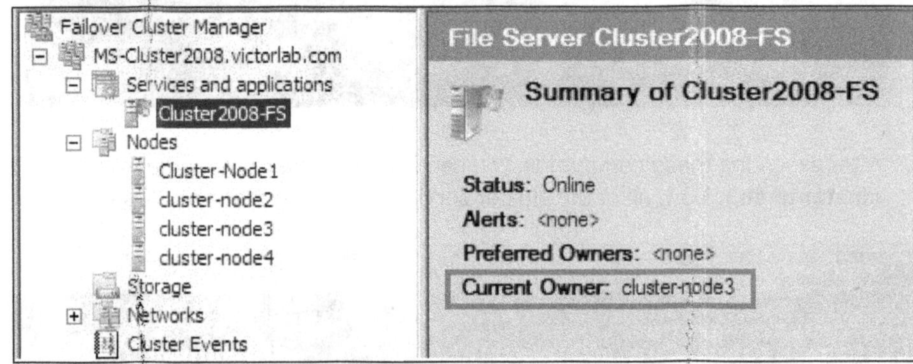

2. Right-click **Cluster2008-FS** and choose **Move this service or application to another node** | **4 - Move to node cluster-node4**:

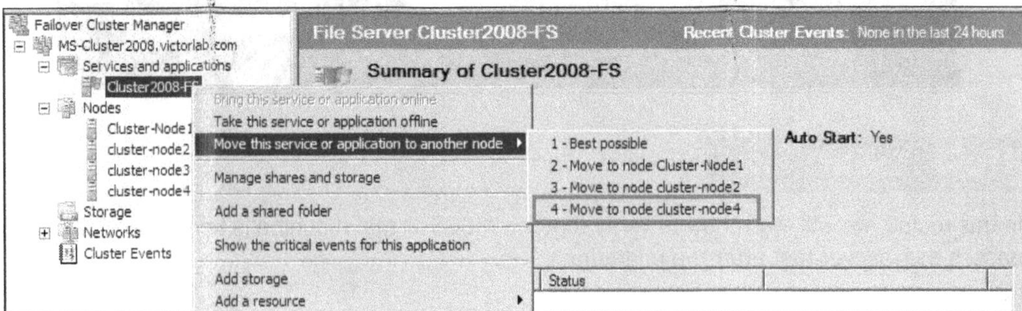

3. After that, you should see that the current owner of **Cluster2008-FS** has been changed to **cluster-node4**. The MSCS failover has been completed successfully:

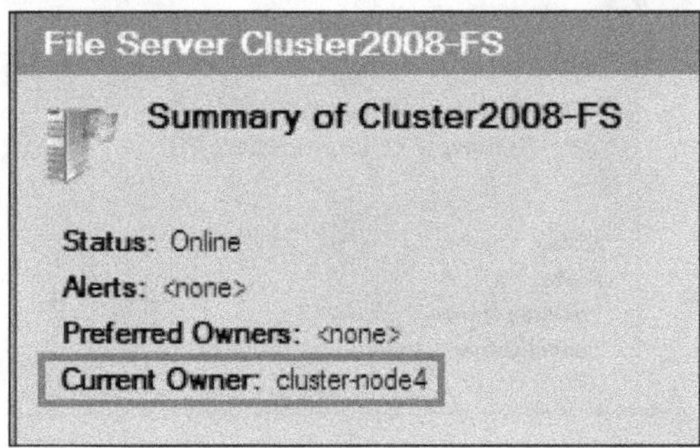

4. Finally, you need to remove the two source Windows 2008 R2 (**Cluster-Node1** and **Cluster-Node2**) from MSCS 2008. Right-click on **Cluster-node1** and select **Stop Cluster Service** then click on **Evict**:

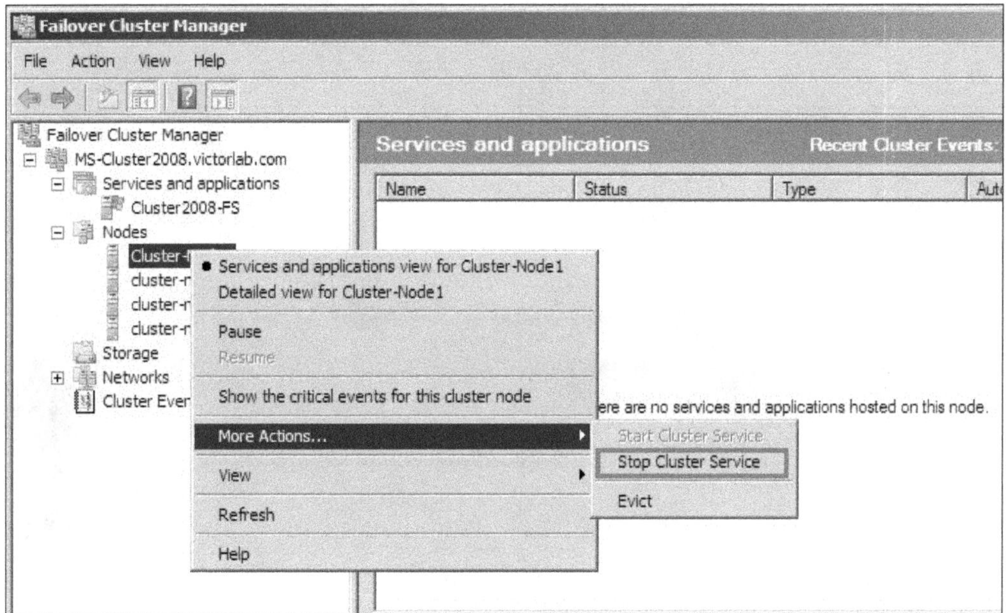

5. Repeat Step 4 to remove **Cluster-Node2** from MSCS 2008. Finally, you should see two nodes MSCS 2008. The cluster service **Cluster2008-FS** is running on **cluster-node3** and **cluster-node4**:

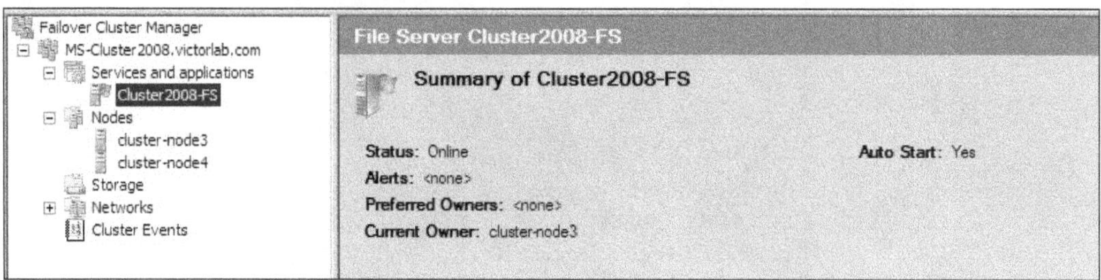

5
System Integration on Cisco UCS

In this chapter, we will cover the following topics:

- Installation and configuration of the UCS Management Pack in VMware vROps
- Installation and configuration of Cisco UCS Central
- Installation and configuration of Cisco UCS Central in Cluster mode
- Installation and configuration of EMC Storage Integrator
- Installation and configuration of EMC Connectrix Manager
- Installation and configuration of Cisco VM-FEX
- Installation and configuration of VMware VSAN into Cisco UCS

Introduction

In this chapter, you will learn how to accomplish tasks related to system integration on Cisco UCS, how to configure the UCS Management Pack in VMware vRealize Operation Manager, Cisco UCS Central in Standalone mode and Cluster mode, and Cisco VM-FEX and VMware VSAN in Cisco C-Series Server. You will also learn how to configure EMC management tools to integrate them into a Cisco UCS B-Series Server, such as the EMC Storage Integrator and EMC Connectrix Manager.

Installation and configuration of the UCS Management Pack in VMware vROps

In this recipe, we will learn how to install the Cisco UCS Manager Adapter for VMware vRealize Operations Manager 6.

Getting ready

The Cisco UCS Manager Adapter for VMware vRealize Operations Manager enables you to monitor the UCS domains on vRealize Operations Manager. The pack uses the XML API exposed by Cisco UCS Manager to collect the monitoring data from UCS domains. This enables you to monitor the health and faults of the various resources in the UCS domain and its impact on the virtual infrastructure that is running on it. Before you configure the Cisco UCS Manager adapter, assume that the VMware vRealize Operations Manager (Virtual Appliance) is already integrated into the VMware environment and there is one Cisco UCS domain (2 Fabric Interconnect 6248UP connected to one Cisco UCS 5108 chassis) is running on your environment. The details of infrastructure are shown in the following diagram:

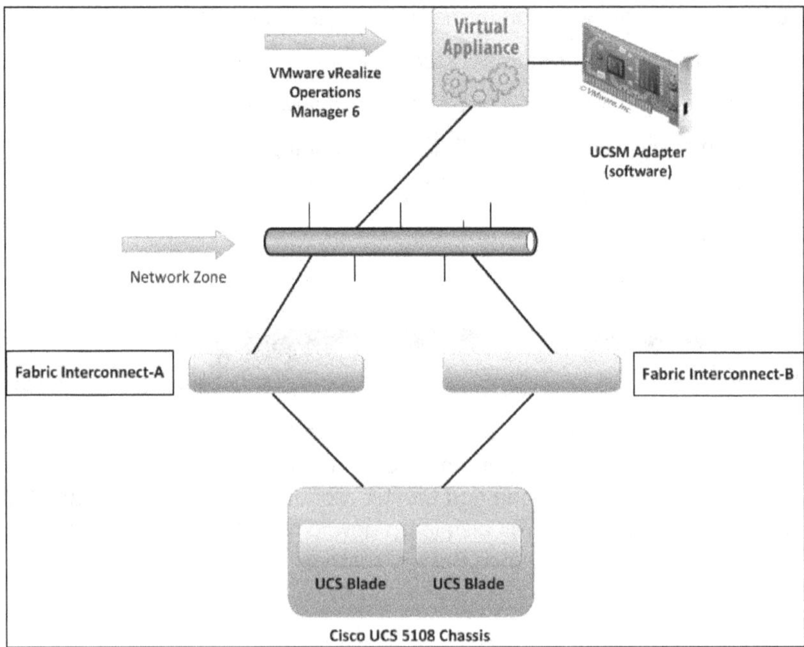

How to do it...

In this recipe, we will learn how to download and install the Cisco UCS Manager Adapter on VMware vRealize Operations Manager.

Follow these steps to download and install the Cisco UCSM Adapter on VMware vRealize Operations Manager:

1. Download the Cisco UCSM Adapter and navigate to `https://software.cisco.com/download/release.html?mdfid=286282669&flowid=72562&softwareid=286283872&release=1.1.1&relind=AVAILABLE&rellifecycle=&reltype=latest`. Log in to your **My Cisco** account and select **UCSMAdapter-1.1.1.pak**. The details are given in the following screenshot:

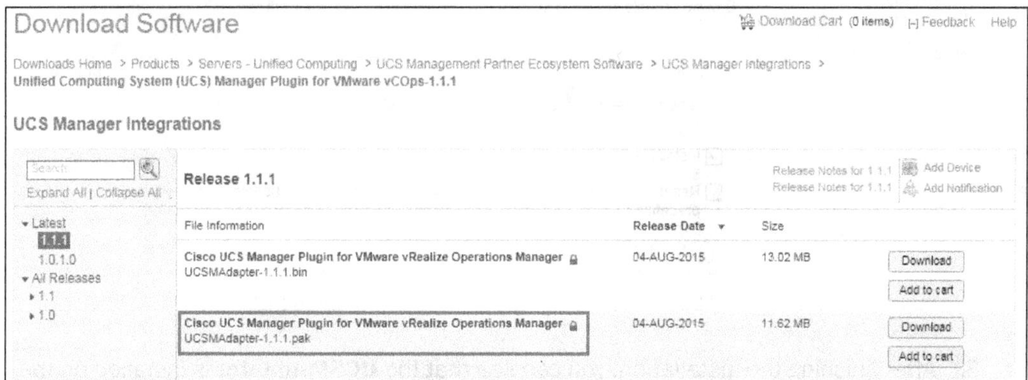

Note: Access to download UCSM Adapter is limited to Cisco users.

2. Open the Web browser and input the IP address of **VMware vRealize Operations Manager** (**vROps**). Log in as an administrator and then select **Administrator** and choose **Solutions**. You can see that it doesn't install any third party plugin on vROps; it has only installed two VMware plugins. Now, we start to install the Cisco UCSM Adapter on vROps:

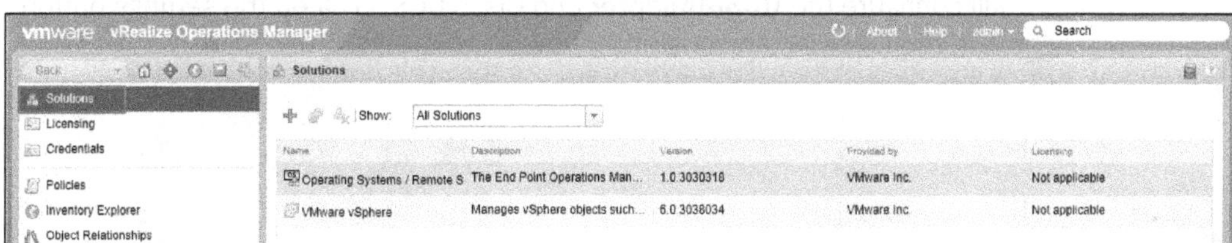

3. Then click on the **+** button to install the UCSM Adapter:

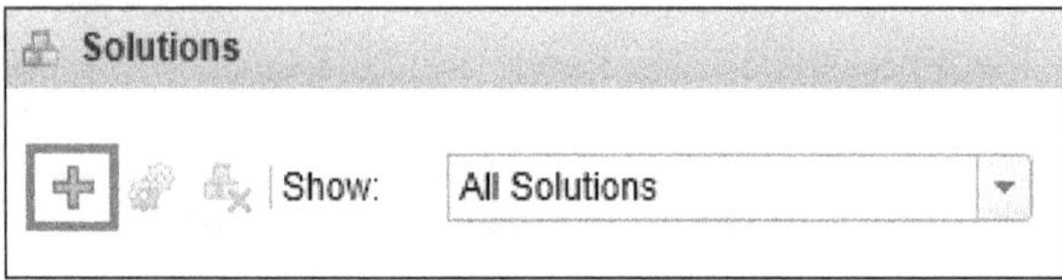

4. Browse to the **UCSMAdapter-1.1.1.pak** and click on the **Upload** button to upload it on vROps. Then click on **Next** to start the installation:

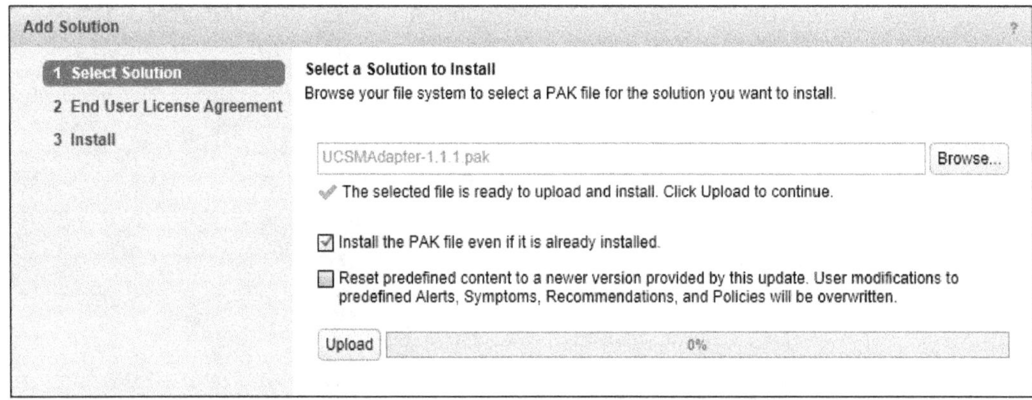

5. After finishing the installation, you can see that the **UCSMAdapter** is installed on the **Solutions** tab:

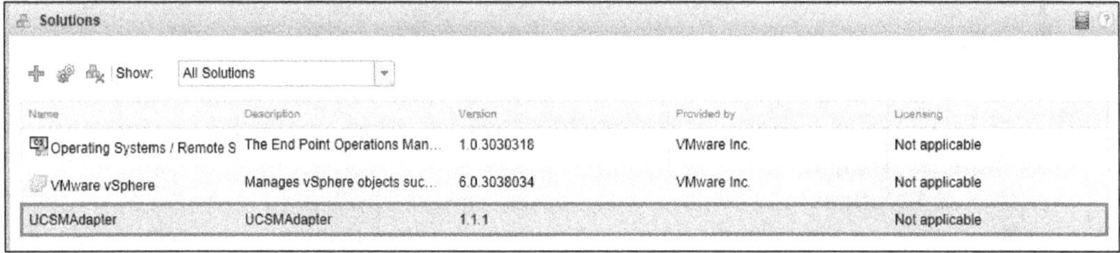

6. Now, we will configure the **UCSMAdapter** and Cisco UCS; click on the settings button highlighted in the following screenshot:

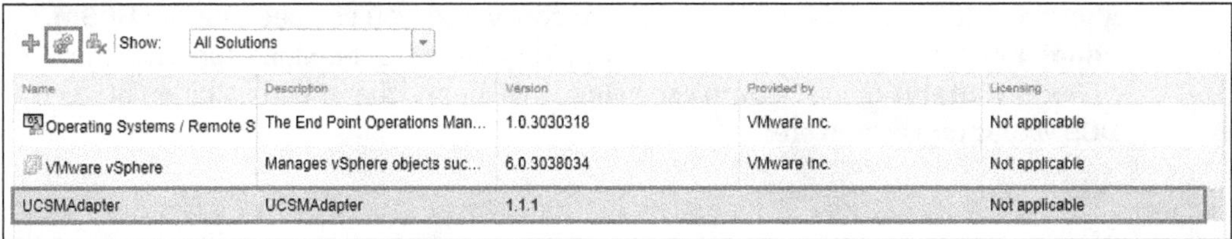

The Cisco UCSM Adapter is a free Management and Monitoring software.

7. Input the following information and then click on **Save Settings**:

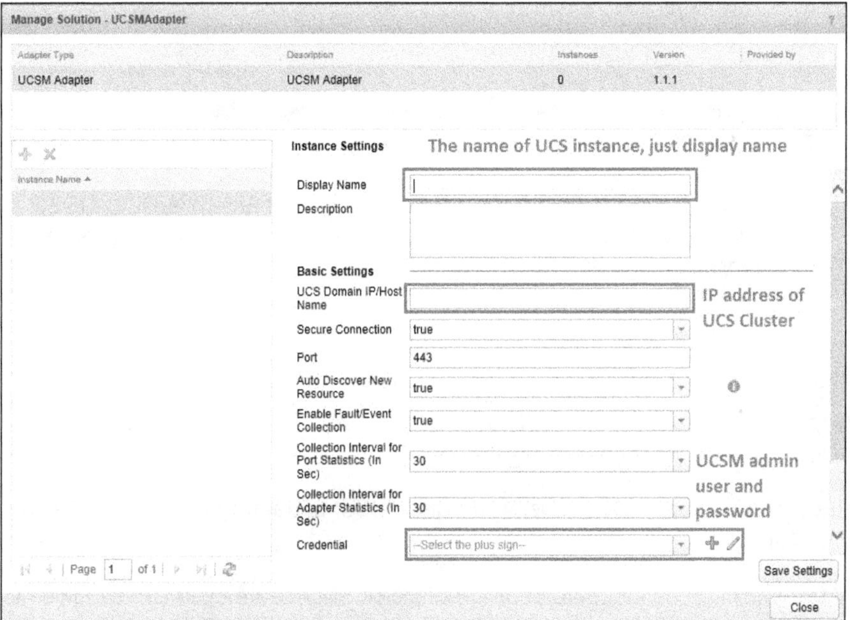

8. After the UCSMAdapter and Cisco UCS are configured, you can see that the **UCSM Adapter** instance starts to collect the data from Cisco UCSM. Make sure that the **Collection Status** displays **Data receiving**. This means that the installation of **UCSMAdapter** is complete:

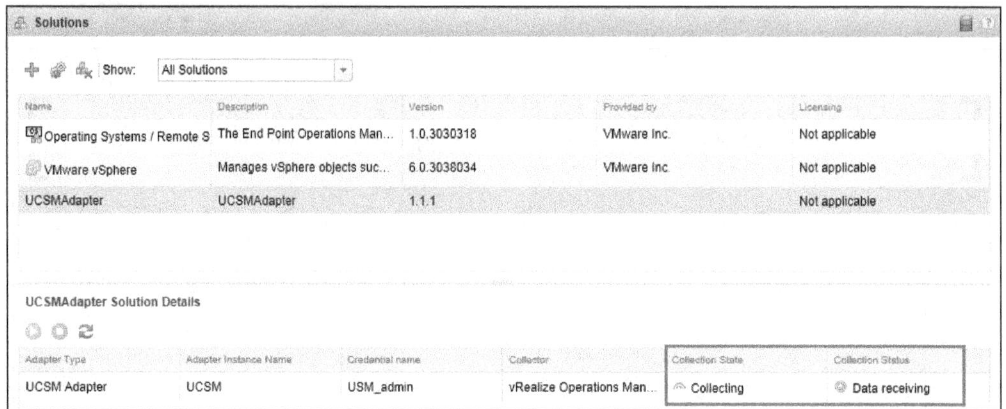

The license edition of vROps must be Advanced or Enterprise if it is to be extensible with third-party management packs for Infrastructure (Network, Storage, and Physical Servers).

How it works...

In this recipe, we will learn how to verify the status of the Cisco UCSM Adapter on VMware vRealize Operations Manager.

Follow these steps to verify the status of the Cisco UCSM Adapter on VMware vRealize Operations Manager:

1. After finishing the installation of the Cisco UCSM Adapter, you can see five new dashboards (**UCSM Dashboard**, **Fabric Interconnect Traffic Statistics**, **Server Traffic Statistics**, **UCS Server Motherboard Statistics**, and **UCS PSU and Fan Statistics**) in the **Dashboard List**:

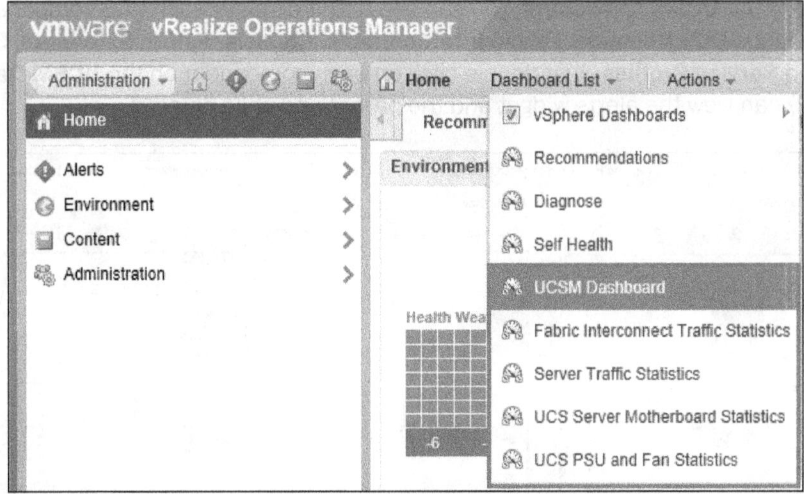

The following table lists the function description of each dashboard:

Dashboard Name	Description
UCSM Dashboard	The vRealize Operations Manager generates events based on the type of fault generated by the Cisco UCS Manager. These events are visible and can be viewed on the alerts widget on the UCSM Dashboard.
Fabric Interconnect Traffic Statistics	Displays Fabric Interconnect Traffic statistics
Server Traffic Statistics	Displays UCS Server Traffic statistics
UCS Server Motherboard Statistics	Displays UCS Server Motherboard statistics
UCS PSU and Fan Statistics	Displays UCS PSU and Fan statistics

2. Go to the **UCSM Dashboard**; you can see that it displays each UCS component, which includes **UCS Domains**, **Fabric Interconnects**, **Chassis**, **Fabric Extenders**, **Servers**, and **Service Profiles**. Just double-click on each component on the **UCSM Dashboard**. You can view the alerts widget and the parent and child objects:

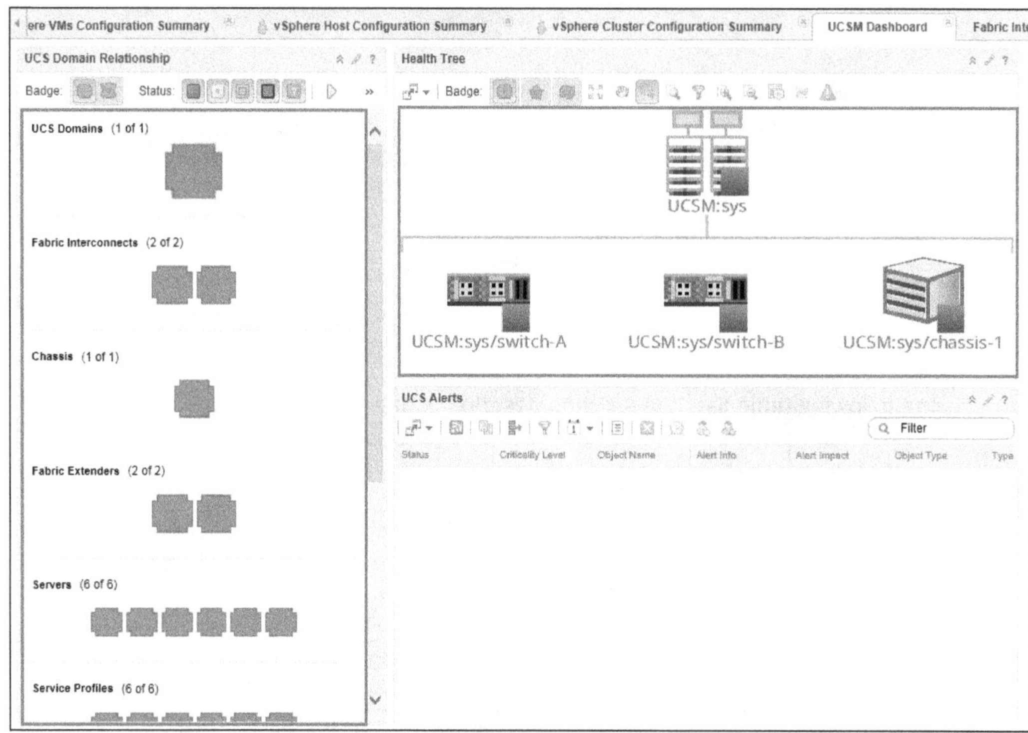

Installation and configuration of Cisco UCS Central

In this recipe, we will learn how to install and configure the Cisco UCS Central in Standalone mode.

Getting ready

The Cisco UCS Central software is used to manage multiple Cisco UCS domains on a single management control panel. The Cisco UCS Central integrates with Cisco UCS Manager and provides global configuration for service pools, policies, firmware, and so on. We deploy Cisco UCS Central on the VMware ESX environment, where a Cisco UCS domain is ready, which is included in the 2 Fabric Interconnect 6248UP, 1 UCS 5108 Chassis, and some UCS B-Series Blade Servers. The details are shown in the following diagram:

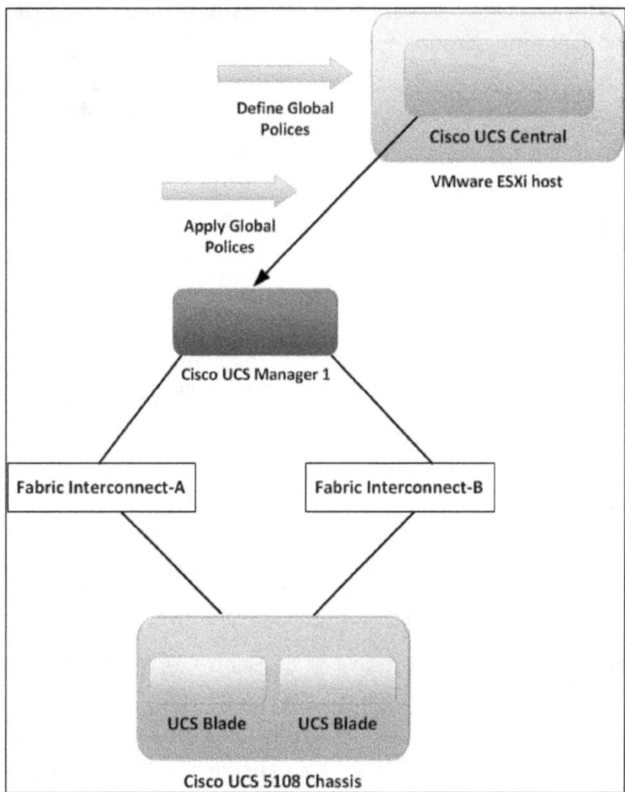

How to do it...

In this recipe, we will learn how to download and install **Cisco UCS Central** (**UCSC**).

Follow these steps to download and install UCSC:

1. Download the Cisco UCS Central and navigate to `https://software.cisco.com/download/release.html?mdfid=284308174&softwareid=284308194&release=1.3(1c)&relind=AVAILABLE&rellifecycle=&reltype=latest&i=rm` and log in to the **My Cisco** account. Select **ucs-central.1.3.1c.ova**; the details are as shown in the following screenshot:

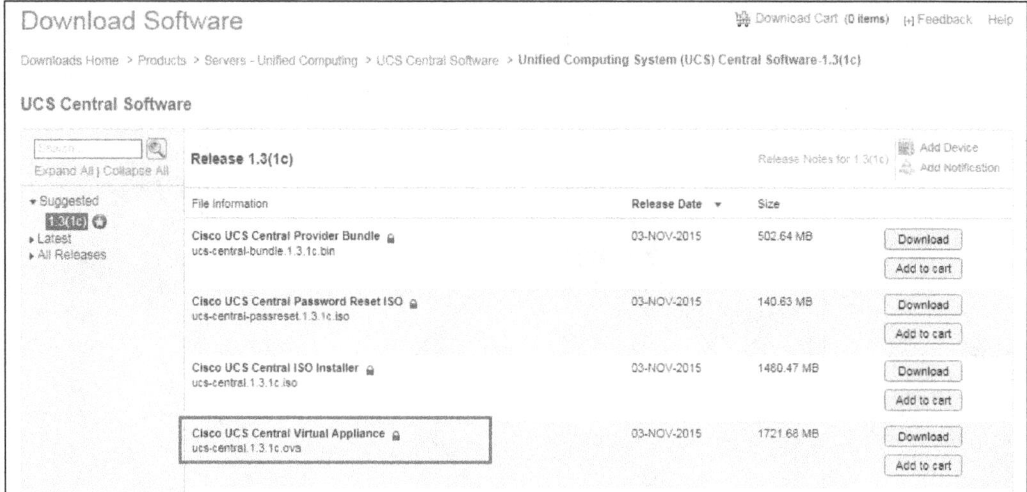

Note: Access to download Cisco UCS Central virtual appliance is limited to Cisco users.

2. Deploy the Cisco UCS Central Virtual Appliance in the VMware ESX environment. This table lists the VMware ESX requirements of Cisco UCS Central:

Requirement	**VMware ESX Minimum Requirement**
ESXi version	ESX 5.0 U3 or above
Disk space	80 GB
RAM	12 GB Memory
vCPU	4 vCPU (cores)

3. Assume that the ESX is managed by vCenter Server, log in to the ESX host using the VMware vSphere Client. Then select **Deploy OVF Template...** on the **File** tab:

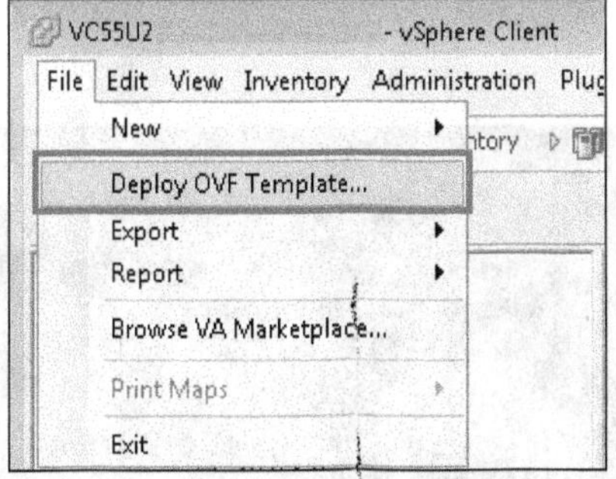

4. **Browse...** to **ucs-central.1.3.1c.ova** and input the UCS Central name. Navigate to **Resource Pool** | **Target ESX Datastore** | **Thick Provision Lazy Zeroed** | **Map the virtual network** | **Finish**:

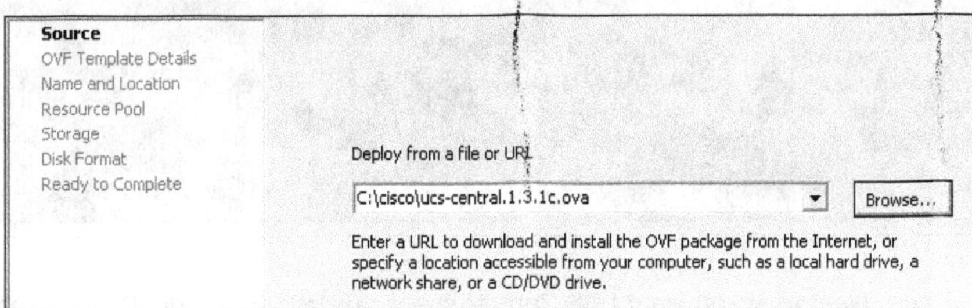

The virtual network of Cisco UCS Central is required to access the management network of Cisco UCS Manager.

5. Once the UCS Central virtual appliance is deployed and the VM is powered ON, open the console of the UCS Central virtual machine and start configuring the UCS Central VM by the following procedure:
   - Set up a new configuration or restore the full-state configuration from a backup; type `setup`:

```
Validating the installation medium's disk (/dev/mapper/VolGroup01-LogVol00) spee
d
Average disk read speed measured: 306
Disk speed validation - Succeeded
Setup new configuration or restore full-state configuration from backup[setup/re
store] - setup_
```

- Specify the IP address, Netmask, and the Default Gateway for the **UCS Central VM**:

```
File  View  VM
                                                            [  OK  ]
Starting monitoring for VG VolGroup01:   1 logical volume(s) in volume group "Vo
lGroup01" monitored
                                                            [  OK  ]
Starting snmpd:                                             [  OK  ]
Starting sshd:                                              [  OK  ]
Starting xinetd:                                            [  OK  ]
Starting pmon:                                              [  OK  ]
Starting postgresql service:                                [  OK  ]
Starting console mouse services:                            [  OK  ]
Starting crond:                                             [  OK  ]
Shutting down pmon:                                         [  OK  ]
Validating the installation medium's disk (/dev/mapper/VolGroup01-LogVol00) spee
d
Average disk read speed measured: 306
Disk speed validation - Succeeded
Setup new configuration or restore full-state configuration from backup[setup/re
store] - setup

Enter the UCS Central VM eth0 IPv4 Address  : 10.2.2.63
Enter the UCS Central VM eth0 IPv4 Netmask  : 255.255.255.0
Enter the VM IPv4 Default Gateway  : 10.2.2.254


Is this VM part of a cluster(select 'no' for standalone) (yes/no)  ? no_
```

- Type `no`, if you want UCS Central in a `standalone` mode. If you want `cluster` mode, type `yes`
- Specify a hostname to the **UCS Central VM**
- Specify the IP address of the **Domain Name Server** (**DNS**) as required
- Specify the domain name as required
- Specify the admin password and the shared secret
- Type `yes` if Statistics collection is required; if not, type `no`
- Type `yes` in order to proceed with the configuration

6. Once the configuration of the UCS Central VM is completed, it will reboot automatically.

According to Cisco best practice, the UCS Central VM should be deployed outside UCS Domains.

How it works...

In this recipe, we will learn how to configure Cisco UCS Central integrated with Cisco UCS Manager.

Follow these steps to configure Cisco UCS Central integrated with Cisco UCS Manager:

1. Open the Web browser and enter the IP address of **Cisco UCS Manager** (**UCSM**), then log in to it as an administrator. Go to the **UCS Central** option on the **Admin** tab and click on **Register With UCS Central**:

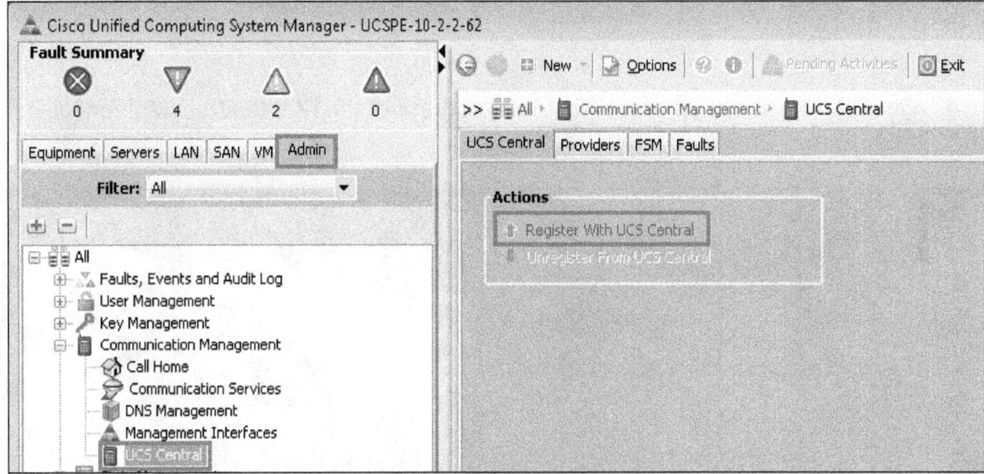

2. Input the **Hostname/IP Address** and **Shared Secret** of the UCS Central VM, which was specified in the UCS Central installation in Step 4, then click on **OK**:

3. After UCSM is registered successfully with UCS Central, the **Registration Status** should display **Registered**, as shown in the following screenshot:

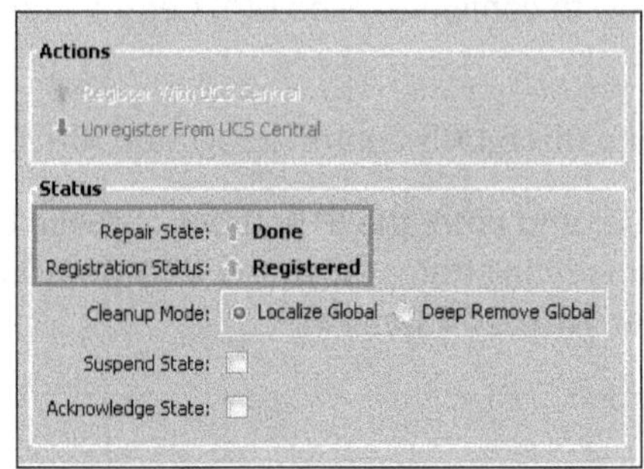

4. Open the Web browser and enter the IP address of the UCS Central VM, then log in to Central VM as administrator:

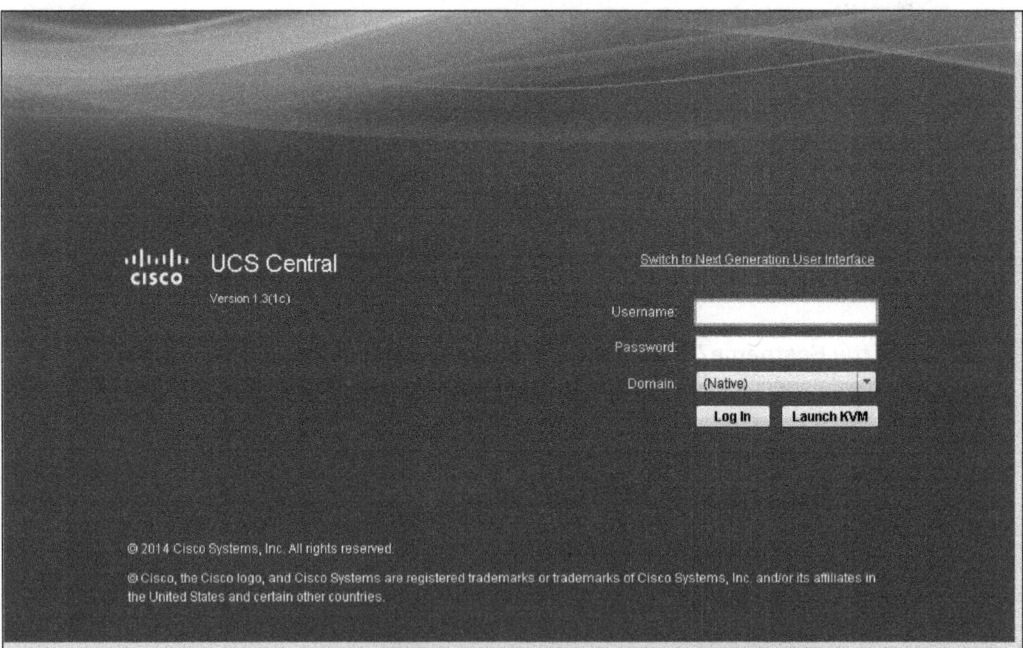

5. You can see that UCSM **UCSPE-10-2-2-62** has been registered with UCS Central in **Ungrouped Domains**, as shown in the following screenshot:

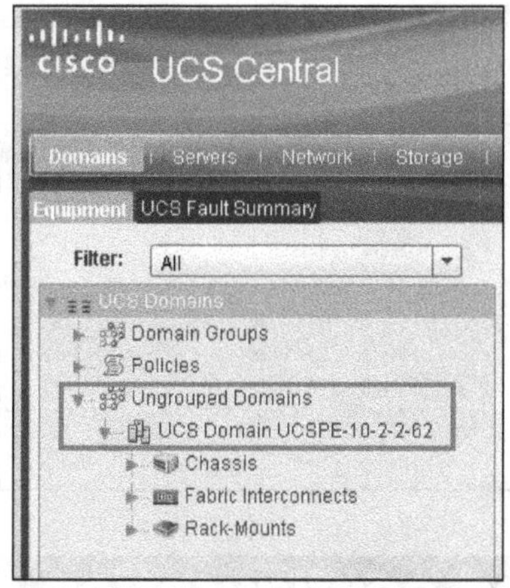

Move the **UCS Domain UCSPE-10-2-2-62** to **Domain Groups** and click on **Change Group Assignment** in the **General** tab, as shown:

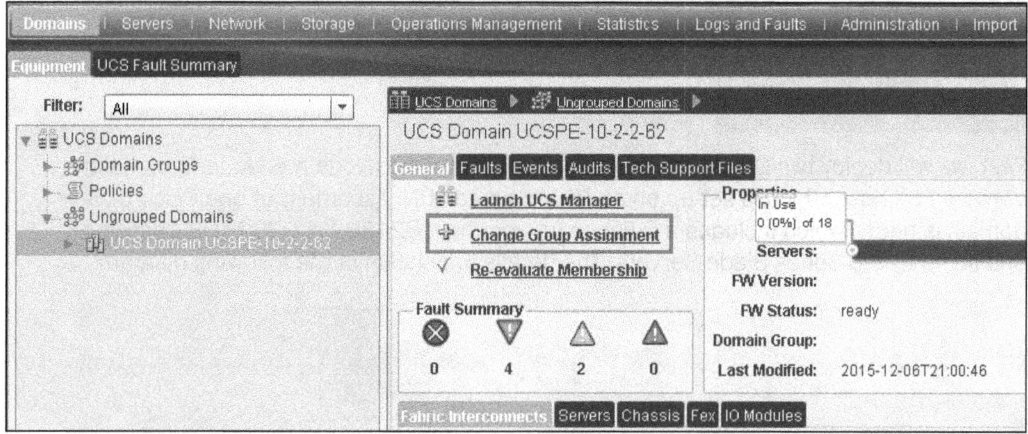

6. Select **Domain Group root** and click on **OK**, as shown:

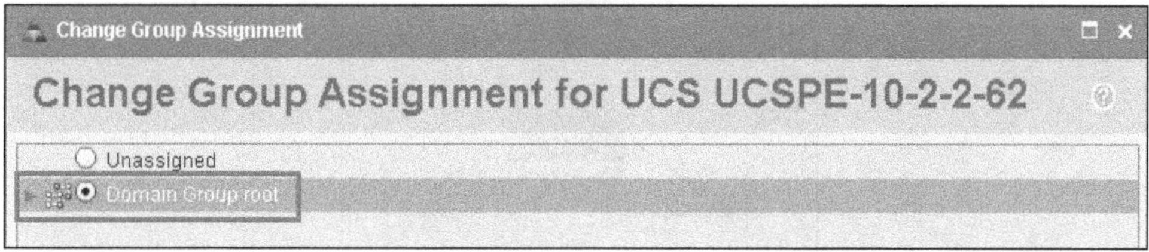

7. Finally, **UCS Domain UCSPE-10-2-2-62** has been successfully moved to **Domain Group root**, as shown:

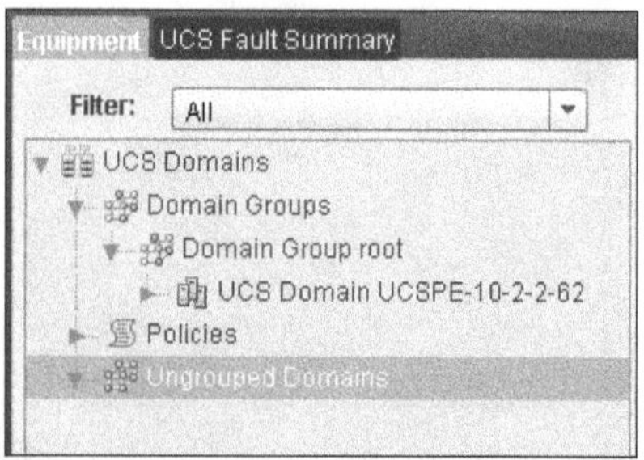

Installation and configuration of Cisco UCS Central in Cluster mode

In this recipe, we will learn the concept of how to install and configure Cisco UCS Central in Cluster mode.

Getting ready

First, we will deploy two Cisco UCS Central virtual machines (Node A & Node B) on each VMware ESX host, which is set up on an RDM Shared LUN. Assume that one Cisco UCS domain is ready, which includes a 2 Fabric Interconnect 6248UP, 1 UCS 5108 Chassis, and some UCS B-Series Blade Servers. The details are shown in the following diagram:

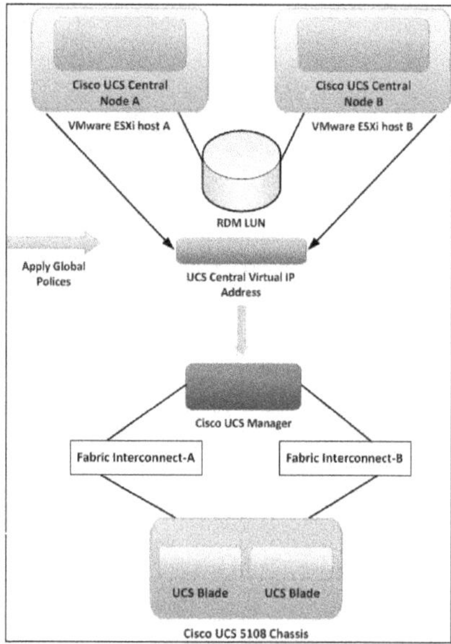

How to do it...

In the following recipe, we will learn how to download and install UCSC in Cluster mode.

Follow these steps to download and install UCSC in Cluster mode:

1. Download Cisco UCS Central and go to `https://software.cisco.com/download/release.html?mdfid=284308174&softwareid=284308194&release=1.3(1c)&relind=AVAILABLE&rellifecycle=&reltype=latest&i=rm` and log in with the **My Cisco** account, and select **ucs-central.1.3.1c.ova**, as shown in the following screenshot:

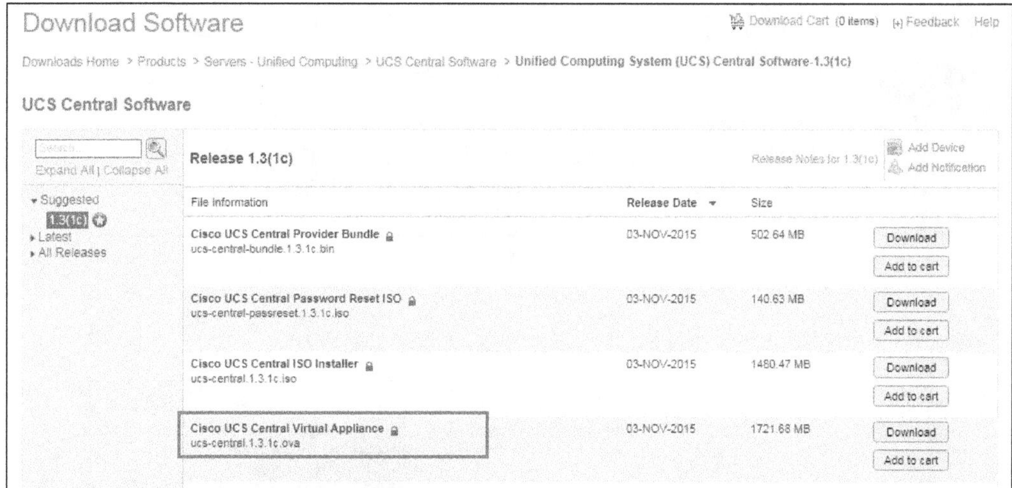

Note: Access to download Cisco UCS Central virtual appliance is limited to Cisco users.

2. The deployment of the Cisco UCS Central virtual appliance into VMware ESX A, and the requirement of VMware ESX is listed in the following table:

Requirement	VMware ESX Minimum Requirement
ESXi version	ESX 5.0 U3 or above
Disk space	80 GB
RAM	12 GB Memory
vCPU	4 vCPU (cores)
RDM Shared LUN	Disk read speed is required to be 75 MB/sec for UCS Central Deployment. The capacity of RDM is required to be more than 80 GB

3. Assume that both ESX hosts A and B are managed by vCenter Server; log in to the ESX host by VMware vSphere Client, then choose **Deploy OVF Template...** on the **File** tab to deploy the UCS Central Node A:

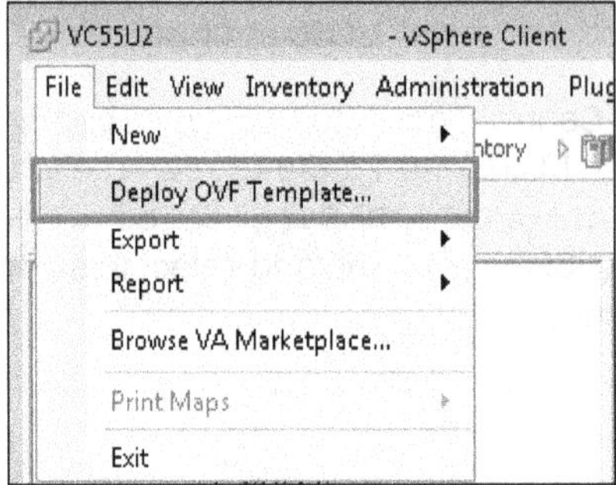

4. **Browse... ucs-central.1.3.1c.ova** and input the name of UCS Central. Navigate to **Resource Pool** | **Target ESX Datastore** | **Thick Provision Lazy Zeroed** | **Map the virtual network** | **Finish**. Repeat this procedure for UCS Central Node B deployment:

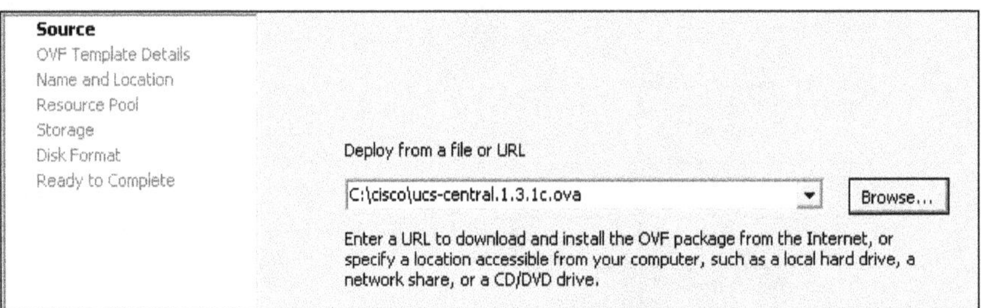

The virtual network of Cisco UCS Central is required to access the management network of Cisco UCS Manager.

5. Once both the UCS Central virtual appliances are deployed, start adding the RDM Shared LUN into UCS Central Node A. You need to create a 100 GB RDM Shared LUN and map it to ESXi host A and ESXi host B. Now, start adding this 100 GB RDM LUN into Node A by the following procedure:

    - Right-click on the **VM** and add a **Disk**, select **Raw Device Mappings** and **Physical Compatibility Mode**:

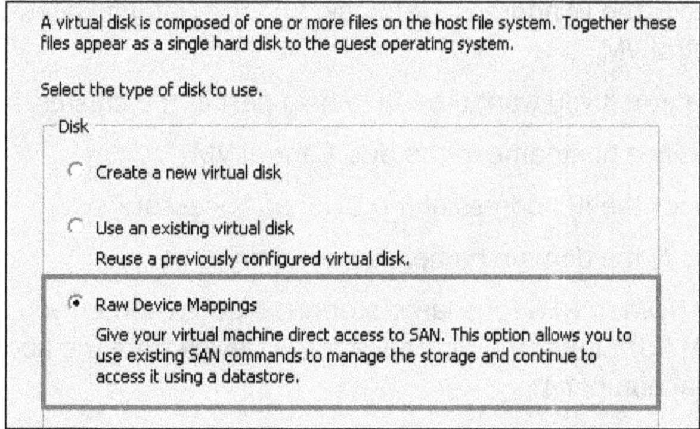

A virtual disk is composed of one or more files on the host file system. Together these files appear as a single hard disk to the guest operating system.
Select the type of disk to use.
Disk
Create a new virtual disk
Use an existing virtual disk
Reuse a previously configured virtual disk.
Raw Device Mappings
Give your virtual machine direct access to SAN. This option allows you to use existing SAN commands to manage the storage and continue to access it using a datastore.

- Now, add an RDM Shared LUN and make sure that the path of the RDM is changed to **Fixed** because it is not supported in multipath. Click on **Edit VM Settings**, select **RDM**, and click on **Manage Paths**. Change the **Path Selection** policy of raw device mapping hard disk to **Fixed (VMware)**. Right-click on all the additional paths and click on **Disable**:

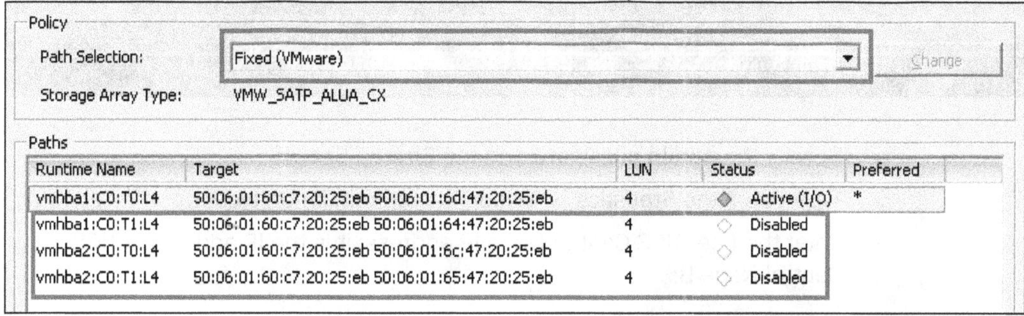

- Repeat the preceding procedure to configure the RDM Shared LUN into UCS Central NodeB.

6. Once the configuration of RDM Shared LUN is complete, power ON UCS Central Node A and open the console of the UCS Central virtual machine. Then, you can start configuring the UCS Central VM according to the following procedure:
    - Set up a new configuration or restore a full-state configuration from a backup; type `setup`:

```
Validating the installation medium's disk (/dev/mapper/VolGroup01-LogVol00) spee
d
Average disk read speed measured: 306
Disk speed validation - Succeeded
Setup new configuration or restore full-state configuration from backup[setup/re
store] - setup_
```

- Specify the IP address, Netmask, and the Default Gateway for the UCS Central VM
- Type `yes` if you want the VM to be a part of the cluster
- Specify a hostname to the UCS Central VM
- Specify the IP address of the DNS, as necessary
- Specify the domain name, as necessary
- Use RDM or NFS for shared storage, type `rdm`. Then you can see a 100 GB RDM LUN. Enter the Shared Storage Device from the above list and type serial number `1`:

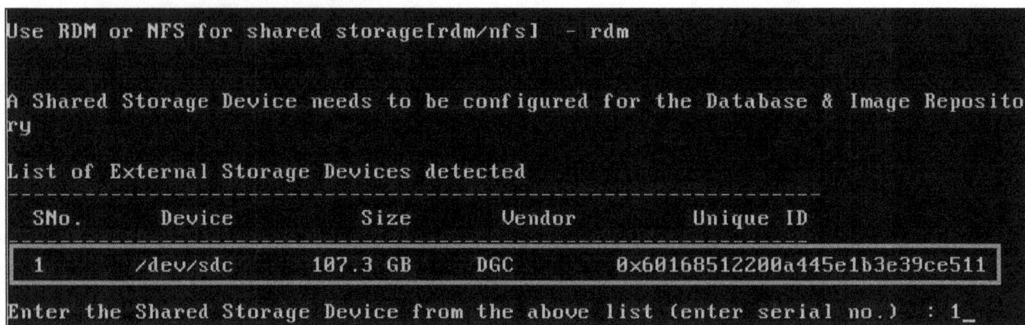

- Specify the **admin password** and the **Shared Secret**
- Type `yes` if the Statistics collection is required; if not, type `no`
- Enter the Peer UCS Central Node IP address; it is the IP address of UCS Central Node B:

```
Performance of system is not guaranteed. Do you want to continue installation.
 [yes/no]  yes
Continuing Installation...
Enforce Strong Password (yes/no)  ? yes
Enter the admin Password   :
Confirm admin Password :
Enter the Shared Secret   :
Confirm Shared Secret :
Enter the Peer UCS Central Node IPv4 Address   : _
```

- Enter the virtual IP address of UCS Central
- Type `yes` in order to proceed with the configuration

7. Once the configuration of UCS Central Node A is complete, it will reboot automatically.

8. Open UCS Central Node B; you can now start configuring UCS Central Node B according to the following procedure:
    - Set up a new configuration or restore the full-state configuration from the backup; type `setup`
    - Specify the IP address, Netmask, and the Default Gateway for UCS Central VM
    - Type `yes` if you want the VM to be a part of the cluster
    - Type `no` if you want to add it to an existing cluster
    - Enter the Peep UCS Central Node IP address; it is the IP address of UCS Central Node A
    - Enter the admin username on Peer UCS Central Node; it is the admin username for Central Node A
    - Enter the admin password on Peer UCS Central Node; it is the admin password for Central Node A
    - Type `yes` in order to proceed with the configuration
9. Once the configuration of UCS Central Node B is completed, it will reboot automatically.

How it works...

In this recipe, we will learn how to configure Cisco UCS Central integrated with Cisco UCS Manager.

Follow these steps to configure Cisco UCS Central integrated with Cisco UCS Manager:

1. Open the Web browser and enter the IP address of UCSM and then login into it as an administrator. Go to **UCS Central** on the **Admin** tab, click on **Register With UCS Central**:

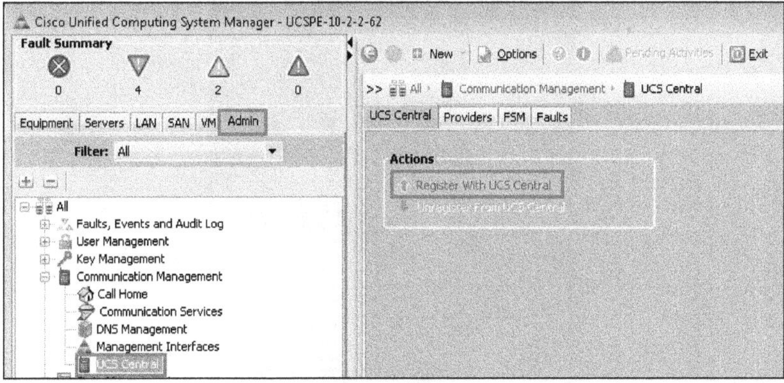

2. Input **Hostname/IP Address** and **Shared Secret** of the UCS Central VM (virtual IP address), which was specified in Step 5 of the preceding UCS Central installation, and then click on **OK**, as shown:

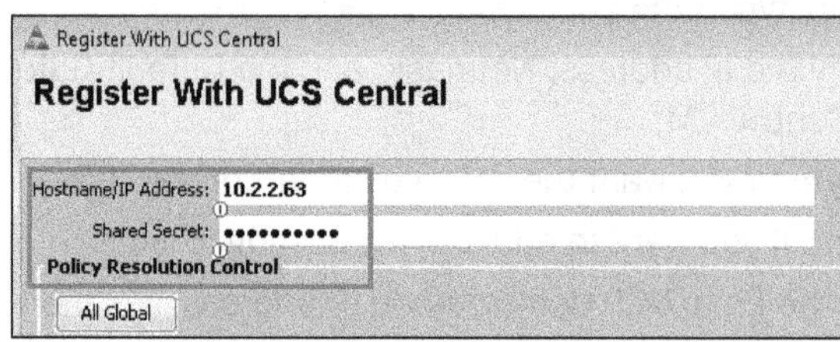

3. When UCSM is successfully registered with UCS Central, the **Registration Status** displays **Registered**:

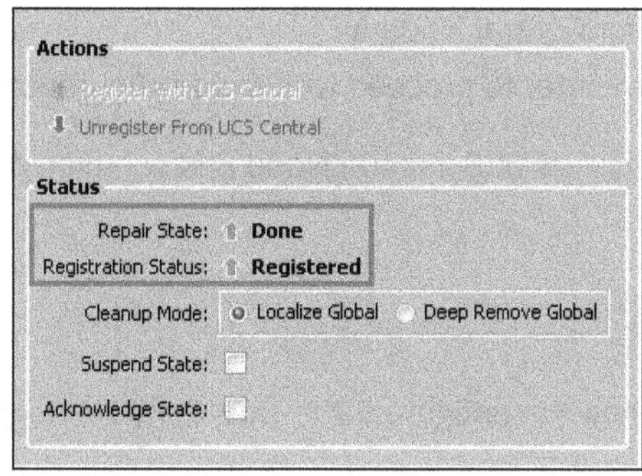

4. Open the Web browser and enter the virtual IP address of the UCS Central VM, then log in to the Central VM as an administrator.
5. You can see that UCSM **UCSPE-10-2-2-62** has been registered with UCS Central on **Ungrouped Domains**, as shown:

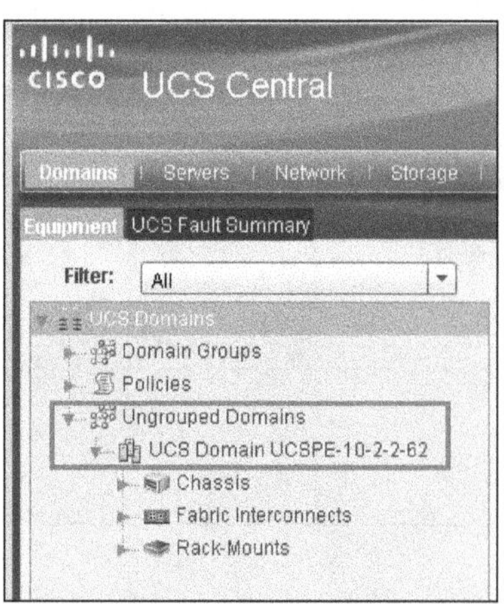

6. Move the **UCS Domain UCSPE-10-2-2-62** to **Domain Groups** and click on **Change Group Assignment** on the **General** tab, as shown:

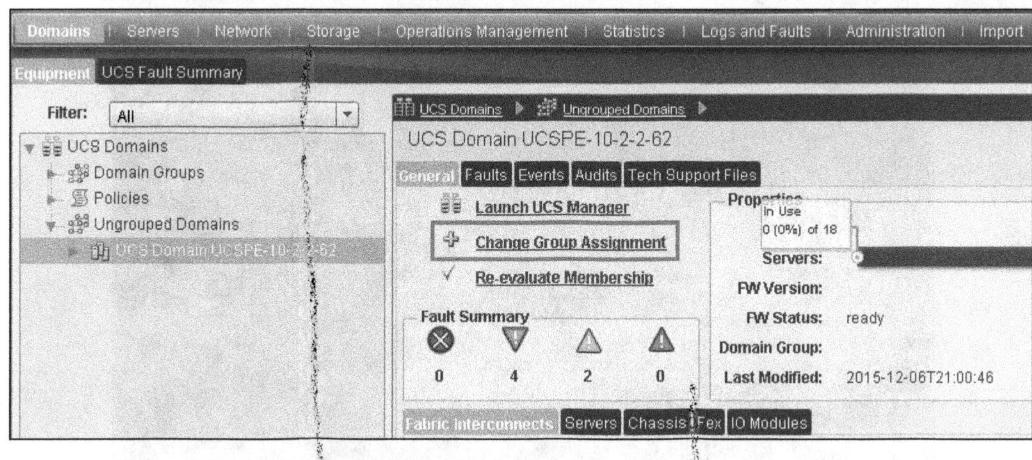

7. Select **Domain Group root** and click on **OK**.

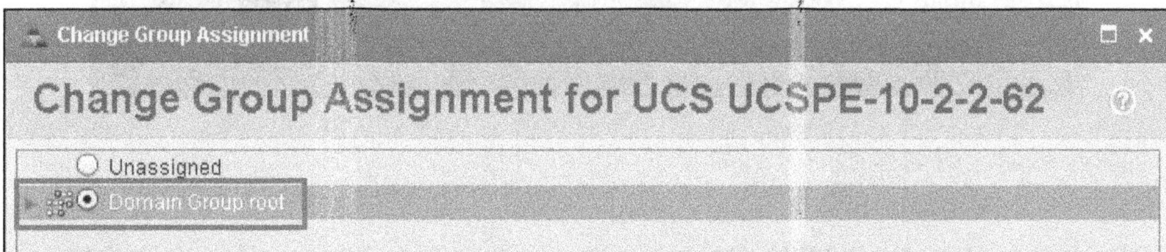

8. Finally, the **UCS Domain UCSPE-10-2-2-62** has been moved to **Domain Group root** successfully:

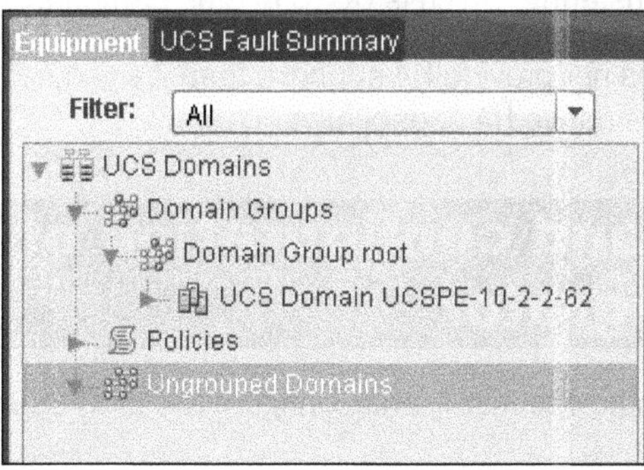

9. Log in to UCS Central A as an **admin** and execute the command `show cluster state`; you can see that Node **A** is **PRIMARY**, Node **B** is **SUBORDINATE**, make it display **HA Ready**. The installation of UCS Central in Cluster mode is complete:

```
UCSCVM-A login: admin
Password:
Last login: Tue Dec  8 05:46:55 on tty1
Logged in from tty1
Cisco UCS Central
TAC support: http://www.cisco.com/tac
Copyright (c) 2011-2014, Cisco Systems, Inc. All rights reserved.
The copyrights to certain works contained in this software are
owned by other third parties and used and distributed under
license. Certain components of this software are licensed under
the GNU General Public License (GPL) version 2.0 or the GNU
Lesser General Public License (LGPL) Version 2.1. A copy of each
such license is available at
http://www.opensource.org/licenses/gpl-2.0.php and
http://www.opensource.org/licenses/lgpl-2.1.php

UCSCVM-A# show cluster state
Cluster Id: 0xd502ab989cfb11e5-0x9f0d49d5dcb87a33

A: UP, PRIMARY
B: UP, SUBORDINATE

HA READY
UCSCVM-A# _
```

There's more...

UCSC has native **High Availability** (**HA**) features, which are provided primarily for deployments where hypervisor-based HA (for example, VMware ESXi or Microsoft Hyper-V) is not available. In general, hypervisor-based HA should be used, if available. In cases where native hypervisor HA is available and active, UCS Central can safely run in a Standalone mode without using UCS Central's native HA clustering, which is UCSC in Cluster mode.

If your host hypervisor does not provide HA support, then it's generally a good idea to take advantage of UCS Central's native HA capabilities.

Installation and configuration of EMC Storage Integrator

In this recipe, we will learn how to install and configure the EMC Storage Integrator on the Cisco UCS Server.

Getting ready

Assume that Microsoft Windows 2008 R2 is installed into Cisco UCS B200 M3 in local boot, which is installed on Cisco VIC 1240. This Cisco UCS B200 is now connected to EMC CLARiiON CX4-240 storage, and also installed EMC Powerpath software on Microsoft Windows 2008 that is running on Cisco UCS B200. EMC Powerpath is an EMC multipath software. Before installing ESI, the host has to fulfill the following requirements. The details are listed in the following diagram:

- Install the .NET framework 4.5 on the host on which the EMC Storage Integrator runs
- Ensure that Microsoft PowerShell 4.0 is installed on the host
- Install the latest version of EMC PowerPath 5.x or **Microsoft Multipath I/O** (**MPIO**)

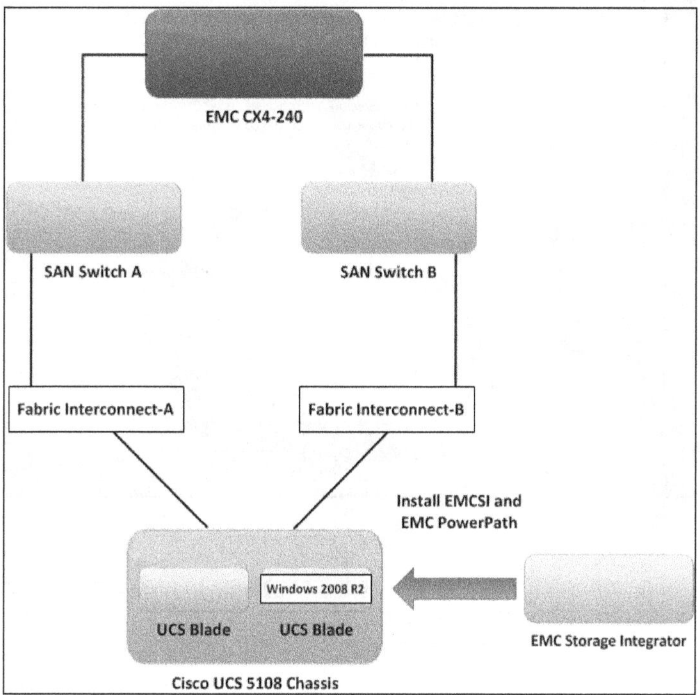

How to do it...

In this recipe, we will learn how to install EMC Storage Integrator 3.6 on Microsoft Windows 2008 R2.

The **EMC Storage Integrator** (**ESI**) for Windows Suite is a set of tools for Microsoft Windows. This tool includes the ESI RecoverPoint Adapter, ESI Microsoft SharePoint Adapter, ESI SQL Server Adapter, and ESI Microsoft Exchange Adapter. The suite also includes the ESI **System Center Operations Manager** (**SCOM**) Management Packs and the ESI PowerShell Toolkit. This tool enables us to view, provision, monitor, and manage EMC block and file storage for Microsoft Windows, Microsoft SharePoint, Microsoft SQL Server, and Microsoft Exchange, respectively. It also supports storage provisioning and discovery for Windows virtual machines running on Microsoft Hyper-V and VMware vSphere.

Following are the steps to install ESI:

1. Run the **EMC Storage Integrator** installer and click on **Next**, as shown:

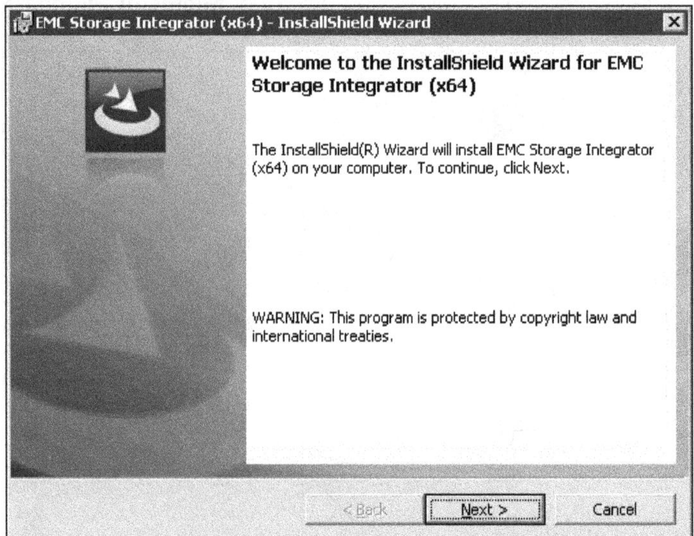

The ESI is a freeware tool. The latest version of EMCSI is `3.9`. EMCSI `3.7` or higher and it is no longer supported by EMC CLARiiON CX4 storage. For the details, you can check the release notes of EMCSI.

2. Keep the default settings and click on **Next**.
3. Select the **Active Directory** and click on **Next**:

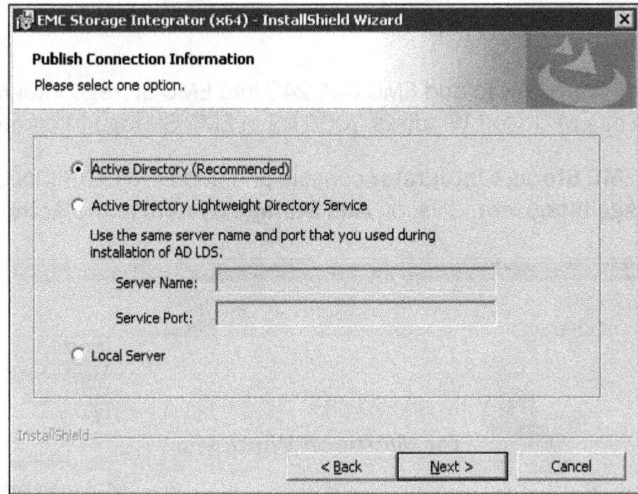

4. Click on the **Install** button:

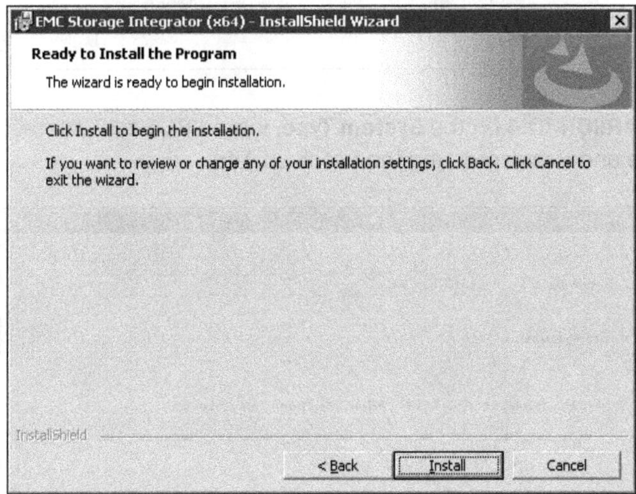

5. Finally, click on the **Finish** button.

How it works...

In this recipe, we will learn how to add EMC CX4-240 into EMC Storage Integrator and provision EMC LUN into Microsoft Windows 2008 R2 in EMC Storage Integrator.

1. Open the **EMC Storage Integrator** console and add EMC CLARiiON CX4-240 into the **EMC Storage Integrator**. Click on **Add Storage System** in the **Actions** menu:

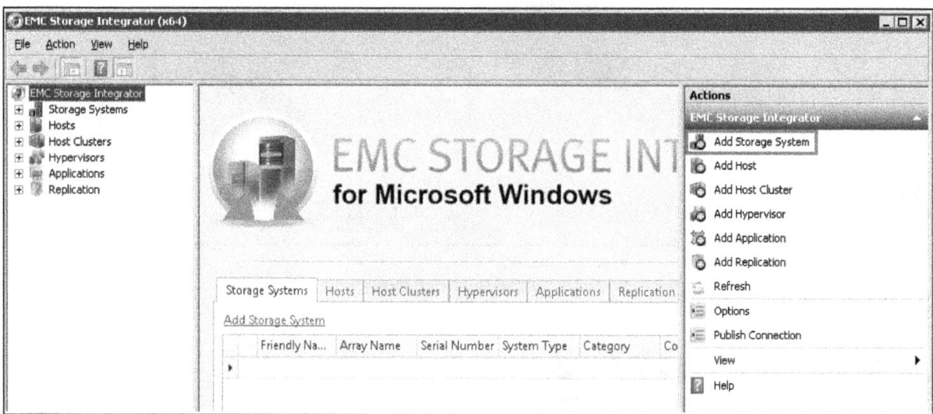

2. Select **CLARiiON-CX4** on the **System Type**, input SPA/B's IP address of CX4-240, **Username** and **Password,** and then click on **Add**:

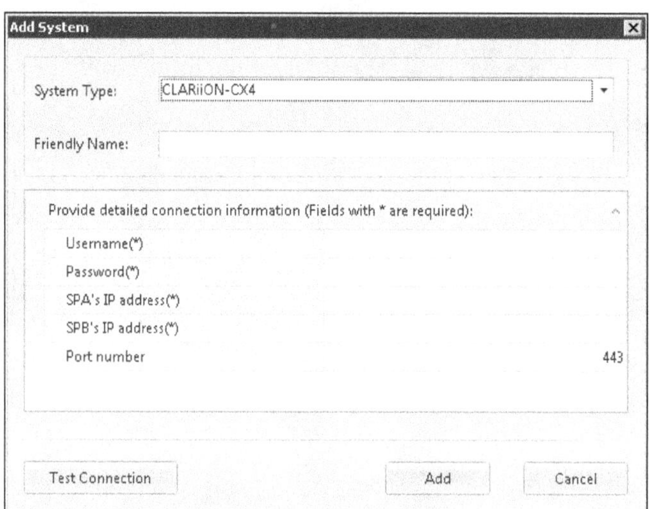

The firmware requirement of EMC CLARiiON CX4 storage is Flare 04.30.

3. Then CX4-240 is added into ESI and you can see the information of each Raid Group for the **CX4-240** model on the **Storage Systems** menu:

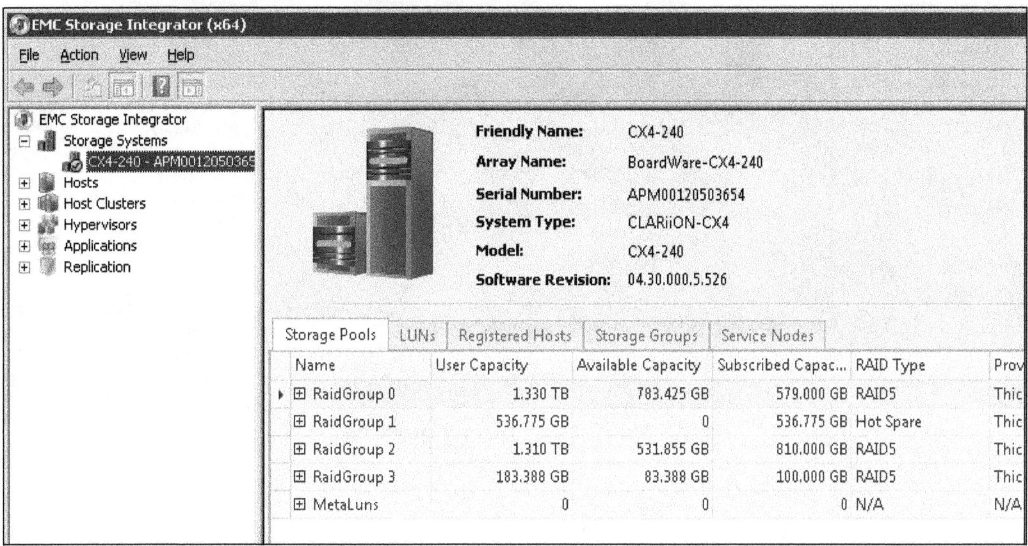

4. Click on **Add Host** on the **Action** menu and input the **IP address/Name** of the host you want to add into ESI. Input the **Username** and **Password** of that host and click on **Add**, as shown:

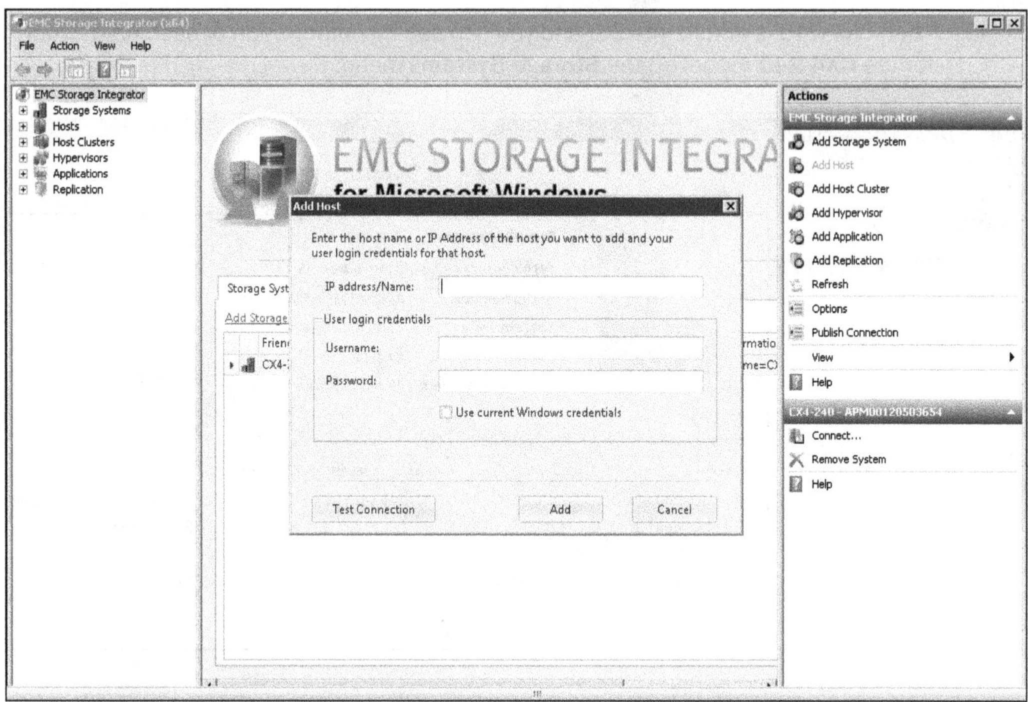

5. Then the host is added into ESI and you can see the disk information of the host, that is, one **90.000GB** drive and one **100.000GB** drive:

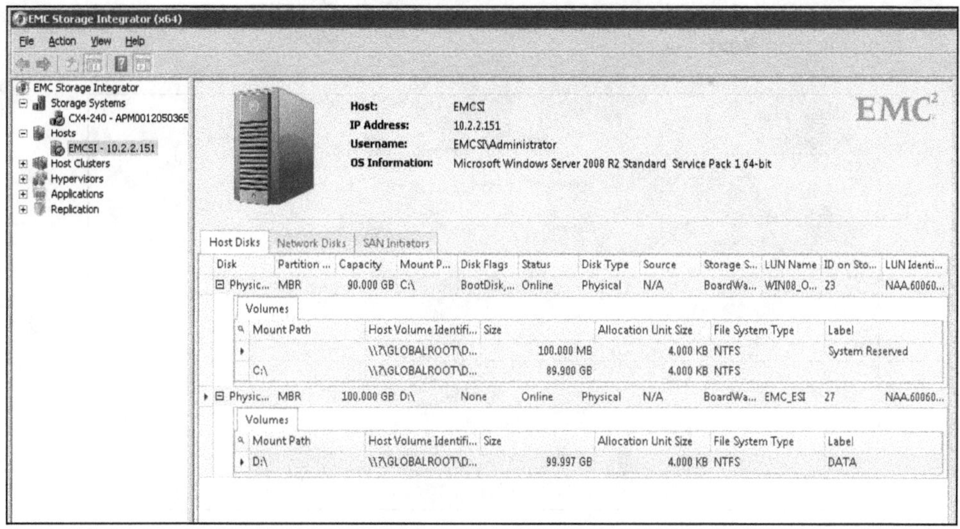

6. After host and EMC storage is added into ESI, you can start to provision the EMC LUN into this host; right-click on the host and select **Create Disk**:

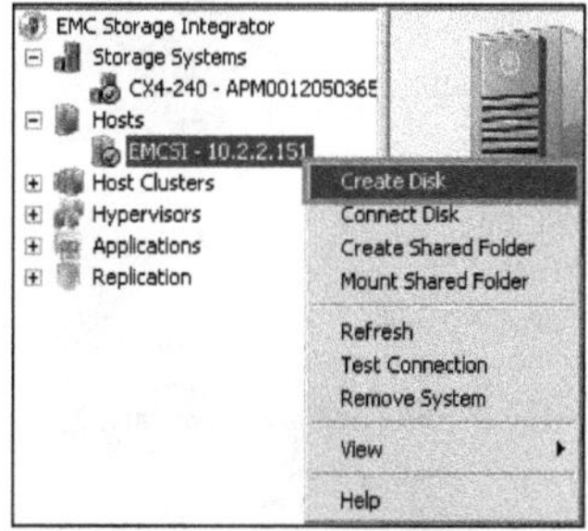

7. You can see the existing Raid Group on CX4-240; now it has three Raid Groups. Select **RaidGroup0** and click on **Next**:

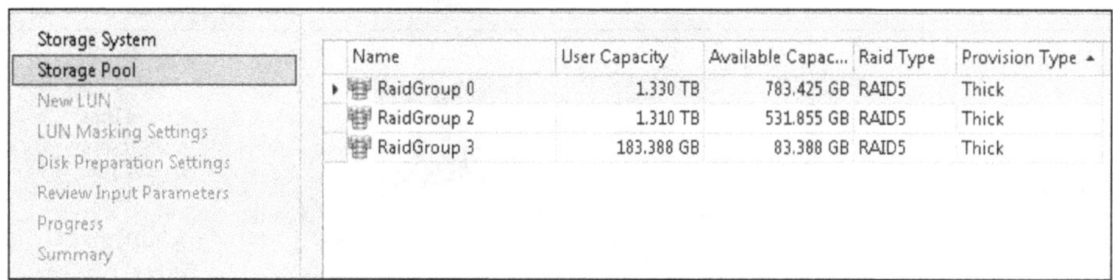

8. Input the LUN **Name** and LUN **Size**; for example, **EMC_TEST_LUN** and **80 GB** and then click on **Next**:

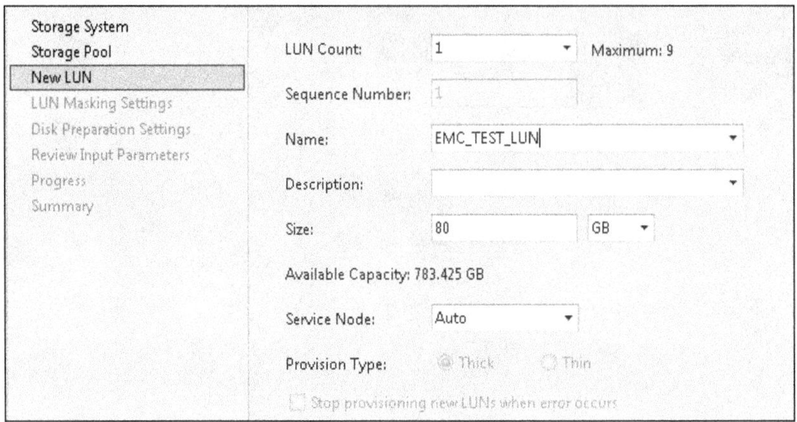

9. Select **Drive Letter** as **G** drive and click **Next**:

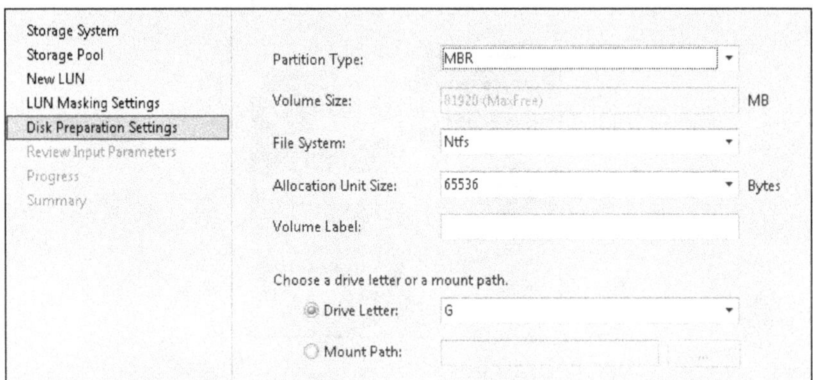

10. After all tasks have been completed, click on **Next** and then on **Finish**:

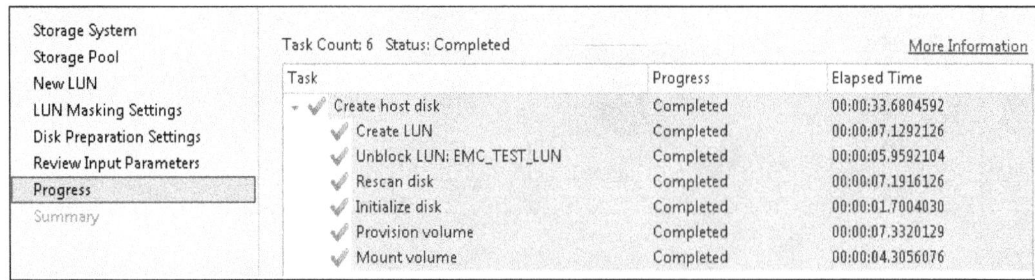

11. Finally, the new LUN is presented to the host and mounted as a G-drive:

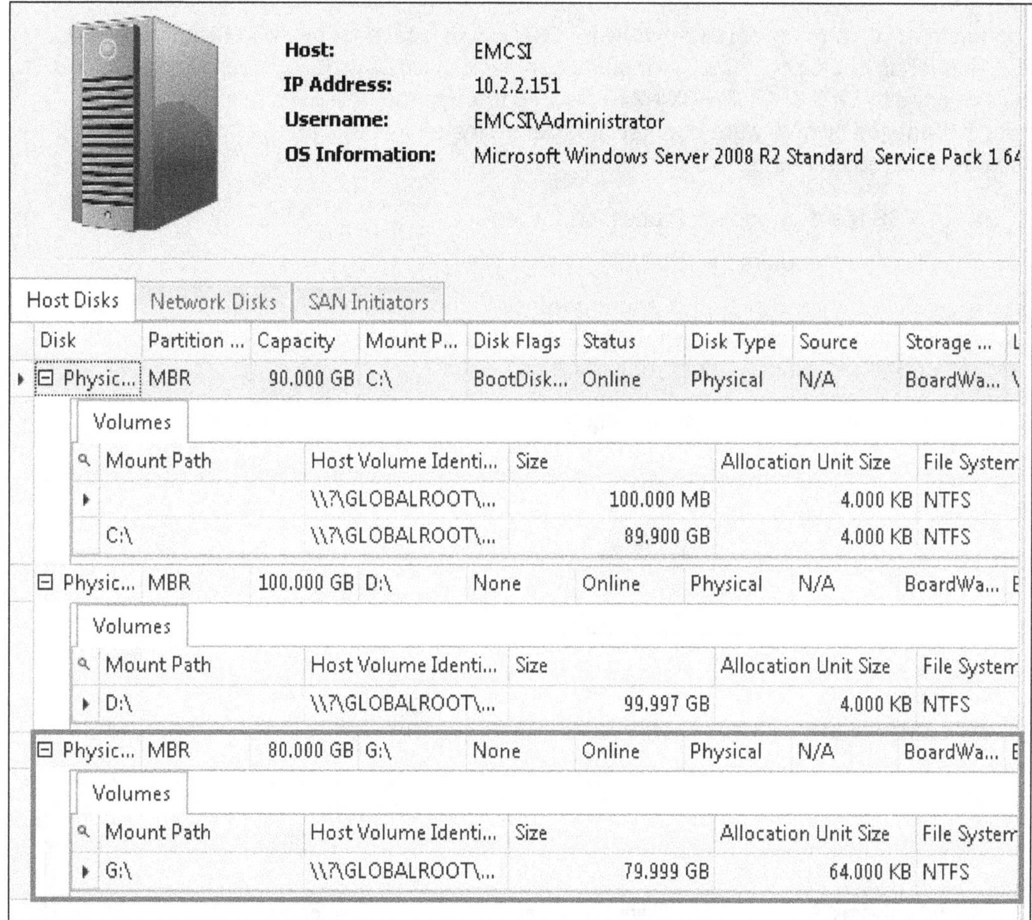

Installation and configuration of EMC Connectrix Manager

In this recipe, we will learn the concept of how to install and configure EMC **Connectrix Manager Converged Network Edition** (**CMCNE**).

Getting ready

Assume that you already deployed VMware ESXi 5.5 in local boot on each Cisco UCS B200 M3, and it has one Cisco VIC 1240 installed on each Cisco UCS B200. Each Cisco UCS B200 is connected to EMC CLARiiON CX4-240 storage through the SAN Switches. The ESXi 5.5 host is managed by a VMware vCenter 5.5. Before installing CMCNE, the host has to fulfill the following requirements:

- 16 GB Memory and 1 x Processor (2 core).
- Disk space required is 20 GB.
- CMCNE Professional Plus and Enterprise Editions are only supported on 64-bit Windows operating systems. CMCNE Professional Edition is supported on 32-bit and 64-bit Windows operating systems.

The details are shown in the following diagram:

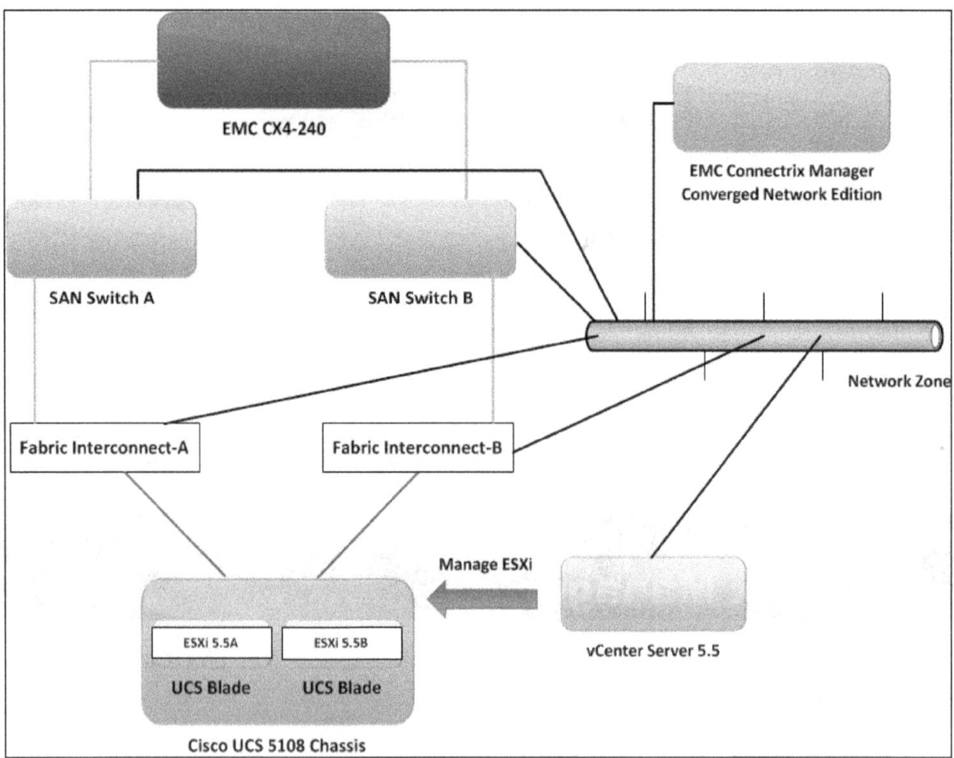

How to do it...

In this recipe, we will learn the concept of how to install CMCNE Professional Edition on Microsoft Windows 2008 R2.

The EMC CMCNE provides a comprehensive fabric management framework for the end-to-end management of the data. CMCNE provides health checks and a performance dashboard with a user-friendly **Graphical User Interface** (**GUI**). CMCNE has three editions, Professional, Professional Plus, and Enterprise Edition. The limitations of the feature are dependent on the edition of CMCNE; you can reference the release notes of CMCNE.

CMCNE Professional Plus and Enterprise Editions require the license key to enable the features, whereas CMCNE Professional does not require any license to be enabled.

Follow these steps to install CMCNE Professional Edition on Microsoft Windows 2008 R2:

1. Execute the EMC CMCNE installer and click on **Next**:

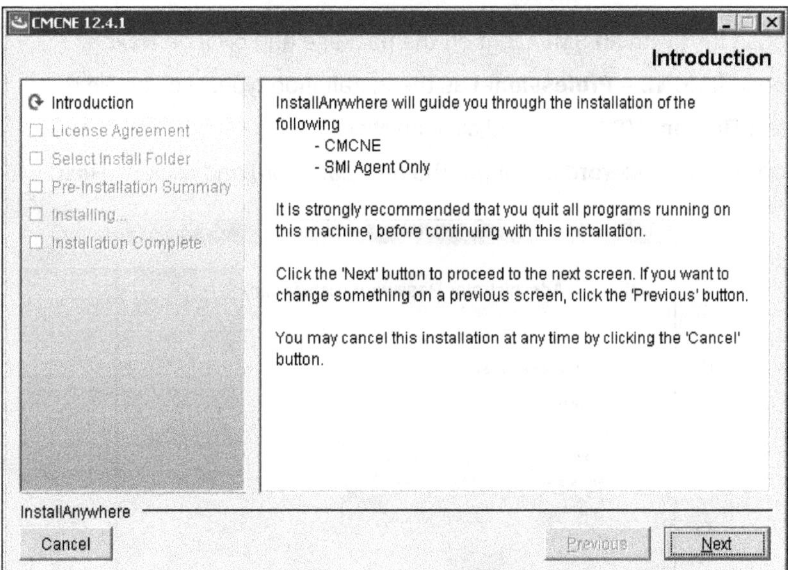

2. Accept the license agreement and keep the default setting; click on **Install**.
3. After finishing the installation, the CMCNE shortcut is displayed on the desktop automatically.

4. Execute the CMCNE shortcut and continue to install CMCNE; click on **Next**.
5. Select **No, don't copy any data and settings** and click on **Next**:

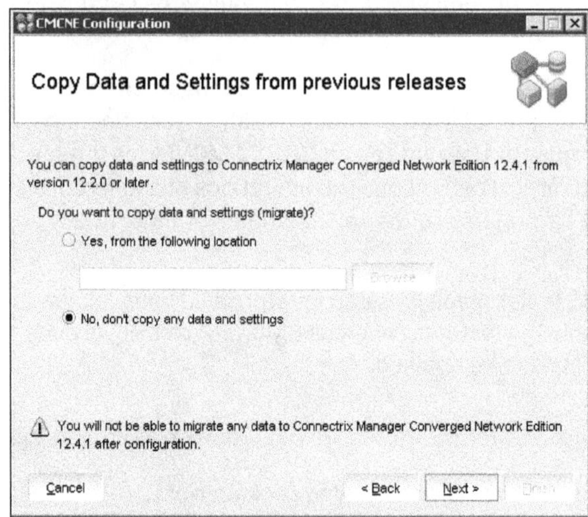

6. Choose **SAN** with an SMI Agent on the package and click on **Next**.
7. Choose **CMCNE – Professional** as the installation type, click on **Next**.
8. Select **Built-in FTP** Server and click on **Next**.
9. Choose **New password** and input the new password and click on **Next**:

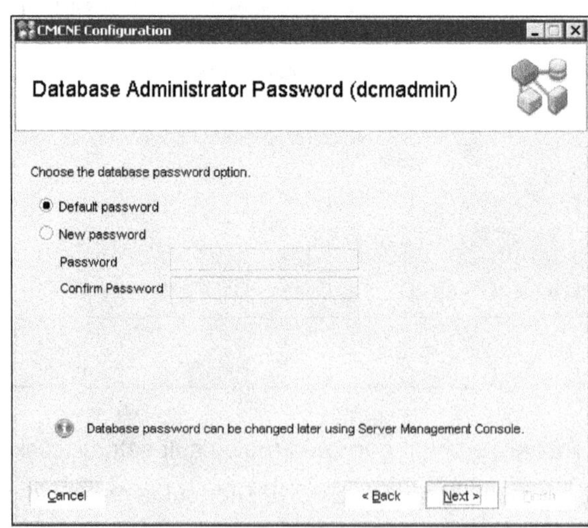

10. Keep the default setting and click on **Install**.

11. After finishing the installation, the CMCNE client starts automatically. Input the **User ID** and **Password** and then click on **Login**. The **User ID** is **administrator** and the password is modified in Step 9:

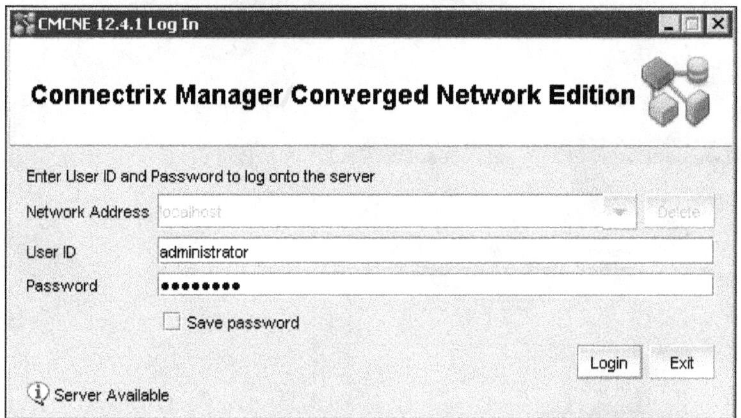

The default User ID is administrator and the Password is password.

How it works...

In this recipe, we will learn the concept of how to add Brocade SAN Switch and VMware ESXi 5.5 into EMC CMCNE.

1. Open the CMCNE client, log in to the CMCNE Server as an administrator and select **Fabrics** on the **Discover** menu:

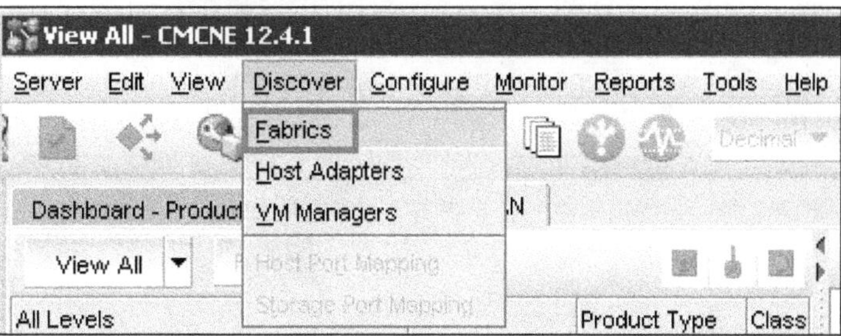

2. Click on the **Add** button, then input the **Fabric Name**, **IP address** of Brocade SAN Switches, and the **User ID** and **Password**. Click **OK**:

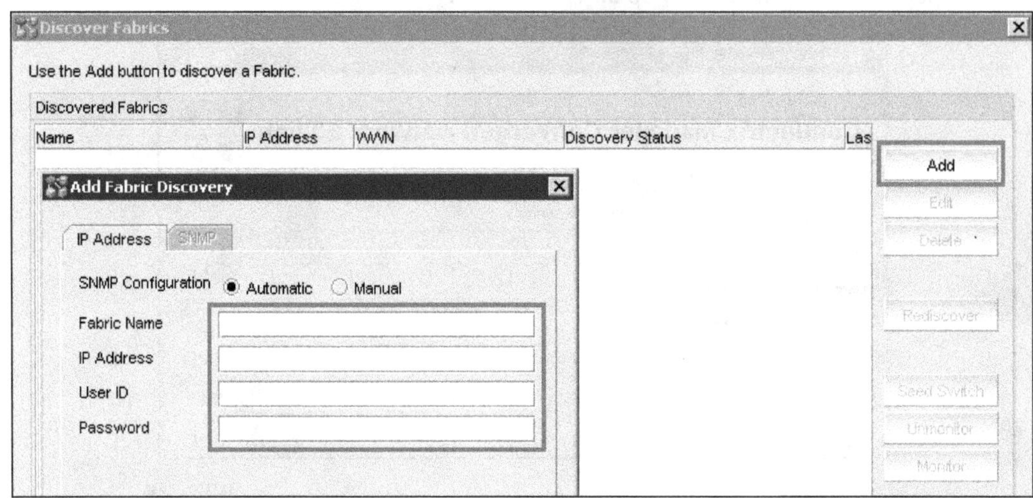

3. After this, add the Brocade SAN Switches; you can see that the **Discovery Status** displays **Discovered: Seed Switch**:

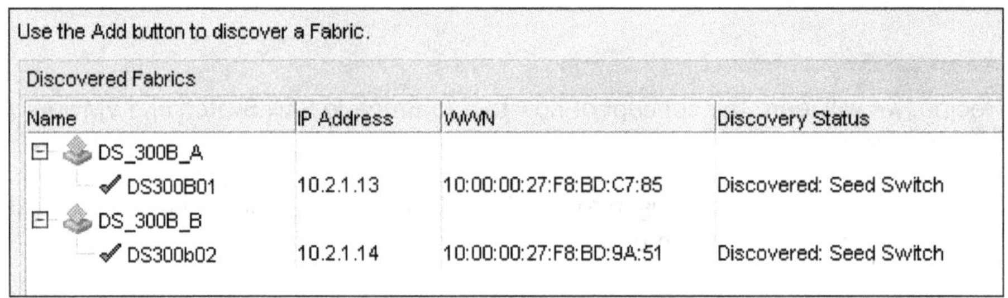

4. Then add the VMware vCenter 5 into CMCNE and select **VM Managers** on the **Discover** menu:

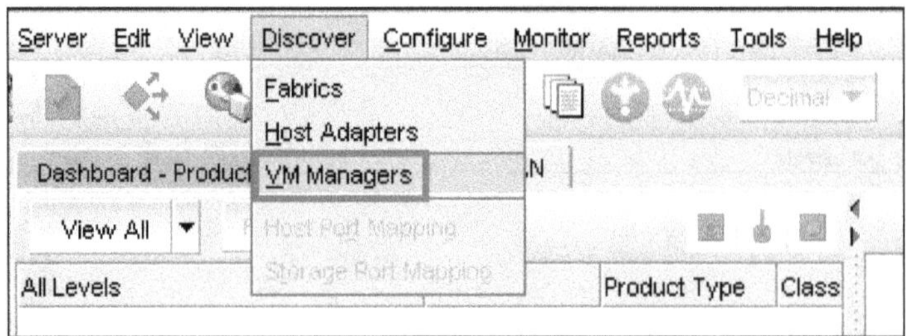

5. Click on **Add** button and input the **Network Address** of the vCenter Server, **User ID** and **Password**. Click on **OK**:

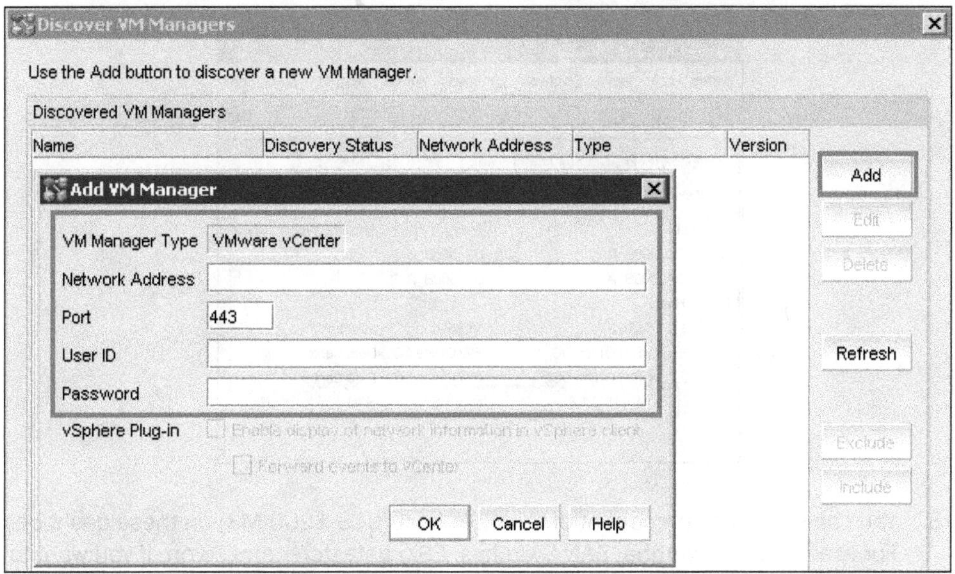

6. Now add the vCenter Server 5.5; you can see that the **Discovery Status** of the vCenter Server **VC55U2** displays **Active**. Assume that there are three ESXi hosts managed by this vCenter 5.5, so that you can see three hosts are managed under **VC55U2**:

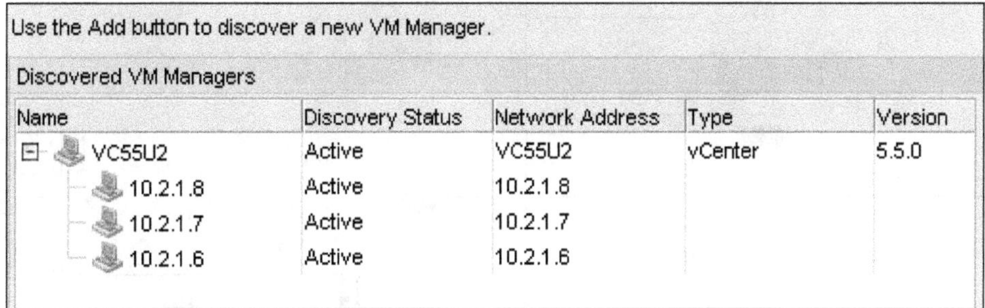

7. Go to the **SAN** dashboard; you can see the Brocade SAN Switches **DS_300B_A** and **DS_300B_B** and the vCenter Server **VC55U2** in the **SAN** dashboard. Select ESXi host **10.2.1.8**:

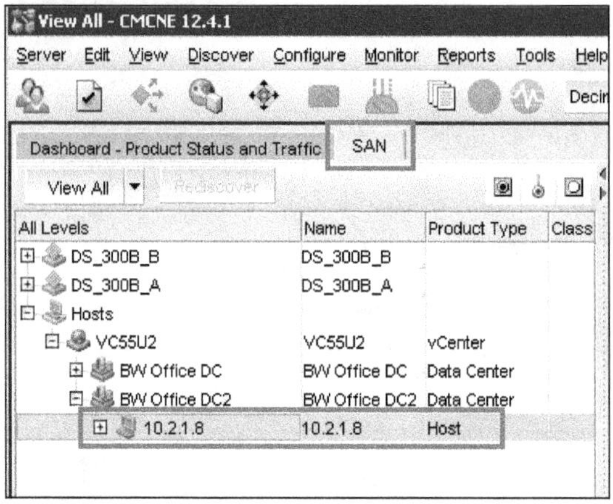

8. You can see each component of this ESXi host (UCS B200 M3) on these dashboards. For example, vnic, vmhba, SAN Switches, ESXi datastore, and so on. If you want to review the information of WWPN information of each vmhba, you also can review it on the SAN Switches **DS_300B_A** and **DS_300B_B** dashboard:

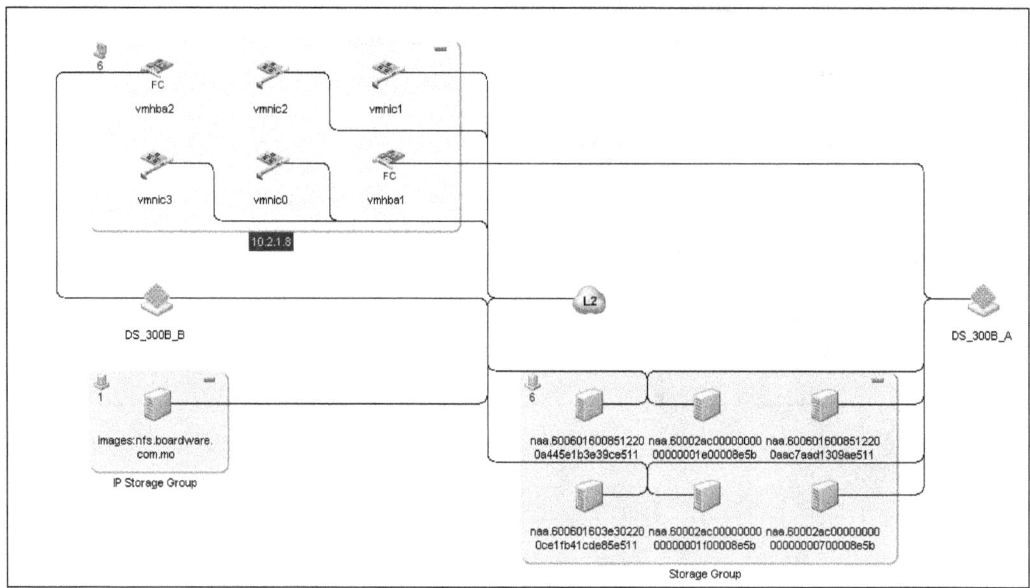

There's more...

The EMC CMCNE also supports the FC Zoning configuration. You can also create a zone on each Brocade SAN Switch, which is added into the CMCNE on one Central Management Server. The SAN administrator is not required to create zoning on each Brocade SAN Switch individually:

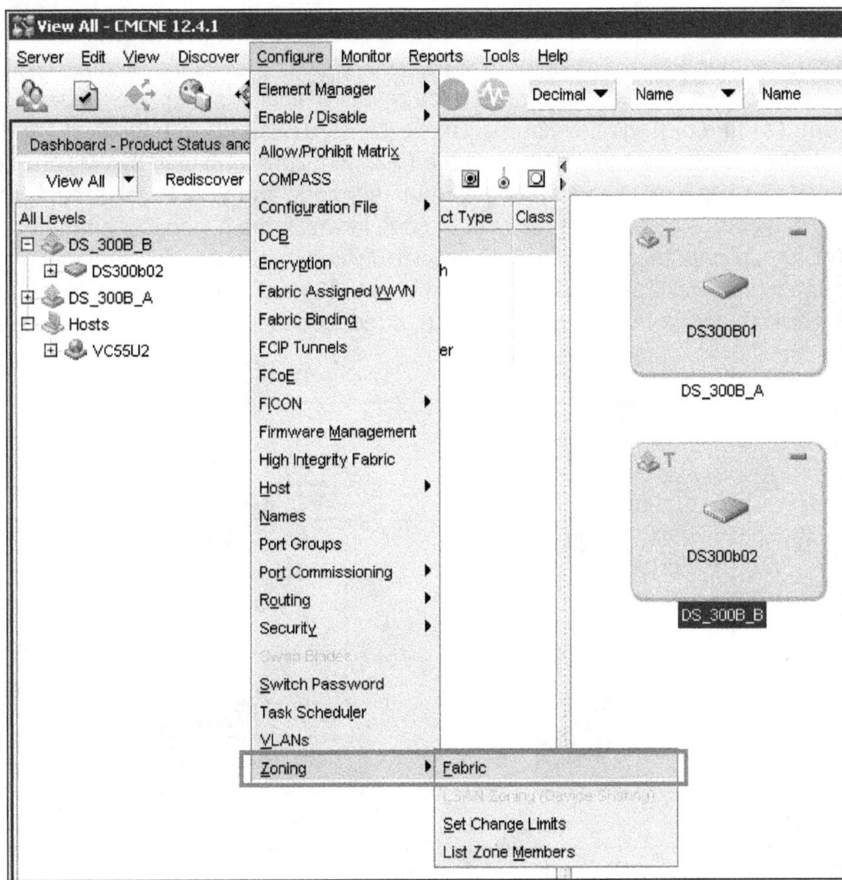

Installation and configuration of Cisco VM-FEX

In this recipe, we will learn how to install and configure Cisco VM-FEX.

Getting ready

Cisco **Virtual Machine Fabric Extender** (**VM-FEX**) collapses the virtual switching infrastructure and physical switching infrastructure into a single and easy to manage environment. Assume that you have prepared two VMware ESXi 5.5 with Cisco VIC and running Enterprise Plus License. These VMware ESXi hosts are managed by VMware Center 5.5. Cisco VM-FEX has two different modes: Emulated mode and PCIe Pass-Through or VMDirectPath mode. The emulated mode is the one in which the hypervisor emulates a physical NIC to replicate the hardware, which is virtualized for the guest virtual machine. PCIe Pass-Through or VMDirectPath mode is that VMware VMDirectPath technology to implement PCIe Pass-Through across the hypervisor layer and reduces the associated I/O overhead. The details are shown in the following diagram:

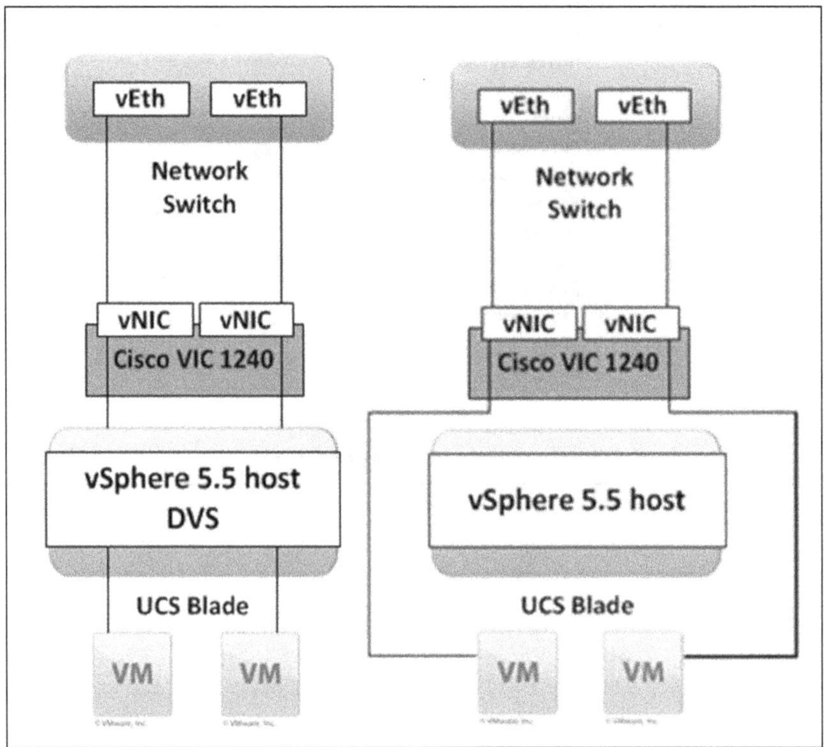

VM-FEX Emulated mode and VM FEX PCIe Pass-Through or VMDirectPath mode

How to do it...

In this recipe, we will learn how to install and configure Cisco VM-FEX in the Emulated mode.

Assume that you have prepared a Cisco service profile that can boot up a VMware ESXi 5.5 in the local drive. Now, Shut down ESXi 5.5 and disassociate this service profile.

Follow these steps to install and configure a Cisco VM-FEX in the Emulated mode:

1. First, log in to Cisco UCS Manager and go to the **LAN** tab in the navigation pane.
2. Create a new dynamic vNIC connection policy, input the policy **Name** and **Number of Dynamic vNICs**, which depends on the number of cables between the IOMs and FI. Select the **Adapter Policy** as **VMWarePassThru** and select **Protection** as **Protected**:

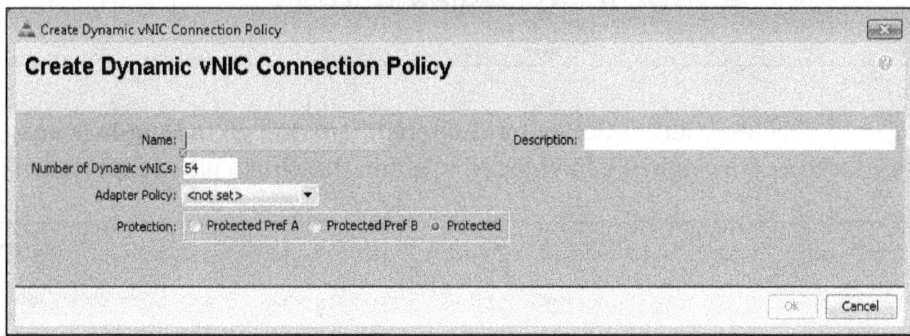

3. Create QoS polices on the **LAN** tab in the navigation pane. Input the policy **Name** and select **Best Effort** on the **Priority** menu:

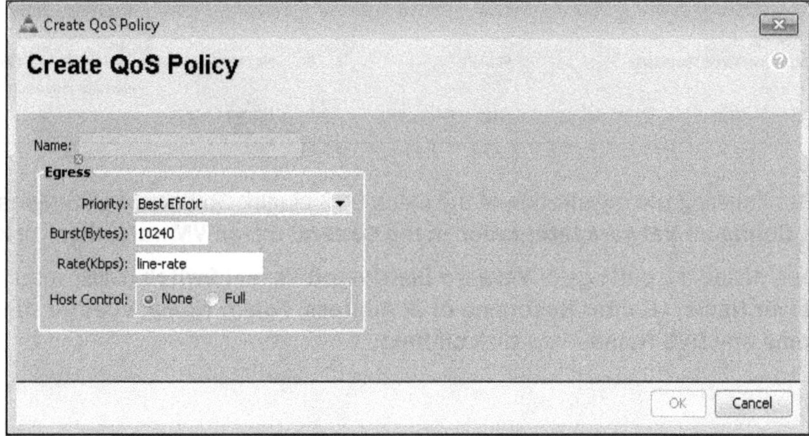

4. The Added Dynamic vNIC Connection Policy and QoS Policies service profile associates this service profile to the UCS Blade Server. Boot up the ESXi 5.5 again.

5. Go to the **VM** tab in the navigation pane and select **VMware**, then **Export vCenter Extension** to download a single UCS extension file:

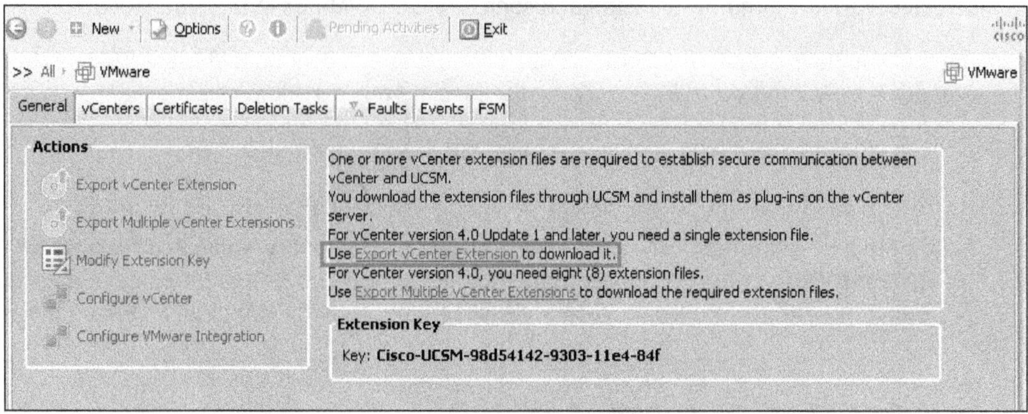

6. Log in to VMware vCenter Server by vSphere Client and go to **Plug-in Manager**. Register the UCS plugin file to VMware vCenter, the plugin file is exported in Step 5:

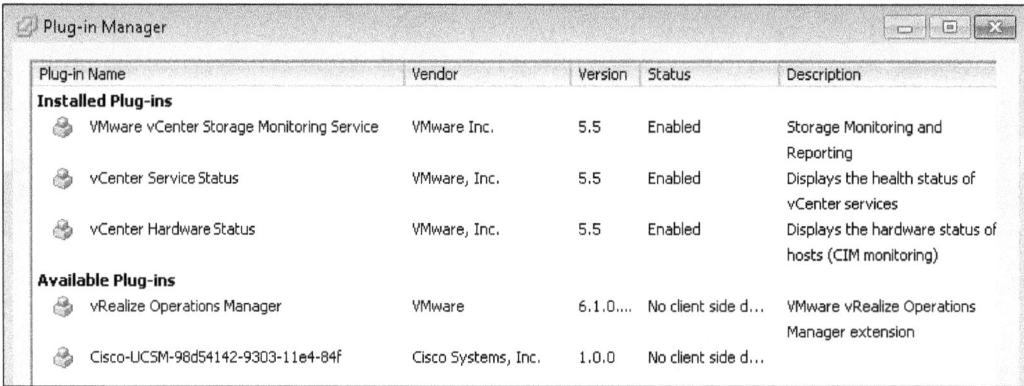

7. After finishing the registration of the Cisco UCS plugin. Go back to UCS Manager, click on **Configure VMware Integration** in the **General** tab on **VMware**, then click on **Next**.

8. Then define the settings of **VMware Distributed Virtual Switch** (**DVS**), input **vCenter Server Name**, **vCenter Hostname or IP Address**, **Folder Name**, **vCenter Datacenter Name** and **DVS Name**, then click on **Next**:

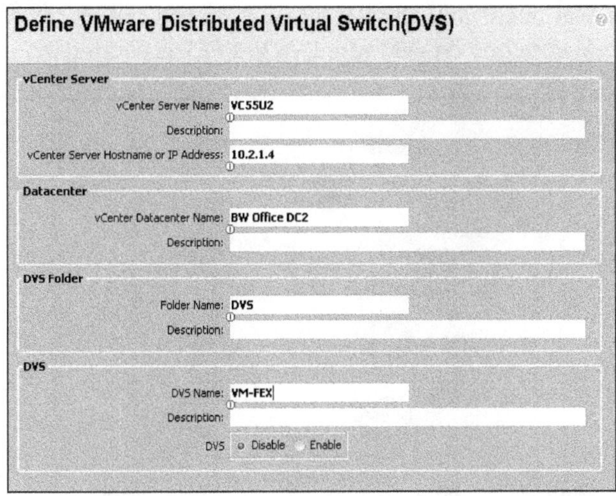

9. Input the **Port Profile Name** and the **QoS Policy** that was created in Step 3, the **VLANs**, and **Profile Client Name**, **Datacenter**, **Folder**, and the **Distributed Virtual Switch** that was created in Step 7, then click on **Next** and **Finish**:

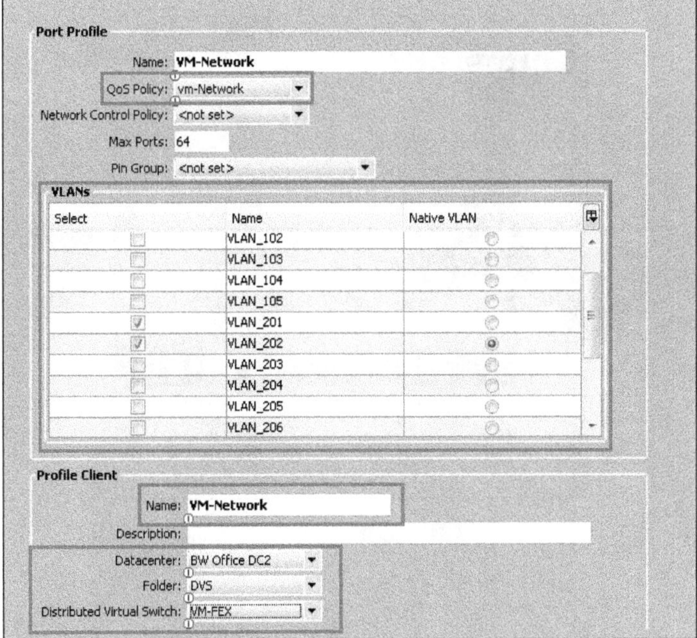

10. After the configuration, go to the **VM** tab and you can see that the **vCenter VC55U2** is added into **VMware** and one VMware DVS **VM-FEX** is created in **Folder DVS**:

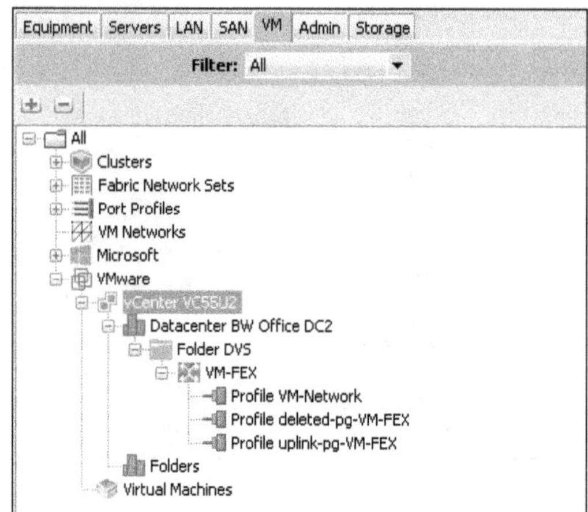

11. Log in to vCenter Server VC55U2 by **vSphere Web Client** and go to **Networking**. You can see that a VMware DVS **VM-FEX** is created in the **DVS** folder:

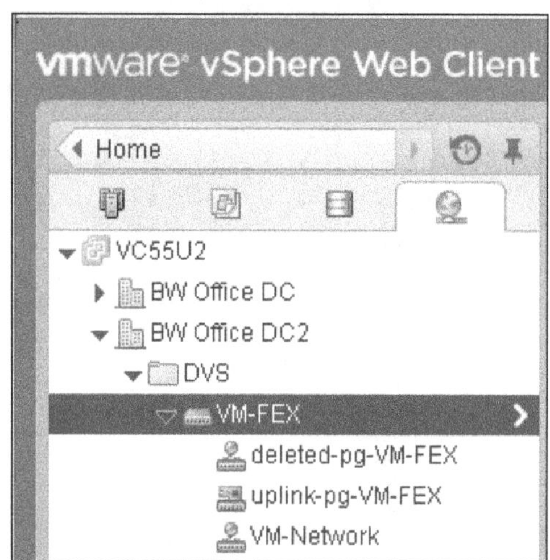

How it works...

In this recipe, we will learn the concept of how to create and configure the port profiles in Cisco VM-FEX.

1. Log in to the Cisco UCS Manager and go to the **VM** tab. Select **Port Profiles** and right-click to create a new port profile:

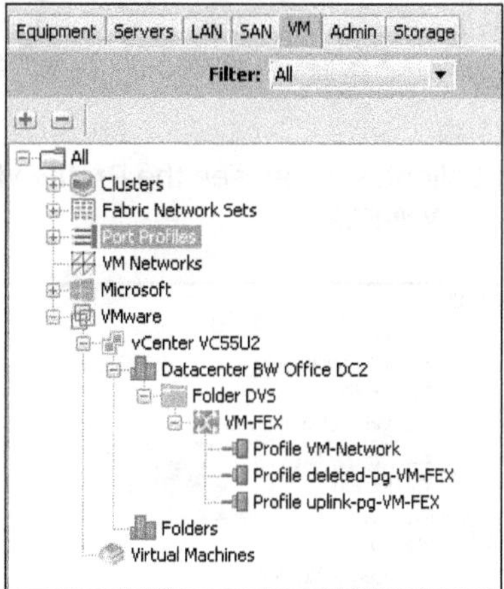

2. Input the port profile **Name**, select the **QoS Policy** and **VLANs** and then click on **OK**:

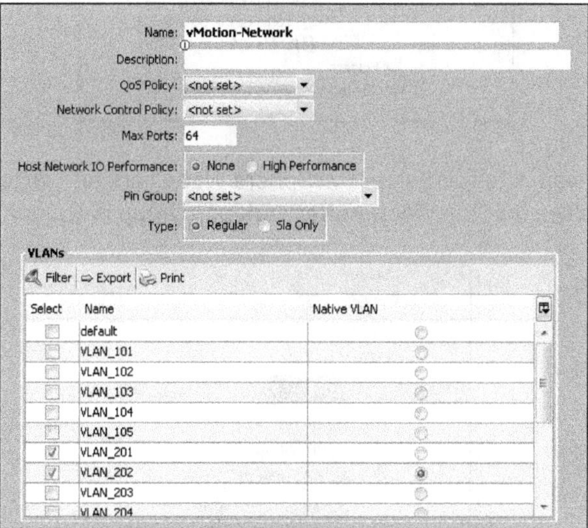

3. After we create the port profile, right-click on that port profile and create a profile client. Input the profile client **Name** (DVS Port Group Name), select **Datacenter**, **DVS** as the **Folder**, and **Distributed Virtual Switch**; click on **OK**:

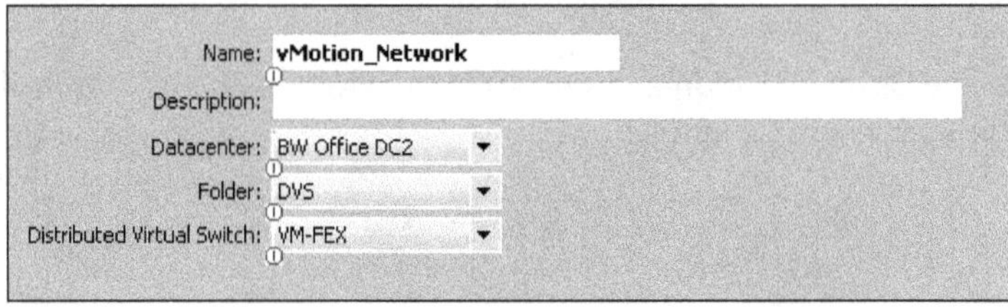

4. After we create the port client, you can see the **Profile vMotion-Network** port client, which is listed under DVS **VM-FEX**:

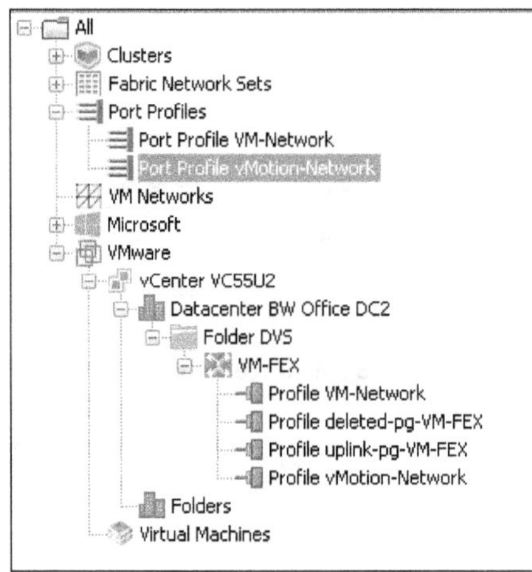

5. Log in to VMware vCenter Server by vSphere Web Client and go to **Networking**. You can also see that the **vMotion-Network** port group is created on DVS **VM-FEX**:

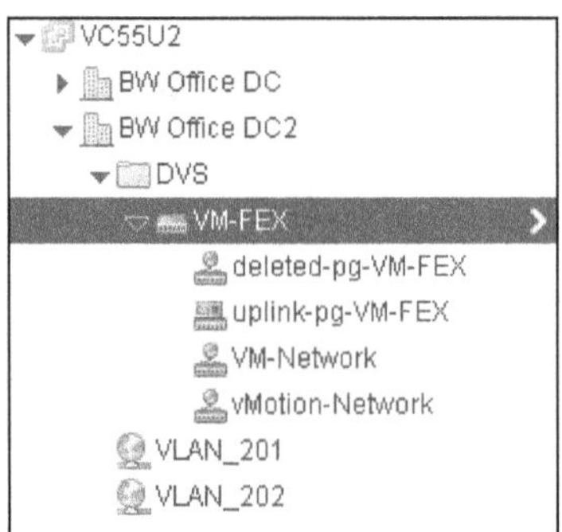

Installation and configuration of VMware VSAN into Cisco UCS

In this recipe, we will learn the concept of how to install and configure VMWare VSAN into Cisco UCS C-Series Server.

Getting ready

First, prepare 2 Cisco UCS 6248UP Fabric Interconnects, which are connected to Cisco Fabric Extender and 3 Cisco C-Series C240 Servers, which are connected to each Cisco Fabric Extender by FC cables through Cisco **Virtual Interface Card** (**VIC**). The following is the diagram of VMware VSAN in a Cisco UCS C-Series Rack Server:

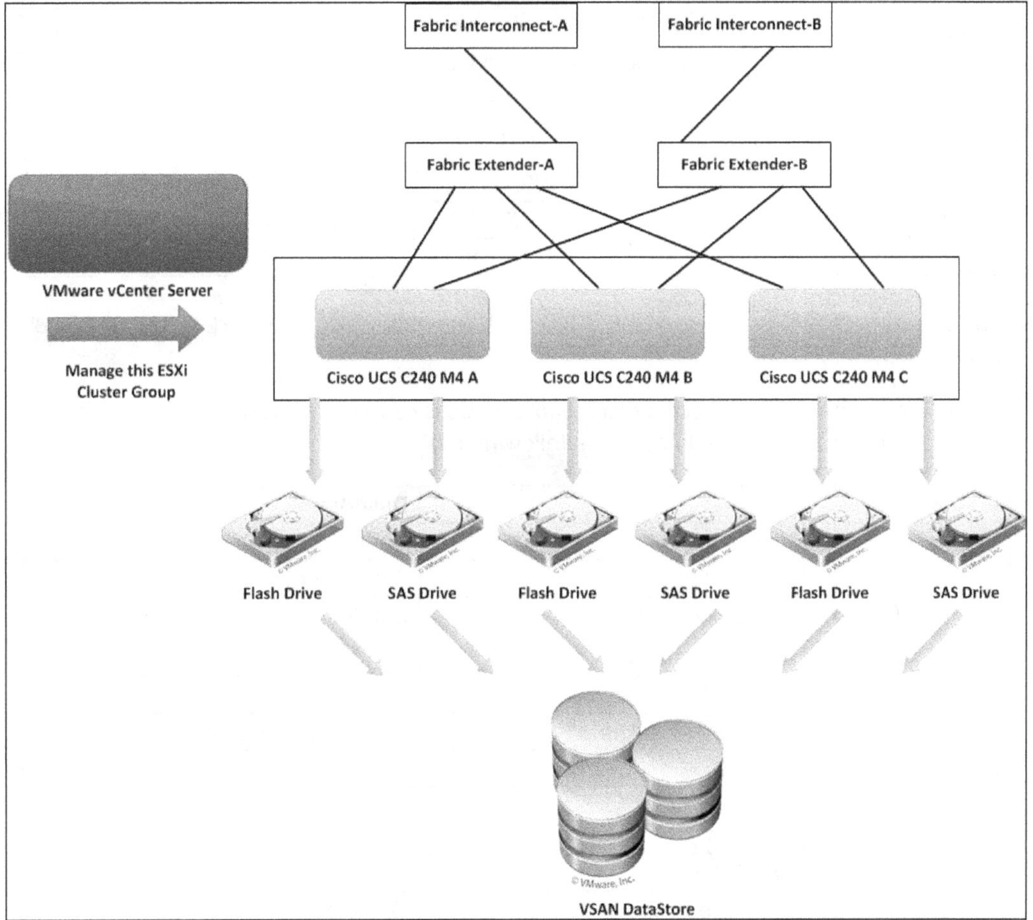

How to do it...

In this recipe, we will learn the concept of how to prepare a Cisco service profile for VMware **Virtual SAN** (**VSAN**) deployment.

The following table is lists the hardware and software requirements for Cisco UCS with VMware Virtual SAN architecture:

Component	Description
Cisco UCS	3 x Cisco UCS C240 M4 Rack Servers, each with 2 x Intel Xeon E5-2600 CPUs 24 x 16 GB DDR3 RDIMMs 6 x 900 GB SAS drives 1 x 200 GB SAS SSDs 1 x LSI MegaRAID SAS controller 1 x Cisco UCS VIC 1227
VMware Software	VMware vCenter 5.5 U3 VMware ESXi 5.5 U3
Fabric Interconnects	2 x Cisco UCS 6248UP 32-Port Fabric Interconnect
Fabric Extender	2 x Nexus 2232PP with 16 FET

Assume that there are three Cisco UCS C240 Rack Servers, which can be detected on Cisco UCS Manager.

1. First prepare some Cisco service pool and policy setting for Cisco service profile, the requirements are listed in the following table:

Parameter Type	Parameter	Description
Service Pools	UUID	Obtained from defined UUID Pool
	Mac address	Obtained from defined MAC Pool
	Worldwide port name (WWPN) Worldwide nod name (WWNN)	Obtained from defined WWPN and WWN Pools
	Boot Policy	Boot Order
	Disk Policy	Local RAID configuration
Fabric	LAN	Virtual NICs, vNICs, and VLANs
	SAN	Virtual Host Bus Adapters, vHBAs, and VSANs
	QoS Policy	Ethernet uplink traffic
Operation	Firmware Policy	Firmware version setting
	BIOS Policy	BIOS version setting

2. The following screenshot is the key parameter setting for VMware VSAN in a Cisco service profile:

   For the Boot Policy setting, create a local drive as the first boot option.

   For the Disk Policy setting, create a local drive with **RAID 1 Mirrored Mode** by two SAS local drives:

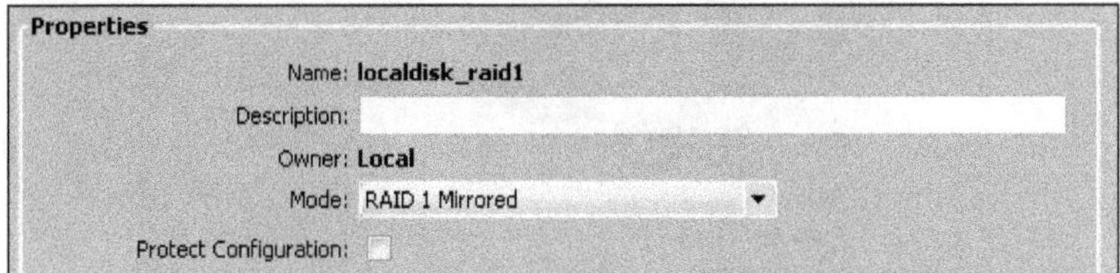

   For the BIOS Policy setting, the following setting can achieve high performance for the VMware Virtual SAN environment:

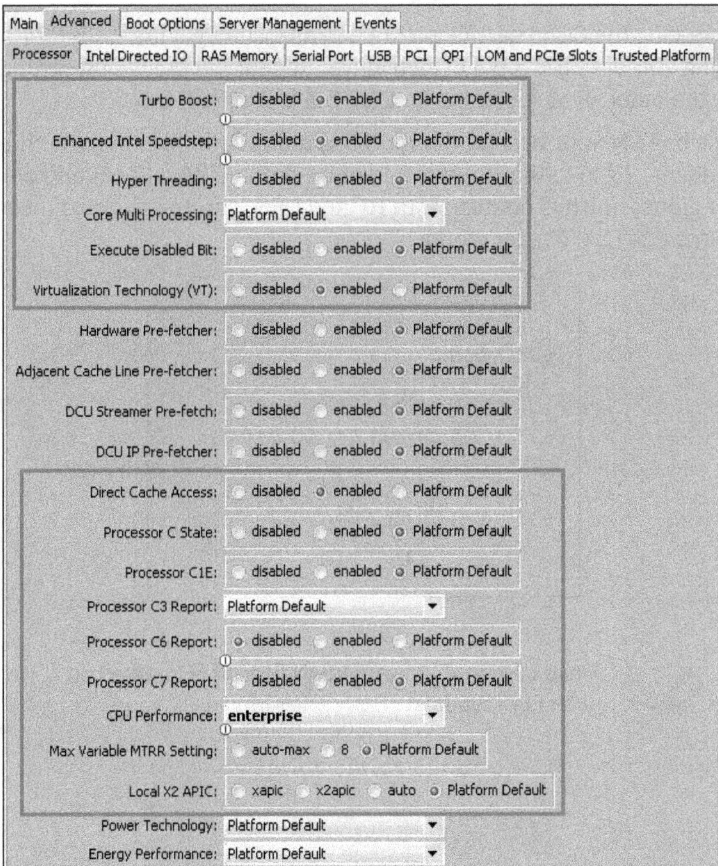

For the vNIC setting, each vNIC is configured for FI Fabric A and Fabric B. You can also enable the Jumbo Frames on each vNIC, which can improve the throughput and the MTU size can be set to 9000:

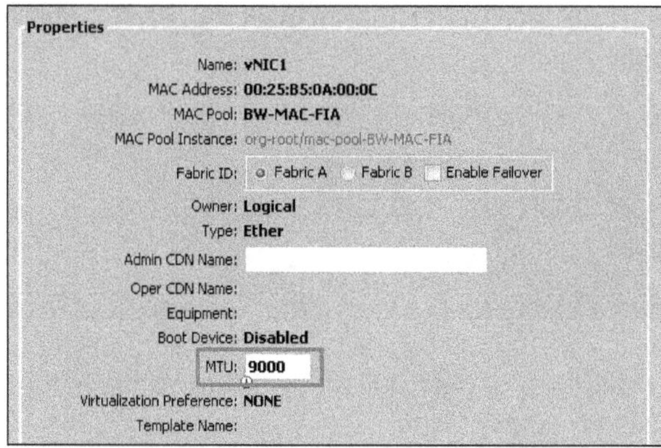

3. After creating the Cisco service profile and associating it into UCS C240, start installing VMware ESXi 5.5 A in local drive. Repeat the preceding settings to create the other service profiles for ESXi 5.5 B and ESXi 5.5 C.
4. Assume one VMware vCenter Server 5.5 is ready. After finishing the three ESXi 5.5 installations, log in to the vCenter Server by vSphere Web Client and create an ESXi cluster group, which is enabled with HA and DRS features and add these three ESXi hosts into this ESXi cluster group:

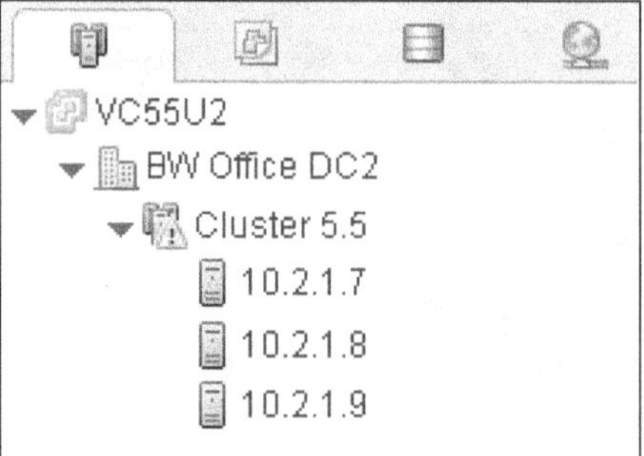

Make sure that VMware VSAN license is enabled on each ESXi 5.5 host.

5. Go to **Networking** for ESXi host and start creating a **VMkernel Network Adapter** for VSAN and then click on **Next**:

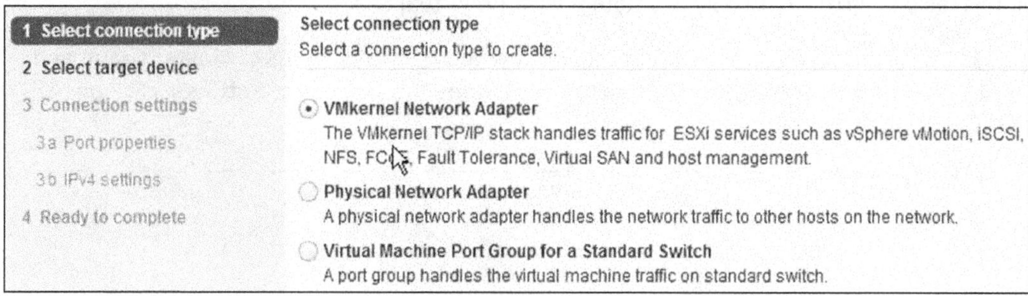

6. Create a VSAN port group and enable the **Virtual SAN traffic** and then click on **Next.**
7. Assign an IP address, Netmask, and Gateway for this VSAN network and click on **Finish**:

According to Cisco and VMware best practices, it is highly recommended that there are two NICs added into VSAN virtual switch and the network speed of each NIC is 10 GB.

8. Repeat Step 4 to 6 to create a VSAN network for the other ESXi hosts.
9. After finishing the VSAN network on all ESXi hosts, now you are ready to enable VMware Virtual SAN on each ESXi host.

How it works...

In this recipe, we will learn how to create a VMware Virtual SAN Cluster.

1. Now you can Turn ON the Virtual SAN feature, right-click on **ESXi Cluster Group** and select **Edit Settings...**. Then go to the **Manage** tab and select **Settings**, click on **Edit...**:

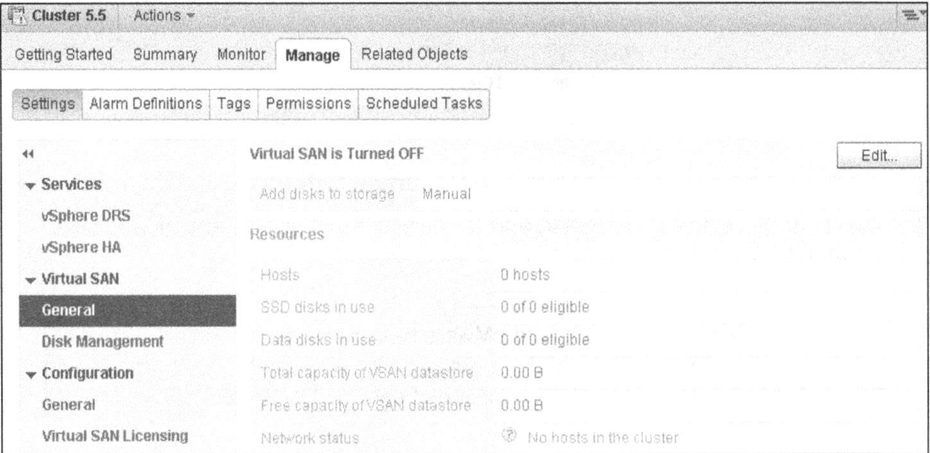

2. Select **Turn ON Virtual SAN** and click **OK**. It starts to create a **VSAN Cluster**:

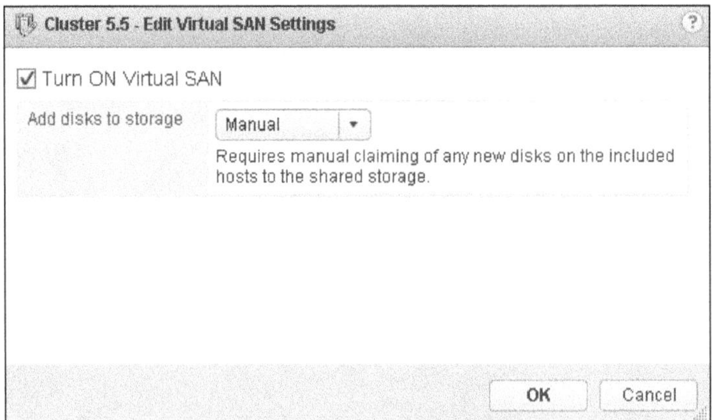

Make sure that a VMware Virtual SAN license is enabled on each ESXi host before turning on Virtual SAN.

3. After finishing the enabling of the VSAN Cluster, go to **Disk Management** on the **Settings** tab and select each ESXi host, then click on the button in the red square to add all SAS drives and flash drives into the **Disk Groups**:

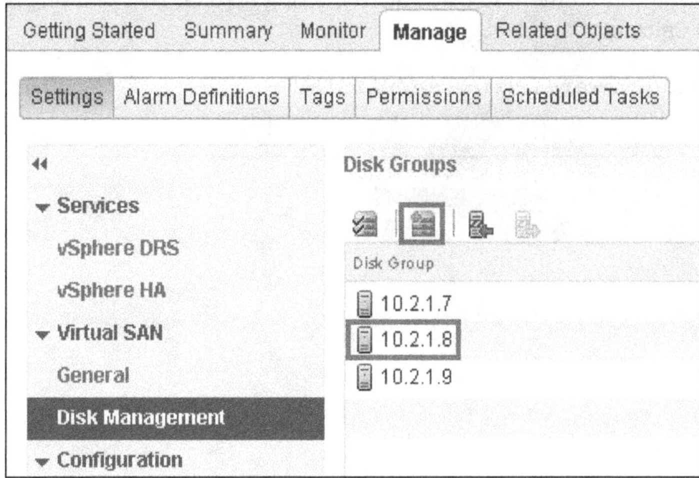

4. After adding all SAS drives (12 x 900 GB) and Flash drives (3 x 200 GB) into **Disk Group**, you can see a new datastore, **vsanDatastore**, with a capacity of around **10.75 TB** on the **Datastores** tab:

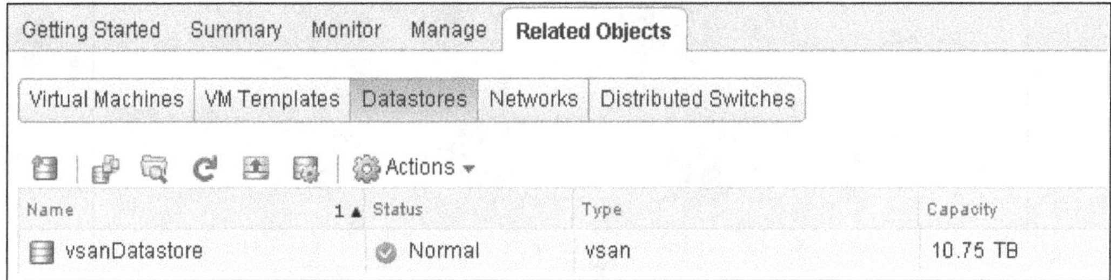

There's more...

The VMware also provides a Virtual SAN TCO Calculator, which is a Web-based system; you can input your VSAN requirement to calculate the sizing results. The following is the URL of a Virtual SAN TCO Calculator:

`https://vsantco.vmware.com/vsan/SI/SIEV`

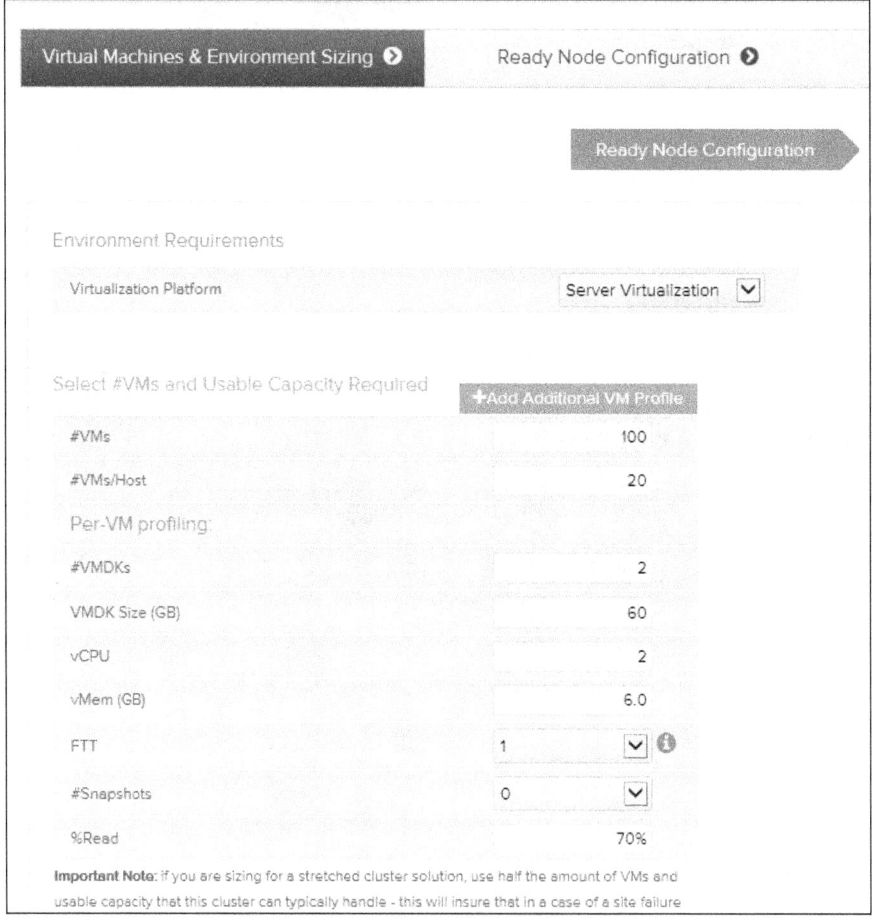

Create a user account if you want to save or download your results.

6

Cisco UCS Site Planning

In this chapter, we will cover the following topics:

- The Cisco UCS Power Calculator
- The Cisco UCS Manager Interoperability Utility
- The EMC E-Lab Interoperability Navigator
- HP Single Point of Connectivity Knowledge (SPOCK)
- The VMware Compatibility Guide
- The IBM System Storage Interoperation Center (SSIC)

Introduction

In this chapter, you will learn how to accomplish the tasks related to Cisco UCS Site Planning; for example, the UCS Power Calculation and how to check Cisco UCS compatibility Support Matrix. We will also learn about other vendor compatibility checking tools, such as EMC E-lab, HP **Single Point of Connectivity Knowledge** (**SPOCK**), VMware Compatibility Guide, and IBM **System Storage Interoperation Center** (**SSIC**).

The Cisco UCS Power Calculator

In this recipe, we will learn how to use the Cisco UCS Power Calculator and export the Power Summary Report result.

Getting ready

Cisco UCS Power Calculator is a free web-based system that is used to provide a power estimate. The user can select different models of Cisco UCS hardware, Cisco Fabric Interconnect, UCS B-Series, and C-Series Server. The user can then input the power consumption and provide the checking result. You also can export a file in the CSV or PRJ format; you can access this tool if you have internet access.

How to do it...

In this recipe, you will learn how to select the Cisco UCS Fabric Interconnect, UCS Chassis 5108, and UCS B-Series in the Cisco UCS Power Calculator, input the power consumption, and export the result. The following table is an example of the Cisco UCS components for a Power Calculator:

Cisco UCS Component	Detail
Cisco UCS Fabric Interconnect 6248UP x 2	2 x Power Supply 2 x Ports Configured Redundancy Mode: N+N 50% Power Consumption
Cisco UCS 5108 Blade Chassis x 1	4 x Power Supply Redundancy Mode: N+N IO Module: 2208
Cisco UCS B200 M4 x 4	2 x Processor: Intel E5-2680 v3 2.5 GHz 24 x 16 GB DDR4 Memory 2 x 600 GB SAS 6 GB 10K RPM SFF HDD 1 x Cisco VIC 1340 Adapter

According to the preceding table, you can calculate the Cisco UCS power consumption using the following procedure:

1. Open your Web browser and go to `http://ucspowercalc.cisco.com/`.
2. Click on **New Project** and select **Fabric** and click on **Fabric Interconnect | 6248UP** and then click on **Configure and Add**, as shown in the following screenshot:

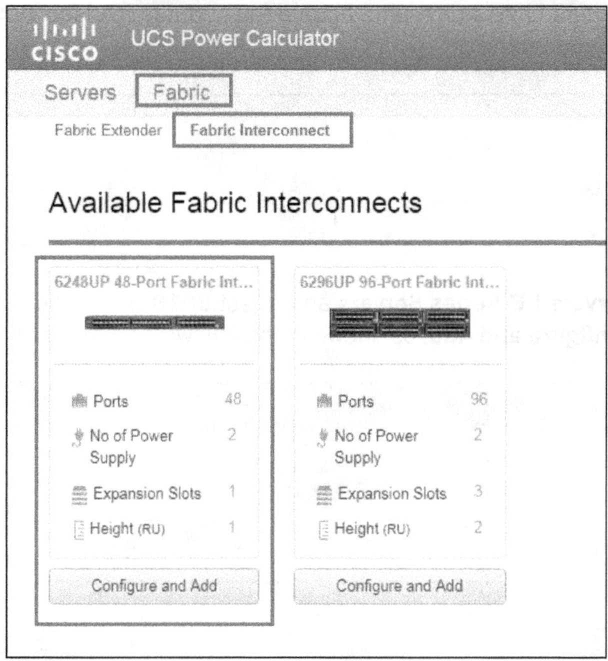

3. Assume that the power consumption is 50% and 12 FI ports are configured, select **Redundancy Mode** as **N+N**, **Input Voltage** as **220 VAC**, **Power Supply** as **2** and **750W PSU**, no **Expansion Modules**; then click on **Add to Project**:

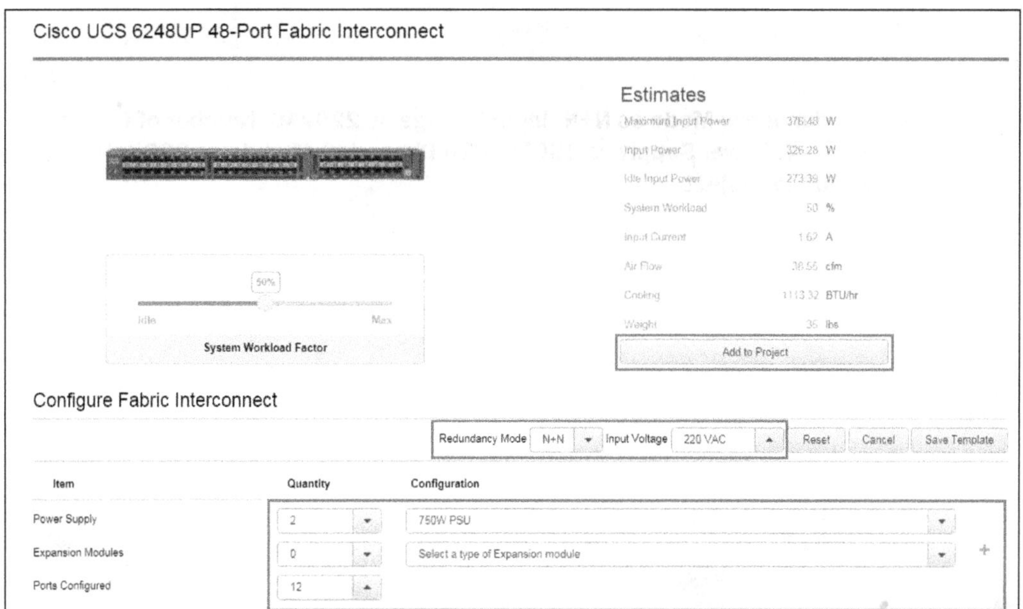

4. Now, in the right-hand side menu, update the quantity of **Cisco UCS 6248UP 48-Port Fabric Interconnect** to 2:

5. Click on **Servers** | **B-Series Servers** and select **5018 Blade Chassis (AC) V2** and click on **Configure and Add**, as shown in the following screenshot:

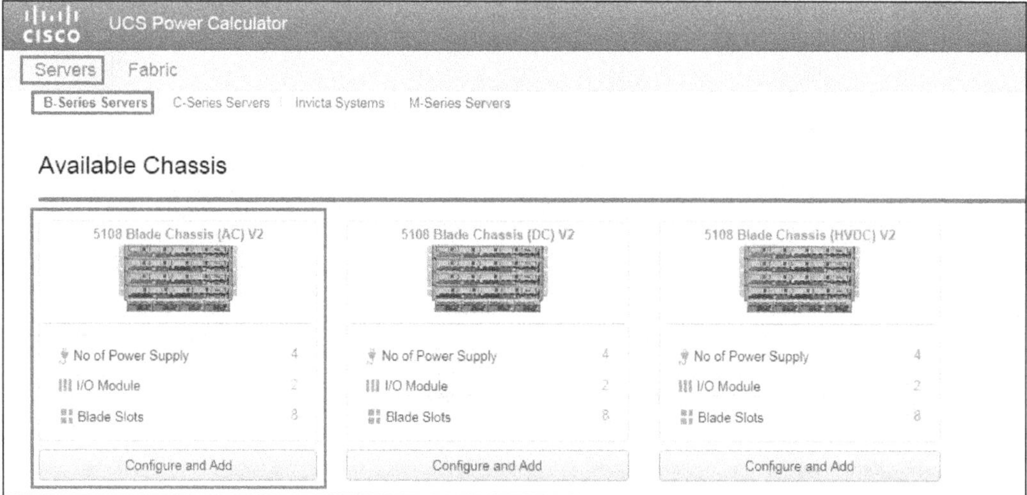

6. Select **Redundancy Mode** as **N+N**, **Input Voltage** as **220VAC**, **Number of Power Supplies** as **4**, **Power Supply** as **2500W PSU DV**, and **IO Module** as **2208**. Then click on **Add to Project**:

7. Click on **Add blade to chassis**:

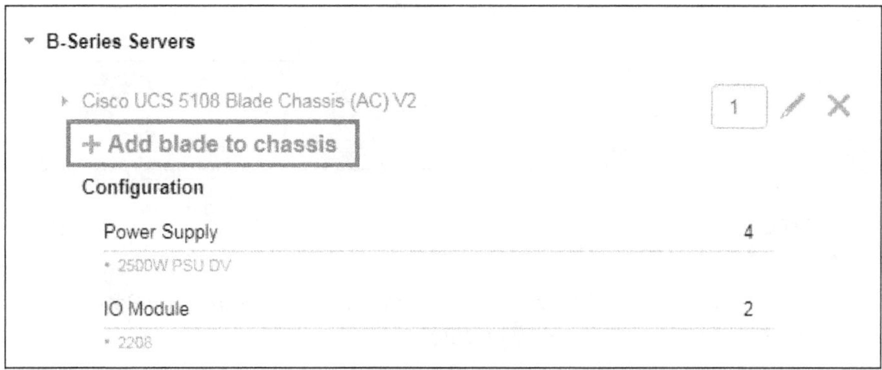

8. Select **B200 M4** and click on **Add to Project**.

9. Assume that the power consumption is 50%, input **Quantity** and **Configuration** of **Processor**, **Memory**, **Storage**, and **Adapter** and then click on **Add to Chassis**:

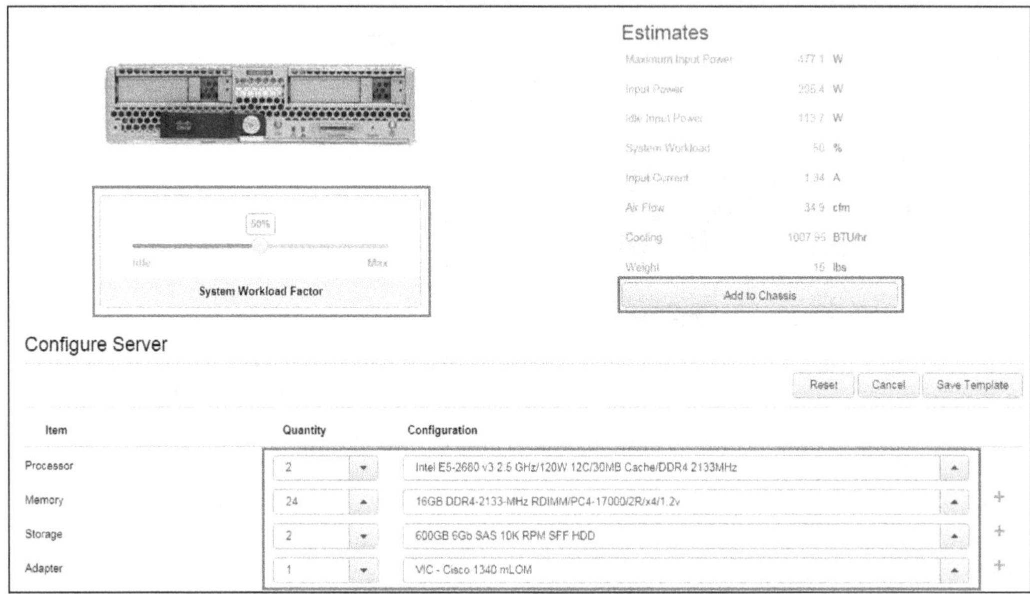

10. After this, update the quantity of **Cisco UCS B200 M4** to `4` in the right-hand side menu. Finally, you can see that all the Cisco UCS components are added to this project:

How it works...

In this recipe, we will learn the concept of how to view the Power Summary Report result and export the result to a file in the CSV or PRJ format.

1. After you input the Cisco UCS hardware requirements into the Cisco UCS Power Calculator, click on the **View Detail Result** button to view the result:

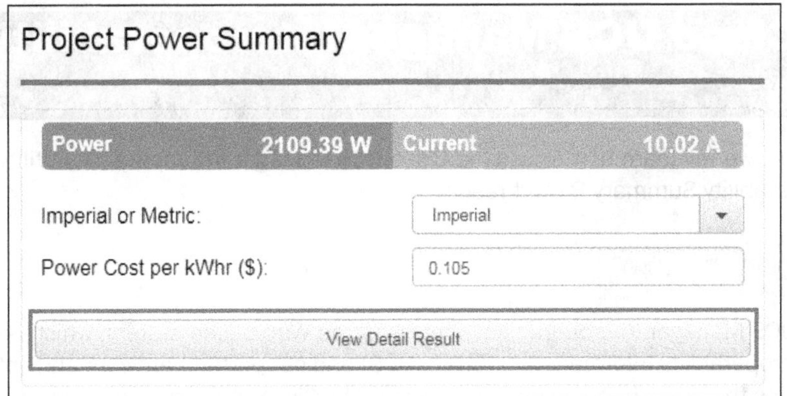

2. You can see the detail of **Max Power (W)** and the **Cooling System Workflow (BTU/hr)** for each Cisco UCS, **Fabric** and **B-Series Servers**, as shown in the following screenshot:

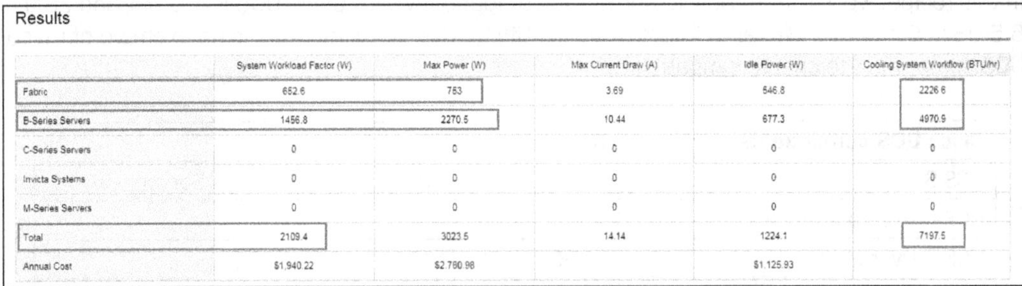

Results

	System Workload Factor (W)	Max Power (W)	Max Current Draw (A)	Idle Power (W)	Cooling System Workflow (BTU/hr)
Fabric	652.6	763	3.69	546.8	2226.6
B-Series Servers	1456.8	2270.5	10.44	677.3	4970.9
C-Series Servers	0	0	0	0	0
Invicta Systems	0	0	0	0	0
M-Series Servers	0	0	0	0	0
Total	2109.4	3023.5	14.14	1224.1	7197.5
Annual Cost	$1,940.22	$2,780.98		$1,125.93	

3. If you want to export the result into one file, you can select the **Export** option in the top right-hand side menu and save it in either `.csv` or `.prj` format:

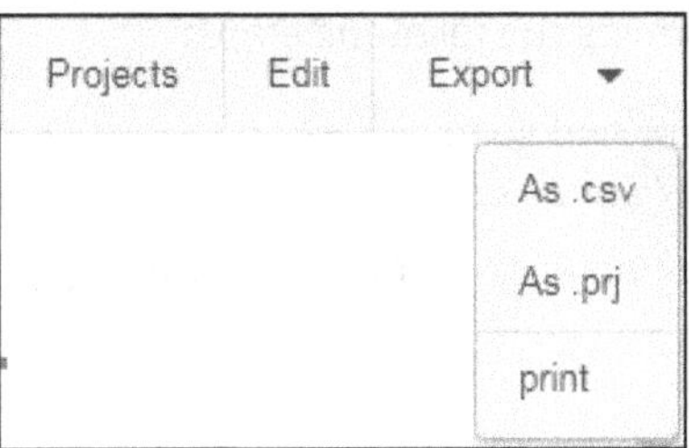

The Cisco UCS Manager Interoperability Utility

In this recipe, we will learn how to use the Cisco UCS Manager Interoperability Utility and view the Interoperability Summary Report result.

Getting ready

The Cisco UCS Manager Interoperability Utility is a free Web-based system, which is used to provide interoperability information for Cisco (UCS) and supported hardware and software configurations that have been tested and validated by Cisco. You can access this tool if you have internet access.

How to do it...

In this recipe, we will learn how to check the compatibility with Cisco UCS B200 M4 and ESXi 5.5 U3 in Cisco UCS Manager Interoperability Utility. The following table is an example of Cisco UCS component to check compatibility.

Cisco UCS components	Detail
UCS Series	B-Series and UCSM-Managed C-Series Servers
UCS firmware release	2.2(6)
UCS Server Model	B200 M4
OS Platform	VMware ESXi 5.5 U3
UCS CNA Adapter	UCS 1380 Virtual Interface Card

According to the preceding table, you can input the UCS component into the UCS Manager Interoperability Utility by performing the following steps:

1. Open your Web browser and go to `http://www.cisco.com/web/techdoc/ucs/interoperability/matrix/matrix.html/`.
2. Select the requirement on each menu, as shown:

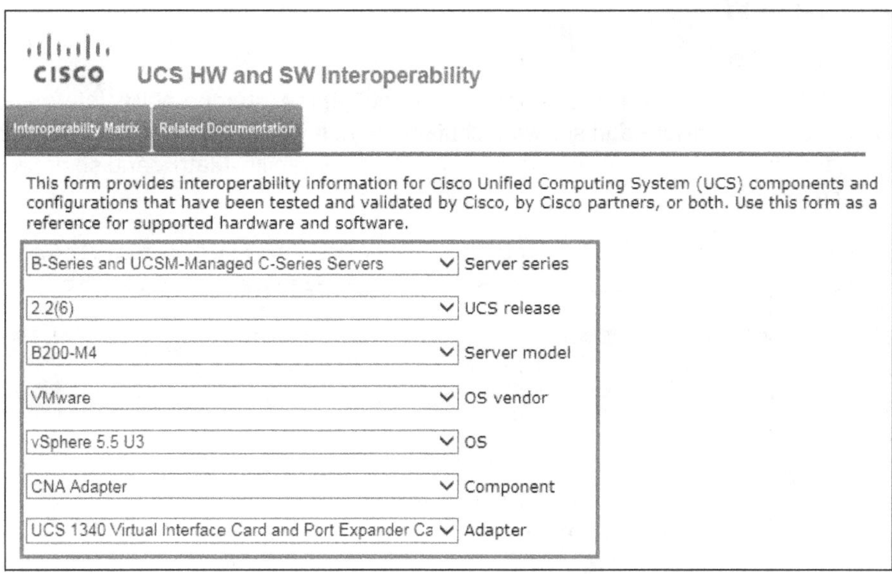

3. The tool will display the result automatically after you input the requirements. You can see the supported **Adapter Driver** and **Adapter Firmware** for VMware ESXi 5.5 U3.

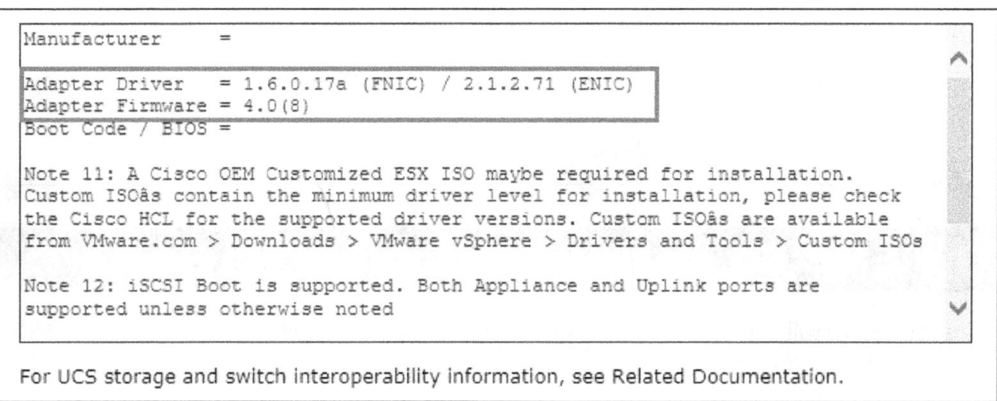

Cisco UCS Manager Interoperability Utility is used to check the hardware and software compatibility for the UCS B-Series, C-Series, and M-Series Servers.

How it works...

You can start the platform installation on UCS once you get the interoperability information of Cisco UCS for the hardware and software configuration. If you want to get the compatibility information for Cisco VM-FEX, Storage Array, Switch Interoperability Matrix, and so on; you can download the technical references from the following link:

`http://www.cisco.com/c/en/us/support/servers-unified-computing/unified-computing-system/products-technical-reference-list.html`

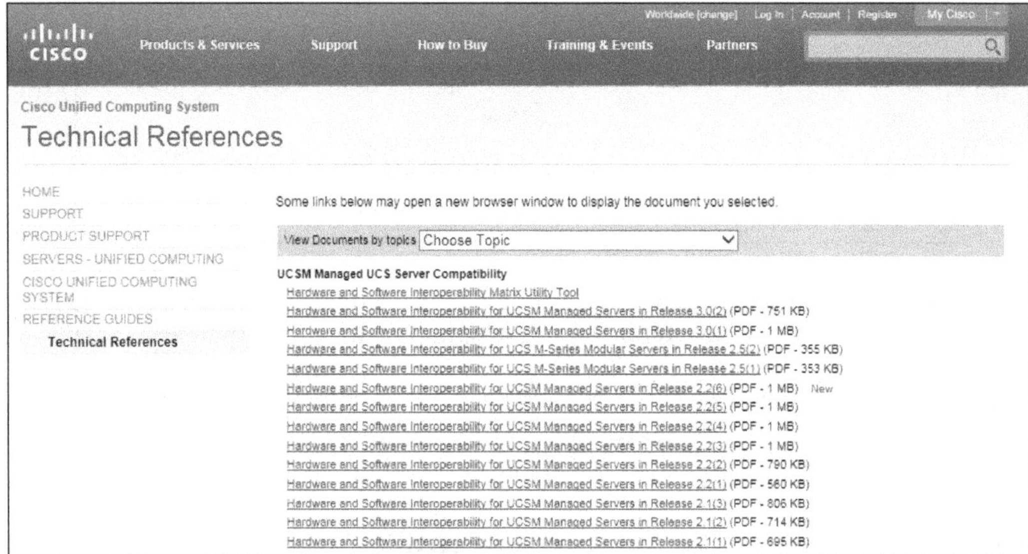

The EMC E-Lab Interoperability Navigator

In this recipe, we will learn how to use EMC E-LAB Interoperability Navigator and check EMC interoperability information.

Getting ready

EMC E-Lab Interoperability Navigator is a Web-based system, which is used to provide interoperability information to support hardware and software configurations that have been tested and validated by EMC. EMC E-Lab's Database stores millions of qualified configuration of EMC and third party hardware and software. You can access this tool if you have internet access.

You need an EMC partner or employee's account to access the EMC E-Lab Interoperability Navigator tool.

How to do it...

In this recipe, we will learn how to check the compatibility between Cisco UCS B200 M4 and EMC VNX 5200 (Block) Storage in an EMC E-Lab Interoperability Navigator. The following table is an example of the Cisco UCS component used for compatibility checking:

Component Type	Detail
Storage Array	EMC VNX5200 (Block)
Host System	Cisco UCS B200 M4
Operation System	Windows Server 2012 R2
Switch	Brocade 300
Host Bus Adapter	Cisco VIC 1340

According to the preceding table, you can input each component into an EMC E-Lab Interoperability Navigator by performing the following steps:

1. Open your Web browser and go to `https://elabnavigator.emc.com/`.
2. After logging in your EMC SSO account, you can enter EMC **E-LAB INTEROPERABILITY NAVIGATOR**:

3. Then choose **ADVANCED QUERIES** from the **QUERIES** menu:

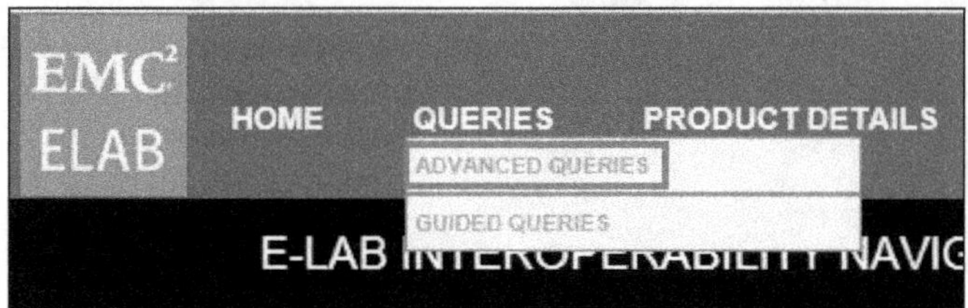

4. Based on the preceding table, input your component to be checked:

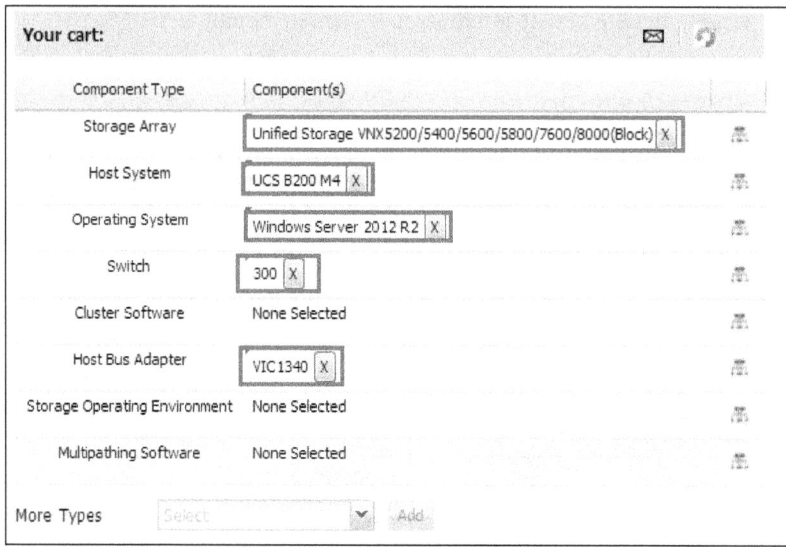

5. After you input your requirement, you can see that the checking result will be displayed at the bottom of the page. You can select the configuration you want; for basic host connectivity, you can select **Base Connectivity** and **Path Management Software** and then click on the **Get Results for Selected Configurations** button:

6. You can then view the details of each configuration on EMC VNX and Cisco UCS, for example base connectivity of EMC VNX and Cisco UCS. If you want to export the configuration into a file in a PDF format, you can click on the **Export All** button:

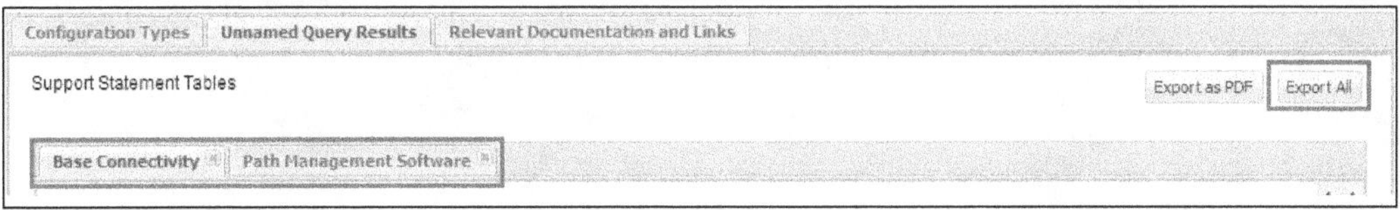

[Click on the **Export as PDF** button, you can only export selected tab information as one PDF. Click on the **Export All** button, you can export all tab info as one PDF.]

How it works...

You can start the platform installation on UCS and host connectivity after you get the interoperability information for Cisco UCS of hardware and software configuration. If you want the compatibility information for Cisco UCS **Blades Chassis Switch Modules**, you can go to the EMC E-Lab home page and download the Blade Chassis Switch Modules Support Matrix on **EMC STORAGE SIMPLE SUPPORT MATRICES** (**ESSMs**); this matrix includes the information of all Blade Chassis; for example, HP, Cisco, IBM, and Dell:

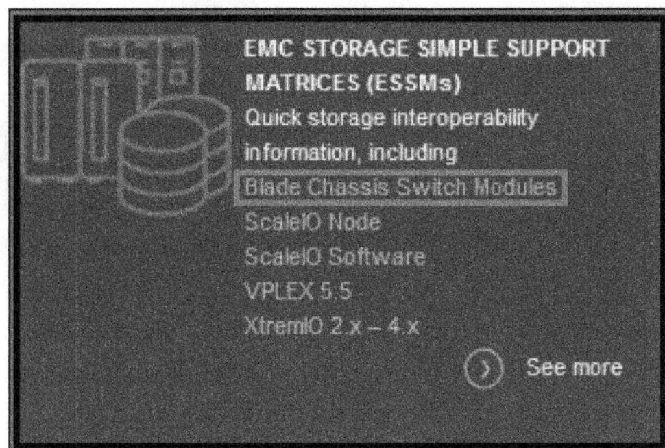

This **Blade Chassis Switch Modules** support matrix is regularly updated:

HP Single Point of Connectivity Knowledge (SPOCK)

In this recipe, we will learn how to use HP SPOCK and check the interoperability information.

Getting ready

HP SPOCK is an authoritative source of interoperability information for HP storage products. A particular configuration is supported if and only if it is listed on SPOCK. You can access this tool if you have Internet access.

You need an HP partner or employee's account to access HP SPOCK.

How to do it...

In this recipe, we will learn how to check the compatibility of Cisco UCS and HP 3PAR Operating System Software 3.2.2 in HP SPOCK. The following table is an example of the Cisco UCS component to check compatibility:

Cisco UCS Components	Detail
UCS Series	B-Series
UCS firmware release	2.0(x), 2.1(x), 2.2(x)
UCS Server Model	B200 M4
OS Platform	Microsoft Windows Server 2012 R2
UCS CNA Adapter	UCS 1340 Virtual Interface Card

According to the preceding table, you can get interoperability information on HP SPOCK by performing the following steps:

1. Open your Web browser and go to `https://h20272.www2.hp.com/SPOCK/` and then click on **Log in to SPOCK now**, as shown in the following screenshot:

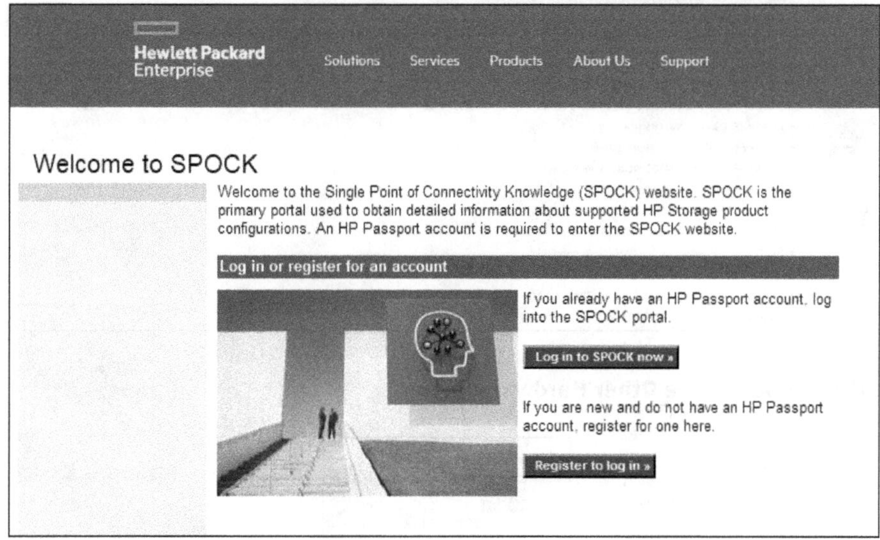

2. After logging into HP SPOCK, you can see the documentation menu on the left-hand side of the screen, as shown in the following screenshot:

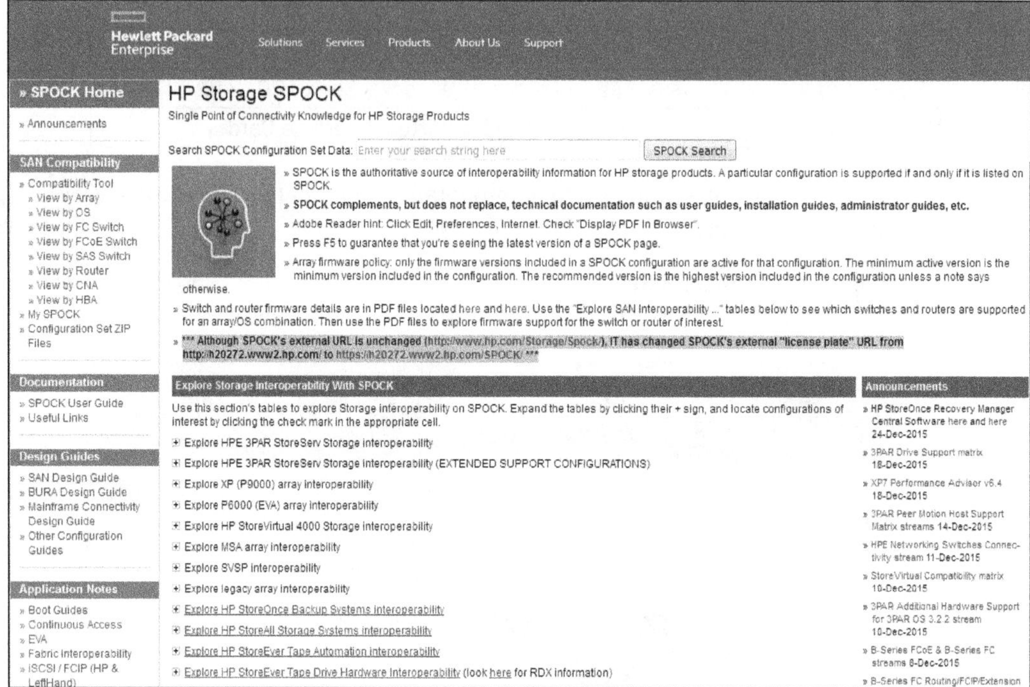

3. Go to **3PAR** on the **Other Hardware** menu:

4. You can download **HP 3PAR Additional Hardware Support for 3PAR OS 3.2.2** (Version number may vary):

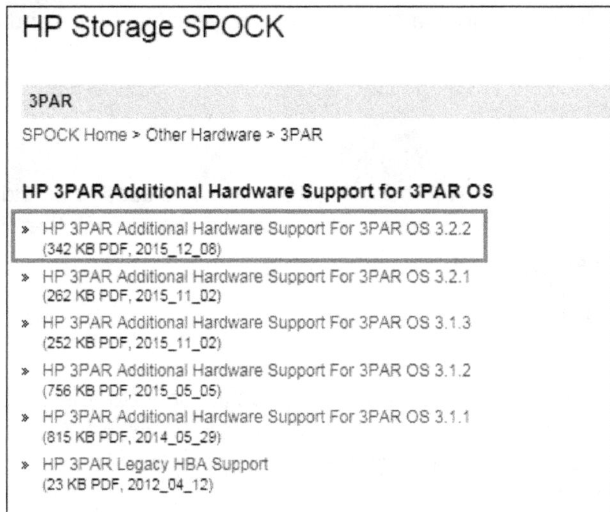

5. This HP 3PAR Support Matrix includes Cisco UCS 2.0(x), 2.1(x), 2.2(x), and 3.0(x); the details of which are shown in the following table:

In addition to the Cisco HCL support, please also refer to the below notes for HP 3PAR support:
Notes
Microsoft Windows Server Operating System, Red Hat Enterprise Linux (RHEL), SUSE Linux Enterprise Server (SLES), VMware vSphere (ESX/ESXi), Oracle Solaris, Citrix XenServer
Microsoft Windows Server Operating System, Red Hat Enterprise Linux (RHEL), SUSE Linux Enterprise Server (SLES), VMware vSphere (ESX/ESXi), Oracle Solaris
Cisco UCS 6200 Series Fabric Interconnects (6248 & 6296)
B-Series blade servers and adapters: M1, M2 with M71KR-E, M71KRQ, M72KR-E, M72KR-Q, M81KR, & VIC1280
B-Series blade servers and adapters: M1, M2, M3 with M71KR-E, M71KRQ, M72KR-E, M72KR-Q, M81KR, VIC1240 & VIC1280
Boot From SAN (BFS)
8GB FC storage target connectivity ONLY (FCoE and iSCSI storage target connectivity is NOT supported)
Please refer to the *Switch Interoperability Matrix* section in the Cisco HCLs
OS Specfic Support Notes
Windows Server (w/Hyper-V) 2008R2SP1 x64 with adapters M81KR, VIC1280 using driver 2.1.0.17 only supported on Qlogic fabric.
Windows Server (w/Hyper-V) 2008R2SP1 x64 with adapters M81KR, VIC1240, VIC1280 using driver 2.1.0.17 only supported on Qlogic fabric.
Windows Server (w/Hyper-V) 2008R2SP1 x64 with adapters M81KR, VIC1240, VIC1280 using driver 2.1.0.18 only supported on Qlogic fabric.
Windows Server (w/Hyper-V) 2008SP2 x64, 2008R2SP1 x64 with UCS adapters M81KR, VIC1240 and VIC1280 using driver 2.1.0.20 only supported on Qlogic fabric.
Windows Server (w/Hyper-V) 2012 x64 with adapters MK81KR, VIC1240, VIC1280 using driver 2.2.0.9 only supported on Qlogic Fabric and Cisco Fabric where Persistent FCID is NOT enabled
Redhat compatible kernel only supported with Oracle Linux.
Refer to Cisco HCL for BFS patch requirements for SLES 11 SP1 x64
ESX 4.x only supported with adapters MK81KR, VIC1240, VIC1280 using driver 1.4.0.201 on Qlogic Fabric, Brocade Fabric and Cisco Fabric where Persistent FCID is NOT enabled
ESX 4.x only supported with adapters MK81KR, VIC1240, VIC1280 using driver 1.4.0.213 on Qlogic Fabric, Brocade Fabric and Cisco Fabric where Persistent FCID is NOT enabled

How it works...

You can start the platform installation on UCS and host connectivity based on the interoperability information of Cisco UCS for hardware and software configuration.

The VMware Compatibility Guide

In this recipe, we will learn how to use the VMware Compatibility Guide and check the interoperability information.

Getting ready

VMware Compatibility Guide is a Web-based system, which is used to provide interoperability information and the supported hardware and software configurations that have been tested and validated by VMware.

How to do it...

In this recipe, we will learn how to check the compatibility between Cisco UCS B200 M4 and VMware ESXi 5.5 U3 and Cisco UCS B200 M4, and EMC VNX5400 Storage Array in VMware Compatibility Guide. The following tables are examples of Cisco UCS component for checking compatibility.

Cisco UCS B200 M4 and VMware interoperability information is as follows:

VMware components	**Detail**
What are you looking for	Systems/Servers
Product Release Version	ESXi 5.5 U3
Partner Name	Cisco
System Blade	B200 M4
CPU Series	Intel Xeon E5-2600-v3 Series
Keyword	M4

EMC VNX 5400 Array and VMware interoperability information as follows:

VMware components	**Detail**
What are you looking for	Storage/SAN
Product Release Version	ESXi 5.5 U3
Partner Name	EMC
Array Type	All
Keyword	5400

According to the preceding table, you can get the interoperability information on VMware Compatibility Guide by performing the following steps. The following is an example of checking the Cisco UCS B200 M4 and VMware Interoperability information:

1. Open your Web browser and go to `http://www.vmware.com/resources/compatibility/search.php`; select your requirements and click on the **Update and View Results** button:

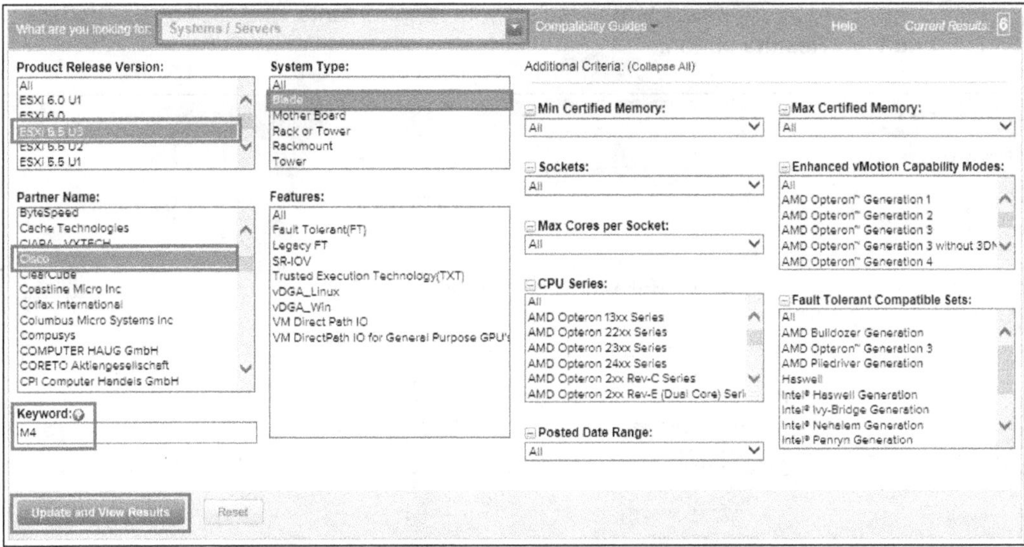

2. After that you can see the search result at the bottom of the page. You can also see that the **UCS B200 M4** model with **Intel Xeon E5-2600-v3 Series** is supported by VMware ESXi 5.5 U3.

   The following screenshot is the checking result for the VMware Compatibility Guide:

Search Results: Your search for " Systems / Servers " returned **6 results** Back to Top Turn Off Auto Scroll Display: 10

Partner Name	Model	CPU Series	Supported Releases				
Cisco	UCS - B200-M4	Intel Xeon E5-2600-v3 Series	ESXi	6.0 U1	6.0	5.5 U3	5.5 U2
Cisco	UCS - B260 M4	Intel Xeon E7-8800/4800-v3	ESXi	6.0 U1	6.0	5.5 U3	5.5 U2
Cisco	UCS - B260 M4	Intel Xeon E7-8800/4800/2800-v2	ESXi	6.0 U1	6.0	5.5 U3	5.5 U2
Cisco	UCS - B420 M4	Intel Xeon E5-4600-v3 Series	ESXi	6.0 U1	6.0	5.5 U3	5.5 U2
Cisco	UCS - B460 M4	Intel Xeon E7-8800/4800-v3	ESXi	6.0 U1	6.0	5.5 U3	5.5 U2
Cisco	UCS - B460 M4	Intel Xeon E7-8800/4800/2800-v2	ESXi	6.0 U1	6.0	5.5 U3	5.5 U2

You can also export the search result as a file in the CSV format.

3. The following is an example of how to search the EMC VNX 5400 Array and VMware Interoperability information:

   Open your Web browser and go to `http://www.vmware.com/resources/compatibility/search.php`, select your requirements, and click on the **Update and View Results** button:

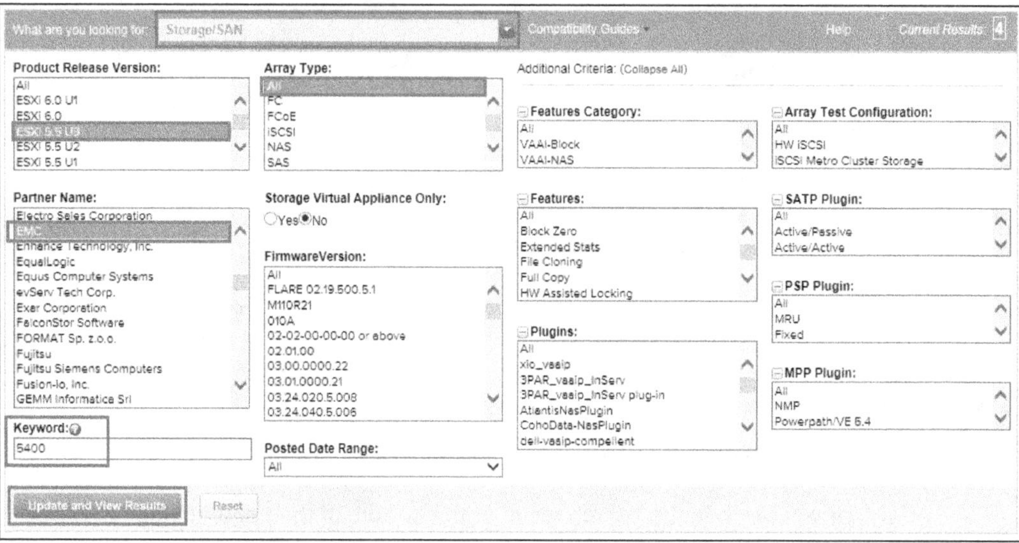

4. After this, you can check the result at the bottom of the page. You can see **EMC VNX 5400** with **FC** connection is supported by VMware ESXi 5.5 U3.

   The following is the search result from the VMware Compatibility Guide:

Bookmark | Print | Export to CSV

Search Results: Your search for " Storage/SAN " returned **4 results**. Back to Top Turn Off Auto Scroll Display: 10

Partner Name	Model	Array Type	Supported Releases				
EMC	VNX5400	iSCSI	**ESX**	4.1 U3	4.1 U2	4.1 U1	4.1
			ESXi	6.0 U1	6.0	5.5 U3	5.5 U2
EMC	VNX5400	FC	**ESX**	4.1 U3	4.1 U2	4.1 U1	4.1
			ESXi	6.0 U1	6.0	5.5 U3	5.5 U2
EMC	VNX5400	NAS	**ESX**	4.1 U3	4.1 U2	4.1 U1	4.1
			ESXi	6.0 U1	6.0	5.5 U3	5.5 U2
EMC	VNX5400	FCoE	**ESX**	4.1 U3	4.1 U2	4.1 U1	4.1
			ESXi	6.0 U1	6.0	5.5 U3	5.5 U2

[You also can export the checking result as a file in the CSV format.]

How it works...

You can start the platform installation of the UCS and host connectivity after you get the interoperability information of Cisco UCS for the hardware and software configurations.

The IBM System Storage Interoperation Center (SSIC)

In this recipe, we will learn how to use the IBM SSIC and check the interoperability information.

Getting ready

The IBM SSIC is a Web-based system, which is used to provide interoperability information and supported hardware and software configurations that have been tested and validated by IBM.

How to do it...

In this recipe, we will learn how to check the compatibility with Cisco UCS B-Series, IBM Storwize v7000, and VMware ESXi 5.5 U2 with the IBM SSIC. The following table is an example of a Cisco UCS component for compatibility checking.

The IBM Storage Array, Cisco UCS, and VMware Interoperability information are as follows:

IBM Components	Detail
Storage Family	IBM System Storage Midrange Disk
Storage Model	Storwize V7000
Host Platform	Cisco UCS
Server Model	Cisco B-Series UCS Servers (Blade)
Operating System	VMware vSphere/ESXi 5.5 U2
Adapter (HBA, CAN, etc)	Cisco UCS VIC 1340
SAN or Networking	Brocade 300
Switch Module	Cisco UCS 6248UP
Connectivity	Fibre Channel

According to preceding table, you can get the interoperability information on IBM SSIC by performing the following steps:

1. Open your Web browser and go to `https://www-304.ibm.com/systems/support/storage/ssic/interoperability.wss`, select your requirements, and click on the **Submit** button:

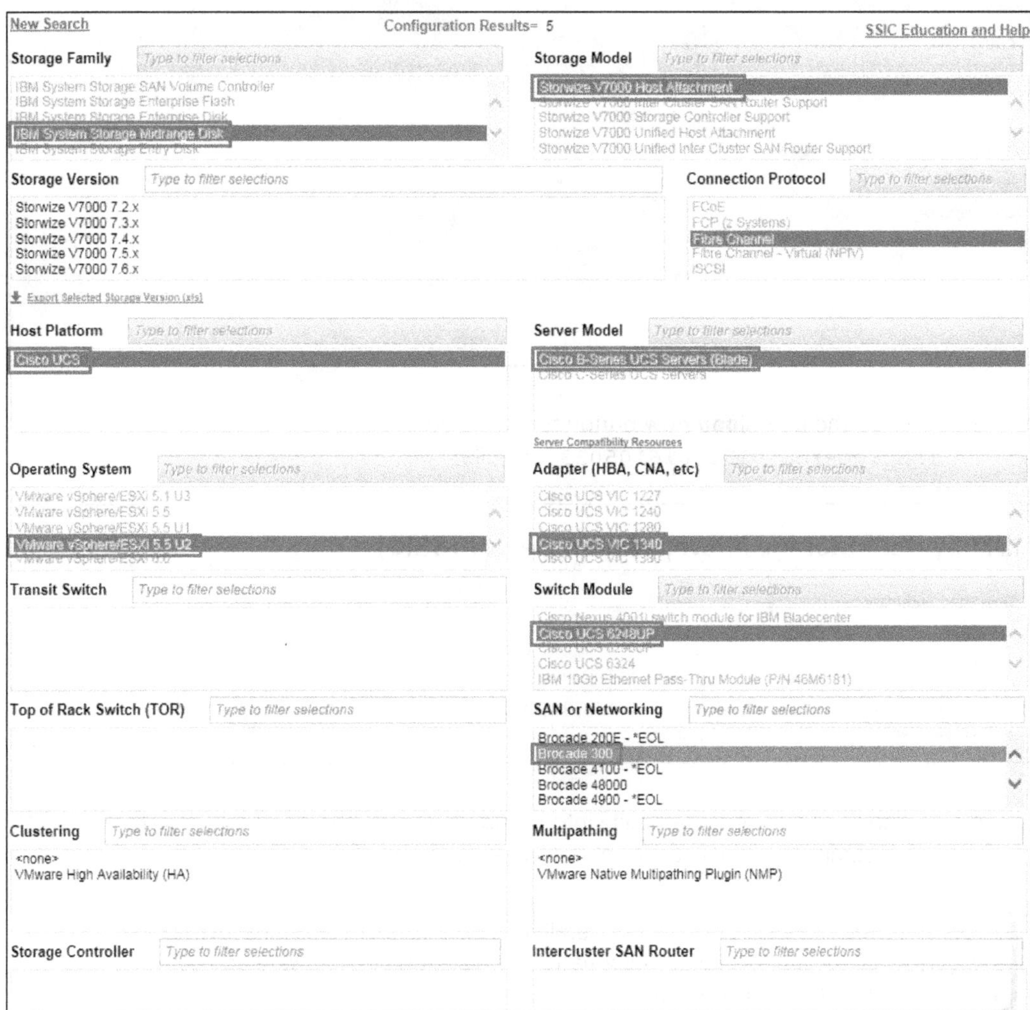

2. Now, you can see the checking result and also export data in the XLS format:

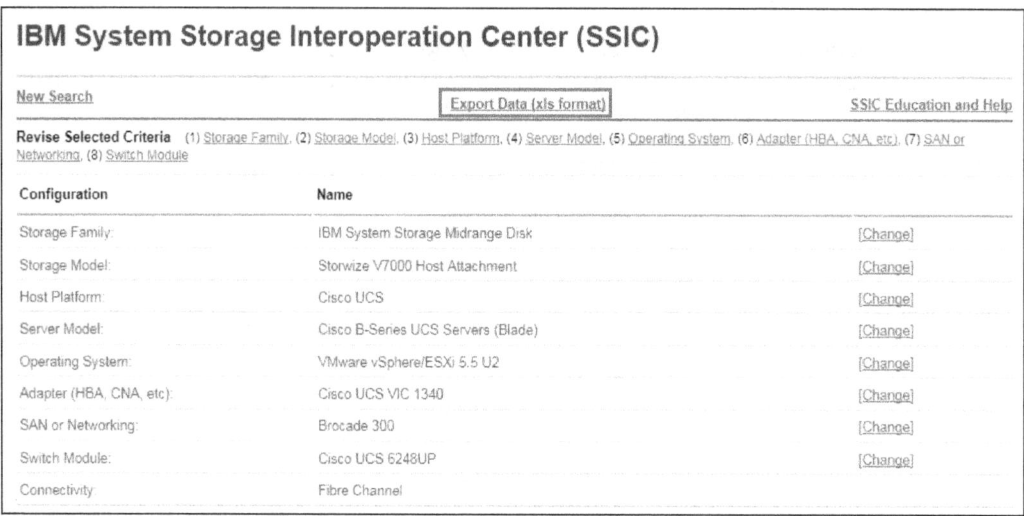

3. Click on the **Download now** button to download the `IBM_Interop_01042016105053.xls` file:

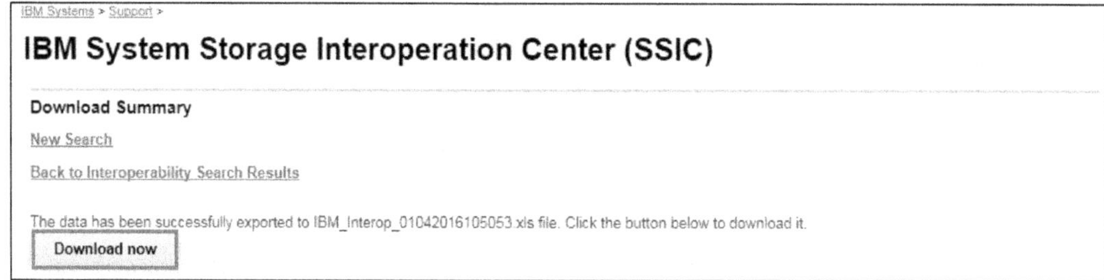

4. You can see the Interoperability information of Cisco UCS in this file, for example, the recommended HBA driver and firmware version.

[You can start the platform installation on UCS and host connectivity based on the interoperability information for Cisco UCS of hardware and software configuration, which you get.]

7

Cisco UCS Backup Solutions

In this chapter, we will cover the following topics:

- Backup and restoration of Cisco UCS configuration
- Backup and restoration of vSphere's virtual machine on Cisco UCS
- Cloning vSphere's virtual machine in EMC Storage
- Cloning vSphere's virtual machine in HP 3PAR Storage
- Replicating vSphere's virtual machine to remote site's Cisco UCS using EMC MirrorView
- Replicating Microsoft Windows Server to remote site's Cisco UCS using EMC MirrorView
- Replicating Microsoft Windows Server to remote site's Cisco UCS using HP 3PAR Remote Copy

Introduction

In this chapter, you will learn how to accomplish tasks related to Cisco UCS backup solutions; for example, backup and restoration of Cisco UCS configurations, and backup and restoration of the virtual host on Cisco UCS using VMware Data Protection. Using Storage's cloning feature to clone the virtual machine on Cisco UCS, and how to replicate the physical host and virtual host to the remote site's UCS host using storage array's replication features; for example, HP 3PAR Remote Copy, EMC MirrorView/S synchronization, and MirrorView/A asynchronization.

Backup and restoration of Cisco UCS configuration

In this recipe, we will learn how to backup and restore Cisco UCS configuration on Cisco UCS.

Getting ready

Assume that two Cisco UCS Fabric Interconnects are running in a Cluster mode and are connected to a Cisco UCS 5108 Chassis. A Cisco UCS B200 M3 is installed into this chassis. You have already installed the VMware ESXi on the Cisco UCS B200. There are two ports that are configured as Server ports on both Fabric Interconnects for the uplink connection between each Fabric Interconnect and each IO Module on chassis. The following diagram shows the details:

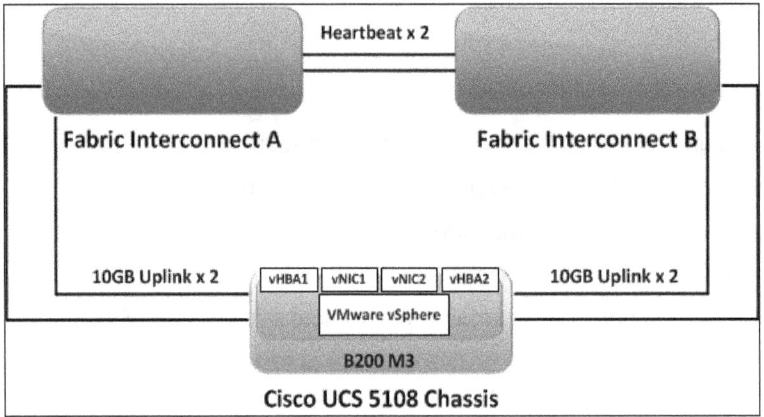

How to do it...

In this recipe, we will learn how to backup Cisco UCS configuration on a Cisco UCS Manager:

Perform these steps for backing up the Cisco UCS configuration on the Cisco UCS Manager:

1. Open the Web browser and input the IP address of the Cisco UCS Manager. Go to the **Admin** tab in the navigation pane and click on **Backup Configuration**, as shown in the following screenshot:

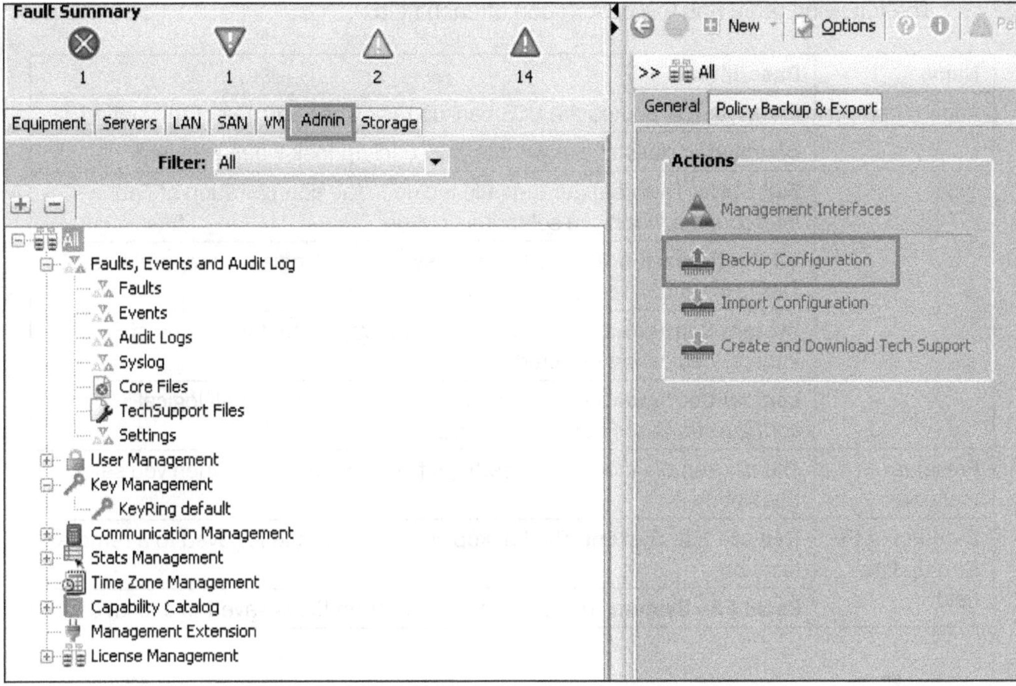

2. Click on **Create Backup Operation** in **Backup Configuration**:

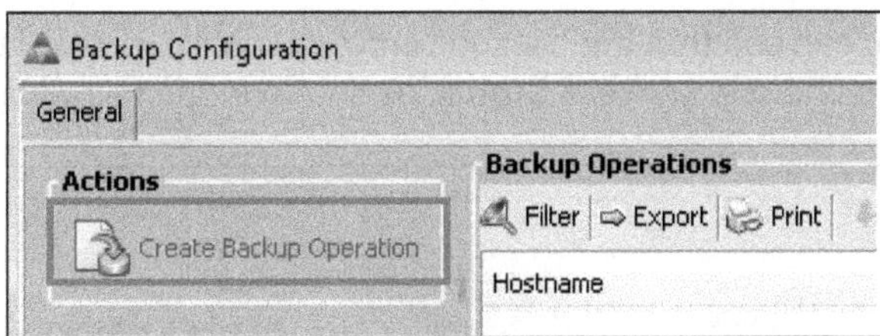

3. Choose the **Type** and the **Location of the Backup file** and then click on the **OK** button:

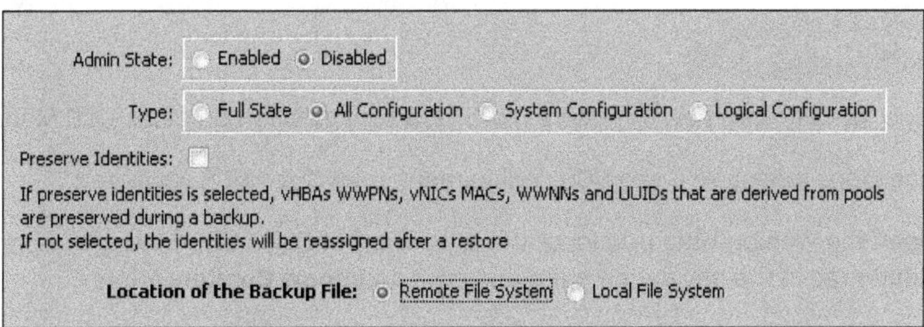

The following table has the description of each field:

Name	Description
Admin State	**Enabled**: It executes the UCS backup task when you select this option
	Disabled: It doesn't execute the UCS backup task when selected
Type	**Full State**: This configuration file includes the configuration of Fabric Interconnect when you select this option
	All Configuration: This includes all system and logical configurations of Fabric Interconnect when selected
	System Configuration: This includes all system configurations of Fabric Interconnect when selected
	Logical Configuration: This configuration file includes all logical configurations of Fabric Interconnect when selected
Preserve Identities	The backup file includes all settings from service pools when you select this option
Location of the Backup File field	**Remote File System**: The backup configuration file is saved to a remote location
	Local File System: The backup configuration file is saved to a local drive

For a remote file system, it is supported by FTP, TFTP, SCP, and SFTP protocol.

4. After this, you can see that the backup configuration file is saved to your selected location and it shows a **success Status**, as shown in the following screenshot:

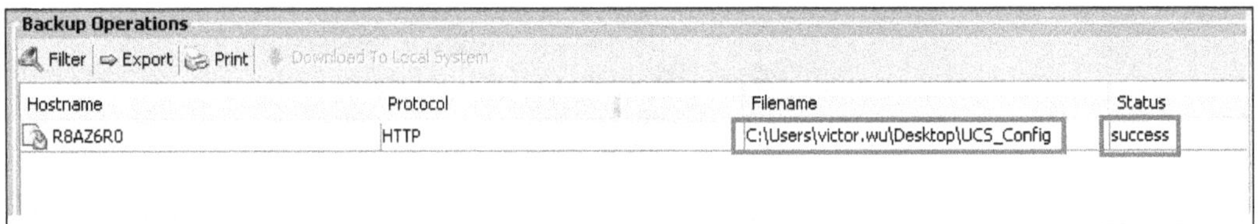

How it works...

In this recipe, we will learn how to restore Cisco UCS configuration on Cisco UCS Manager.

Follow these steps to restore Cisco UCS configuration on a Cisco UCS Manager:

1. Open the Web browser and input the IP address of Cisco UCS Manager. Go to the **Admin** tab in the navigation pane and click on **Import Configuration**:

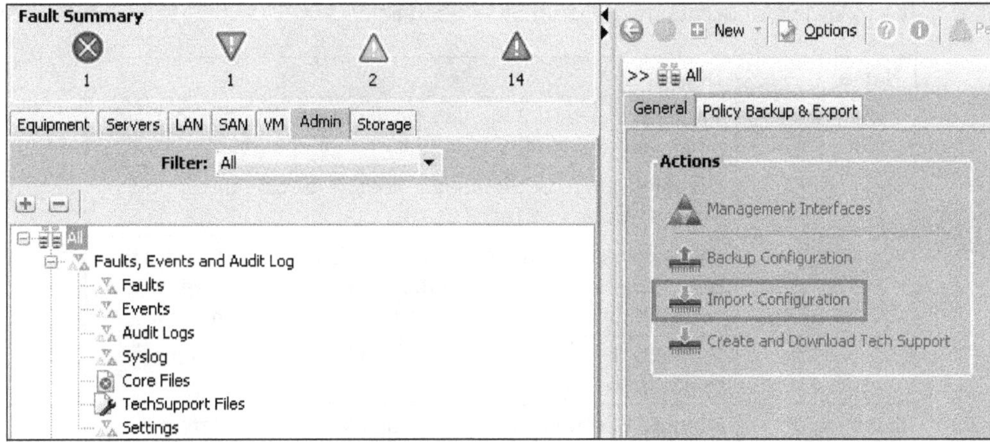

2. Click on **Create Import Operation** in **Import Configuration**:

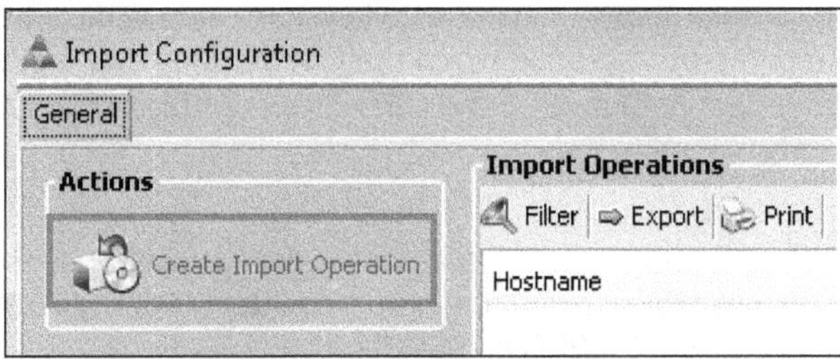

3. Import your backup configuration on **Location of the Import File**, and click on **OK**:

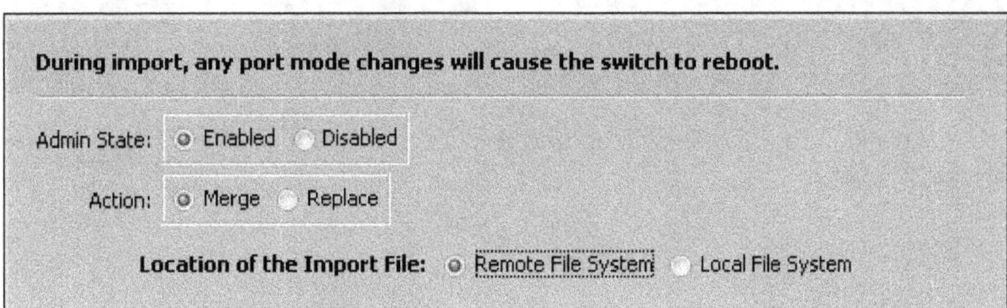

The following table lists the description of each field:

Name	Description
Admin State	**Enabled**: Cisco UCS Manager executes the import operation when you click on **OK**.
	Disabled: Cisco UCS Manager doesn't execute the import operation when you click on **OK**.
Action	**Merge**: The imported confirmation file is compared with the existing confirmation file. If there are conflicts, it overwrites the existing information on the Cisco UCS domain.
	Replace: The current configuration is replaced with the imported configuration file.
Location of the Import File	**Remote File System**: The backup file is imported from a remote server.
	Local File System: The backup file is imported locally

The imported configuration file includes all system and logical configurations. You can execute the import operation when the Cisco UCS is running. Some modifications caused a UCS reboot or disrupted the traffic; for example, a change in the number of vNIC or vHBA to a Server.

You cannot import configurations from a higher release to a lower release. For a remote file system, it is supported by the FTP, TFTP, SCP, and SFTP protocols.

Backup and restoration of vSphere's virtual machine on Cisco UCS

In this recipe, we will learn how to backup and restore a VMware vSphere's virtual machine into a Cisco UCS Server.

Getting ready

Assume that you have already installed VMware vSphere host on a Cisco UCS B200 M3 and some virtual machines are running on this vSphere host. The VMware **vSphere Data Protection** (**VDP**) 5.5 Virtual Appliance is installed on the other VMware vSphere host. Each VMware vSphere is managed by the same VMware vCenter and can access the same SAN shared ESXi Datastore. The following diagram shows the details:

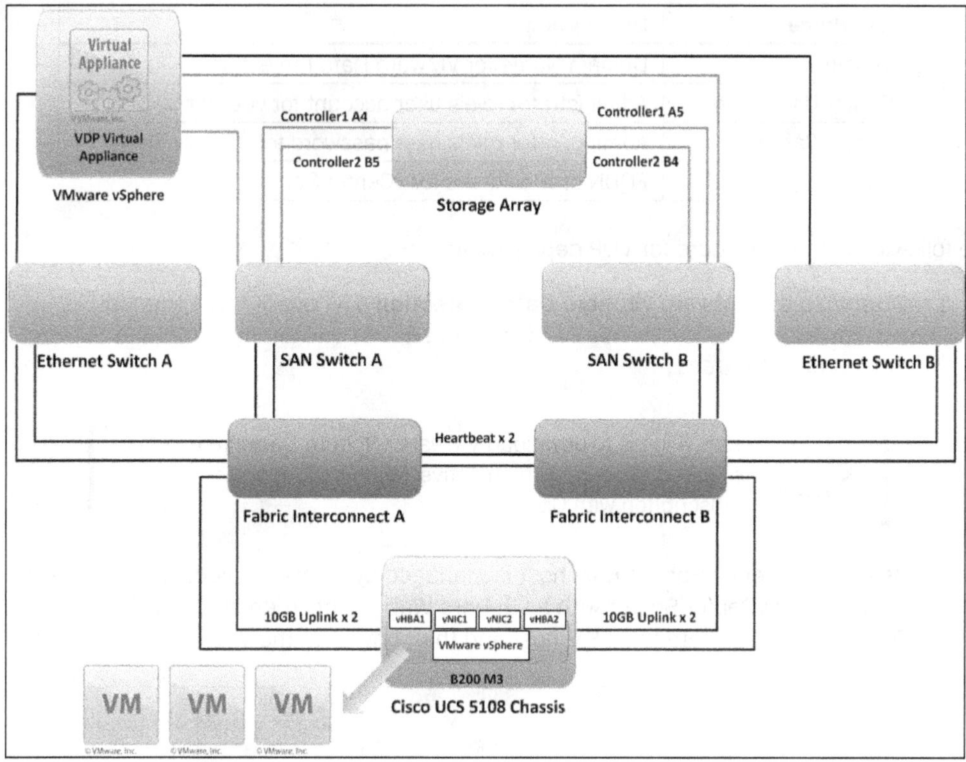

How to do it...

In this recipe, we will learn how to deploy a VDP. A VMware vSphere Data Protection is a backup and recovery solution. It is fully integrated with the VMware vCenter Server and VMware vSphere Web Client, providing a disk-based backup of virtual machines. The VMware vSphere Data Protection is based on the industry-leading EMC Avamar backup and recovery solution.

The following table lists the required items for VMware vSphere Data Protection deployment:

Item Name	Description
IPv4 for VDP	Management Network for VMware Data Protection
Netmask	Network Netmask for VMware Data Protection
Gateway	Management Network for VMware Data Protection
Primary DNS	Primary DNS for VMware Data Protection
Hostname	Hostname for VMware Data Protection

Item Name	Description
Domain	Domain Name for VMware Data Protection
vCenter Username	Administrator role's user account for vCenter Server
vCenter Password	Administrator role's user password for vCenter Server
vCenter FQDN or IP	FQDN or IP address for vCenter Server

The following is the procedure for VDP deployment:

1. Download the **VMware vSphere Data Protection** `5.5` ova file type from `https://my.vmware.com/web/vmware/details?downloadGroup=VDP55_11&productId=353&rPId=9681`.

Note: Access to download VMware vSphere Data Protection is limited to users with an active Technical Support Subscription with Cisco.

2. Assume that one vSphere ESXi host is managed by a VMware vCenter Server, and log in to this vCenter Server with a vSphere Web Client. Then import VMware Data Protection ova file into this ESXi host and then power on the VDP virtual appliance:

3. After this you can start to configure VMware vSphere Data Protection. Open the Web browser and input `https://<IP of VDP>:8543/vdp-configure/`. The default password is `changeme`:

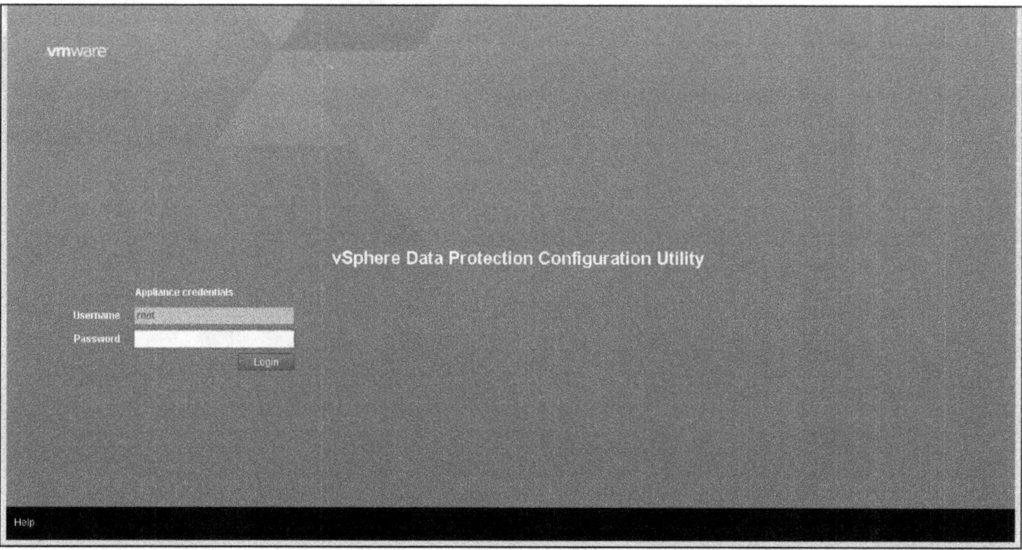

4. According to the preceding table, input the requirement information to complete the VDP configuration. The VDP will start to integrate with VMware vCenter Server and it reboots automatically after finishing the integration.

> It requires 10 minutes for VDP and VMware vCenter Server integration. VMware vSphere Data Protection does not require any license to enable the features. If you install the Advanced VMware vSphere Data Protection, it requires the license to enable its features.

5. Then log in to vCenter Server by **vSphere Web Client**; you can see **vSphere Data Protection 5.5** on the **Home** menu:

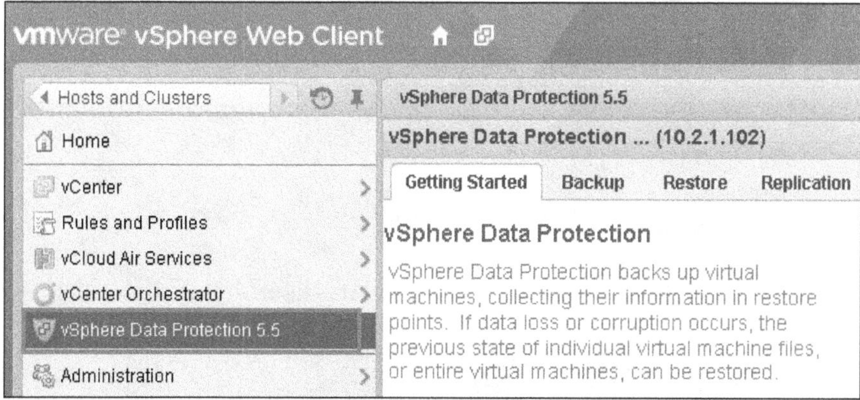

How it works...

In this recipe, we will learn how to backup and restore VMware vSphere's virtual machine in full image into Cisco UCS Server using VMware VDP.

Perform the following steps to backup the virtual machine using VDP:

1. Log in to vCenter Server with a **vSphere Web Client**, and go to the **Getting Started** tab on **vSphere Data Protection**. Click on **Create Backup Job**:

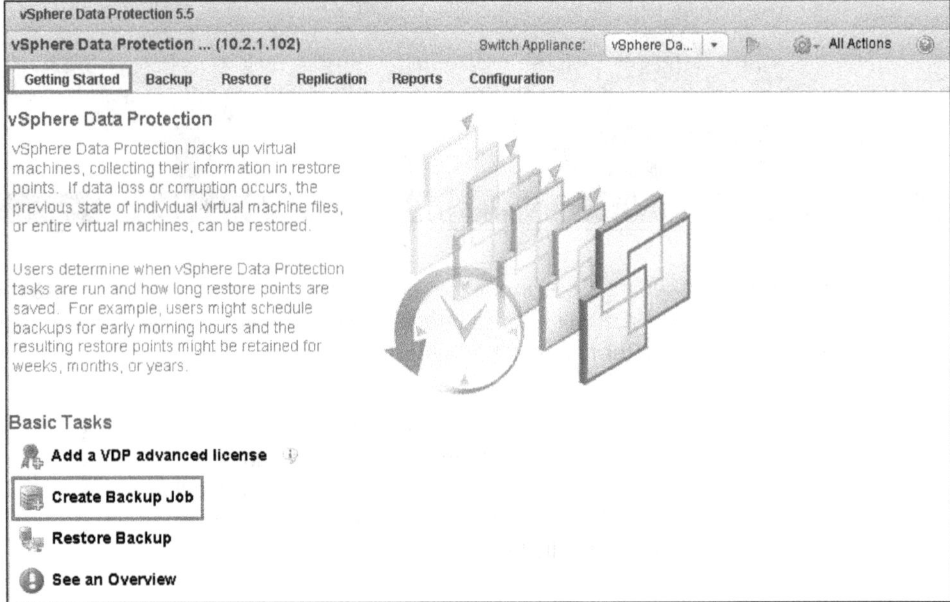

2. Select **Full Image** on **Data Type** and choose your backup target virtual machine on the Cisco UCS Server:

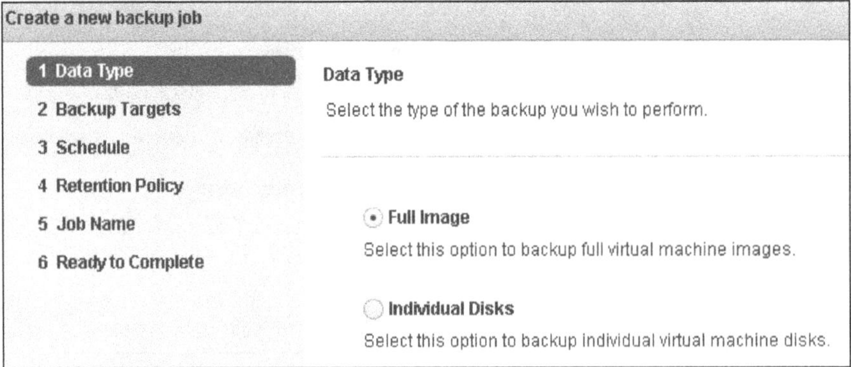

3. Select your **Backup schedule**, then click on **Next**:

Schedule

The schedule determines how often your selections will be backed up. Backups will occur as close to the start of the backup window as possible.

Backup schedule: Daily

Weekly performed every Sunday

The first Sunday of every month

Start Time on Server: 8 : 00 PM

4. Select the **Retention Policy** you want for the virtual machine, click on **Next**:

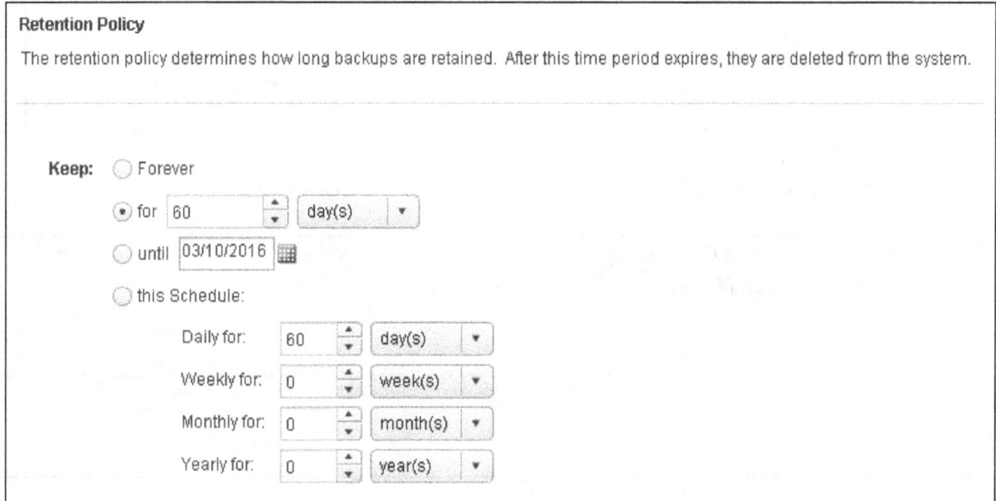

The following table lists the description of each backup retention policy:

Name	Description
Forever	All backup jobs for the virtual machine that will never expire
For	All backups for the virtual machine that will expire after you specify the time
Until	All backups for the virtual machine will expire on the specified date

Name	Description
This Schedule	You can specify the retention time for backup: ▸ Daily: Schedule the backup on each day ▸ Weekly: Schedule the backup on each week ▸ Monthly: Schedule the backup on each month ▸ Yearly: Schedule the backup on each year

1. Input the **Name** of the backup job, click on **Next**, and then click on **Finish** to create the backup job:

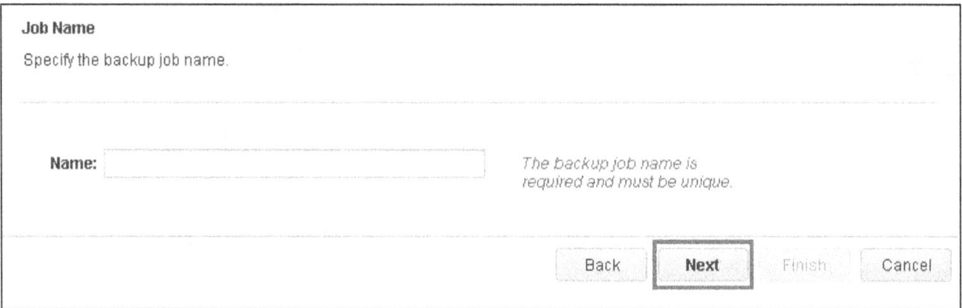

2. Go to the **Backup** tab, you can see the status of the backup job:

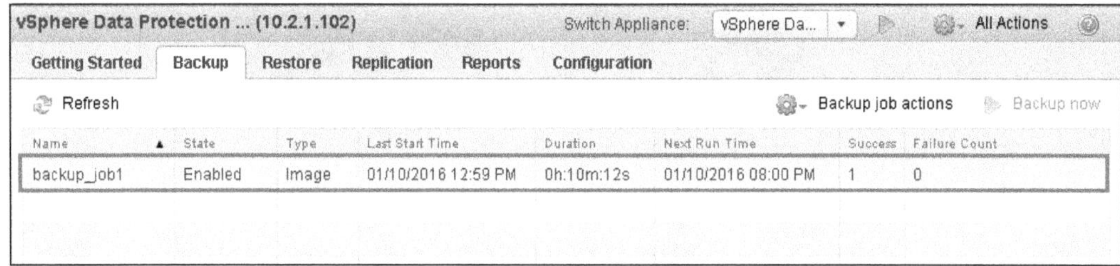

The following is the procedure to restore the virtual machine using vSphere Data Protection. Assume that you plan to restore the virtual machine on Windows2008:

1. Log in to vCenter Server with a **vSphere Web Client**, go to the **Restore** tab on vSphere Data Protection. Select the image of virtual machine **Windows2008** to restore into the target Cisco UCS (vSphere ESXi host), you can see this virtual machine has three backup images; then, click on the **Restore** button:

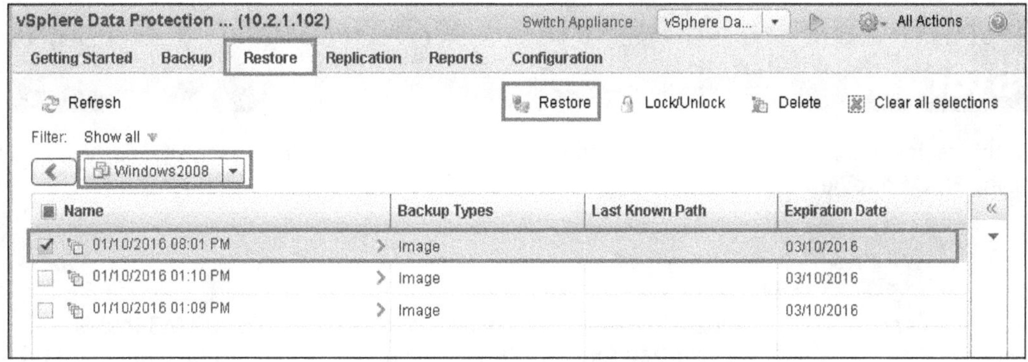

2. You can see the selected image and then click on **Next**:

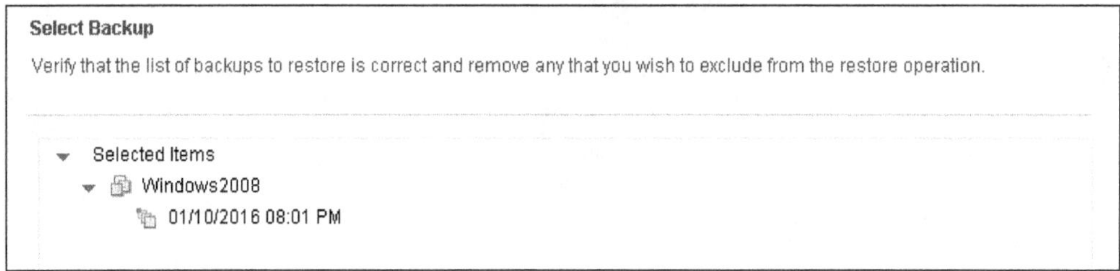

3. You can select the **Restore to original location** option or other **Datastore** for the target destination, click on **Next**, and then click on **Finish** to confirm this restore task:

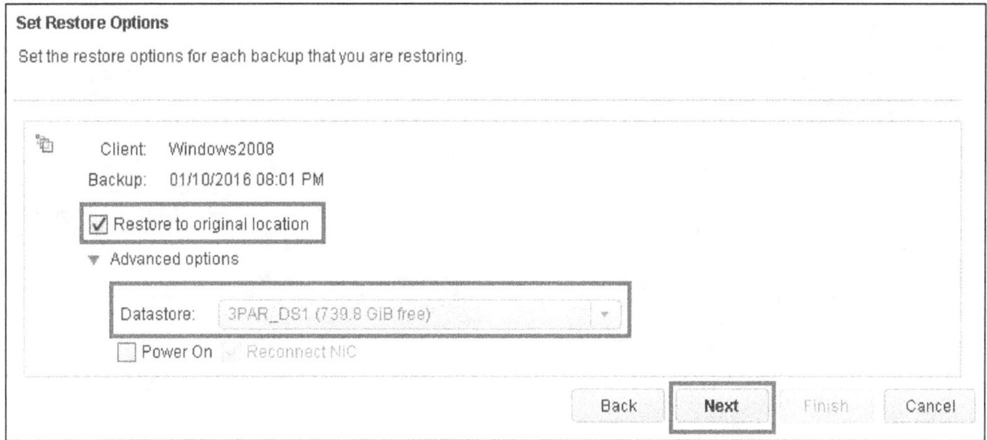

The virtual machine can power on at once after finishing the restore if you select **Power On**.

Cloning vSphere's virtual machine in EMC Storage

In this recipe, we will learn how to clone vSphere's virtual machine on a Cisco UCS Server using EMC SnapView Clone.

Getting ready

Assume that you have installed a VMware vSphere host on a Cisco UCS B200 M3 that is connected to EMC CLARiiON CX4-240 Storage. The virtual machines are running an EMC LUN. The following diagram shows the details:

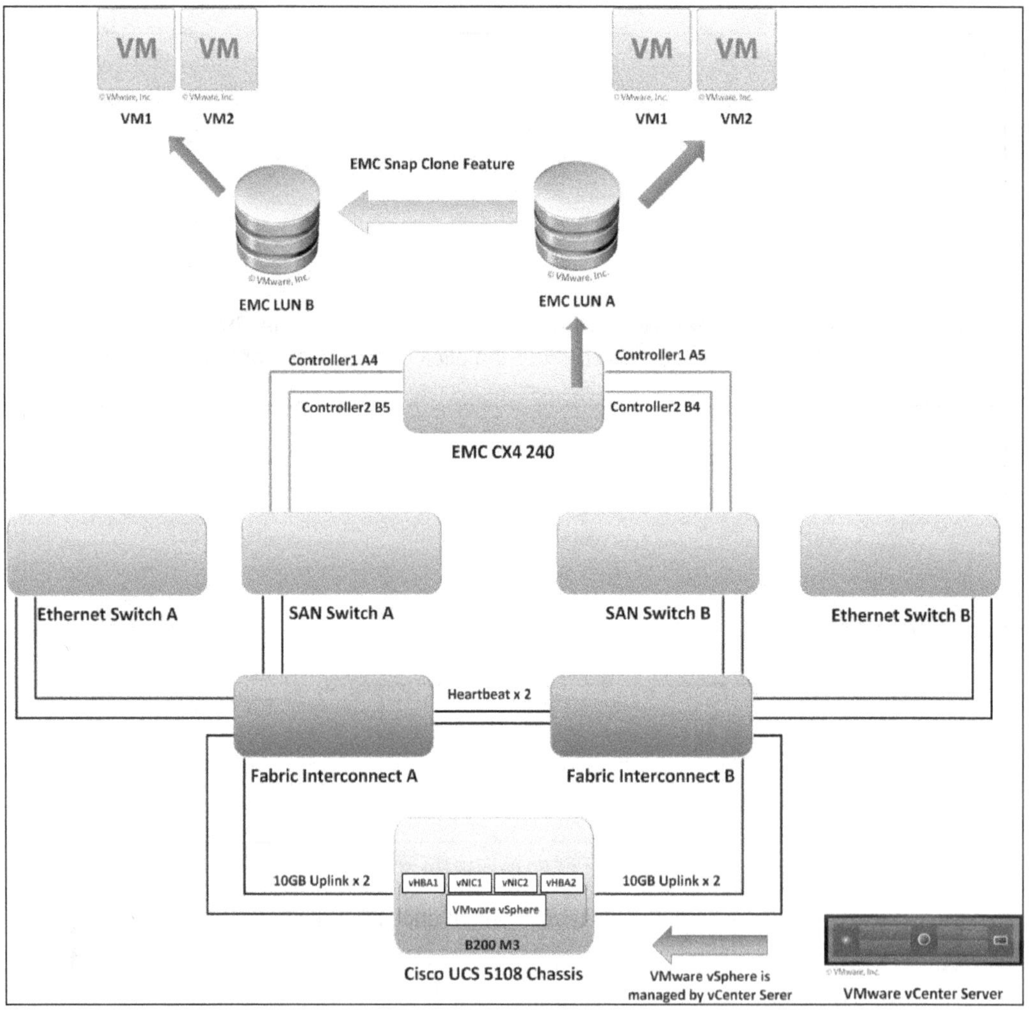

How to do it...

In this recipe, we will learn how to create a SnapView Clone group on EMC CX4-240 storage.

EMC SnapView Clone is the optional software for EMC CLARiiON storage products, it can provide point-in-time copies of LUNs (logical units) and provide a full clone from source LUNs to destination LUNs. It also allows incremental synchronization between the source and destination LUNs. The EMC SnapView also includes another feature, it is SnapView Snapshot that can provide a pointer-and-copy design, referred to as copy on first write. Make sure that SnapView is enabled on the EMC CLARiiON storage, then you can provide the SnapView Clone and Snapshot features. You can see that **SnapView** displays an **Active** status on the **Software** tab of **Storage System Properties** if the EMC SnapView feature is enabled:

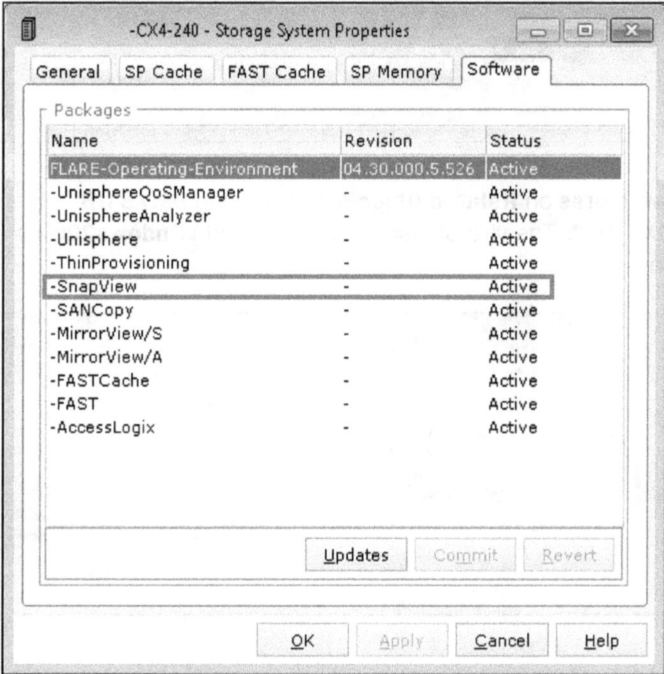

The following table lists the information of each component for the SnapView cloning operation:

Component Name	Detail
VC55U2	vCenter Server 5.5
10.2.1.8	VMware vSphere 5.5: Cisco UCS B200 M3
Demo, Windows2008	Virtual machines are running on
CX4_DS1	ESXi Datastore: EMC LUNs CX4_DS1

Following are the steps to create a the SnapView Clone group on EMC CX4-240 storage:

1. First, you can collect the information of virtual machine that is needed to be cloned in vCenter. Log in to the vCenter Server by a **vSphere Web Client** and select host **10.2.1.8**; you can see two virtual machines, **Demo** and **Windows2008**, on the **Virtual Machines** tab of **Related Objects**:

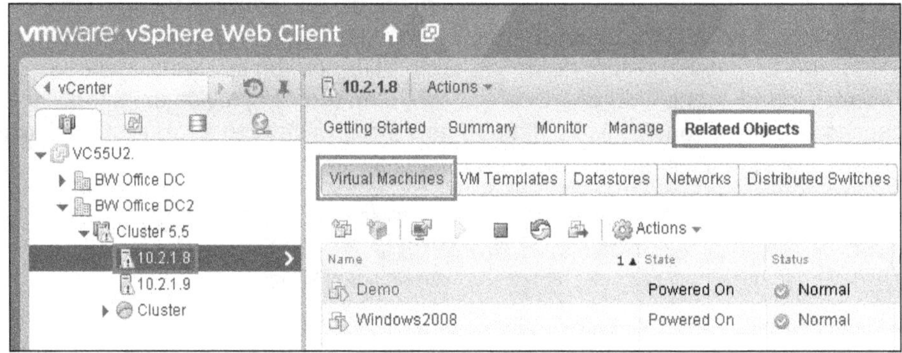

2. Select **Datastores** on **Related Objects**, there is one **99.75 GB** datastore, named **CX4_DS1**. The virtual machines **Demo** and **Windows2008** are stored on this datastore:

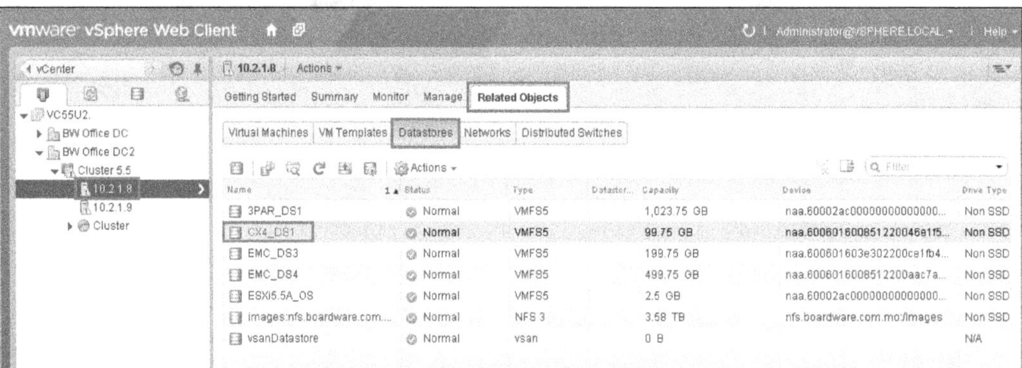

3. Open the Web browser and input the IP address of EMC Unisphere Manager, which is the management console of CX4-240 storage. Select the **LUNs** on the **Storage** menu and choose the LUNs you plan to clone:

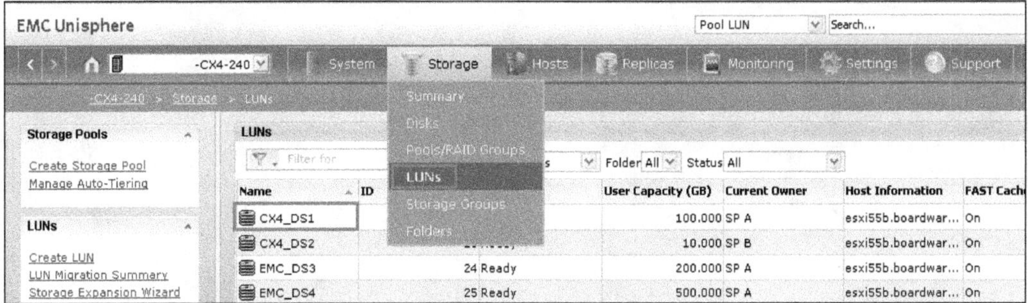

4. Right-click on **CX4_DS1** and select **SnapView** and choose the **Create Clone Group**. Then input **Clone Group Name** as `CX4_DS1_Clone` and click on **OK**.
5. Go to the **Replicas** tab and select clone, you can see that the **Clone Group Name** is **CX4_DS1_Clone**, which was created in Step 4:

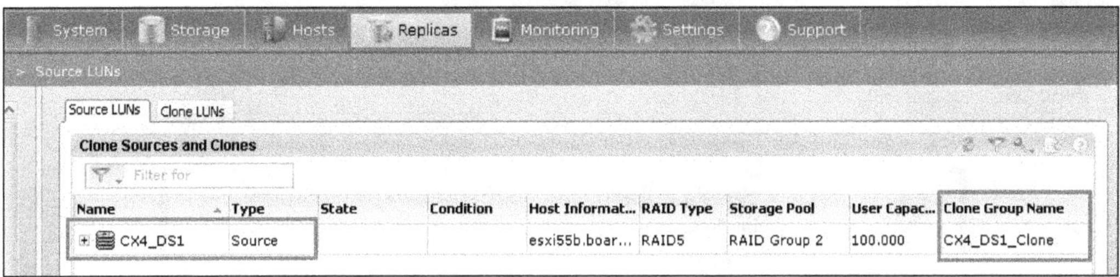

6. Assume that two free LUNs are created for **Clone Private LUNs** (**CPLs**), then the CPLs are configured using the **Configure Clone Settings** menu:

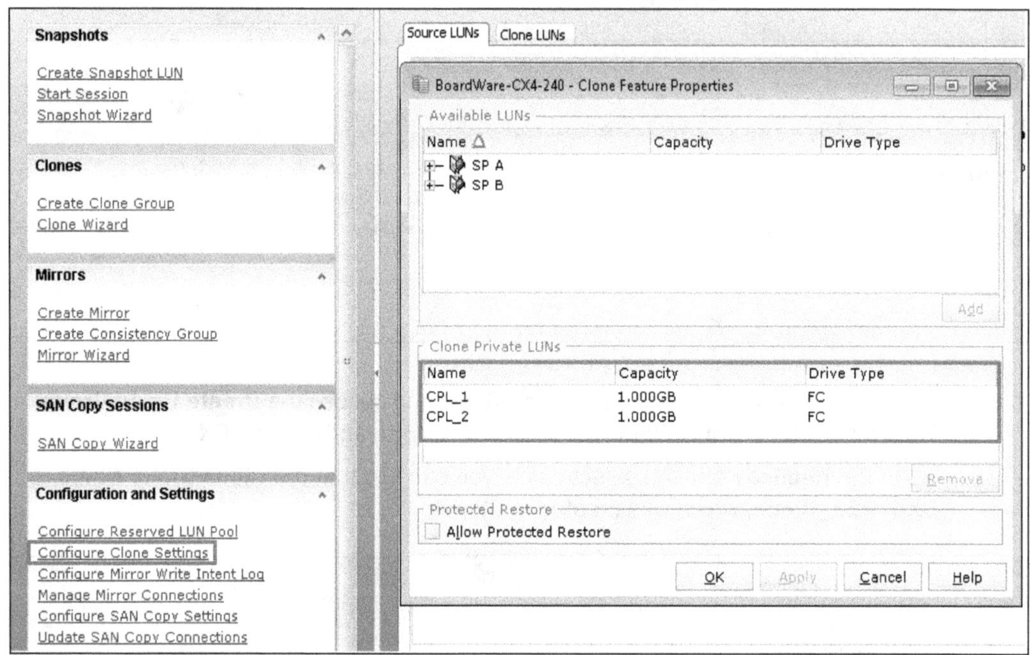

Only classic LUNs (LUNs configured in RAID Group) are eligible to be CPLs. CPLs must be 1 GB or larger.

7. Right-click on the **CX4_DS1** of **Source LUNs** tab on clone group and select **Add Clone**:

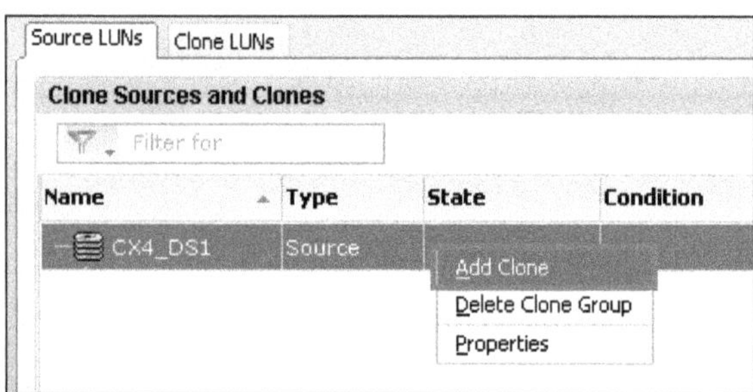

8. Before adding the target clone LUN into **Clone Group**, you need to create new LUNs as target LUNs. Assume that the target LUN is **CX4_DS1_Clone**, select this target LUN and click on **Apply**:

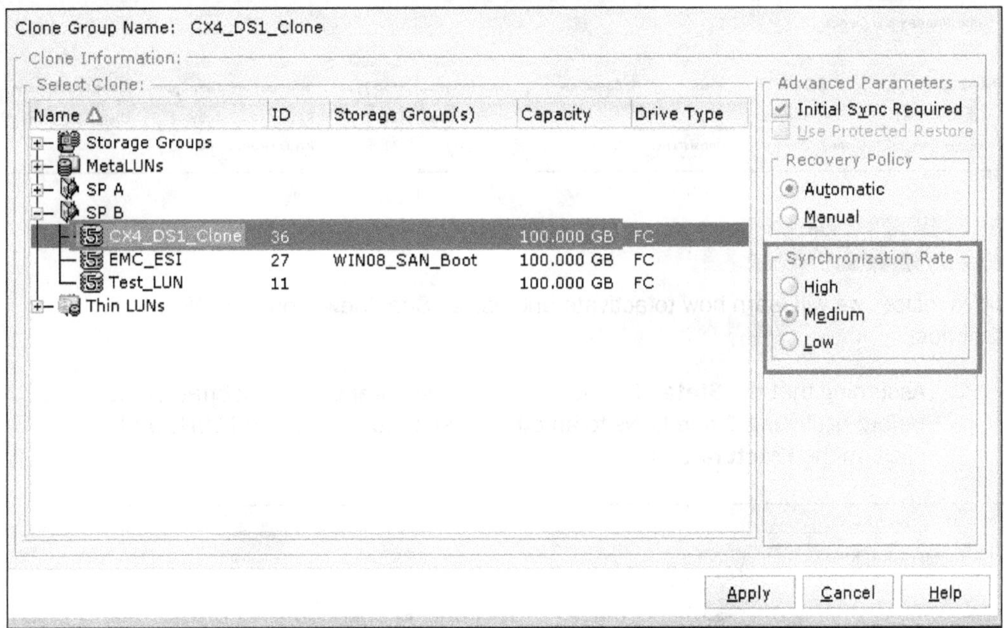

The EMC SnapView Cloning has three rate options for synchronization: **High**, **Medium**, and **Low**.

The size capacity of target LUNs can be the same or bigger than the source LUNs.

9. After this you can see that the source LUN **CX4_DS1** starts to clone data into the target LUN **CX4_DS1_Clone**:

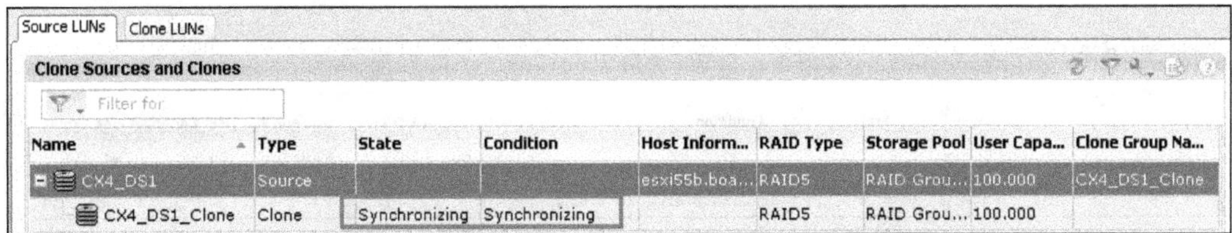

10. When the **State** of the **Clone LUNs** is changed to **Consistent**, the cloning is completed:

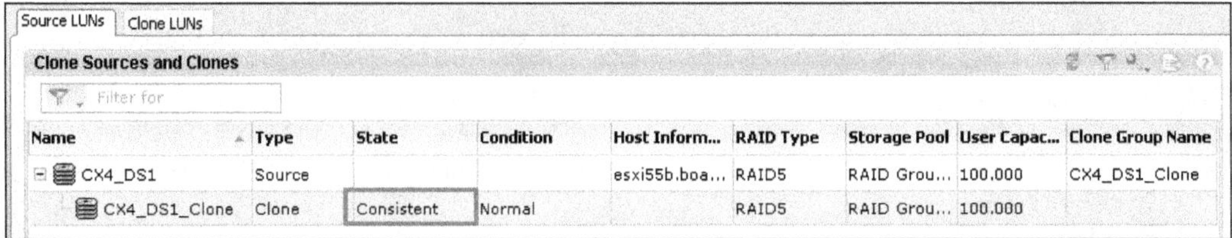

How it works...

In this recipe, we will learn how to activate and assign SnapView Clone's LUNs into an other host.

1. Assuming that the **State** of clone's LUNs is **Consistent**, you must fracture it before assigning **Clone** LUNs to an other host. Select the cloned LUNs and click on the **Fracture** button:

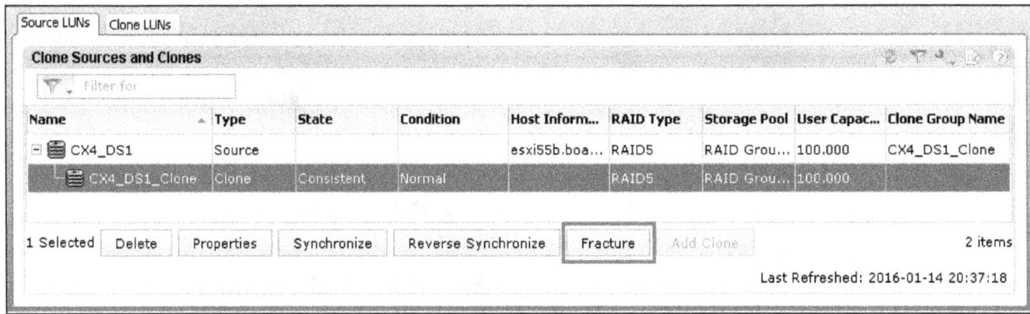

2. After fracturing the **Clone** LUNs, the **Condition** is changed into **Administratively Fractured**. Then you can assign this **Clone** LUNs into an other host:

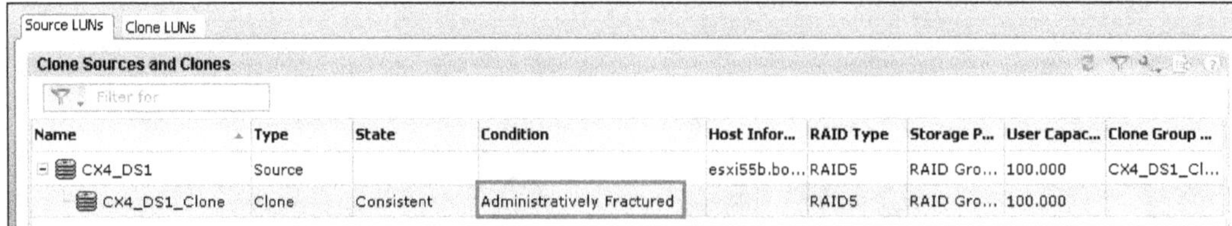

3. Go to **Storage Groups** on the **Hosts** tab and create a new storage group:

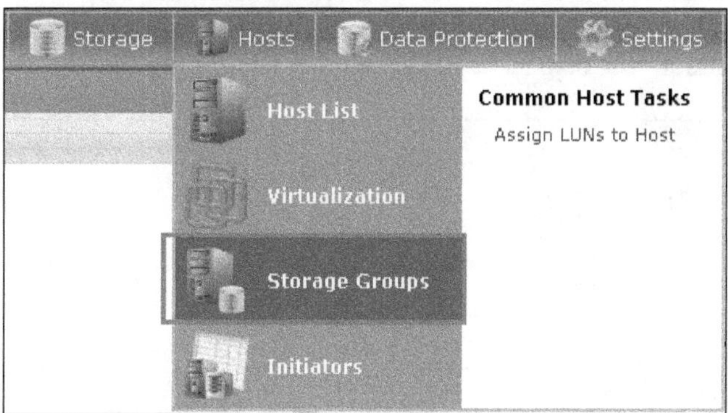

4. After that, right-click this new storage group and select **Properties**. Go to the **LUNs** tab, select the clone LUNs **CX4_DS1_Clone** on **Available LUNs** and add it into **Selected LUNs**:

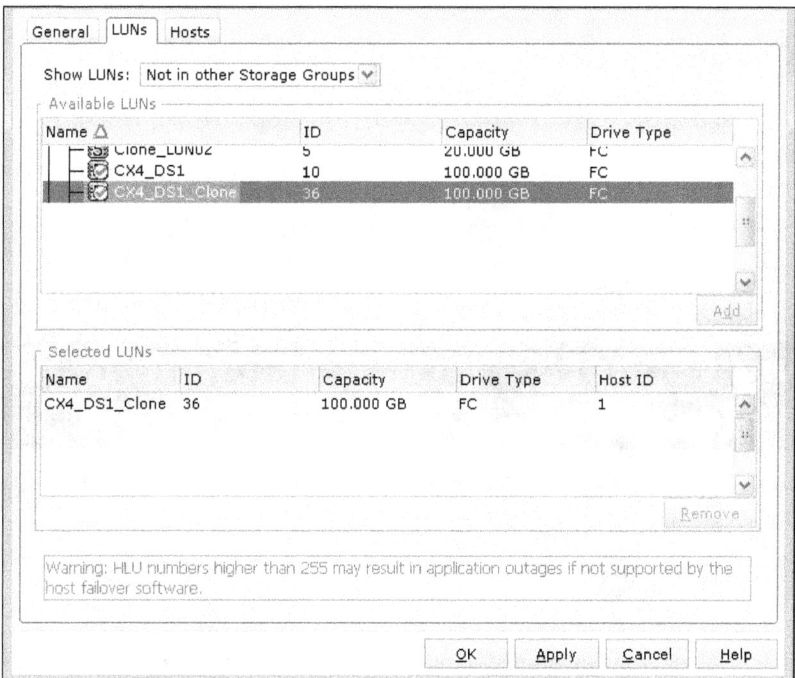

5. Then go to the **Hosts** tab, select the test host on **Available Hosts**. Assume that **esxi55.testlab.com** is the test host. Select this host and click on the right hand sign button to move **esxi55.testlab.com** into **Hosts to be Connected**, then click on **Apply**. Finally, the test host **esxi55.testlab.com** can access the Clone LUN.

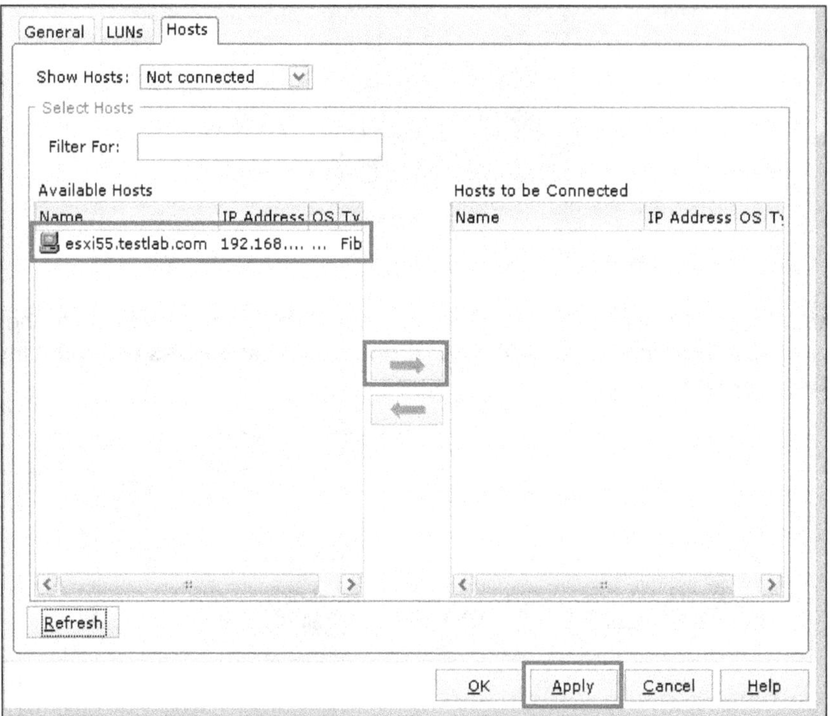

Cloning vSphere's virtual machine in HP 3PAR Storage

In this recipe, we will learn how to clone vSphere's virtual machine on Cisco UCS Server using HP 3PAR's Physical Copy.

Getting ready

Assume that you have already installed VMware vSphere host on one Cisco UCS B200 M3 which is connected to HP 3PAR 7200 Storage. The virtual machines are running one virtual volume. The following diagram shows the details:

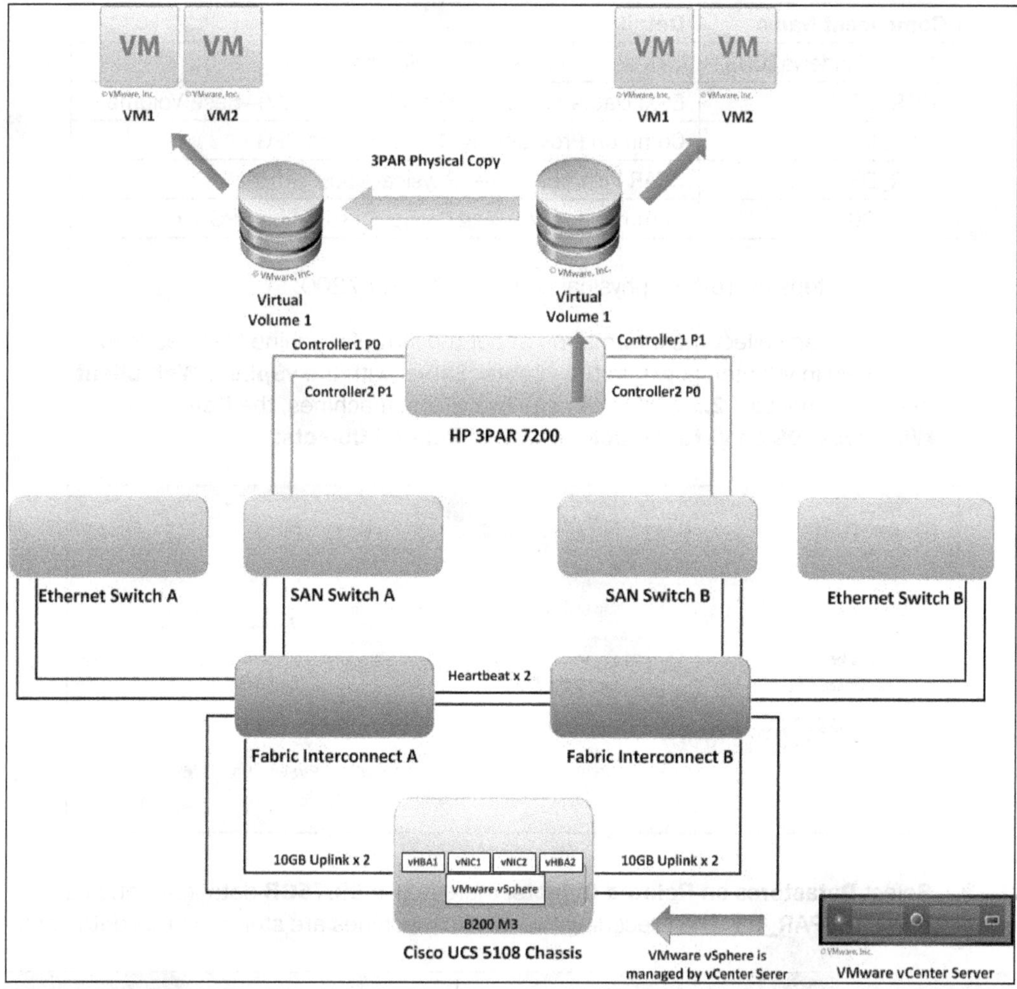

How to do it...

In this recipe, we will learn how to create a physical copy on HP 3PAR 7200. HP 3PAR's physical copy feature duplicates all the data from a base volume to a destination volume. The base volume is the original volume that is copied to the destination volume. The physical copy on the destination volume remains available if the original base volume becomes unavailable. The following table lists the information of each component for HP 3PAR physical copy operation:

Component Name	Detail
VC55U2	vCenter Server 5.5
10.2.1.8	VMware vSphere 5.5: Cisco UCS B200 M3

Component Name	Detail
Demo, Windows2008	Virtual machines are running on
3PAR_DS	ESXi Datastore: 3PAR Virtual Volume (VV)–Base Volume
CPG_FC5	Common Provisioning Group: Source CPG
3PAR_DS_Copy	3PAR Virtual Volume: Physical Copy
CPG_FC6	Common Provisioning Group: Destination CPG

Following are the steps to create a physical copy on HP 3PAR 7200:

1. First, you can collect the information about the virtual machine that needs to be cloned in vCenter. Log in to the vCenter Server with the **vSphere Web Client** and select host **10.2.1.8**. You can see two virtual machines, the **Demo** and **Windows2008** on **Virtual Machines** tab of **Related Objects**:

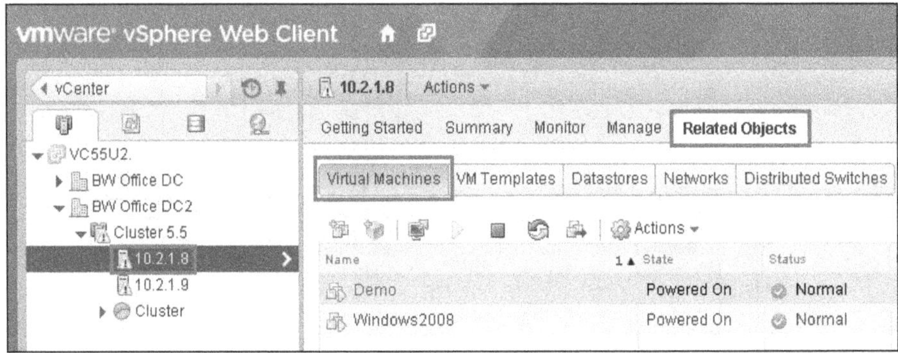

2. Select **Datastores** on **Related Objects**, there is one **99.75GB** datastore, and its name is **3PAR_DS**. The preceding two virtual machines are stored on this datastore:

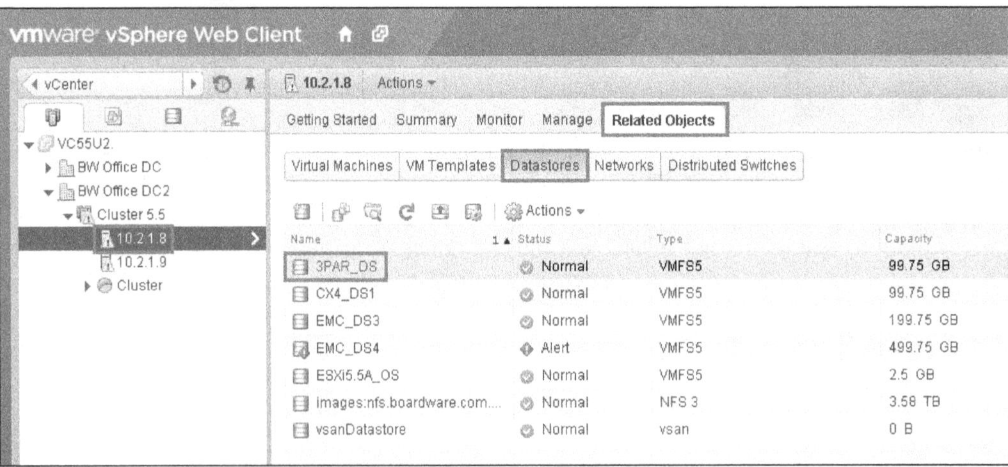

3. Log in to HP 3PAR 7200 by **HP 3PAR Management Console** that is the HP 3PAR management tool. Then go to **Provisioning** and select **CPGs**, the **Virtual Volume** (**VV**) **3PAR_DS** is allocated into **CPG_FC5**:

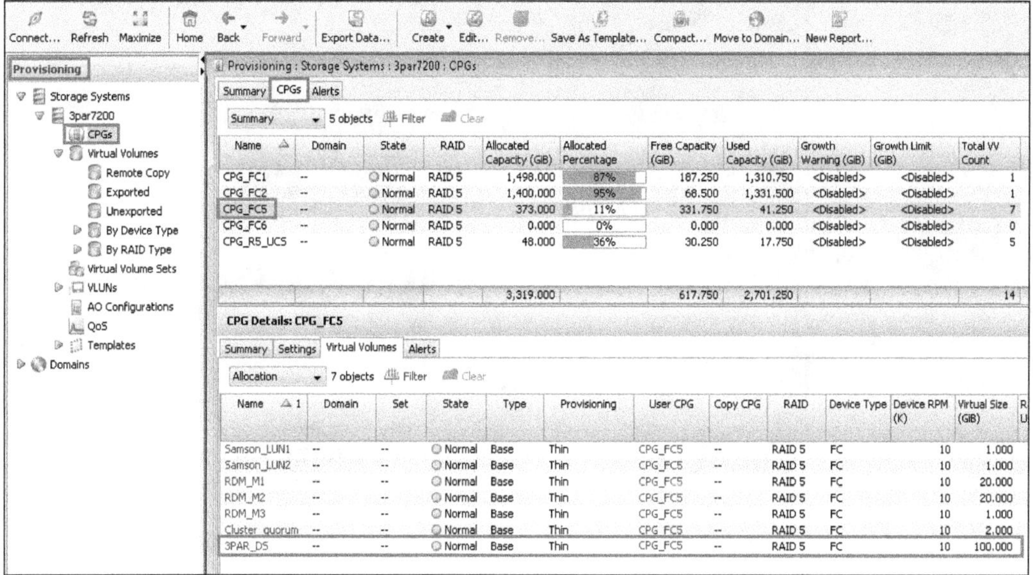

HP 3PAR **Common Provisioning Group** (**CGP**) is a virtual pool of logical disks that allocates space to virtual volumes on demand.

4. Then prepare the destination virtual volume for the physical copy on the other CPG **CPG_FC6**, right-click on **CPG_FC6** and select **Create Virtual Volume...**:

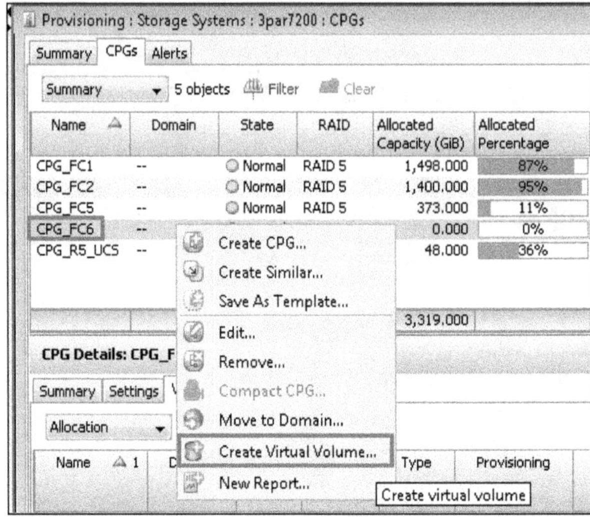

5. Input the **Name** of the virtual volume and its **Size**, then click on **Finish**:

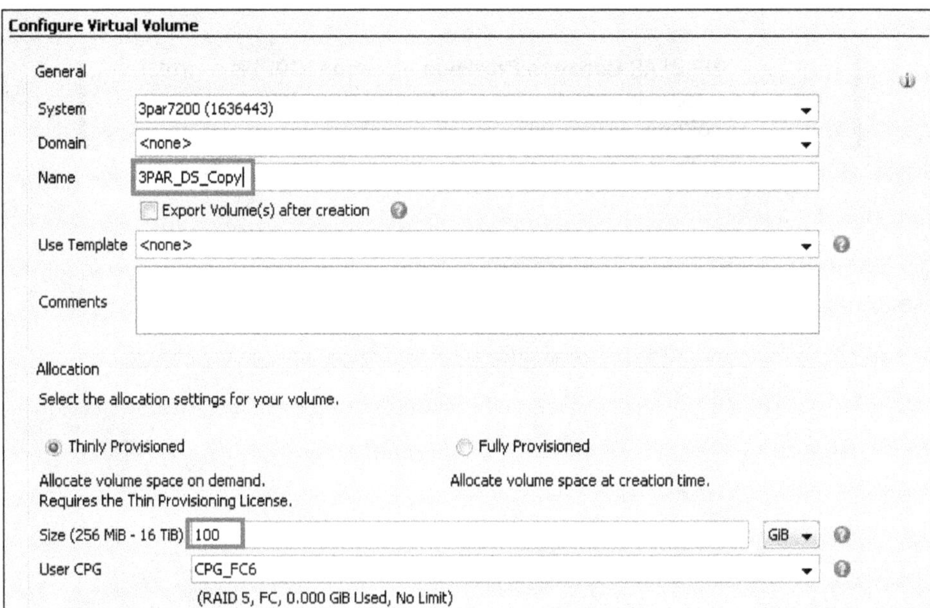

The size of destination virtual volume is same as the base virtual volume.

6. Go to **Virtual Volumes** on **Provisioning** and select the virtual volume **3PAR_DS**, make sure that the base virtual volume is already enabled with the **Copy CPG** feature before starting the physical copy, right-click on the virtual volume and select the destination CPG if it is not enabled:

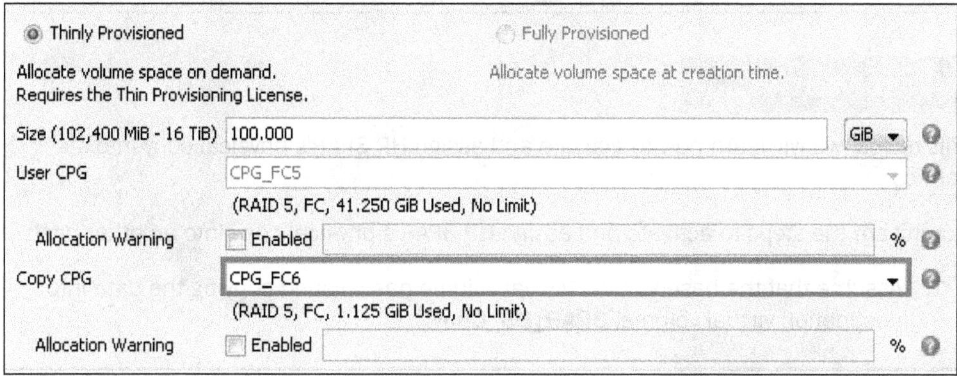

7. Right-click on the base virtual volume **3PAR_DS** and select **Create Physical Copy...**:

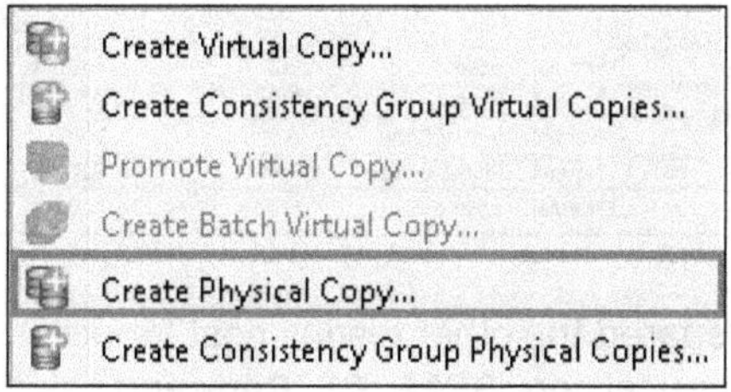

8. Select **3PAR_DS** on **Parent Volume** menu and **3PAR_DS_Copy** on **Destination Volume** menu and click on **OK**:

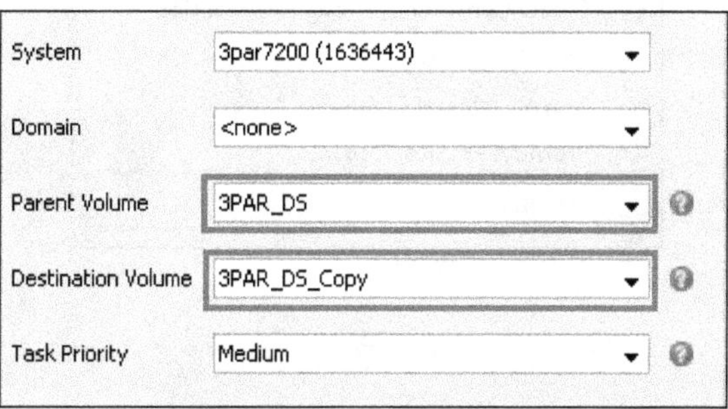

9. The base virtual volume starts to synchronize to the destination virtual volume:

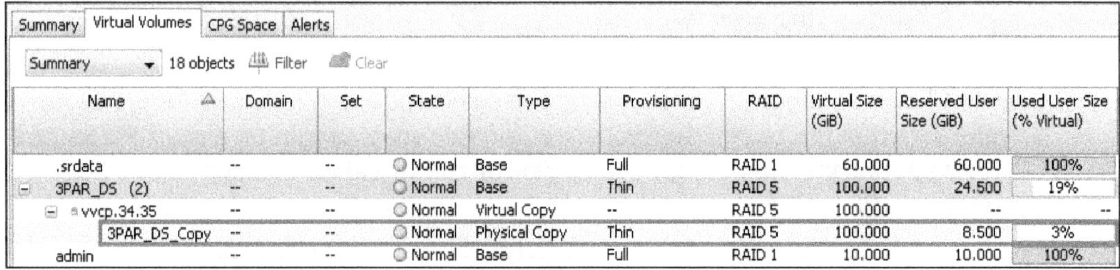

Name	Domain	Set	State	Type	Provisioning	RAID	Virtual Size (GiB)	Reserved User Size (GiB)	Used User Size (% Virtual)
.srdata	--	--	Normal	Base	Full	RAID 1	60.000	60.000	100%
3PAR_DS (2)	--	--	Normal	Base	Thin	RAID 5	100.000	24.500	19%
vvcp.34.35	--	--	Normal	Virtual Copy	--	RAID 5	100.000	--	--
3PAR_DS_Copy	--	--	Normal	Physical Copy	Thin	RAID 5	100.000	8.500	3%
admin	--	--	Normal	Base	Full	RAID 1	10.000	10.000	100%

How it works...

In this recipe, we will learn how to activate and assign HP 3PAR's physical copy into an other host.

Following are the steps to activate and assign HP 3PAR's physical copy into an other host:

1. Assume that the base volume virtual volume has finished copying the data into destination virtual volume, **3PAR_DS_Copy**:

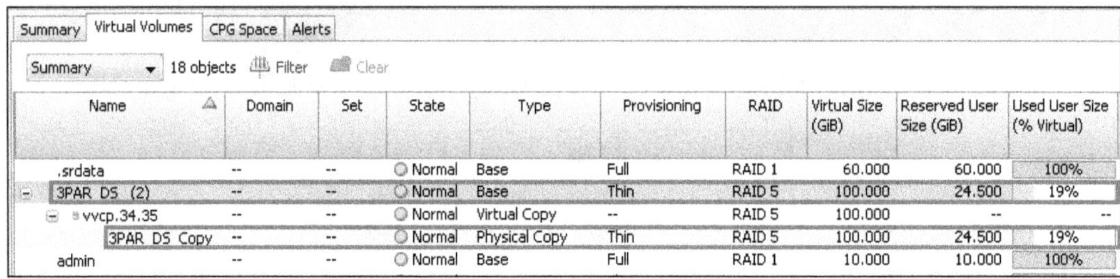

Name	Domain	Set	State	Type	Provisioning	RAID	Virtual Size (GiB)	Reserved User Size (GiB)	Used User Size (% Virtual)
.srdata	--	--	Normal	Base	Full	RAID 1	60.000	60.000	100%
3PAR_DS (2)	--	--	Normal	Base	Thin	RAID 5	100.000	24.500	19%
vvcp.34.35	--	--	Normal	Virtual Copy	--	RAID 5	100.000	--	--
3PAR_DS_Copy	--	--	Normal	Physical Copy	Thin	RAID 5	100.000	24.500	19%
admin	--	--	Normal	Base	Full	RAID 1	10.000	10.000	100%

2. Assume that you prepared the other testing host for accessing this physical copy. Right-click on the physical copy **3PAR_DS_Copy** and select **Export...**. You can export this volume into the testing host, for example, other Cisco UCS Blades:

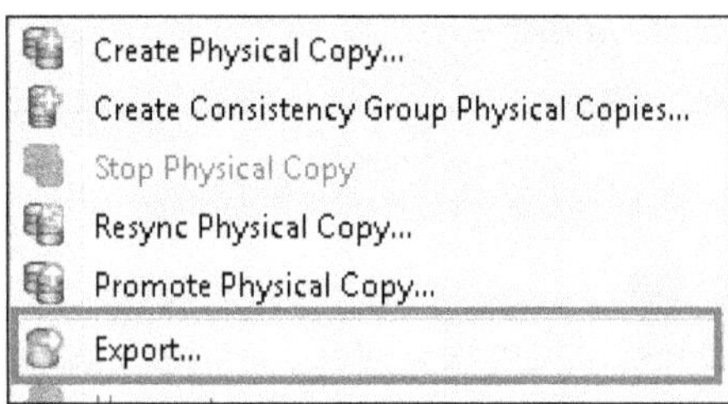

Replicating vSphere's virtual machine to remote site's Cisco UCS by using EMC MirrorView

In this recipe, we will learn the concept of how to replicate vSphere's virtual machine to remote site's Cisco UCS Server using EMC MirrorView/S.

Getting ready

In this example, there are two datacenters, local and remote sites. Assume that these are installed one Cisco UCS 5108 Chassis with some Cisco UCS B200 M3 and two Cisco UCS 6248 Fabric Interconnect in each site. Each Fabric Interconnect is connected to two pairs of FC SAN Switches and two pairs of Ethernet LAN Switches. The EMC VNX5200 is connected to Cisco UCS B200 M3 through two FC SAN Switches. You have installed VMware vSphere 5.5 on each UCS B200 M3 in local boot. The hardware configuration of the remote site is same as the local site, and there are two pairs **Inter-Switch Links** (**ISL**): its the **Dark Fibre** on each FC Switch between both local and remote sites. The following diagram shows the details:

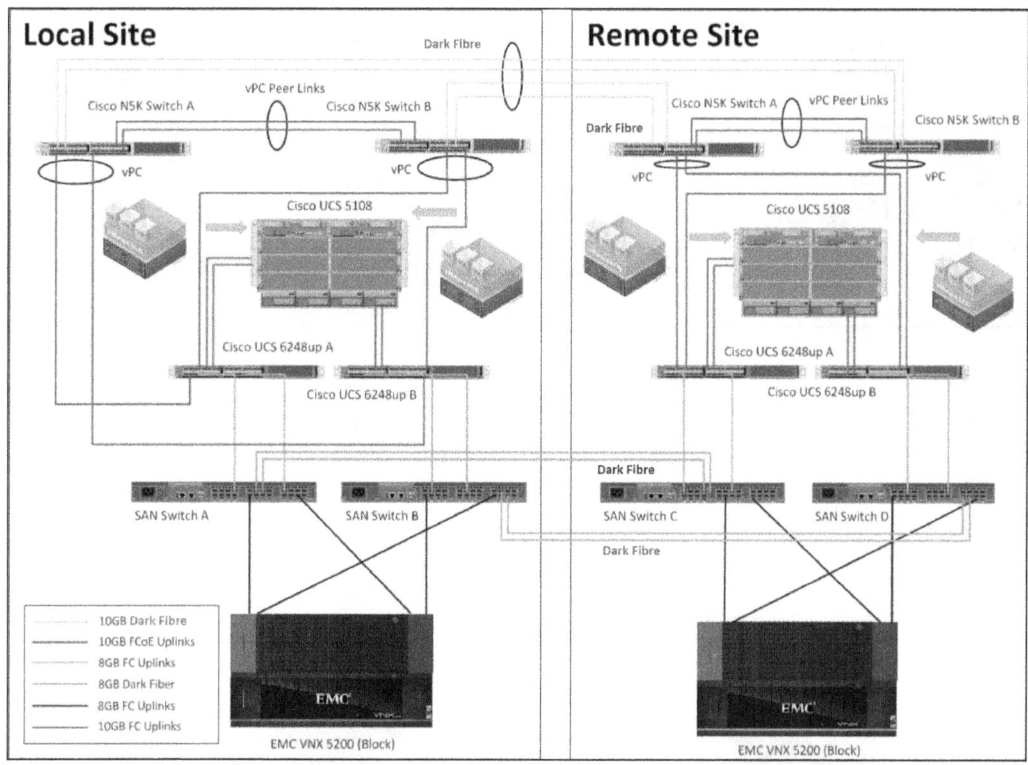

The following table lists the details of each device component:

Sites	**Device component**	**Detail**
Production	Cisco UCS 5018 Chassis 1	Cisco UCS 5108 Chassis with two Cisco UCS 2204XP Fabric Extender
	Cisco UCS B-Series B200 1	▸ Cisco UCS B-Series B200 with 1 1240 VIC adapter ▸ Two Processors: Intel E5-2680 v3 2.5 GHz ▸ 2416 GB DDR4 Memory ▸ 2 600 GB SAS 6 GB 10K RPM SFF HDD
	Cisco UCS 6248UP x 2	▸ 12 ports are enabled on each Cisco UCS 6248UP ▸ Two ports as Server port ▸ Two ports as Ethernet uplink ports ▸ Two ports as FC uplink ports
	SAN Switches 2	▸ Brocade 300B SAN Switch, 16 ports are enabled on each one ▸ Two ports as EMC VNX5200 frontend port ▸ Two ports as UCS FC uplink ports ▸ Two ports as ISL connection ports between two sites
	Cisco N5K LAN Switches x 2	▸ 16 ports are enabled on each one ▸ Two ports as Cisco vPC uplinks ▸ Two ports as vPC peer links
	VMware vSphere 5.5	It is installed into Cisco UCS B200 M3 in local boot
	EMC VNX5200 (Block) x 1	EMC Remote Protection Suite is required to enabled

Sites	Device component	Detail
Remote	Cisco UCS 5018 Chassis x 1	Cisco UCS 5108 Chassis with two Cisco UCS 2204XP Fabric Extender
	Cisco UCS B-Series B200 x 1	▸ Cisco UCS B-Series B200 with one 1240 VIC adapter ▸ Two Processors: Intel E5-2680 v3 2.5 GHz ▸ 24 16 GB DDR4 Memory ▸ Two 600 GB SAS 6 GB 10K RPM SFF HDD
	Cisco UCS 6248UP x 2	▸ 12 ports are enabled on each Cisco UCS 6248UP ▸ Two ports as Server port ▸ Two ports as Ethernet uplink ports ▸ Two ports as FC uplink ports
	SAN Switches x 2	▸ Brocade 300B SAN Switch, 16 ports are enabled on each one ▸ Two ports as EMC VNX5200 frontend port ▸ Two ports as UCS FC uplinks port ▸ Two ports as ISL connection ports between two sites
	Cisco N5K LAN Switches x 2	▸ 16 ports are enabled on each one ▸ Two ports as Cisco vPC uplinks ▸ Two ports as Cisco vPC peer links
	VMware vSphere 5.5	It is installed into Cisco UCS B200 M3 in local boot
	EMC VNX5200 (Block) 1	EMC Remote Protection Suite is required to enabled

How to do it...

In this recipe, we will learn how to create EMC MirrorView/S on EMC VNX5200 between two sites by FC connection.

EMC MirrorView software provides two kinds of storage-based remote mirroring features, they are **MirrorView/Synchronous** (**MirrorView/S**) and **MirrorView/Asynchronous** (**MirrorView/A**). For EMC VNX2/VNX1 storage, remote protection suite are included MirrorView/S and MirrorView/A. EMC MirrorView/S is a synchronous software that mirrors data in real time between local site and remote storage systems. EMC MirrorView/A is an asynchronous software that provides replication based on a periodic incremental update. Both MirrorView/S and MirrorView/A are supported into Fibre Channel and iSCSI connections. Make sure that MirrorView/S and MirrorView/A are enabled on both local and remote EMC VNX storage systems, then you can provide MirrorView/S and MirrorView/A features.

You can see **MirrorView/S** and **MirrorView/A** displays an **Active** status on the **Software** tab of **Storage System Properties**, if the EMC MirrorView feature is enabled:

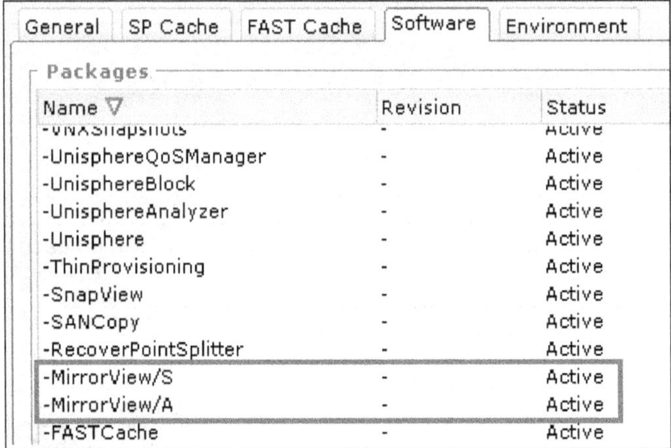

EMC MirrorView/S and MirrorView/A need to be enabled individually on EMC VNX storage by using different license files.

1. Assume that there is one ESXi host connected to an EMC LUNs in local VNX5200, which has one ESXi datastore; now replicate this datastore to a secondary VNX5200 in the remote site. First, please add the local VNX5200 and the remote VNX5200 into the same domain in the Unisphere Manager. Open the Web browser and input the management of the IP address of the local VNX5200, then go to the **Domains** tab and click on **Manage Multi-Domain Configuration**:

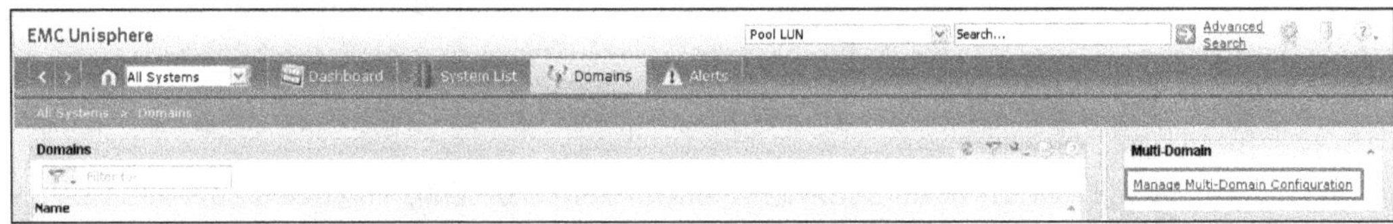

2. Input the management **IP address** of local VNX5200 and remote VNX5200 into the same domain, then click on **Apply**:

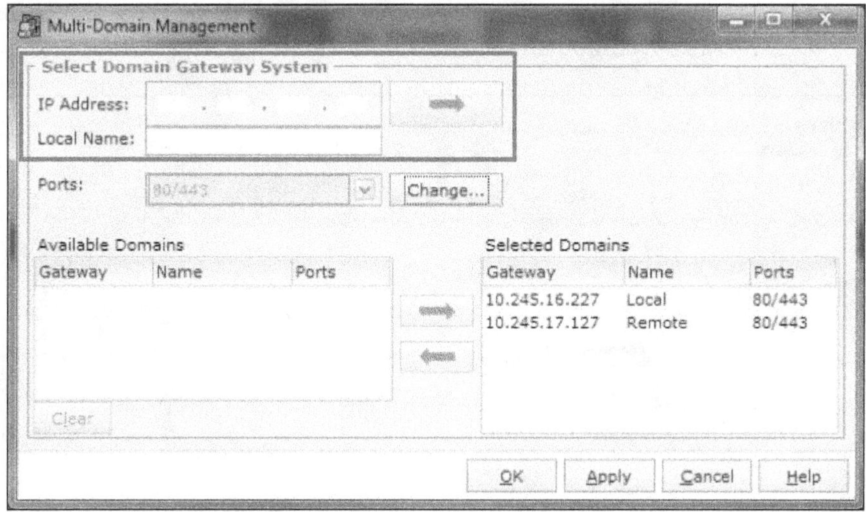

Make sure the management network of both the local VNX5200 and the remote VNX5200 can access each other.

3. Start to prepare MirrorView connections, you need to create the following on each FC SAN Switch:

Switch name	Port number	Detail	FC Zone
Local site - SAN Switch A	0	A0: Port 0 of first I/O module for FC of controller A (local VN5200)	MVS_Zone (members: A0, A0)
Remote site - SAN Switch C	0	A0: Port 0 of first I/O module for FC of controller A (remote VN5200)	
Local site - SAN Switch B	0	B0: Port 0 of first I/O module for FC of controller B (local VN5200)	MVS_Zone (members: B0, B0)
Remote site - SAN Switch D	0	B0: Port 0 of first I/O module for FC of controller B (remote VN5200)	

For the VNX2 series, port 0 of the first I/O Module for FC and iSCSI port is automatically assigned as the MirrorView port, other ports are not assigned as MirrorView port.

4. After creating MirrorView Zoning on each SAN Switch, go to the **Data Protection** tab on the local site's VNX5200 and select **Mirrors**:

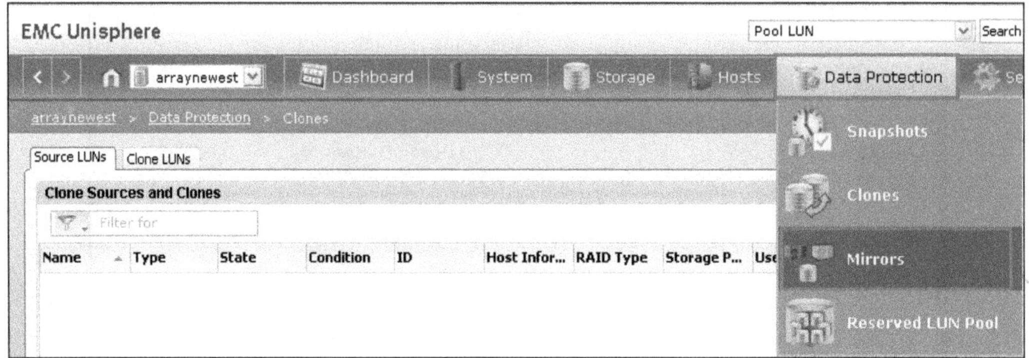

5. Click on the **Manage Mirror Connections** in the **Protection** menu:

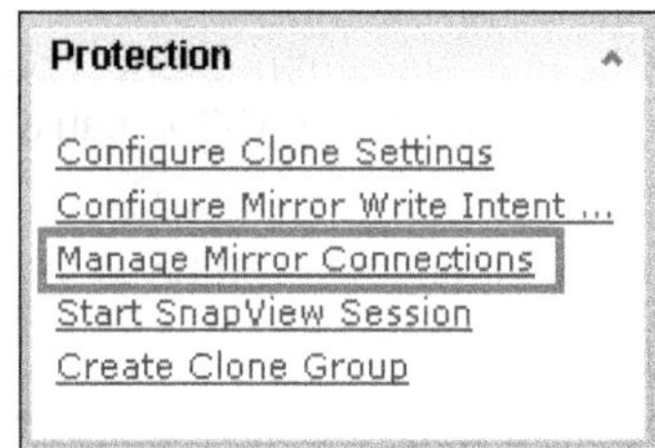

6. Select the FC type MirrorView and click **Enable**, then you can see **SPA** and **SPB** display a **Y** status:

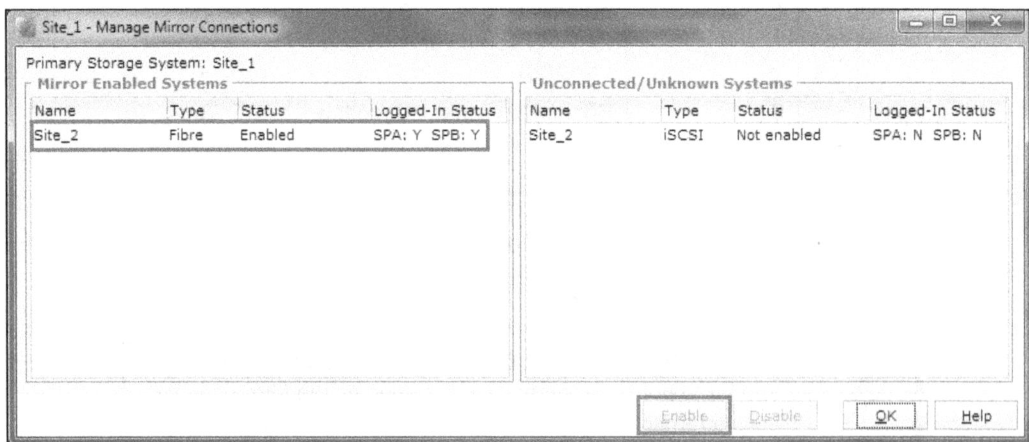

7. Before creating the MirrorView/S session, you must click on **Configure Mirror Write Intent Log** on the **Protection** menu. You can assign two new LUNs for Mirror Write Intent Log:

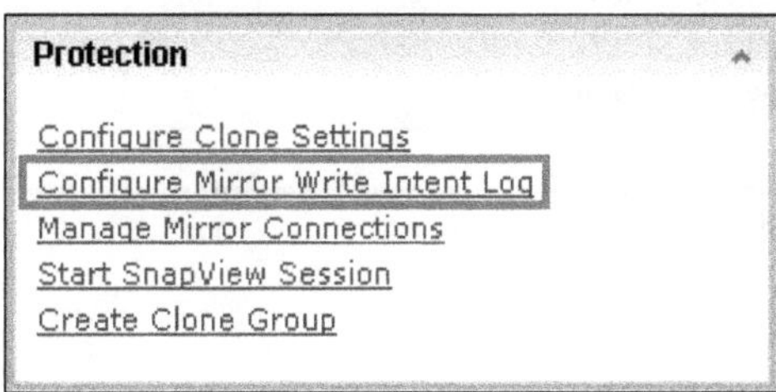

The capacity of Mirror Write Intent Log is 1 GB or greater.

8. Go to the **LUNs** on the **Storage** tab, right-click on the source LUN **VNX_DS1** and select **MirrorView** | **Create Remote Mirror**.

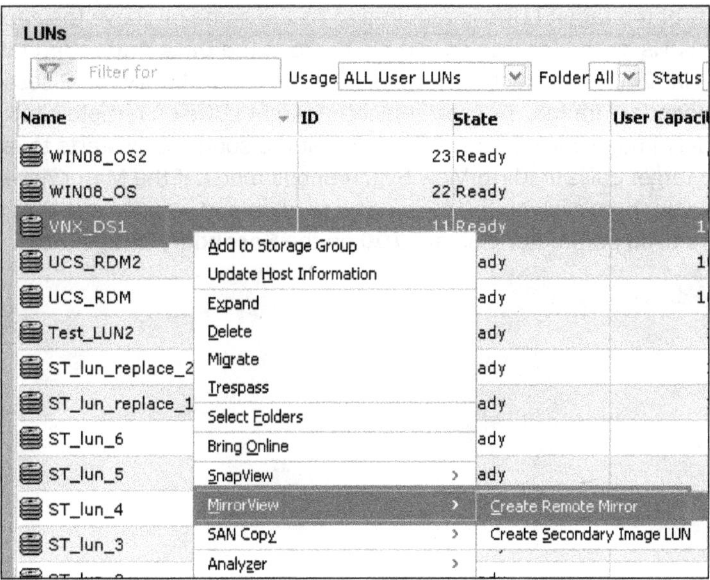

9. Select **Synchronous** on the **Mirror Type** menu and input the **Name** of the MirrorView session as `MirrorView_Session`, click on **Ok**:

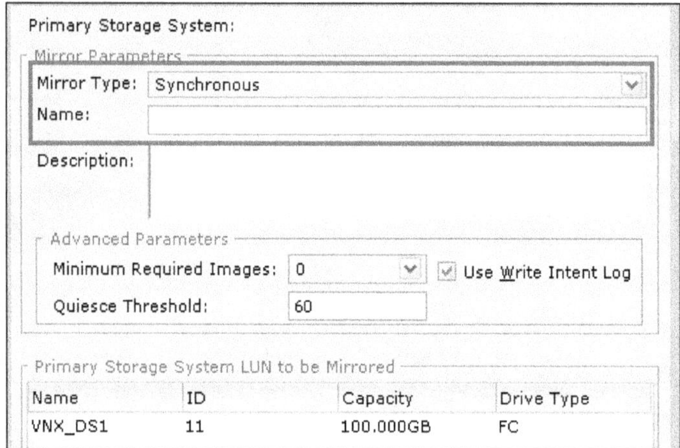

10. Assume that you prepared the target LUNs on the remote site's VNX5200. The capacity of the target LUNs is required to be the same or above the capacity of the source LUNs on the local site's VNX5200. Go to the **Data Protection** tab on local site's VNX5200 and select **Mirrors**, right-click on the MirrorView/S session and select **Add Secondary Image**. You can select the target LUNs on remote site's VNX5200 as secondary image and click on **OK**. After that the source LUN starts to replicate the data to target LUNs in MirrorView Synchronous mode. If the MirrorView/S replication is complete, right-click on the MirrorView session and you can see that the % **Synchronized** parameter displays **100** on the **Secondary Image** tab:

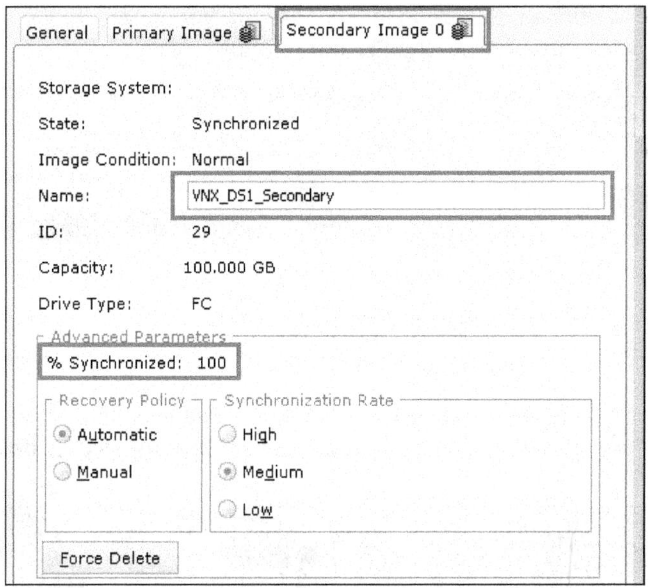

It has three Synchronization rates, **High**, **Medium** and **Low** for each MirrorView session, it is supported to change the synchronization rate during the replication process.

How it works...

In this recipe, we will learn how to activate the secondary image of the MirrorView/S session and present it to an other host on a remote site.

1. Go to the **Data Protection** tab on local site's VNX5200 and select **Mirrors**:

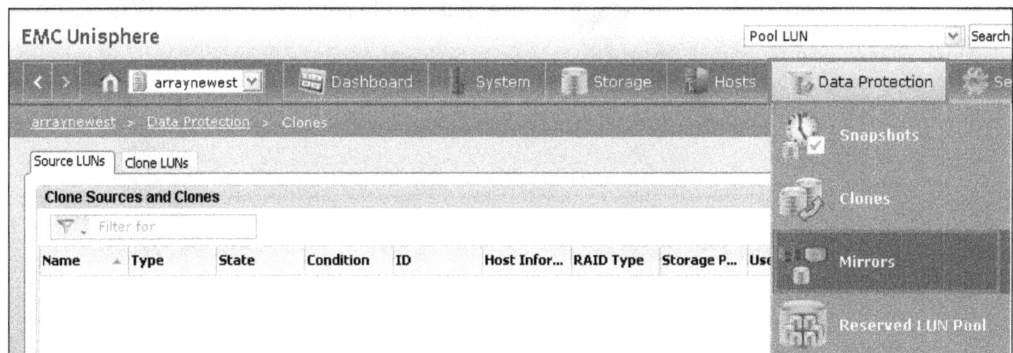

2. Select the MirrorView/S session and choose the **Secondary Image** on **Primary and Secondary Images**. Click on the **Fracture** button:

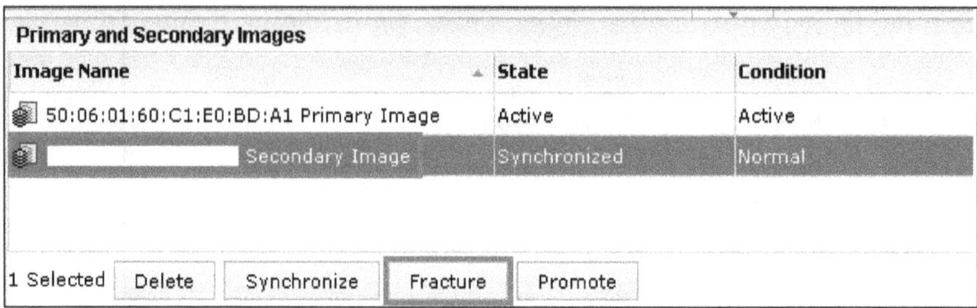

3. Assume that there are some ESXi hosts (UCS) is ready on the remote site. After fracturing the secondary image, you can present this image into the other ESXi host.

Replicating Microsoft Windows Server to remote site's Cisco UCS using EMC MirrorView

In this recipe, we will learn how to replicate Microsoft Windows Server to a remote site's Cisco UCS Server by using EMC MirrorView/A.

Getting ready

In this example, there are two datacenters, local and remote sites. Assume that they are installed on a Cisco UCS 5108 Chassis with a Cisco UCS B200 M3 and two Cisco UCS 6248 Fabric Interconnect on each site. Each Fabric Interconnect is connected to two pairs of FC SAN Switches and two pairs of Ethernet LAN Switches. EMC VNX5200 is connected to Cisco UCS B200 M3 through two FC SAN Switches. You have installed Microsoft Windows 2008 R2 on each UCS B200 M3 in SAN boot.

The hardware configuration of the remote site is the same as the local site and there are two pairs of ISL, which is the **Dark Fibre** on each FC Switch between both local and remote sites. The following diagram shows the details:

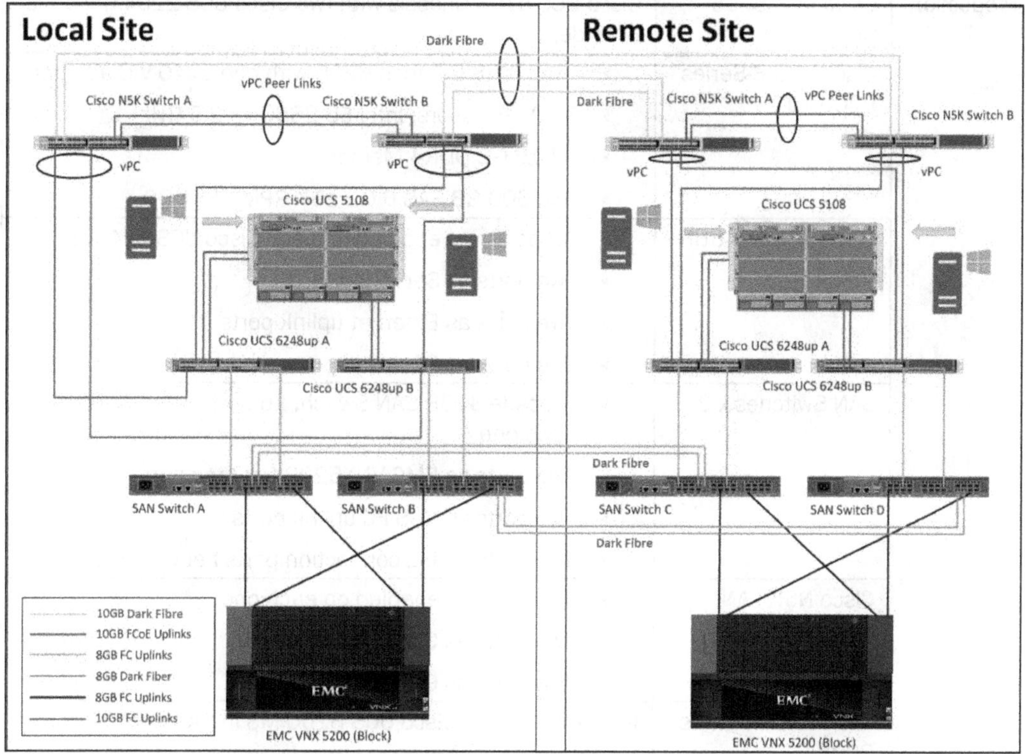

The following table lists the details of each device component:

Sites	**Device component**	**Detail**
Production	Cisco UCS 5018 Chassis x 1	Cisco UCS 5108 Chassis with two Cisco UCS 2204XP Fabric Extender
	Cisco UCS B-Series B200 x 1	▸ Cisco UCS B-Series B200 with one 1240 VIC adapter ▸ Two Processors: Intel E5-2680 v3 2.5 GHz ▸ 24 16 GB DDR4 Memory ▸ Two 600 GB SAS 6 GB 10K RPM SFF HDD
	Cisco UCS 6248UP x 2	▸ 12 ports are enabled on each Cisco UCS 6248UP ▸ Two ports as Server ports ▸ Two ports as Ethernet uplink ports ▸ Two ports as FC uplink ports
	SAN Switches x 2	▸ Brocade 300B SAN Switch, 16 ports are enabled on each one ▸ Two ports as EMC VNX5200 frontend port ▸ Two ports as UCS FC uplink ports ▸ Two ports as ISL connection ports between two sites
	Cisco N5K LAN Switches x 2	▸ 16 ports are enabled on each one ▸ Two ports as Cisco vPC uplinks ▸ Two ports as Cisco vPC peer links
	Microsoft Windows 2008 R2	It is installed into Cisco UCS B200 M3 in SAN boot. EMC PowerPath 6.0 installed on Microsoft Windows 2008 R2 for multipath I/O feature.
	EMC VNX5200 (Block) x 1	EMC Remote Protection Suite is required to enabled

Sites	Device component	Detail
Remote	Cisco UCS 5018 Chassis x 1	Cisco UCS 5108 Chassis with two Cisco UCS 2204XP Fabric Extender
	Cisco UCS B-Series B200 x 1	▸ Cisco UCS B-Series B200 with one 1240 VIC adapter ▸ Two Processors: Intel E5-2680 v3 2.5 GHz ▸ 24 16 GB DDR4 Memory ▸ Two 600 GB SAS 6 GB 10K RPM SFF HDD
	Cisco UCS 6248UP x 2	▸ 12 ports are enabled on each Cisco UCS 6248UP ▸ Two ports as Server ports ▸ Two ports as Ethernet uplink ports ▸ Two ports as FC uplink ports
	SAN Switches x 2	▸ Brocade 300B SAN Switch, 16 ports are enabled on each one ▸ Two ports as EMC VNX5200 frontend ports ▸ Two ports as UCS FC uplink ports ▸ Two ports as ISL connection ports between two sites
	Cisco N5K LAN Switches x 2	▸ 16 ports are enabled on each one ▸ Two ports as Cisco vPC uplinks ▸ Two ports as Cisco vPC peer links
	Microsoft Windows 2008 R2	It is installed into Cisco UCS B200 M3 in SAN boot. EMC PowerPath 6.0 installed on Microsoft Windows 2008 R2 for multipath I/O feature.
	EMC VNX5200 (Block) x 1	EMC Remote Protection Suite is required to enabled

How to do it...

In this recipe, we will learn how to create the EMC MirrorView/A on EMC VNX5200 between two sites by FC connection.

EMC MirrorView software provides two kinds of storage base remote mirroring features, they are MirrorView/S and MirrorView/A. For VNX2/VNX1 storage, remote protection suite are included MirrorView/S and MirrorView/A. For the EMC MirrorView/S is a synchronous software that mirrors data in real time between local site and remote storage systems. EMC MirrorView/A is asynchronous software that provide replication based on a periodic incremental update. Both MirrorView/S and MirrorView/A are supported into Fibre Channel and iSCSI connections. Make sure that MirrorView/S and MirrorView/A enabled on both local and remote EMC VNX storage systems, then you can provide **MirrorView/S** and **MirrorView/A** features.

You can see **MirrorView/S** and **MirrorView/A** displays **Active** status on the **Software** tab of **Storage System Properties** if the EMC MirrorView feature is enabled:

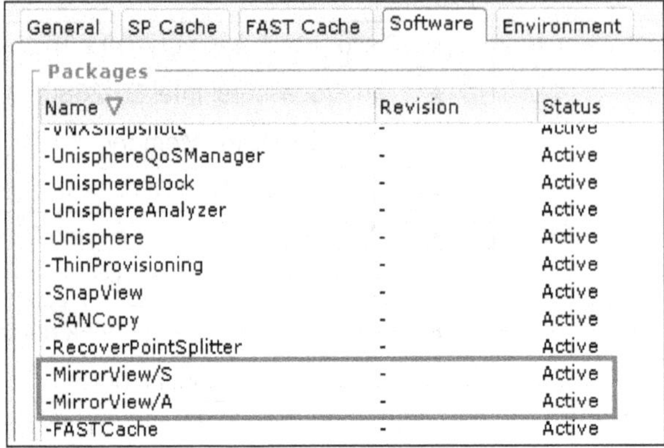

The EMC MirrorView/S and MirrorView/A are required to be enabled individually on EMC VNX storage by using different license files.

1. Assume that there is a Microsoft Windows 2008 R2 in a EMC LUNs SAN boot in local VNX5200. Now replicate this EMC LUN to the secondary VNX5200 on a remote site. First, add a local VNX5200 and a remote VNX5200 into the same domain in Unisphere Manager. Open a Web browser and input the management IP address of the local VNX5200, then go to the **Domains** tab and click on **Manage Multi-Domain Configuration**:

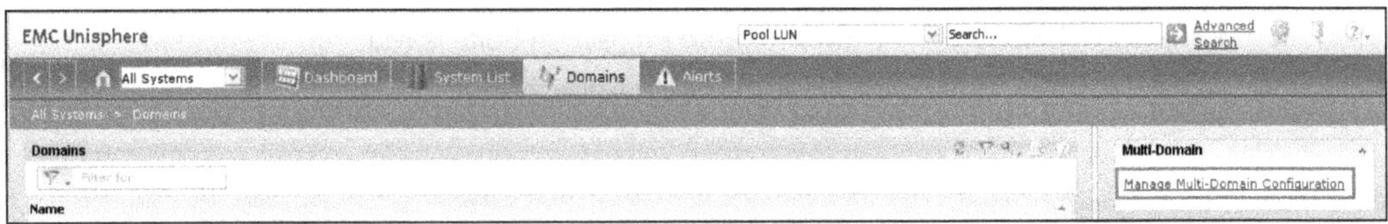

2. Input the management **IP Address** of local VNX5200 and remote VNX5200 into the same domain, then click on **Apply**:

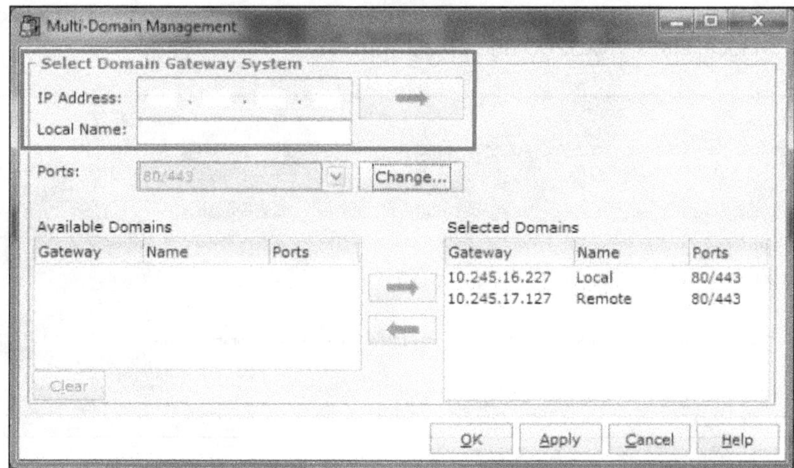

Make sure the management network of both local VNX5200 and remote VNX5200 can access each other.

3. Start preparing the MirrorView connections, you need to create the following on each FC SAN Switch:

Switch name	Port number	Detail	FC Zone
Local site - SAN Switch A	0	A0: Port 0 of first I/O module for FC of controller A (local VN5200)	MVA_Zone (members: A0, A0)
Remote site - SAN Switch C	0	A0: Port 0 of first I/O module for FC of controller A (remote VN5200)	
Local site - SAN Switch B	0	B0: Port 0 of first I/O module for FC of controller B (local VN5200)	MVA_Zone (members: B0, B0)
Remote site - SAN Switch D	0	B0: Port 0 of first I/O module for FC of controller B (remote VN5200)	

For the VNX2 series, port 0 of the first I/O module for FC and iSCSI port is automatically assigned as the MirrorView port, other ports are not assigned as MirrorView port.

4. After creating the MirrorView Zoning on each SAN Switch, go to the **Data Protection** tab on local site's VNX5200 and select **Mirrors**:

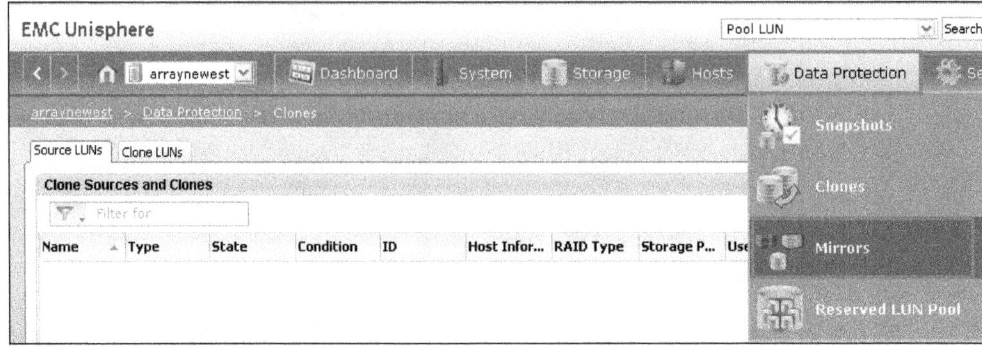

5. Click on **Manage Mirror Connections** in the **Protection** menu:

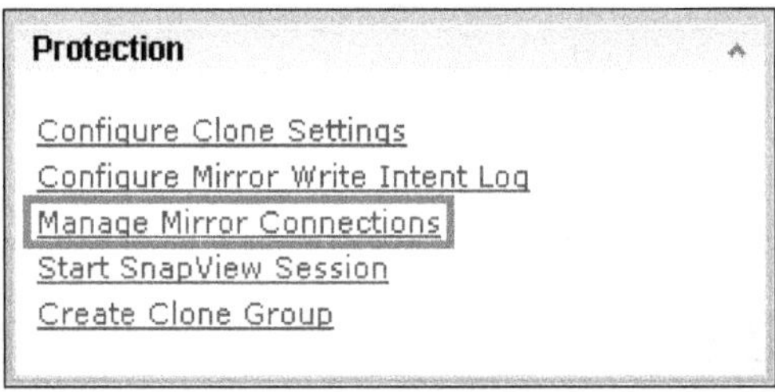

6. Select the FC type MirrorView and click on **Enable**, then you can see that the **SPA** and **SPB** display a **Y** status:

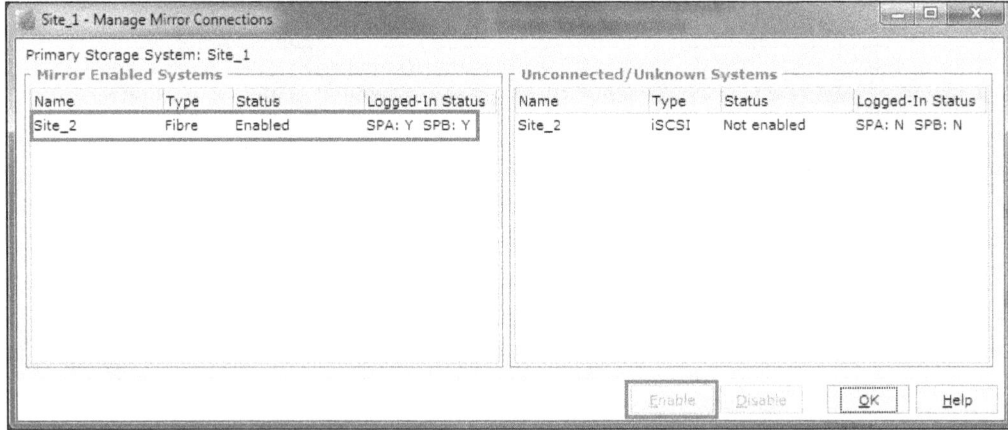

7. Before creating the MirrorView/A session, you must configure some free LUNs into the **Reserved LUN Pool** (**RLP**) for the MirrorView/A relationship on the primary and secondary array. Go to **Data Protection** and select **Reserved LUN Pool**:

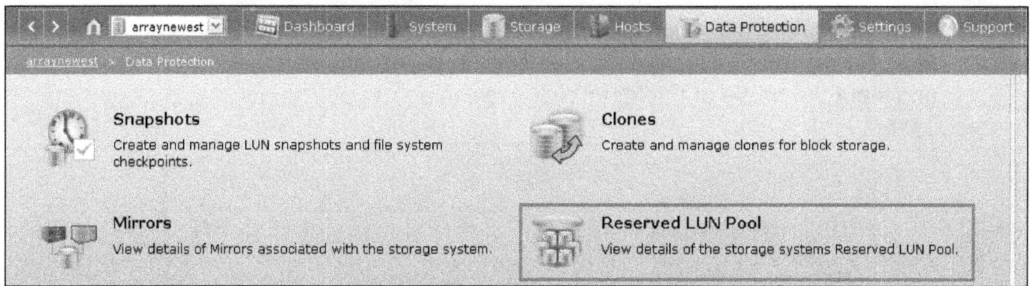

Reserved LUN capacity for the primary and secondary images is set at 20 percent of the image LUN size.

8. Go to the **Free LUNs** tab and click on **Configure**:

9. Assume that you have created two free LUNS for RLP. Select the free **Available LUNs** and click on **Add LUN**, then **OK**:

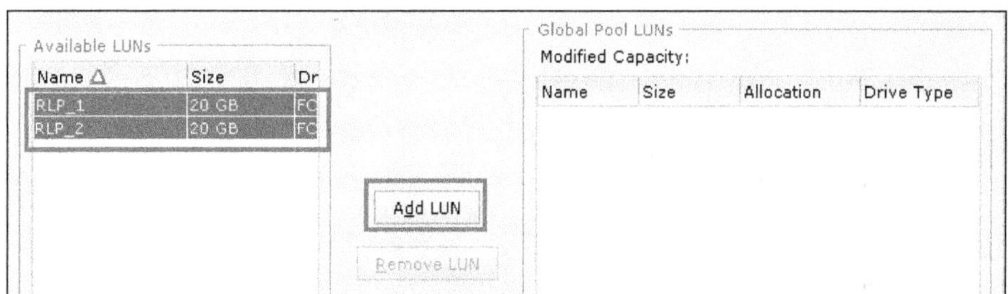

Due to the capacity of source LUN being 100 GB, 20 percent of the source LUN is 20 GB.

10. After this, go to **LUNs** on the **Storage** tab, right-click on the source LUN and select **MirrorView**, create a remote mirror. Select **Asynchronous** on the **Mirror Type** menu and input the **Name** of the MirrorView session as `Mirror Group 1`, click on **Ok**:

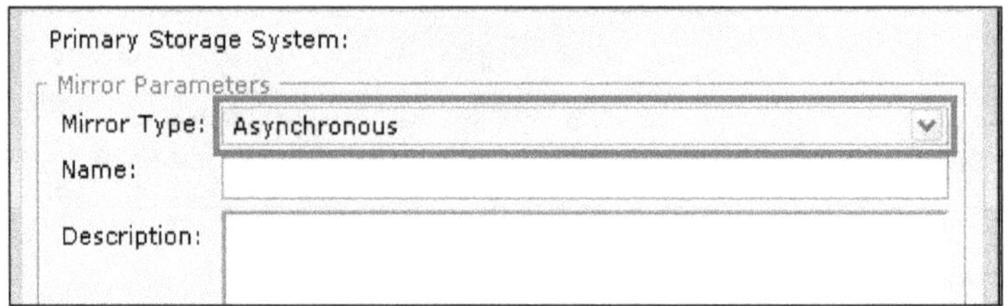

Assume that you have prepared the target LUNs on the remote site's VNX5200. The capacity of target LUNs is required to be the same or greater than the source LUNs on local site's VNX5200. Go to the **Data Protection** tab on local site's VNX5200 and select **Mirrors**. Select the MirrorView/A session **Mirror Group 1** and click on **Add Secondary**. You can select the target LUNs on remote site's VNX5200 as the secondary image and click **OK**:

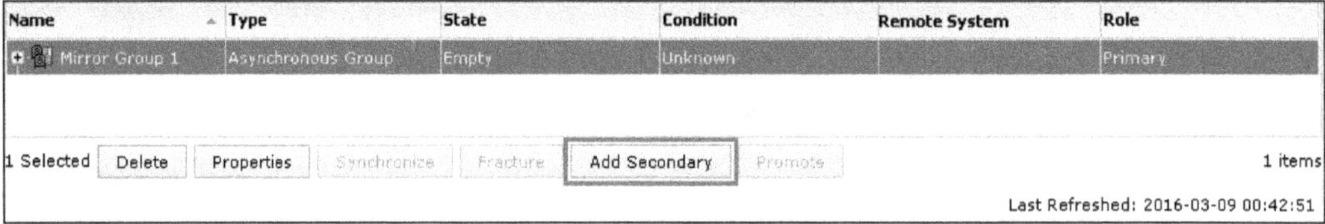

After that the source LUN starts to replicate the data to target LUNs in MirrorView/A mode. If the MirrorView/A replication is complete, right-click the MirrorView session and you can see **% Synchronized** displays **100** on the **Secondary Image** tab:

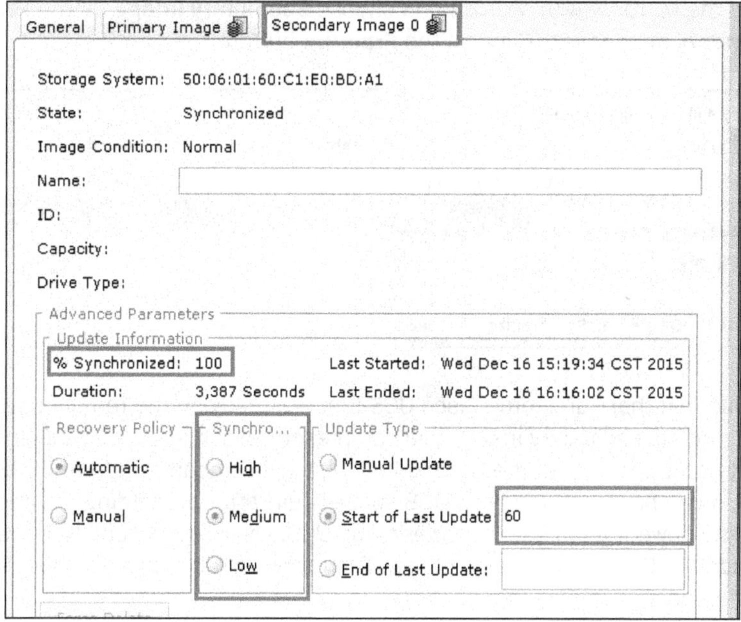

It has three synchronization rates that are **High**, **Medium** and **Low** for each MirrorView session, it is supported to change the synchronization rate during the replication process.

By default, each MirrorView/A session update the delta change once every 60 minutes.

How it works...

In this recipe, we will learn how to activate the secondary image of the MirrorView/A session and present it to the other host on the remote site.

1. Go to the **Data Protection** tab on the local site's VNX5200 and select **Mirrors**:

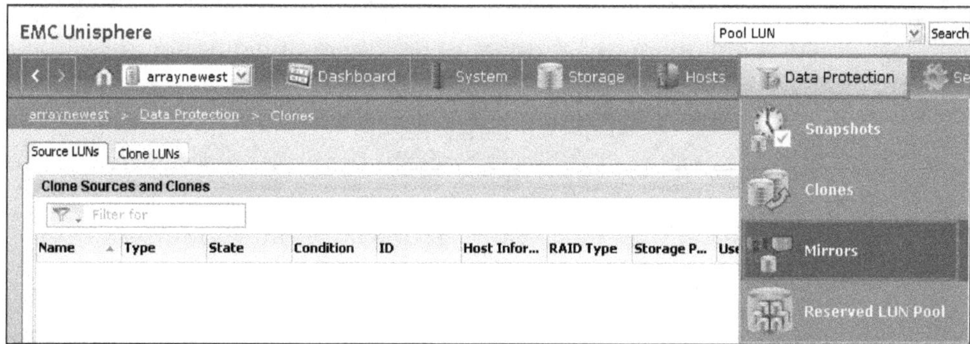

2. Select the MirrorView/A session and choose **Secondary Image** on the **Primary and Secondary Images** tab. Click on the **Fracture** button:

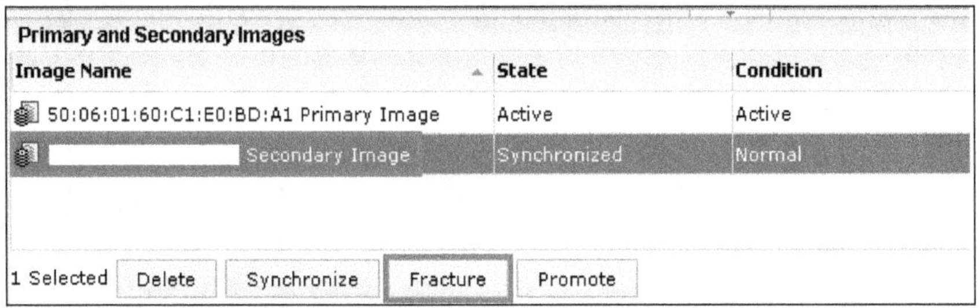

3. Assume that there are some Cisco UCS that are ready on the remote site. After fracturing the secondary image, you can present this image into the Cisco UCS on the remote site. Due to this, the secondary image is Microsoft Windows 2008 R2 boot LUNs. It can boot up Windows 2008 successfully after presenting the image to Cisco UCS and powering up. Before powering up UCS, you need to configure the boot policy and add the Cisco UCS service profile. The following table lists the sample boot policy for reference:

SAN boot policy	vHBA	SAN target	Target WWN	Remote site - Storage port
SAN boot	vHBA1-FIA	SAN target primary	WWN of Controller1-A4	Controller1-A4
		SAN target secondary	WWN of Controller2-B5	Controller2-B5
	vHBA2-FIB	SAN target primary	WWN of Controller2-B4	Controller2-B4
		SAN target secondary	WWN of Controller1-A5	Controller1-A5

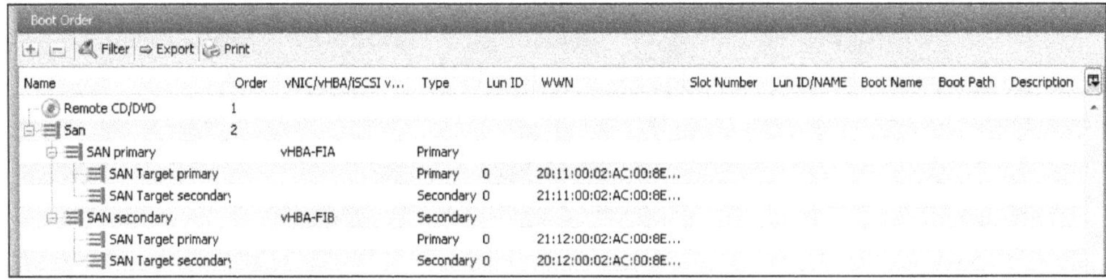

Replicating Microsoft Windows Server to remote site's Cisco UCS using HP 3PAR Remote Copy

In this recipe, we will learn how to create a 3PAR Remote Copy on HP 3PAR StoreServ 7200 between two sites by IP connection.

Getting ready

In this example there are two datacenters, local and remote . Assume that they have a Cisco UCS 5108 Chassis with some Cisco UCS B200 M3 and two Cisco UCS 6248 Fabric Interconnects on each site. Each Fabric Interconnect is connected to two pairs of FC SAN Switches and two pairs of Ethernet LAN Switches. HP 3PAR Storeserv 7200 is connected to Cisco UCS B200 M3 through two FC SAN Switches. You have installed Microsoft Windows 2008 R2 on each UCS B200 M3 in SAN boot. The hardware configuration of remote site is the same as local site. There are two 1 GB Ethernet connections between both local and remote site's 3PAR 7200. The following diagram shows the details:

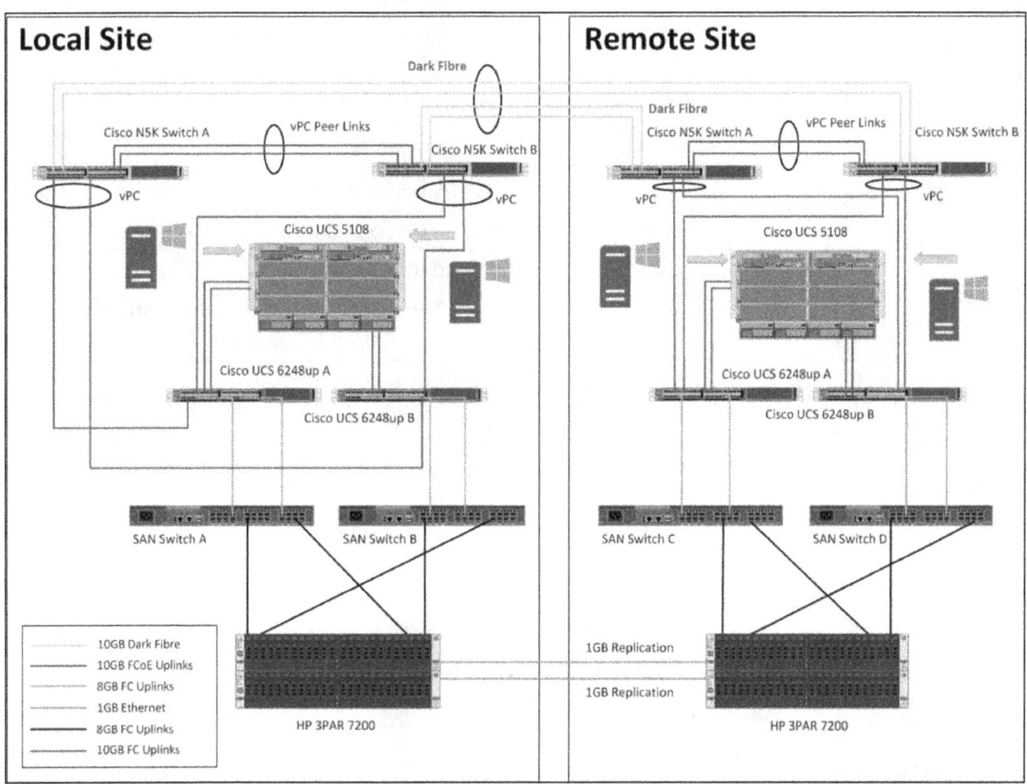

The following table lists the details of each device components:

Sites	Device components	Detail
Production	Cisco UCS 5018 Chassis x 1	Cisco UCS 5108 Chassis with two Cisco UCS 2204XP Fabric Extenders
	Cisco UCS B-Series B200 x 1	Cisco UCS B-Series B200 with one 1240 VIC adapter Two Processors: Intel E5-2680 v3 2.5 GHz 24 16 GB DDR4 Memory Two 600 GB SAS 6 GB 10K RPM SFF HDD
	Cisco UCS 6248UP x 2	12 ports are enabled on each Cisco UCS 6248UP Two ports as Server ports Two ports as Ethernet uplink ports Two ports as FC uplink ports
	SAN Switches x 2	Brocade 300B SAN Switch, 16 ports are enabled on each one: ▶ Two ports as EMC VNX5200 frontend ports ▶ Two ports as UCS FC uplink ports ▶ Two ports as ISL connection ports between two sites
	Cisco N5K LAN Switches x 2	16 ports are enabled on each one Two ports as Cisco vPC uplinks Two ports as Cisco vPC peer links
	Microsoft Windows 2008 R2	It is installed into Cisco UCS B200 M3 in SAN boot. EMC PowerPath 6.0 installed on Microsoft Windows 2008 R2 for multipath I/O feature.
	HP 3PAR Storeserv 7200 x 1	A Remote Copy license is enabled. Remote Copy port is configured (IP)

Sites	Device components	Detail
Remote	Cisco UCS 5018 Chassis x 1	Cisco UCS 5108 Chassis with two Cisco UCS 2204XP Fabric Extenders
	Cisco UCS B-Series B200 x 1	▸ Cisco UCS B-Series B200 with one 1240 VIC adapter ▸ Two Processors: Intel E5-2680 v3 2.5 GHz ▸ 24 16 GB DDR4 Memory ▸ Two 600 GB SAS 6 GB 10K RPM SFF HDD
	Cisco UCS 6248UP x 2	▸ 12 ports are enabled on each Cisco UCS 6248UP ▸ Two ports as Server ports ▸ Two ports as Ethernet uplink ports ▸ Two ports as FC uplink ports
	SAN Switches x 2	Brocade 300B SAN Switch, 16 ports are enabled on each one: ▸ Two ports as EMC VNX5200 frontend ports ▸ Two ports as UCS FC uplink ports ▸ Two ports as ISL connection ports between two sites
	Cisco N5K LAN Switches x 2	16 ports are enabled on each one Two ports as Cisco vPC uplinks Two ports as Cisco vPC peer links
	Microsoft Windows 2008 R2	It is installed into Cisco UCS B200 M3 in SAN boot. EMC PowerPath 6.0 installed on Microsoft Windows 2008 R2 for multipath I/O feature.
	HP 3PAR Storeserv 7200 x 1	A Remote Copy license is enabled. Remote Copy port is configured (IP)

How to do it...

In this recipe, we will learn how to create an HP 3PAR Remote Copy connection between two sites with a 1 GB Ethernet connection.

HP 3PAR StoreServ Remote Copy is a replication technology that allows you to replicate the virtual volume to the local or remote's 3PAR StoreServ storage in either synchronous mode or asynchronous mode.

The replication is supported into FC channel and IP connection. The 1 Gb/s Ethernet Remote Copy port is bydefault built-in on 3PAR 7200 storage. The red connections are for Remote copy for both local and remote 3PAR 7200:

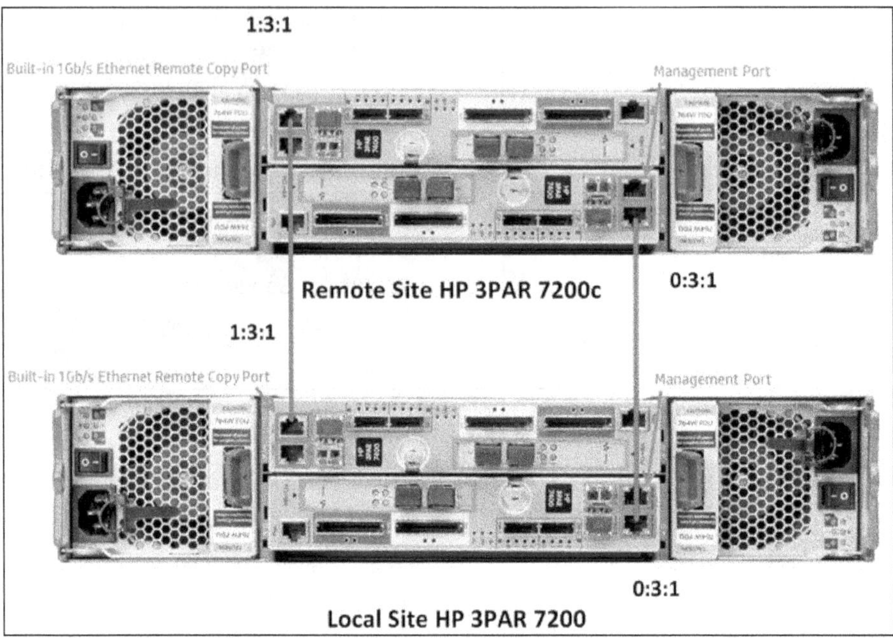

The below table lists the configuration of the local and remote 3PAR 7200:

Site	Model	Management IP	Remote Copy Port	License
Local	7200	10.2.1.15	0:3:1 - 192.168.1.10 1:3:1 - 192.168.1.11	Remote Copy is enabled
Remote	7200c	10.2.1.16	0:3:1 - 192.168.1.12 1:3:1 - 192.168.1.13	Remote Copy is enabled

1. Assume that you have already installed HP 3PAR Management Console onto your workstation. Log in to the 3PAR 7200 storage by HP 3PAR Management Console, input both 3PAR management IPs on **IP Address or Name** field and then you can log in to both HP storage in the same time:

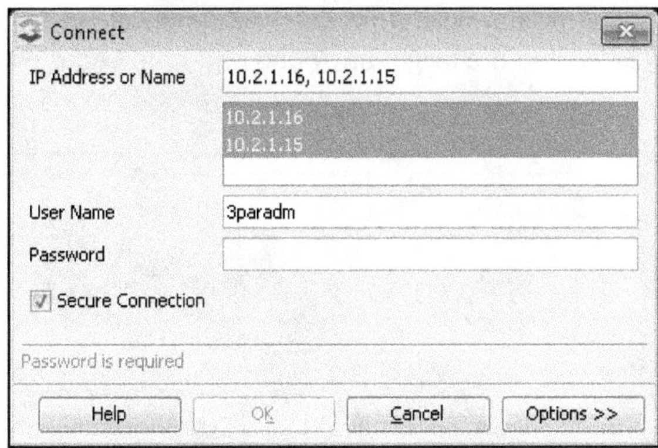

Assume the administrator is the same account on both local & remote 3PAR 7200.

2. After this you can see both the 3PAR displays on the left menu, select **Remote Copy** and click on **New Configuration...** on the **Common Actions** menu:

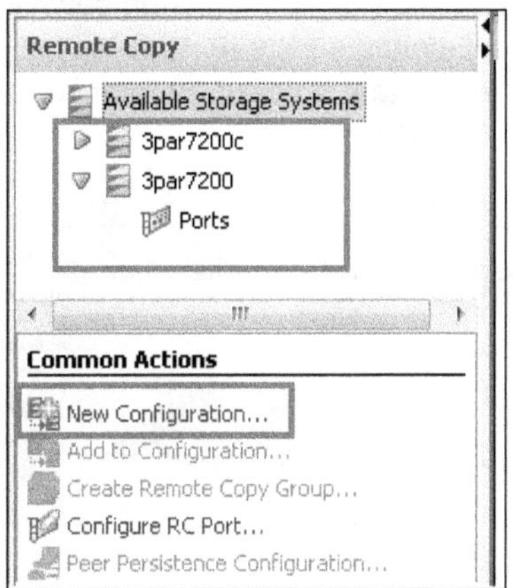

3. Select **1:1** for Remote Copy configuration, then right-click on the array to configure it as the primary array and the target array and enter the **Location** of each array, then click on **Next**:

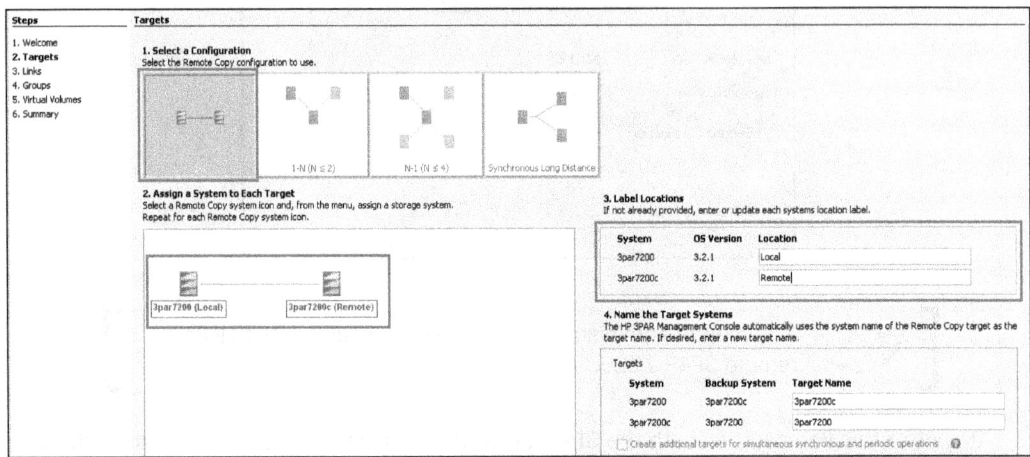

4. Select the **IP** address and make the connection between port **0:3:1** (local array) and port **0:3:1** (remote array), configure the **IP Address** for each Remote Copy port and click **Ping** for the connection test. Repeat the procedure to configure port **1:3:1** and port **1:3:1**, then click on **Next**:

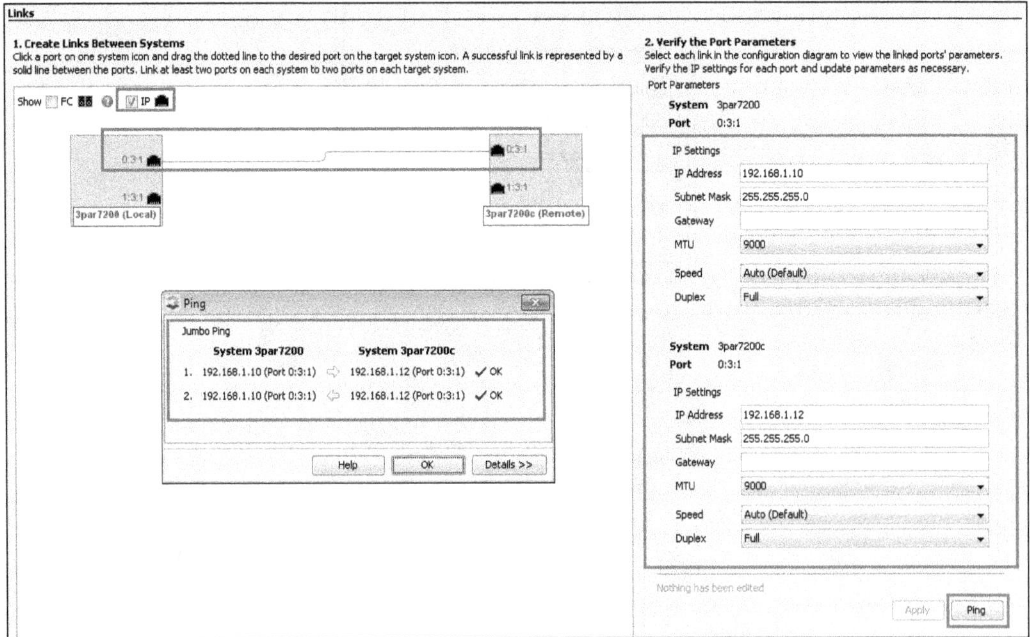

5. Select **3par7200** in the **Source System** menu and **3par7200c(RCIP)** in the **Backup Target Name** menu, select **Synchronous** from the **Mode** menu, input the remote group name in **Group** as `RemoteCopy` and click on **Add**, then **Next**:

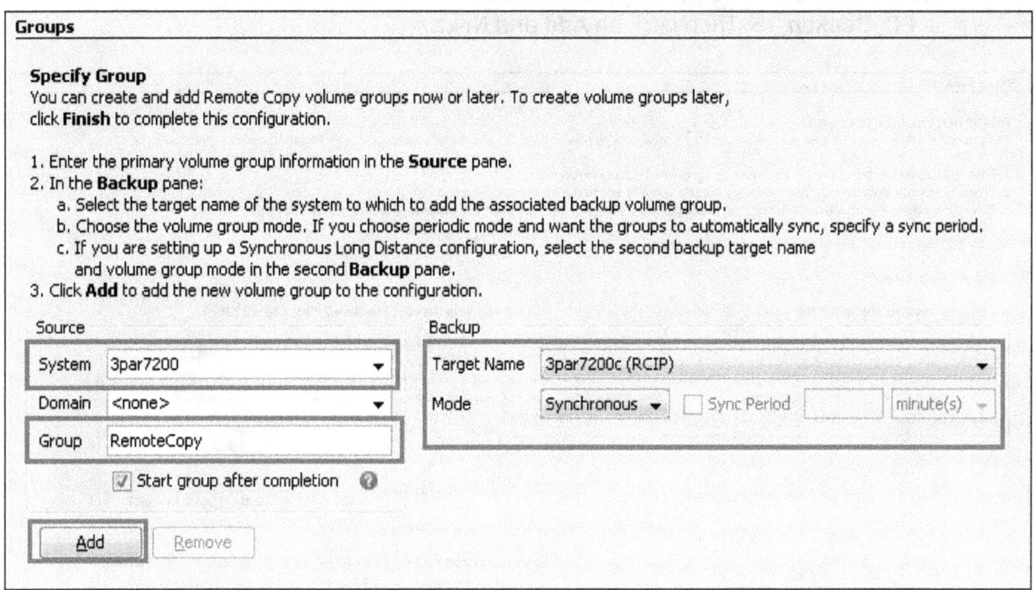

Groups
Specify Group
You can create and add Remote Copy volume groups now or later. To create volume groups later, click Finish to complete this configuration.
1. Enter the primary volume group information in the Source pane.
2. In the Backup pane:
a. Select the target name of the system to which to add the associated backup volume group.
b. Choose the volume group mode. If you choose periodic mode and want the groups to automatically sync, specify a sync period.
c. If you are setting up a Synchronous Long Distance configuration, select the second backup target name and volume group mode in the second Backup pane.
3. Click Add to add the new volume group to the configuration.
Source
System 3par7200
Domain <none>
Group RemoteCopy
Start group after completion
Add
Remove
Backup
Target Name 3par7200c (RCIP)
Mode Synchronous
Sync Period
minute(s)

6. Assume that **3PAR_DS** is the source virtual machine, select it and click on **Create new volume** on target **3par7200c** and input the backup volume name as `3PAR_DS_Secondary`. When you create the new backup volume, you specify which **CPG** to use for the **User CPG** and the **Copy CPG**. Assume that **User CPG** is **FC_r5**, and **Copy CPG** is **FC_Backup_r5**. Then click on **Add** and **Next**:

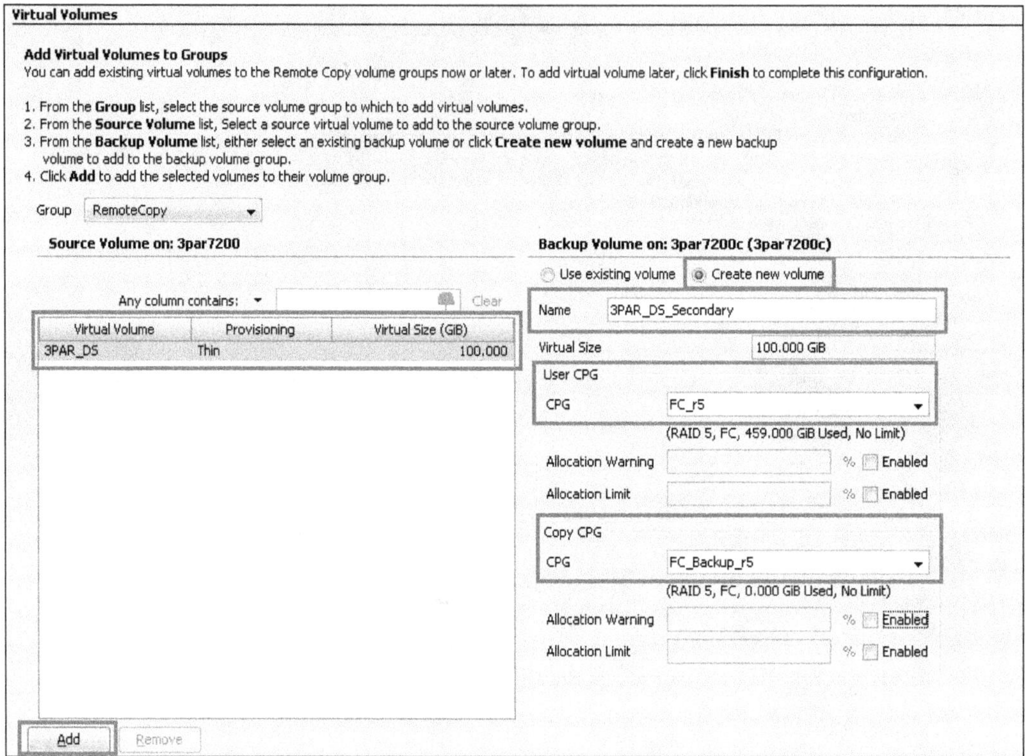

You must create two CPGs for backup volume on target 3PAR storage before setting up the 3PAR remote copy connection.

7. It displays the **Summary** of Remote Copy configuration, next click on **Finish** to create the Remote Copy configuration:

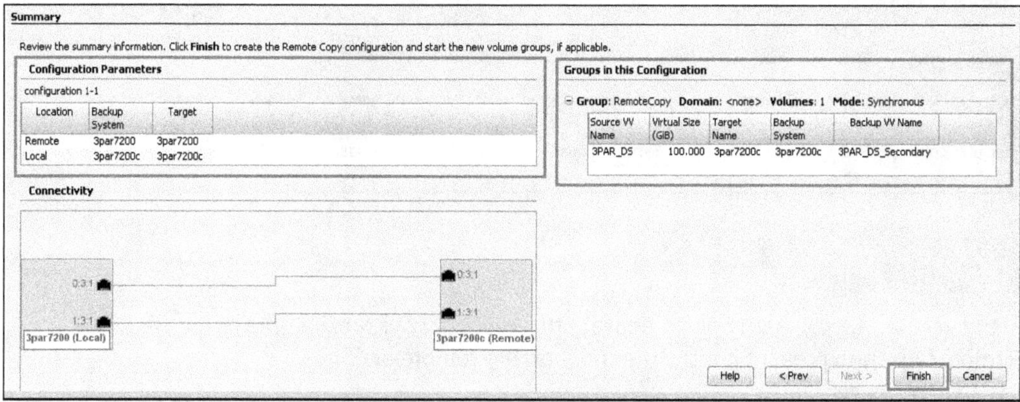

8. Then the remote copy group **RemoteCopy** starts replicating. It displays the replication status in the **Sync Percent** column when you select **Groups** in the **Remote Copy Configuration** menu:

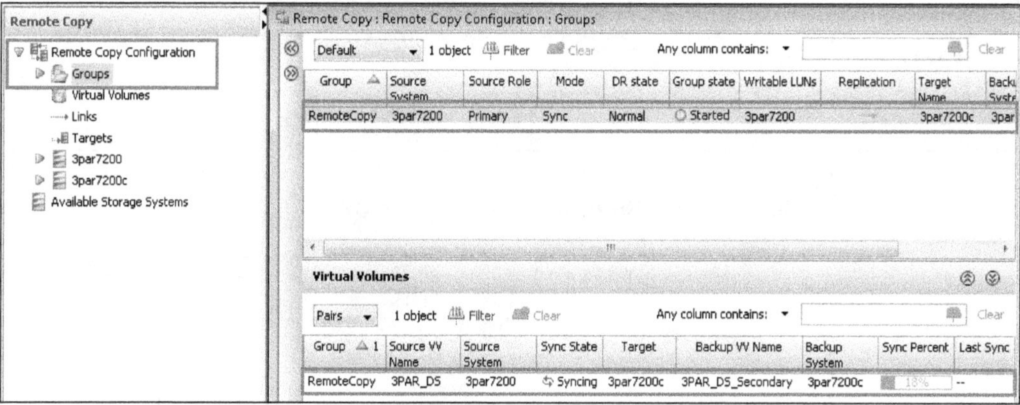

9. When the replication has completed successfully, the **Sync State** displays **Synced**:

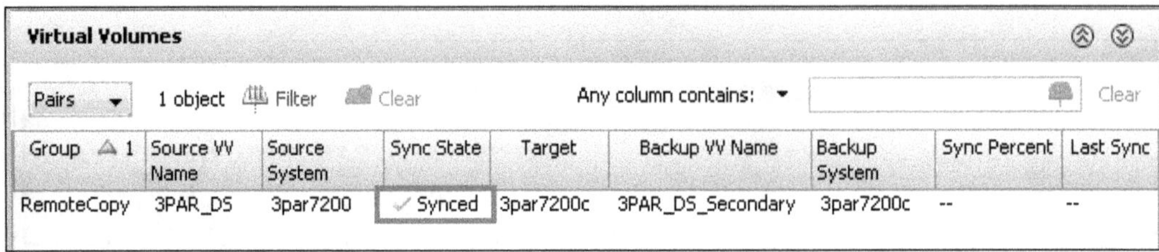

How it works...

In this recipe, we will learn how to activate the secondary virtual volume of the HP 3PAR Remote Copy and present it into other host on the remote site.

1. Go to the **Remote Copy Configuration** menu, right-click on the Remote Copy group **RemoteCopy**:

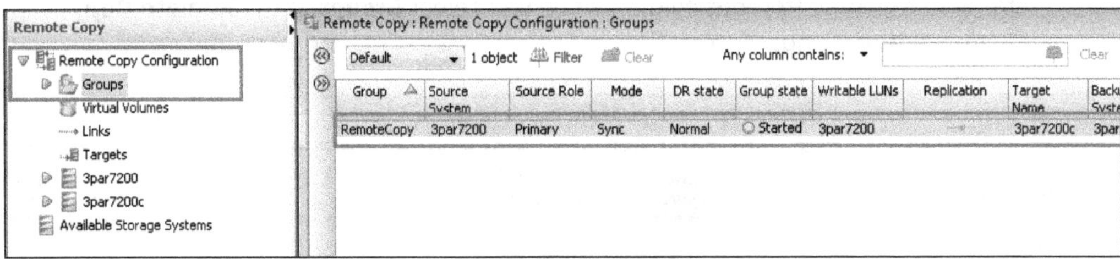

2. Select **Stop Remote Copy Group(s)...**, then click on **OK**:

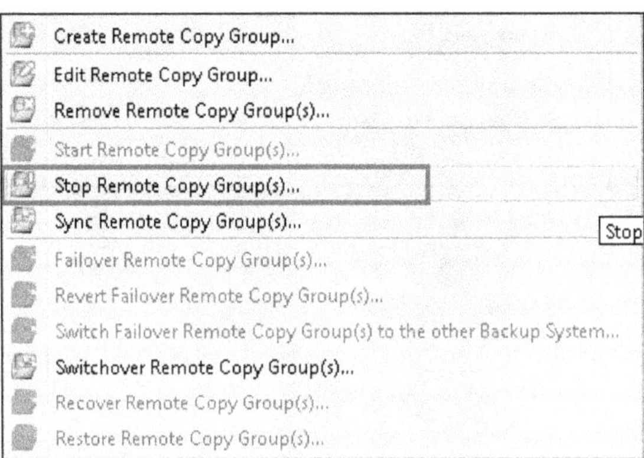

3. The **Group state** changes to **Stopped**:

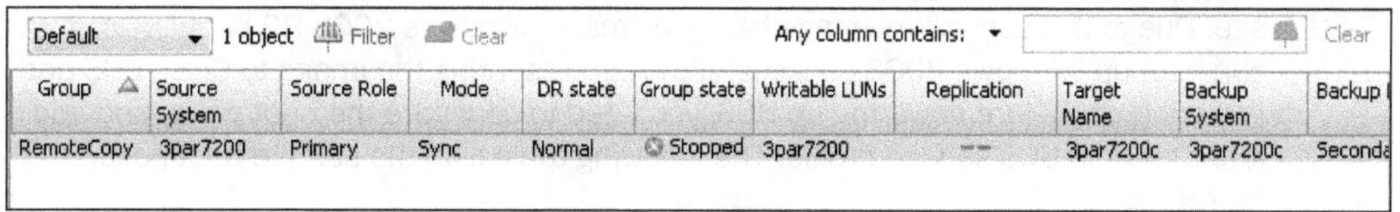

Default | 1 object | Filter | Clear | Any column contains: | Clear

Group	Source System	Source Role	Mode	DR state	Group state	Writable LUNs	Replication	Target Name	Backup System	Backup
RemoteCopy	3par7200	Primary	Sync	Normal	Stopped	3par7200	--	3par7200c	3par7200c	Second

4. Right-click on **RemoteCopy** and select **Failover Remote Copy Group(s)...**. Then click on **Yes**:

Remote Copy failover is about to be executed for the selected groups, virtual volume will be writable from the host on Array 3par7200c and the original source Array 3par7200.

5. The **Backup Role** of **3par7200** changes to **Primary-Rev**, then you can export this virtual volume **3PAR_DS_Secondary** to an other host (Cisco UCS) on the remote site:

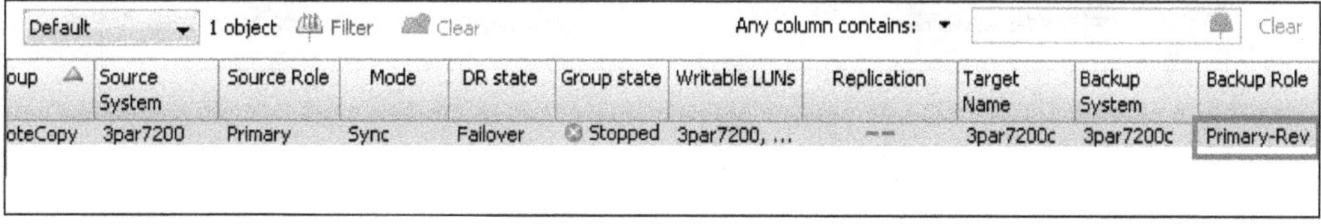

Default | 1 object | Filter | Clear | Any column contains: | Clear

oup	Source System	Source Role	Mode	DR state	Group state	Writable LUNs	Replication	Target Name	Backup System	Backup Role
oteCopy	3par7200	Primary	Sync	Failover	Stopped	3par7200, ...	--	3par7200c	3par7200c	Primary-Rev

6. Assume that there is some Cisco UCS ready in the remote site. After failover Remote Copy group **RemoteCopy**, you can present this image to the Cisco UCS on the remote site. Due to this secondary image being Microsoft Windows 2008 R2 boot LUNs, it can boot up Windows 2008 successfully after presenting the image to Cisco UCS and powering up. Before powering up UCS, you need to configure the boot policy and add it to the Cisco UCS service profile. The following table lists the sample boot policy for reference:

SAN boot policy	vHBA	SAN target	Target WWN	Remote site - Storage port
SAN boot	vHBA1	SAN target primary	WWN of Controller1-P1	Controller1-P1
		SAN target secondary	WWN of Controller2-P2	Controller2-P2
	vHBA2	SAN target primary	WWN of Controller2-P1	Controller2-P1
		SAN target secondary	WWN of Controller1-P2	Controller1-P2

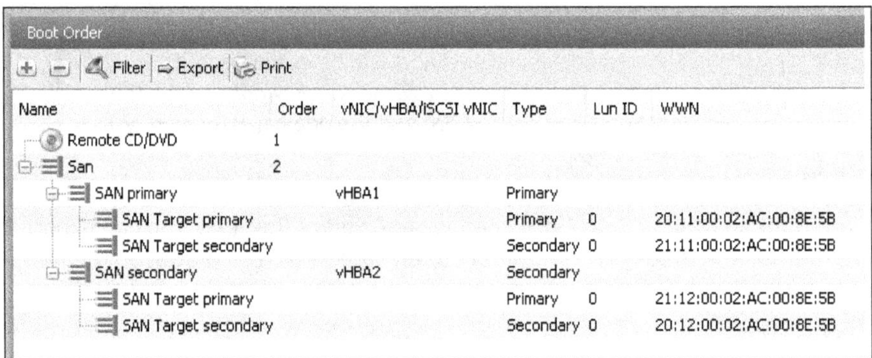

Index

E

F

G

H

I

T

U

V

W

www.ingramcontent.com/pod-product-compliance
Lightning Source LLC
Chambersburg PA
CBHW062052050326
40690CB00016B/3061

* 9 7 8 1 7 8 5 8 8 8 9 8 4 *